D0215382

INFLATION TARGETING

INFLATION TARGETING

LESSONS FROM THE INTERNATIONAL EXPERIENCE

Ben S. Bernanke

Thomas Laubach

Frederic S. Mishkin

Adam S. Posen

PRINCETON UNIVERSITY PRESS   PRINCETON, NEW JERSEY

Copyright © 1999 by Princeton University Press
Published by Princeton University Press, 41 William Street,
Princeton, New Jersey 08540
In the United Kingdom: Princeton University Press, Chichester, West Sussex
All Rights Reserved

Library of Congress Cataloging-in-Publication Data

Inflation Targeting : lessons from the international experience / Ben
 S. Bernanke . . . [et al. } .
p.   cm.
Includes bibliographical references and index.
ISBN 0-691-05955-1 (cl : alk. paper)
1. Inflation (Finance)—Government policy—Case studies.
2. Monetary policy—Case studies.   I. Bernanke, Ben.
HG229.I457 1999
332.4'1—dc21   98-39632

This book has been composed in New Baskerville

Princeton University Press books are printed
on acid-free paper and meet the guidelines
for permanence and durability of the Committee
on Production Guidelines for Book Longevity
of the Council on Library Resources

http://pup.princeton.edu

Printed in the United States of America

10 9 8 7 6 5 4 3 2 1

Contents

List of Figures   vii

Preface   ix

PART ONE: INFLATION TARGETING: THE ISSUES   1

1. Introduction   3
2. The Rationale for Inflation Targeting   10
3. Issues of Design and Implementation   26

PART TWO: CASE STUDIES AND EMPIRICAL EVIDENCE   39

4. German and Swiss Monetary Targeting: Precursors to Inflation Targeting   41
5. New Zealand: Inflation-Targeting Pioneer   86
6. Canada: Inflation Targets as Tools of Communication   115
7. United Kingdom: The Central Bank as Counterinflationary Conscience   145
8. Sweden: Searching for a Nominal Anchor   172
9. Three Small Open Economies: Israel, Australia, and Spain   203
10. Inflation Targeting: How Successful Has It Been?   252

PART THREE: CONCLUSIONS   285

11. What Have We Learned?   287
12. Inflation Targeting for the United States and the European Monetary Union   309

Notes   335

References   355

Index   367

List of Figures

Figure 4.1	German Economic Indicators	48
Figure 4.2	Swiss Economic Indicators	54
Figure 5.1	New Zealand Economic Indicators	103
Figure 6.1	Canadian Economic Indicators	131
Figure 7.1	United Kingdom Economic Indicators	160
Figure 8.1	Swedish Economic Indicators	175
Figure 9.1	Israeli Economic Indicators	215
Figure 9.2	Australian Economic Indicators	230
Figure 9.3	Spanish Economic Indicators	238
Figure 10.1	Inflation Forecasts from Phillips Curves	265
Figure 10.2	Consensus Forecasts of Inflation	267
Figure 10.3	Interest Rate Differentials	272
Figure 10.4	Dynamic Simulations	277
Figure 10.5	Dynamic Simulations	278
Figure 10.6	Dynamic Simulations	279

Preface

THIS PROJECT was a natural outgrowth of the authors' immersion—as researchers and as policy advisers—in the process of making monetary policy. Our experience has created a shared concern that, despite the great success of U.S. monetary policy in recent years, too little consideration is being given to ensuring that future policy will be equally (or even more) effective. In particular, the United States has lagged behind other industrial countries in considering monetary-policy frameworks and institutions that might help ensure good economic performance in the long term.

Because monetary policy is, notoriously, an art rather than a science, there is much to be learned from observing the experiences of other practitioners. Most of this book is simply that: our observations of what other countries' policy-makers have done and how well their methods have worked. Our hope is that both policy-makers and the general public will learn from these studies of the international experience, and that the result will be more intelligent and more coherent policy-making, in the United States and elsewhere.

This project was initiated at the Federal Reserve Bank of New York while Frederic Mishkin was an executive vice president and Director of Research at the Bank and Adam Posen was an economist in the Bank's Research and Markets Analysis Group. The other two co-authors also had affiliations with the New York Fed at that time: Ben Bernanke was a Visiting Scholar, and Thomas Laubach served as a graduate student intern at the Bank while completing his Ph.D. in Economics at Princeton. We owe a deep debt of gratitude to the New York Fed for providing us with the resources to undertake this project and for the assistance of many individuals at the bank. In particular, we would like to thank Dorothy Sobol and Valerie LaPorte of the Publications function for their comments and editorial suggestions, and Laura Brookins for research assistance. We also want to thank without implicating Peter Fisher, executive vice president and head of the Markets Group, and William McDonough, president of the Federal Reserve Bank of New York, for many valuable, but more general, discussions about inflation targeting and monetary policy.

We also benefited from detailed comments provided by central bankers who read the case studies for their respective countries. We particularly would like to thank Otmar Issing of the Deutsche Bundesbank; Michel Peytrignet, Erich Spoerndli, and especially Georg Rich of the Swiss National Bank; Donald Brash of the Reserve Bank of New Zealand; Kevin Clinton and Charles Freedman of the Bank of Canada; Andrew Haldane, Neal Hatch, and Mervyn King of the Bank of England; Claes Berg of the Swedish Riksbank; Ohad Bar-Efrat of the Bank of Israel; Jose Viñals of the Banco de España; and Guy Debelle, Steve Grenville, and Glenn Stevens of the Reserve Bank of Australia. We are also grateful to all the central banks whose experiences we report here for their willing provision of data and documentary materials.

Several other researchers and central bankers commented on part or all of the manuscript. We want to thank Charles Goodhart of the London School of Economics and John Taylor of Stanford University for commenting on the entire manuscript. Others providing helpful comments on various aspects of this research included Alan Blinder, John Crow, Brad DeLong, Richard Freeman, Donald Kohn, Alan Krueger, Bennett McCallum, Julio Rotemberg, Lars Svensson, and Tim Taylor. We also benefited from comments in seminars given at the Federal Reserve Bank of New York, the Federal Reserve Bank of San Francisco, Columbia University, Georgetown University, Johns Hopkins University, the National Bureau of Economic Research, the Bank of Canada, the Bank for International Settlements, the Bank of England, Rutgers University, and the Swiss National Bank.

Finally, we want to extend a special thanks to Peter Dougherty, our editor at Princeton University Press, his assistant David Huang, and our development editor, Everett Sims, for their help and advice. Of course, all errors are our own. All views expressed in this book are those of the authors and are not necessarily those of Princeton University, Columbia University, the Institute for International Economics, the National Bureau of Economic Research, the Federal Reserve Bank of New York, the Federal Reserve Bank of Kansas City, or the Federal Reserve System.

Part One ————————————————————————

INFLATION TARGETING: THE ISSUES

1

Introduction

AT THE END of the twentieth century, with communism largely gone and with state-dominated strategies being replaced everywhere by market-oriented reforms, there is a consensus that prosperity and economic growth are created primarily by private enterprise and free markets. It would be a mistake, however, to conclude that no room is left for government policy to promote economic growth and stability. The government, through its fiscal, regulatory, trade, and environmental policies and through its role in building infrastructure, both institutional (*e.g.,* the legal system) and physical (*e.g.,* roads and bridges), plays a vital role in creating the conditions that give the power of the market full play.

Monetary policy, whether determined solely by a central bank or by a central bank in conjunction with other officials, has emerged as one of the most critical government responsibilities. One element of the new consensus is that low, stable inflation is important for market-driven growth, and that monetary policy is the most direct determinant of inflation. Further, of all the government's tools for influencing the economy, monetary policy has proven to be the most flexible instrument for achieving medium-term stabilization objectives. Unlike fiscal policy, which has multiple goals and is hostage to the slow and uncertain legislative process, monetary policy can be adjusted quickly in response to macroeconomic developments. Indeed, financial markets often anticipate changes in monetary policy before they are announced. Thus, when governments react to fluctuations in output and employment, monetary policy is usually the favored tool.

Given the heavy burden that has been placed on them, central bankers in the industrialized democracies generally have met their responsibilities well in recent years. Inflation has been lower in most countries than at any time since the 1960s. Moreover, there has been only one mild global recession since the early 1980s, and growth rates have been reasonably good. The United States in particular has been able to combine low levels of inflation with low levels of unemployment. Good economic performance today, however, does not guarantee good performance in the future, as history has shown us many times. Thus central bankers are striving to develop strategies for conducting monetary policy that will "lock in" the gains of recent years and contribute to continued stability and growth in the future.

This book is about one of those strategies, *inflation targeting*. Over the past decade, this strategy has aroused considerable interest among central bankers and monetary economists. Inflation targeting in one form or another has been adopted by a number of industrialized countries, including New Zealand, Canada, the United Kingdom, Sweden, Finland, Israel, Spain, and Australia. Japan has recently announced its intention to adopt inflation targets. Moreover, most of the elements of inflation targeting can be found in the long-standing and well-regarded monetary policy of Germany and Switzerland.[1] In the United States, inflation targeting has attracted some influential advocates, both within and outside the Federal Reserve System. For example, a bill introduced by Congressman Bill Saxton ("The Price Stability Act of 1997") calls explicitly for the use of inflation targets by the Fed.[2] Finally, the Maastricht Treaty, the basis for the proposed European monetary union, mandates price stability as the primary objective of the new European Central Bank. The European Monetary Institute has stated that "the list of potential candidate strategies [for the future ECB] has been narrowed down to two, namely monetary targeting and direct inflation targeting."[3]

What Is Inflation Targeting?

Inflation targeting is a framework for monetary policy characterized by the public announcement of official quantitative targets (or target ranges) for the inflation rate over one or more time horizons, and by explicit acknowledgment that low, stable inflation is monetary policy's primary long-run goal. Among other important features of inflation targeting are vigorous efforts to communicate with the public about the plans and objectives of the monetary authorities, and, in many cases, mechanisms that strengthen the central bank's accountability for attaining those objectives.

A Framework, Not a Rule

A principle theme of this book is that, in practice, inflation targeting serves as a *framework* for monetary policy rather than as a *rule* for monetary policy. This distinction requires a bit of explanation.

Following ideas originally put forward by the so-called Chicago School in the 1930s, monetary economists have long characterized strategies for conducting monetary policy as being a form of either "rules" or "discretion." *Rules* are monetary policies that are essentially automatic, requiring little or nothing in the way of macroeconomic analysis or value judgments by the monetary authorities. A putative example of such a rule is the gold standard, in which the conduct of monetary policy (at least in principle) amounted to little more than maintaining the price of gold at the official parity. Another example is the constant-money-growth rule associated with Milton Friedman, under which some specified measure of the money stock is required to grow by a fixed percentage each year, independent of economic or financial conditions.

Advocates of rules usually speak about the "discipline" or "credibility" they create; by adhering rigorously to a certain rule, the monetary authority supposedly reassures the public that it will not engage in inflationary policies or otherwise abuse its powers (for example, by stimulating the economy in order to help incumbent office holders to get reelected). Critics, however, have argued that any discipline created by rules comes at a high cost, since a rule rigorously followed deprives the central bank of its ability to deal with unusual or unforeseen circumstances, let alone with fundamental changes in the economy.

The polar opposite of a rules-based strategy, according to this traditional classification of policy regimes, is an approach based on *discretion*. A central bank that follows a purely discretionary approach to policy-making makes no public commitments about its objectives or future actions, except perhaps in very vague, general terms. Instead, it reserves the right to set monetary policy from month to month or week to week according to the policy-makers' assessment of current conditions (a "look at everything" strategy). Supporters of this approach argue that discretionary policy-making preserves flexibility and enables the central bank to respond to new information or unexpected developments. The flip side of the coin, as advocates of rules-based policies are quick to point out, is that pure discretion forfeits the discipline inherent in a rules-based approach. The lack of perceived discipline may foster uncertainty in the public mind and increase the economy's propensity toward inflation.

The distinction between rules and discretion has played a major role in debates about monetary policy for many decades. However, in our view, this dichotomy between rules and discretion is just too simple to capture the realities that central bankers face. Specifically, in our view, *there is no such thing in practice as an absolute rule for monetary policy.* For example, even the gold standard permitted moderate policy discretion in practice, particularly for countries with ample gold reserves. Moreover, the gold standard was routinely suspended during wars and other emergencies before it collapsed completely during the Great Depression.[4] More recently, the supposedly "fixed" exchange rates of the European Monetary System did not remain fixed during the exchange-rate crises of 1992 and 1993; instead, the official rates were altered or even abandoned altogether as central bankers reacted to changing conditions. As of this writing, the exchange rates of countries in the EMS are required to be kept only within rather wide bands, leaving considerable scope for variations in monetary policy. In short, in real-life monetary policy-making, the rules-versus-discretion distinction is an empty one; in practice, only discretion prevails.

Though we would argue that all monetary policy regimes are in fact discretionary, it is also true that discretion is a matter of degree. Discretion may manifest itself as the relatively undisciplined approach that we described above, leading to policies that change with the personal views of the central bankers or with the direction of the political winds. Or it may operate within a more clearly articulated framework, in which the general objectives and tactics of the policy-makers—although not their specific actions—are committed to in advance. We will present evidence in this book that, in practice, inflation targeting has provided such a framework, allowing monetary policy to operate in an environment that we call "constrained discretion." *By imposing a conceptual structure and its inherent discipline on the central bank, but without eliminating all flexibility, inflation targeting combines some of the advantages traditionally ascribed to rules with those ascribed to discretion.*

Inflation targeting has had important benefits for the countries that have used it. Inflation-targeting countries have achieved lower inflation rates and lower inflation expectations; they experience less "pass-through" into the inflation rate of shocks to the price level; and they typically enjoy lower nominal interest rates as a result of the lower inflation expectations. (On the other hand, there is little evidence so far that inflation targeting reduces the real economic costs of achieving an initial reduction in the rate of inflation.) There is also evidence that the use of inflation targeting increases public understanding of monetary policy, improves policy-maker accountability, and provides a discipline-enhancing "nominal anchor" for monetary policy (see Chapter 2). On net, the experience of inflation-targeting countries appears to be sufficiently positive to warrant close examination of this new approach to monetary policy. The purpose of this book is to conduct just such an examination.

A Case-Study Approach

Although theory can highlight the supposed strengths and weaknesses of a monetary-policy strategy, there is no substitute for observing how the strategy works in practice. Attempts at formal statistical analysis of the impact of inflation targeting are limited by the fact that most of the national experiences with this approach are short—eight or so years at the most. Moreover, many of the questions of how best to implement inflation targets, and of how the political authorities and the public respond to inflation targeting, cannot be fully addressed by strictly quantitative methods. For these reasons, although we present econometric analyses of the effects of inflation targeting in Chapter 10, we have gone well beyond the purely statistical approach in our research. To learn as much as we can from the available evidence, we have conducted detailed *case studies* of those countries that have had the most extensive experience with inflation targeting. We also consider the experience of Germany and Switzerland, which are not self-described inflation-targeters but whose monetary-policy strategies have much in common with inflation targeting. These case studies, with their analysis and interpretation, form the core of this book.

Although the case-study method has been used only rarely in macroeconomics, it has proved extremely useful in our exploration of inflation targeting. We found that case studies provide invaluable information about the broad features and effects of inflation targeting and about the practical implementation and operation of this approach. For example, analysis of the cases will enable us to address issues such as how the inflation target should be defined, how the responsibility for setting the inflation target should be assigned, how the monetary authorities should deal with various macroeconomic shocks, and how the authorities should communicate their goals and intentions to the public. In addition, the case studies have helped us to understand the political setting of inflation targeting, providing insight on questions such as: What political conditions are conducive to the adoption of inflation targeting as a strategy? How does inflation targeting affect the balance of power between the central bank and the rest of the government regarding control of monetary policy? Does inflation targeting allow the political process to generate more rational policy decisions? Finally, the case studies have suggested why many qualitative aspects of the experience with inflation targeting have been similar across countries.

To facilitate cross-country comparisons and generalizations, we have used a parallel structure for the case studies. Our study of each country begins with a brief introduction and a list of some important themes highlighted by the case. The first section outlines why and under what economic and political circumstances the inflation-targeting regime was adopted. The second section describes the operational framework of the targeting regime in the country under study. The third section provides a narrative review and discussion of the country's actual experience with inflation targets. The final section summarizes the lessons to be drawn from the experiences of the country or countries studied.

By applying the same questions to the experiences of all the countries examined, we bring some measure of rigor to our cross-country comparisons and generalizations. The use of the parallel structure has also allowed us to organize the wealth of institutional and historical information available on recent experiences with monetary policy-making. We hope that this analytical record will be of independent interest. Our case-study-based analysis of inflation targeting is, as far as we are aware, the first to date—and one of the few studies of macroeconomic policy more broadly—in which a single team of authors has examined the experiences undergone by a broad group of countries, as opposed to the usual practice of collecting uncoordinated pieces on individual countries written by economists familiar with each.

A Reader's Guide

The rest of the book proceeds as follows: Chapter 2 considers in greater detail the rationale for inflation targeting. It develops further the idea that inflation targeting is neither an ironclad rule nor a form of unbridled discretion, but rather a framework within which constrained discretion may be exercised. Chapter 3 introduces some important operational issues arising from the use of inflation targeting in practice.

The case studies begin in Chapter 4, where we examine the experience of Germany and Switzerland. Although these countries are not formal adherents of inflation targeting, they have had long experience with many of the features that characterize this approach. The chapters that follow proceed in the order in which the countries adopted inflation targeting: New Zealand (Chapter 5), Canada (Chapter 6), the United Kingdom (Chapter 7), and Sweden (Chapter 8). Chapter 9 recounts the experiences of three relatively small, open economies: Israel, Spain, and Australia. Chapter 10 presents econometric evidence on the success of inflation targeting, using data from the major countries studied in this volume.

The book's two final chapters review and summarize what we have learned, drawing conclusions and making recommendations for the implementation of the inflation-targeting approach. In particular, we consider whether it is desirable for inflation targeting to be embraced by the United States or by the European Monetary Union.

This study is intended not only for monetary economists, but also for central bankers and other policy-makers, practitioners in the financial markets, and students of political science, public policy, contemporary history, and economics. We also hope that general readers interested in current developments in monetary policy, in particular the ways that those who wield this important policy tool are accountable to democratic political institutions, will benefit from this book.

Reflecting the variety of possible audiences, the book can be read on several levels. The reader wanting a quick overview of inflation targeting and the policy recommendations that we draw from our case studies should read Chapters 2, 3, 11, and 12. Those interested primarily in the policy implications of the case studies may wish to review the summary boxes at the beginnings of Chapters 4 through 9, as well as the final sections of those chapters, which outline the key lessons of each case. Finally, those readers most interested in the historical experiences of the various countries might concentrate their reading on the first and third sections of each of Chapters 4-9, which discuss the adoption of inflation targeting and the policy experience under this regime in each country, respectively. Of course, we believe that the case studies will prove most rewarding to those who read them in their entirety.

Some prior knowledge of economics and economic policy will be helpful to the reader, particularly for reading the case studies. However, the only chapter that requires special technical expertise is Chapter 10, which presents econometric evidence to assess the success of inflation targeting. Readers allergic to formal statistics can skip this chapter without loss of continuity.

We hope that in whatever manner the reader chooses to dip into this book, he or she will be rewarded with a deeper understanding of how monetary policy has been conducted in some important industrialized countries and of how the framework and institutions of monetary policy-making can be improved.

2

The Rationale for Inflation Targeting

IN GENERAL, macroeconomic policy has many goals besides low inflation, including high real growth, low unemployment, financial stability, a not-too-excessive trade deficit, and so on. Yet a central tenet of inflation targeting is that price stability must be the primary long-run goal of monetary policy. This emphasis on price stability to the seeming exclusion of other objectives demands some explanation. The inflation targeter's case for stressing long-run price stability in formulating monetary policy, and in communicating policy intentions to the public, rests on three arguments.

First, the increased emphasis on controlling inflation arises not because unemployment and related problems have become less urgent concerns, but because economists and policy-makers are considerably less confident today than they were thirty years ago that monetary policy can be used effectively to moderate short-run fluctuations in the economy, except perhaps fluctuations that are particularly severe or protracted. Further, most macroeconomists agree that, *in the long run,* the inflation rate is the only macroeconomic variable that monetary policy can affect. When monetary policy-makers set a low rate of inflation as their primary long-run goal, to some significant extent they are simply accepting the reality of what monetary policy can and cannot do.

Second, there is by now something of a consensus that even moderate rates of inflation are harmful to economic efficiency and growth, and that the maintenance of a low and stable inflation rate is important, perhaps necessary, for achieving other macroeconomic goals.

Third, and in our view most essentially, the establishment of price stability as the primary long-run goal of monetary policy provides a key conceptual element in the overall framework of policy-making. That framework helps policy-makers to communicate their intentions to the public and to impose some degree of accountability and discipline on the central bank and on the government itself. For example, on those occasions when monetary policy is used to address short-run stabilization objectives, the constraint that long-run inflation goals must not be compromised forces policy-makers to consider the longer-term consequences of those short-run measures, imposing a consistency and rationality on their policy choices that they might not otherwise exhibit. In the jargon of monetary economics, explained further below, an inflation target serves as a *nominal anchor* for monetary policy. In doing so, it provides a focus for the expectations of financial markets and the general public, as well as a reference point against which central bankers can judge the desirability of short-run policies.

We now develop these three arguments in greater detail.

What Monetary Policy Can and Cannot Do

Thirty years ago, policy-makers and most economists supported "activist" monetary policies, which were defined as policies whose purpose was to keep output and unemployment close to their "full employment" levels at all times. Supporters of activism believed that there was a long-run tradeoff between inflation and unemployment, known as the Phillips curve (Phillips, 1958; Samuelson and Solow, 1960). According to this view, the monetary authorities could maintain a *permanently* lower rate of unemployment by accepting some degree of inflation, and vice versa. At about the same time, large econometric models of the U.S. economy became available that promised to give policy-makers the quantitative information they needed to implement economic stabilization policies. To many economists and policy-makers, it seemed possible that actively managed monetary (and fiscal) policies could be used to maintain maximum employment pretty much all the time.

That happy outcome was not to be. The business cycle did not die a quiet death in the 1960s, as had been predicted by the more optimistic proponents of activist policies. Indeed, the recessions of 1973-74 and 1981-82 were the most severe of the postwar period. Nor did inflation vanish: The late 1960s and the decade of the 1970s were plagued with rising and variable rates of inflation, in the United States and in many other countries as well. Further, in the view of most economists, the severe 1981-82 recession was largely the *result* of restrictive monetary policy, which in turn had been made necessary by surging inflation. In short, the activist monetary policies of the 1960s and 1970s not only failed to deliver their promised benefits, they helped to generate inflationary pressures that could be subdued only at high economic cost.

Intellectual developments, too, have contributed to the fading reputation of strongly activist policies. Three such developments have been particularly influential: (1) Milton Friedman's monetarist critique, particularly his observation that monetary policy works only with "long and variable lags"; (2) the conclusion, reached first by Friedman and Edmund Phelps, that there is no long-run tradeoff between inflation and unemployment; and (3) increased understanding of the potential importance of central bank credibility to the effectiveness of monetary policy.

Friedman, the founder of the school of macroeconomic thought known as *monetarism,* never doubted that monetary policy can have powerful effects on the economy. He documented this claim extensively in his path-breaking book, *A Monetary History of the United States, 1867-1960,* co-authored with Anna J. Schwartz. But Friedman also argued that those effects set in only with lags that are both long and variable (that is, varying from episode to episode in essentially unpredictable ways). Consequently Friedman argued that monetary policy, though powerful, is not a tool that can be used with precision.

Friedman's critics pointed out that policy lags, even if they are as long and variable as Friedman claimed, do not rule out the possibility of successful activism; they only make control of the economy technically more difficult. For example, they suggested, the techniques of "optimal control" (the mathematical and engineering methods used in guiding rockets) could be used to compensate for lags between a given policy action and its effect. Policy may be less effective under these conditions, Friedman's critics observed, but the active pursuit of short-run economic stability would still be preferable to passive, non-reactive policy-making.

In turn, various arguments against the optimal control paradigm for monetary policy have been put forward. Notably, 1995 Nobel Prize winner Robert E. Lucas, Jr., pointed out (Lucas, 1976) that there is an important difference between rockets and the people who make up an economy, which is that people try to understand and predict the actions of their "controllers" (the policy-makers), while rockets do not. More specifically, Lucas showed that optimal control methods may be useless for guiding policy if they do not take into account the possibility that the public's expectations about the future will change when policies change. The public's expectations about the future, including expectations about future policy actions, are important because they affect current economic behavior. Consequently, Lucas argued, policy-making takes on elements of a strategic game between the policy-makers and the public. Analyzing such a game is a considerably more difficult problem than guiding a rocket. Moreover, given the difficulty of anticipating changes in public expectations, Lucas's argument implies, it is doubtful that policy-makers will be able to control the economy with any degree of precision.

Lucas's argument has had a major impact in thinking about macro-economic policy, though there is still some disagreement about its empirical relevance. There is, in any case, another explanation of why long and variable lags make activist policy counterproductive—an explanation that, in our view, is possibly more relevant than the more technical explanations (such as Lucas's). This alternative explanation rests on the tendency of the public and politicians in modern democracies to take a myopic view of public policy issues. Given the pressures of frequent elections and the almost instantaneous reporting of poll results, it is difficult for politicians to appreciate that watchful waiting is sometimes the best policy.

Instead, in practice, politicians (and politically influenced central bankers) tend to over-manipulate the levers of monetary policy in attempts to control the economy. They may react to a rise in unemployment, for example, by cutting interest rates sharply, ignoring the possibility that the situation might have righted itself by the time the effects of their action are felt. As a result, the economy may overheat, leading either to a bout of inflation or to another sharp policy shift, which generates more, rather than less, economic instability. Thus, because of the interaction of long policy lags and short political horizons, activist policies may lead to worse results than would a policy of restraint.

The second blow to policy activism also was struck by Friedman, in his 1967 presidential address to the American Economic Association (Friedman, 1968). (Arguments similar to Friedman's were made at about the same time by Edmund Phelps [Phelps, 1968]). In his address, Friedman criticized the assumption that *permanent* reductions in unemployment could be achieved by accepting a higher level of inflation (the Phillips curve tradeoff).[1] He agreed that higher inflation might stimulate the economy and lower unemployment for short periods: For example, if wage rates are fixed by contract and prices unexpectedly rise, then the profit margins of firms will increase, giving them an incentive to produce more goods and services. (This is just one of many stories that have been told to explain why inflation may stimulate the economy.) In effect, firms choose to produce more because unexpected inflation implies an unexpected decline in the real cost of production.

However, Friedman pointed out, workers are no more likely than firms to ignore their own economic interests. Once they realize that inflation has risen, they will demand more rapid wage increases to compensate for their lost buying power. As the rate of increase in wages begins to match the rate of increase in prices, the profit margins of firms, and hence their rate of production, will return to normal. The net result is that, in the long run, only the inflation rate has been affected by the expansionary monetary policy; output and unemployment have returned to their normal, or "natural," rates. Hence, Friedman concluded, the notion that by accepting a rise in inflation the country can buy a long-term decrease in unemployment is wrong: *There is no long-run tradeoff between inflation and unemployment.* Or, if there is such a relationship, Friedman added in his 1977 Nobel lecture (Friedman, 1977), it goes the "wrong" way: Because inflation inhibits economic growth and efficiency, an increase in inflation may in fact lead to slightly higher (rather than lower) unemployment in the long run.

This alleged absence of any long-run relationship between inflation and unemployment has important implications for activist monetary policy. Contrary to what was believed thirty years ago, it appears that the *benefits* of expansionary policies (such as lower unemployment) are largely transitory, whereas the *costs* of expansionary policies (primarily the inefficiencies associated with higher inflation) tend to be permanent, absent any countervailing policies.[2] Thus, long after the benefits of the expansionary policies have disappeared, policy-makers will have to choose between accepting a higher permanent level of inflation (with its negative impact on the economy) and reining in the economy by restrictive policies. Restraining the economy with tight monetary and fiscal policies curtails inflation but may also "give back" much of the employment gains, so that often all that has been accomplished in the long run is to increase the instability of the economy. To put Friedman's point another way, in the long run the only macroeconomic variable that the central bank can affect systematically is the inflation rate. It is unlikely that monetary policy can be used to reduce the unemployment rate *on average* over any substantial period of time.

The third challenge to activist policy arose from the *policy credibility problem* (known also in the technical literature as the "time inconsistency problem"), analyzed in important work by Kydland and Prescott (1977), Calvo (1978), Barro and Gordon (1983), and many subsequent authors. The policy credibility problem has to do with the likelihood that, even if it wants to keep inflation low, an activist central bank will often have a strong incentive to increase the rate of inflation above the level expected by the public. The reason is that in the short run wages and many other input costs are fixed by contract or by informal agreement; hence, by creating more inflation than expected, the central bank can stimulate production, employment, and profits, at least temporarily. Since high rates of employment and profits are popular, the central bank will be tempted to boost inflation.

But will the central bank in fact be able to achieve these short-run gains? Kydland and Prescott and the authors that followed, in an argument reminiscent of Friedman's earlier critique, pointed out that it was unlikely that the central bank could consistently fool workers and firms into expecting inflation lower than what subsequently occurred. Eventually, workers and firms would come to understand the central bank's incentives, leading them to adjust their inflation expectations (and hence their wage- and price-setting behavior) accordingly.[3] The outcome, once the public understands the central bank's behavior, is that output and employment are, on average, no higher than they otherwise would be; but inflation is higher than it otherwise would be, with no benefits to compensate.

The policy credibility argument suggests that activist central banks, no matter how much they declare their intention to keep inflation low, will be over-expansionist and hence inflation-prone in practice. As the public comes to understand and anticipate this behavior, higher inflation will become ingrained in the system, without any compensating increase in output or employment. This "inflation bias" is another possible drawback of an activist monetary policy.

Thus a number of developments have acted to dim the optimistic view of the capabilities of monetary policy that was dominant in the 1960s. We do not want to take this point too far: Despite all we have said, we do not deny that monetary policy can have powerful effects on output and employment, or even that there are times when monetary policy can be used constructively to stabilize output and employment. Moreover, it is unrealistic to think that politicians and policy-makers can ever be induced to abstain completely from activist policies, given the political pressures to "do something" about slowdowns in the economy. Indeed, we will see in this book that even the most avid inflation-targeting central banks can and do use monetary policy to address short-term policy objectives, within a framework of maintaining long-run price stability.

Still, to reiterate, activist policy oriented to keeping the economy continuously at full employment comes with important caveats: First, because of long and variable lags between monetary policy actions and effects, the effectiveness of activist policies may be seriously curtailed; indeed, if these policies are controlled by myopic politicians, they may be destabilizing, rather than stabilizing. Second, the apparent absence of any long-run tradeoff between unemployment and inflation reduces the attractiveness of activist policies, since the benefits of such policies (higher output and employment) are largely transitory, while their costs (higher inflation) are permanent. Indeed, in the long run, the central bank can affect only inflation, and not real variables such as output. Finally, there are reasons to believe that central banks that engage in activist policies may be prone to opportunistic behavior, which leads (once the public has come to understand it) to higher inflation but no higher output or employment (the policy credibility problem). This awareness of what monetary policy can and cannot do has moved many monetary policy-makers toward a greater focus on price stability, particularly in the long run.

To forestall confusion: Our criticisms of "policy activism" does not imply that policy-makers should be reluctant to move the policy levers, but rather that doing so in an attempt to maintain continuous full employment is likely to be counterproductive. Indeed, a focus on price stability, as implied by the inflation-targeting approach, may require active manipulation of monetary policy instruments. Policy activism, in the broader sense of policy reacting sensitively to new information as it arrives, is not ruled out by these arguments.

The Benefits of Low Inflation

Another reason for setting price stability as the primary goal of monetary policy is a growing belief among economists and central bankers that low inflation helps to promote economic efficiency and growth in the long run.

That high inflation is detrimental to the economy has long been recognized. Countries experiencing high inflation (or, in extreme cases, "hyperinflation" of 500% to 1000% or more per year) usually exhibit poor economic performance. Among the costs of high inflation are: over-expansion of the financial system, as individuals and businesses devote more and more of their resources to avoiding the effects of inflation on their cash holdings; an increased susceptibility to financial crisis, as difficulties in adjusting to high inflation make the financial system more fragile; poor functioning of product and labor markets, as prices become noisy measures of the relative economic values of goods and services; the costs of frequent re-pricing, along with the costs of monitoring the prices of suppliers and competitors; and distributional effects, often including the destruction of the middle class (much of whose savings become worthless), with the associated social consequences. Fischer (1993) and others have provided evidence that macroeconomic stability, including control of inflation, is an important precondition for economic growth.

Periods of very rapid inflation are clearly destructive. But whether more moderate inflation (below, say, 10% per year) is harmful, is more controversial. Some economists have argued that the public's consistent antipathy toward inflation (as evidenced by opinion polls, for example) is primarily the result of confusion about what inflation really is. Strictly speaking, inflation is a general rise in all prices, wages, and incomes. As such, it should have little or no effect on real purchasing power or the economic incentives of individuals, since a general rise in prices leaves relative prices unaffected. When members of the public talk about inflation, however, they often stress the effects of changes in relative prices (of food or energy, for example) on their standard of living. These are legitimate concerns, of course, but they are largely independent of the rate of inflation *per se*. Moreover, they are beyond the power of monetary policy to correct. "True" inflation, economists have sometimes suggested, should be no more harmful to the economy than a decision to price all goods and services in terms of dimes instead of dollars.

Yet in recent years economists and central bankers have tended to treat even relatively low rates of inflation as a problem, as evidenced by the aggressive disinflations that policy-makers have undertaken in almost every industrialized country in the past two decades. Somewhat paradoxically, to a degree inflation has become perceived as a serious economic problem precisely because of the public's confusion over what inflation is and about how to make adjustments for it. For example, because people find it difficult to adjust for inflation in their calculations, many of their decisions—particularly long-term decisions, such as how much to save for retirement and how to invest their capital—are less appropriate than they might otherwise be. And it is true, given compound interest, that over a thirty- or forty-year period, even slight differences in annual inflation rates have a large effect on the purchasing power of the dollar. Making it difficult to assess both current relative prices and the future price level, inflation can also distort the decisions of firms about production and investment.

More sophisticated savers, investors, and managers, of course, find ways to insulate themselves from the effects of inflation. But that effort is not without its own economic costs, including costs of attention and calculation as well as the cost of resources devoted to (for example) the development of alternative financial instruments. Less sophisticated individuals are less likely to insulate their income and savings from inflation; their inability to do so represents one of several channels by which inflation induces redistribution of wealth among groups.

Shiller's (1996) opinion surveys of public attitudes toward inflation, while confirming the suspicions of economists that the public is confused about what inflation is, show that people believe inflation to be highly uneven in its distributional impacts and hence corrosive of the social compact.

The absence of complete indexation (automatic adjustments for inflation) in virtually all legal and contractual arrangements (which in turn reflects the many technical difficulties with indexation in the real world) also allows inflation, even at relatively low levels, to have adverse economic effects. The most important costs of inflation at low to moderate levels seem to come from the interaction of inflation with the tax system, which is rarely if ever fully indexed to inflation. For example, the common practice of basing capital depreciation allowances on the historical costs of investments, rather than on current values, implies that inflation erodes a key tax benefit of capital formation, reducing the incentive to invest and perhaps (because of sectoral differences in capital lifetimes and depreciation methods) leading to a misallocation of investment among sectors. Fischer (1994) calculates the social costs of tax-related distortions to be about 2% to 3% of GDP at an inflation rate of 10%, and Feldstein (1997) argues that there would be social gains from reducing inflation even when initial inflation is very low. Even moderate inflation can also produce serious distortions in accounting systems, in labor contracts, and in the risks and returns of financial instruments.

To be sure, obtaining direct empirical confirmation of a link between inflation and the overall economic performance of the economy is very difficult. Inflation is, after all, determined by the interaction of many forces. We rarely see variations in inflation that are not associated with factors such as supply shocks or political instability. Consequently, it is probably impossible to conduct completely "clean" tests of the direct effects of inflation on real economic performance.

Still, a number of econometric studies are available that associate higher inflation with lower productivity and with lower rates of growth (see Andersen and Gruen [1995] for a survey). In one of the most cited articles involving cross-national comparisons of growth rates, Fischer (1993) finds that, on average, a 1-percentage-point rise in the rate of inflation can cost an economy more than one-tenth of a percentage point in its growth rate. The effect on the growth rate often varies significantly with the rate of inflation, according to empirical studies. For instance, Sarel (1996) found that the negative effects of inflation increase sharply at higher rates of inflation but are not important at rates of inflation below 8% or so; and Bruno and Easterly (1998) argue that only "infla-tion crises," when inflation reaches very high levels, have significant nega-tive effects on growth. However, some recent studies suggest that the greater unpredictability of price changes associated with inflation may significantly retard economic growth, even at low levels of inflation (Judson and Orphanides, 1996; Hess and Morris, 1996). The greater the long-term effects of inflation on economic growth, the more reason monetary authorities have to focus on long-run price stability as a policy goal.

The Need for a Nominal Anchor

We have discussed two broad reasons for an increased emphasis on price stability in monetary policy-making; namely, reduced confidence in ac-tivist policies and increased concern about the adverse effects of even moderate rates of inflation. While these developments have increased the receptivity of central bankers to inflation targeting as a strategy for policy, we would argue that neither of these two reasons is absolutely essential for justifying this policy approach. The strongest argument for inflation targeting is, instead, that it can help to provide monetary policy with what economists call a "nominal anchor."

The price of any good—bread, for example—is measured in units of whatever it is that serves as money in the society. For example, under a gold standard, as with any other commodity money standard, the price of bread is measured in ounces of gold.[4] Under a gold standard, it is not difficult to see how the price of bread is determined: Because bread and gold are both intrinsically useful commodities, the price of bread in terms of gold cannot differ by too much from the relative marginal values of the two commodities to their users. If there is a famine, for example, bread will become relatively more valued, and its price in terms of gold will rise; but if gold jewelry becomes more fashionable, the demand for gold will rise, and the price of bread in terms of gold will fall.

How prices are determined under an unbacked paper-money stan-dard, which is the nearly universal type of monetary system at present, is far less obvious. With paper money intrinsically almost worthless, what then determines whether a loaf of bread is worth one dollar or three dollars? The short answer, sweeping a lot of complications under the rug, is that in a paper-money system there is a need for some additional constraint on monetary policy, called a *nominal anchor,* to tie down the price level to a specific value at a given time. A nominal anchor can take the form of a quantity constraint, such as a limit on the amount of paper money that can be put into circulation; or of a price constraint, which legally fixes the value of the paper money in terms of some good or asset (such as gold or a foreign currency). Both types have been used, and both can ensure that the economy's price level takes a well-determined, specific value, despite the fact that paper money itself is intrinsically nearly worthless.

Conducting monetary policy without a firmly established nominal anchor is possible but risky. Suppose, for example, that there is no quantity or price constraint on monetary policy, and that for some reason there is a sharp increase in the rate of inflation expected by the public. (Goodfriend [1993] has called such episodes "inflation scares" and argues that they have occurred frequently in postwar U.S. monetary history.) Such shifts in inflation expectations pose a dilemma for the monetary authorities: Say they accommodate the shift by conducting monetary policy in such a way that the expectations prove correct. By doing so they have not only permitted a rise in inflation, but they have also communicated to the public that there is nothing to prevent inflation from rising still further. If, on the other hand, they resist the rise in inflation expectations by keeping monetary policy tight, they risk putting the economy into a recession. In the absence of a nominal anchor, shifts in inflation expectations could be induced by any number of different factors, making macroeconomic prediction and control exceptionally difficult.

Clearly, then, monetary policy is most effective in the presence of a firmly established nominal anchor, and the more understandable that anchor is to the public the better. An effective commitment to long-run price stability is just such a nominal anchor, since (given the current level of prices), a target rate of inflation communicates to the public the price level the central bank is aiming to achieve at specified dates in the future. We will discuss other possible ways to establish a nominal anchor in a later chapter, when we consider alternatives to inflation targeting. We will see, though, that each of these alternatives has important problems.

As we have emphasized, the fact that inflation targeting may be an effective means of providing a nominal anchor for monetary policy is, we believe, a sufficient reason in itself to consider this approach seriously. In particular, inflation targeting would remain a useful framework for policy even if the inflation targets were set at moderate rather than low levels, perhaps because it may be determined that very low inflation is not beneficial to the economy. And, as we will see repeatedly in this book, inflation targeting does not preclude some degree of policy activism; rather, it provides a framework which allows for the pursuit of objectives other than price stability in a more disciplined and consistent manner. Of the three arguments we have discussed for making the control of inflation the primary long-run goal of monetary policy, the ability of inflation targets to help establish a nominal anchor for the price level seems to us the most essential.

Inflation Targeting: A Framework, Not a Rule

The classification of monetary policy strategies as "rules" or "discretion" (see Chapter 1) has been a major theme in the history of monetary economics, and the current debate over inflation targeting reflects that tradition. Recent critiques have tended to place inflation targeting on the "rule" side of the dichotomy (see, for example, [Benjamin] Friedman and Kuttner [1996]).[5] As we have already noted, we believe that this is not the best way to think about inflation targeting.

If inflation targeting were to be treated as a policy rule in the classical sense (which, again, we do not think it should be), it would indeed be open to some serious criticisms. First, the idea that monetary policy literally has no goals other than to control inflation would find little support from the public, from central bankers, or from monetary economists. Second, given that governments and central banks do care about production, employment, exchange rates, and other variables besides inflation, treating inflation targeting as an ironclad policy rule could lead to very poor economic outcomes. For example, Friedman and Kuttner (1996) emphasize that an exclusive focus of policy on inflation could lead to a highly unstable economy in the event of large supply-side shocks, such as the sharp increases in oil prices that have buffeted the world economy from time to time.

Finally, critics of inflation targeting that characterize this approach as a rule might well ask what would be gained by precommitting monetary policy in such a way. The academic literature argues that "tying the hands" of monetary policy-makers should reduce opportunism and hence the inflation bias associated with the policy credibility problem. It also argues that rules-based policies should diminish the costs of disinflation, since increased credibility leads the public to moderate its inflation expectations more quickly. However, critics point out (and our own analysis will confirm) that, although inflation-targeting countries have generally achieved and maintained low rates of inflation, there is little evidence that inflation targeting has significantly reduced the real costs of bringing inflation down. Even the Deutsche Bundesbank and the Swiss National Bank, whose dogged pursuit of low inflation over the past two decades has presumably given them maximum credibility, have managed to achieve reductions in inflation only at high costs in lost output and employment (Debelle and Fischer, 1994; Posen, 1995a). Nor is there evidence that the introduction of inflation targets *per se* materially affects expectations of inflation, as revealed either by surveys or by the level of long-term nominal interest rates. Inflation expectations have come down, in most cases, only as inflation-targeting central banks have demonstrated that they can achieve, and will maintain, low inflation (as we will discuss in Chapter 10; see also Laubach and Posen [1997a]).

These objections are valid, as far as they go. However, we have already expressed skepticism (in Chapter 1) that any monetary-policy strategy that has actually been used has met the classical criteria for a policy rule. As we will see, that skepticism applies particularly to inflation targeting, at least as it is actually practiced by contemporary central banks. Inflation targeting is not a policy rule in the classical sense, and analyzing it as if it were a strict policy rule leads to important misconceptions.

Why do we believe that it is wrong to think of inflation targeting as a policy rule? First, at a technical level, inflation targeting does not provide simple, mechanical operating instructions to the central bank. Rather, inflation targeting requires the central bank to use structural and judgmental models of the economy, in conjunction with whatever information it deems relevant, to pursue its price-stability objective. In other words, inflation targeting is very much a "look at everything" strategy, albeit one with a focused goal.

Second, and more importantly, inflation targeting as it is actually practiced confers a considerable degree of discretion on policy-makers. As the case studies in this book will document in detail, inflation-targeting central bankers, within the constraints imposed by their medium- to long-term inflation targets, have left themselves considerable scope to respond to unemployment conditions, exchange rate fluctuations, and other short-run phenomena.

But if inflation targeting is not a rule in the classical sense, then what is it, and what good is it? As we have suggested, we find it fruitful to think of inflation targeting not as a policy rule, but as a framework for policy within which "constrained discretion" can be exercised. It is here that the nominal anchor function of inflation targets is central: Like a real-life anchor, inflation targets keep the economic ship in the desired area in the long term, while permitting it to respond in the short run to unpredictable swells and currents. Less fancifully, we see the inflation-targeting framework as serving two important functions: (1) improving communication between policy-makers and the public, and, not unrelatedly, (2) providing discipline and accountability in the making of monetary policy.

The announcement of inflation targets communicates the central bank's intentions to the financial markets and to the public, and in so doing helps to reduce uncertainty about the future course of inflation. Many of the costs of inflation arise from its uncertainty or variability rather than from its level; for example, uncertainty about inflation exacerbates the volatility of relative prices (reducing the information content of prices) and increases the riskiness of non-indexed financial instruments and contracts set in nominal terms. In addition, uncertainty about the intentions of the central bank creates volatility in financial markets—a common phenomenon in the United States, where stock-market analysts parse every sentence uttered by the Federal Reserve chairman in search of hidden meanings. By making explicit the central bank's medium-term policy intentions, inflation targets improve planning in the private sector, enhance the public debate about the direction of monetary policy, and increase the accountability of the central bank. Transparency—clarity and ease of understanding by the public—has been claimed for other policy strategies as well, but the public is far more likely to understand what is meant by the predicted rate of change of consumer prices than, for instance, the growth rate of the M1 money stock.

Consider the familiar scenario in which an upcoming election or a slow economic recovery prompts the government to pressure the central bank to apply some short-run stimulus to the economy. In an inflation-targeting regime, the central bank would be able—indeed, would be required—to make it clear that the short-run benefits of that action (faster real growth) may have to be purchased at the cost of higher inflation in the medium and long terms. The accuracy of the central bank's inflation projections, and the willingness of the government to accept the higher inflation, could then be debated in public. The issue of long-run inflation would be on the table, where it could be seen as a counterweight to the projected short-run benefits of an economic stimulus. Making visible the connection between short-term adjustments of monetary policy and their long-term consequences would clarify for the public and for policy-makers what it is that monetary policy can and cannot do. At the very least, the need to consider long-term consequences might help overcome the myopia of policy-makers and dampen their readiness to over-manipulate the levers of policy in a destabilizing way.

Aggregate supply shocks, such as oil-price shocks, present a thornier problem for inflation targeters (as stressed by Friedman and Kuttner [1996]). Once a severe supply shock hits the economy, keeping inflation close to the target may prove very costly in terms of lost output and employment. As the case studies in this book will show, however, a well-designed inflation-targeting regime can cope with supply shocks fairly well. For example, the inflation target in most countries is designed to exclude at least the first-round effects of certain supply shocks, such as rises in the prices of food or energy, or in value-added taxes. Escape clauses that permit the central bank to change its medium-term targets in response to unexpected developments are another way of coping with supply shocks. As we will see in Chapter 4, following the 1979 oil-supply shock, the Bundesbank raised its one-year inflation goal in order to define a new transition path for inflation. The Bundesbank set its short-term inflation goals so that, over time, the inflation induced by the supply shock was gradually eliminated, until the long-run inflation objective was once again reached. In contrast to a purely discretionary approach, in which the central bankers deal with supply shocks by the seat of their pants, the inflation-targeting framework gives the central bank a better chance of convincing the public that the effects of a supply shock will be limited to a one-time rise in the price level, rather than creating a permanent rise in the inflation rate.

The idea that inflation targeting requires an accounting to the public of the projected long-run implications of its short-run policy actions is also central to the argument that inflation targeting can help to discipline monetary policy. Just who needs "disciplining" may differ from country to country (and from period to period), depending on politics, institutional arrangements, and personalities. In the academic literature on central bank credibility, it is generally assumed that it is the central bank that needs to be disciplined, because it desires an unemployment rate lower than the natural rate. This desire creates an incentive for the central bank to try to engineer "surprise" inflations in order to stimulate production and employment. As we discussed when describing the policy credibility problem, however, since the public cannot be fooled repeatedly, the long-run outcome of such policies is higher-than-necessary inflation, without sustained gains in output and employment.[6]

If this theoretical story is applicable, then an inflation-targeting framework will not *directly* prevent the counterproductive attempts of the central bank to apply short-run stimulus. In this respect, inflation targeting is inferior to an ironclad rule, assuming that such a rule could ever be implemented. However, in contrast to a purely discretionary situation with no explicit targets, under an inflation-targeting regime the central bank would be forced to calculate and publicize the long-run implications of its short-run actions, thus ensuring that they would be subject to public scrutiny and debate. To the extent that the central bank governors dislike admitting publicly that they may miss their long-run inflation targets (or, alternatively, to the extent that they dislike having their inflation projections criticized as biased or manipulated), the existence of an inflation-targeting framework provides an incentive for the central bank to limit its short-run opportunism.

Although economic theorists have typically assumed the central bank is the entity that chooses to inflate opportunistically, the executive and legislative branches of government are more likely in practice to have the greater incentive to engage in (or induce) such behavior. In fact, central bankers tend to view themselves as defenders of the currency. That view may be the result of the appointment of "tough" central bankers (for reasons described by Rogoff [1985]), or it may just be that their professional backgrounds and socialization tend to make central bankers relatively hawkish on inflation. In either case, the existence of inflation targets can help the central bank to protect itself from inflationist pressures exerted by the government. In particular, by pointing out the long-run, as well as the short-run, implications of over-expansionist policies, the central bank may be able to win support from the general public and from the financial community in resisting such policies. Again, the case studies in this book will illustrate this scenario.

To summarize, we see a close relationship between the roles of inflation targeting as a nominal anchor and as the linchpin in a framework for making monetary policy. By linking policy to medium- and long-term horizons, but without crippling the central bank's ability to respond to short-run developments, inflation targeting creates a rough compromise between the discipline and accountability of rigid rules and the flexibility of the discretionary approach. Of course, this claim, whatever its superficial plausibility, needs to be supported by evidence from the field. Moreover, it is important to know a great deal more about the actual design and implementation of successful inflation-targeting regimes. Much of the rest of this book is devoted to addressing these issues.

3

Issues of Design and Implementation

IN THE LAST chapter we outlined some of the potential benefits of inflation targeting as a strategy for monetary policy. Whether those benefits
are realized, however, depends on how effectively the strategy is designed
and implemented. In this chapter we discuss, in a preliminary way, some
of the choices central bankers have faced when they adopted inflation
targeting. As we will see in later chapters, inflation-targeting central banks
have tended to implement this approach in broadly similar ways. That
convergence appears to reflect similar, though often independently derived, judgments about how to handle the tradeoffs raised by the inflation-targeting strategy.

Transparency and flexibility are two major advantages of inflation targeting, in our view, and these features have figured prominently in the
official rationales for adopting this approach. By *transparency* we mean
clear and timely communication of policy objectives, plans, and tactics
to the public. Among the goals of policy transparency are the heighten-
ing of public understanding of what monetary policy can and cannot
do; the reduction of economic and financial uncertainty; and the
strengthening of the accountability to the government and the general
public of the monetary authorities. By *flexibility* we mean the ability of
central banks to react effectively to short-run macroeconomic developments within the broad constraints imposed by the inflation-targeting
framework. Over the long haul, these two features tend to be mutually
reinforcing; in particular, we will see in the case studies how transparency often serves to contribute to flexibility of policy over the long run.
At the level of day-to-day implementation, however, operational choices
that promote transparency sometimes end up reducing flexibility, and
vice versa. Thus, *in the design of an inflation-targeting strategy, often a key
issue is the proper balancing of transparency and flexibility.*

The short-run tradeoff between transparency and flexibility is reminiscent of the rules-versus-discretion debate we discussed in the prior
chapters. Generally, the most transparent policies are simple and largely
non-contingent; in the event that previously announced policies (for
example, adherence to a specific inflation target) have to be changed in

midstream, maximum transparency requires that the change be for clearly specified reasons that are obvious to the public. The most flexible policies, in contrast, require that the central bank be able to respond to unforeseen events as they occur and to the availability of new information that is difficult to explain to the public. How the central bank designs and implements its inflation-targeting strategy has a significant effect on how well transparency and flexibility are balanced.

We now turn to some of the operational issues that arise in inflation targeting, and to the manner in which the central bank might best communicate to the public.

Operational Issues

Key operational issues that arise in the implementation of inflation targeting include: the definition of the target; the choice of the numerical values for the targets; the time horizon over which the target is relevant; the conditions, if any, under which the target should be modified; how to go about hitting the target; and how to handle unintentional target misses.

Which Measure of Inflation Should Be Used?

The first step in designing an inflation-targeting regime is to decide on the price index whose rate of change is to be targeted. For maximum transparency, the price index should be one that people are familiar with and that is broad-based, accurate, and timely. For maximum flexibility, the index should exclude price changes in narrowly defined sectors and one-time price jumps that are unlikely to affect trend or "core" inflation—for example, a rise in a value-added tax or in a sales tax. The index chosen should exclude at least the first-round effects of such changes.

All inflation-targeting central banks have chosen to measure the rate of inflation by reference to some version of the consumer price index (CPI), often a version of the index that excludes certain volatile components in order to focus on "core" inflation. In making that choice, however, the central bank must explain to the public how the price index is constructed and how it is related to the headline CPI index. The public should not get the impression that the central bank has chosen this one index from among alternative indexes in order to guarantee favorable results. For this reason, the index chosen should be used consistently throughout the period for which the target is in effect, and it should be clearly defined and reproducible by others. One way of assuring the public that the central bank is not manipulating the data is to have the data compiled by an agency (such as the Bureau of Labor Statistics in the United States) that is independent of the monetary authorities.

What Numerical Value Should the Target Have?

In choosing a numerical value for an inflation target, central bankers have usually stressed "price stability" as their policy objective. Federal Chairman Alan Greenspan reportedly once defined price stability as a rate of inflation so low that businesses and households do not have to take it into account in making everyday decisions. That definition does not, however, provide much practical guidance in setting inflation targets.

A strict definition of price stability suggests an inflation rate at or very near zero. But targeting the inflation rate at zero would create some serious problems. Recent research suggests that ordinary CPI-based measures of inflation may be biased upward. One reason is that a fixed-weight index does not reflect the possibility that consumers may stop buying goods whose prices are rising and substitute similar goods that sell for lower prices. Another reason is that a fixed-weight index may fail to reflect changes in quality, and price rises due to improved quality should not be counted as inflation. According to studies of inflation in the United States, including the officially commissioned study known as the "Boskin Report," the CPI overstates inflation by from 0.5 to 2.0 percentage points per year (Boskin *et al.*, 1996; Moulton, 1996; and Shapiro and Wilcox, 1996). Few studies are available for other countries, but presumably a similar situation prevails abroad as well. Because of this apparent bias in measurement, even if a central bank decided that its target for the "true" rate of inflation should be zero, the implied target for *measured* inflation would have to be greater than zero.

Putting measurement issues aside, there are probably substantive economic risks to targeting inflation at too low a level, just as there are risks to targeting inflation at too high a level. For example, Akerlof, Dickens, and Perry (1996) point out that if nominal wages are rigid downward, which they argue is consistent with the evidence, then reductions in real wages (wages measured in terms of purchasing power) can occur only through inflation. That means that a very low rate of inflation might prevent real wages from falling in response to declining labor demand in certain industries or regions, thereby leading to increased unemployment and blocking the re-allocation of labor from declining sectors to expanding sectors. Simulations conducted by Akerlof *et al.* suggest that inflation rates close to zero might increase the long-run or "natural" rate of unemployment.

Another argument against setting the inflation target too low (Summers, 1991) is that low inflation will induce a low level of nominal interest rates, leaving the central bank with very little room to lower interest rates in the event of a recession (since nominal rates cannot go below zero).[1] Some Japanese central bankers have claimed that the Summers argument applies to the recent recession in their country, during which nominal interest rates fell below 1%, blunting the ability of monetary policy to support a recovery.

The significance of these arguments should not be overstated. According to Akerlof *et al.*, the inflation rates that would significantly affect the natural rate of unemployment are quite low—that is, measured (as opposed to "true") rates of inflation of 2% per annum or less. Moreover, they do not take into account forces that may work in the opposite direction. For example, Groshen and Schweitzer (1996) point out that high and variable inflation rates may increase the "noise" in relative wages, reducing their information content and hence the efficiency of the process by which workers are allocated across occupations and industries. Thus, according to Groshen and Schweitzer, higher inflation can represent "sand" as well as "grease" in the wheels of the labor market.

Summers' argument about nominal interest rates neglects the fact that monetary policy works through channels other than short-term interest rates (see, for example, Mishkin [1996]). Low interest rates did not prevent the Japanese during their recent recession from engineering a large depreciation of the yen, which helped to stimulate their economy. Further, although nominal interest rates cannot be negative, real interest rates (the nominal interest rate less the inflation rate) can indeed be negative; and standard theory suggests that real, rather than nominal, rates are the more important for aggregate spending and real activity.

A more persuasive argument against aiming for an inflation rate of zero is that such a policy risks tipping the economy into deflation, with the true (as opposed to the measured) price level actually falling. Persistent deflation—particularly if unanticipated—can create serious liquidity and solvency problems that may interfere with the financial system's normal functioning, precipitating or exacerbating an economic contraction (Bernanke and James, 1991; Mishkin, 1991). In short, undershooting a zero inflation target (i.e., deflation) is potentially more costly than overshooting a zero inflation target by the same amount.

These risks suggest that the inflation target should probably be set above zero—say, around 1% to 3% per annum. This has been the practice of all the inflation-targeting central banks we discuss in the chapters to come. One of the advantages of inflation targeting is that it provides a floor as well as a ceiling for the inflation rate. Thus a well-run inflation-targeting regime should be as vigilant in protecting the economy from deflationary forces, and the risks of "too little" inflation, as from the costs of excessive inflation. An interesting historical example is that of Sweden in the 1930s, which adopted a "norm of price stabilization" after leaving the gold standard in 1931. As a result, Sweden escaped the devastating deflation experienced by many other countries during the Great Depression and enjoyed much better economic performance during the 1930s (Jonung, 1979).

A Price-Level Target or an Inflation Target?

There is a lively, ongoing debate over whether targeting should be of the inflation rate *per se* or of the price level.[2] Of course, a targeted price level need not imply a constant price level; the targeted level could be allowed to drift upward over time, analogous to a crawling peg for the exchange rate (Goodhart and Vinals, 1994; Svensson, 1996). The disadvantage of targeting the inflation rate is that unanticipated shocks to the price level may be treated as bygones and never offset. As a result, long-term forecasts of the price level might show a large variance that could impede private-sector planning.[3] The practical import of this phenomenon, so long as inflation remains low, is unclear. On the other hand, strict price-level targeting requires that overshoots or undershoots of the target be fully made up. That requirement reduces the variance of long-run forecasts of the price level but may impart significantly more volatility to monetary policy and the real economy in the short run.[4] In particular, there might have to be periods of deflation to compensate for periods of inflation greater than the target. In practice, central banks set inflation rather than price-level targets but tend to compensate partially for target misses, particularly at shorter horizons.

What Horizons?

Inflation targets can be set for one or more horizons. In practice, targets of less than one year or more than four years are unlikely to be meaningful, the former because inflation is not controllable by monetary policy at such short horizons and the latter because such distant targets would have little credibility. Within the 1-to-4 year range, the central bank's choice of target influences the tradeoff between transparency and flexibility: The more tightly the target is specified over the shorter term, the less ambiguity there is in the central bank's communication with the public, but the greater the constraints on the central bank's freedom of action in the short run. A variety of choices are observed in practice.

As we will see in Chapter 4, the practice of the Bundesbank illustrates one means of combining explicit short-term monetary targets with an explicit long-run inflation goal in an effort to send clear signals to the public about its intentions. Every December, the Bundesbank announces an inflation target for the coming year (now called the "normative rate of price increase"), from which the more well-known monetary targets are derived. This objective, while technically only for the current year, is rarely changed; its function is to inform the public of the level to which the Bundesbank intends to maintain or lower the inflation rate in the short term. It also, however, signals which inflationary shocks the Bundesbank plans to accommodate for a few years and which it will not, depending on whether the target is changed. Thus when a supply shock occurred, as in 1979, the Bundesbank's policy was to acknowledge reality by raising the annual inflation goal, thereby not demanding too-rapid progress on inflation in the short run. On the other hand, by labeling the higher inflation target as the "unavoidable rate of price increase," as the Bundesbank did in the early 1980s, it indicated that it would maintain constant pressure toward the long-run inflation objective, widely known to be about 2% per annum. (Indeed, from 1984 to 1996, when it was lowered to 1.5% to 2%, the Bundesbank's inflation target remained constant at 2% per year.)

The Bundesbank's approach illustrates that sometimes it makes sense to vary inflation targets over time. There are at least two scenarios in which varying targets might prove useful: first, in the transition to a lower rate of inflation at the beginning of an inflation-targeting regime; and second, in response to shocks to the economy that make it too costly to hold to the long-run inflation goal in the short or medium term. We discuss the latter case later in the chapter.

A Point or a Range?

As with the choice of horizon and the numerical values of targets, the inflation-targeting central bank has some discretion about whether to announce its targets as a single point or as a range around some mid-point. The implications of this choice (in terms of how expectations are influenced and how the public responds to a target "miss") are much debated, as we will see. In the event that the central bank chooses to announce a range for its target, a narrower range communicates greater commitment by the central bank to nearing its inflation goal than does a broader range. At the same time (per the usual tradeoff), it somewhat reduces the bank's ability to respond to unforeseen events. Unavoidable errors in controlling inflation may drive inflation outside of its range, despite the best efforts of the central bank. Moreover, the damage to credibility of missing a target range entirely is greater than that of missing a target point.

The spread of the target range communicates useful information about the central bank's assessment of the uncertainty surrounding the effects of its policies. Some authors have estimated the uncertainty associated with inflation outcomes to be quite high (see, for example, Haldane and Salmon [1995], and Stevens and Debelle [1995]), implying that the target range would have to be rather wide—on the order of 5 or 6 percentage points—to account for this factor alone. However, a band that wide might well lead the public and the markets to doubt the central bankers' commitment to the inflation target. It remains to be seen whether uncertainty about inflation will be as high under inflation-targeting regimes as it has been historically; as the public comes to expect that the central bank will act strongly to resist inflationary pressures, the predictability and controllability of inflation may well improve endogenously. There does appear to have been a significant decline in the variability of inflation in nearly all industrial countries, whether inflation-targeting or not, in recent years.

What Information Should Be Used in Policy-Making?

Once the central bank has settled on an inflation target, it must turn to the practical problem of achieving that target. What information should it use in its efforts to keep inflation within the desired range?

The answer to this question is "any information that is relevant to the forecasting of inflation." That answer highlights an important difference between inflation targeting and other monetary-policy strategies. Most other strategies, such as money-growth targeting, make heavy use of so-called *intermediate targets*—variables, such as the money stock, that can be controlled reasonably well by the monetary authorities but which have only an indirect and statistically uncertain relationship to ultimate goal variables, such as inflation. Proponents of such strategies have criticized inflation targeting as being non-operational, since the central bank's control of inflation is relatively tenuous and takes effect only after long lags.

While it is true that it is more difficult to control inflation than to control (say) money growth, that point is of little help in comparing the value of the two approaches. Money growth is of no intrinsic interest, so the fact that it is easier to control is useful only insofar as it is a good forecaster of ultimate goal variables. If the relationship of money growth or other simple intermediate targets with goal variables is unreliable, as has proven to be the case in many countries, then little advantage (in terms of better outcomes for the ultimate objectives) is gained by employing these intermediate targets. Indeed, on the general principle that more information is better than less information, it is almost never desirable to rely entirely on a single intermediate target, since there is likely to be at least some additional information available that can aid in forecasting and controlling the ultimate goal variable(s).

Svensson (1997a) has made this basic point in an interesting way: He suggests that inflation targeting regimes *do* use an intermediate target; but that the intermediate target is an inferred rather than directly observed quantity, namely, the current *forecast* of inflation at the target horizon. In other words, in Svensson's formulation, an inflation-targeting central bank should set its instruments (interest rates, for example) at each date so that the forecast of inflation equals its target level. This formulation highlights the fact that an inflation-targeting central bank uses strictly more information than a central bank employing an intermediate target, except in the extreme case that the intermediate target embodies all information relevant to forecasting the goal variable (in which case the intermediate-targeting regime and inflation targeting are functionally identical).

Although it is undeniable that inflation targeting implies the use of more information than traditional intermediate-targeting strategies, which would seem to be a positive feature of that approach, some caveats must be noted. First, even Svensson's formulation begs the important question of exactly which information the central bank should look at, and how it should react to the information it receives. In particular, as shown formally by Woodford (1994) and Bernanke and Woodford

(1997), it is *not* the case that the inflation-targeting central bank can react mechanically to deviations from the target of a private-sector forecast of inflation or of a forecast made by its own economists. Such an approach risks a perverse circularity, in which forecasters find it optimal always to project inflation equal to the announced target, so that their forecasts provide no information to the central bank.

Alternatively, one can show that under some conditions, tying current monetary policy actions too strongly to forecasts of future inflation can lead to a multiplicity of equilibrium outcomes, in which the actual path of inflation is essentially arbitrary. The reason is that strong dependence of policy on expectations can lead to many different expectations of inflation becoming "self-fulfilling prophecies," as expectations induce the policies necessary to make those expectations come true. Rather than basing policy directly on inflation forecasts, the central bank must use a full structural model capable of analyzing the effects of various policy paths in order to implement its inflation targets (see Bernanke and Woodford [1997] for further discussion). Successful use of a structural model to calculate the policies necessary to target inflation will lead the rational forecast of inflation to equal the target, a la Svensson, but only as a byproduct of the process.

A second caveat arises from the observation that one objective of a monetary policy strategy is to communicate with the public, and in particular to establish credibility for the central bank's announced goals and tactics. It could be argued that the long lags and uncertainty involved in controlling inflation are a problem for a central bank that wants quickly to convince the public that it is serious about meeting its targets, and that it intends to be accountable. For this reason, it would seem that the strategy of targeting a more controllable variable (such as the money supply) might be desirable, since in that case the public will be able to observe in rather short order whether the central bank is meeting its commitments. However, a theoretical analysis by Laubach (1997) shows that this intuition does not necessarily hold true. In particular, if the intermediate target has only weak connections to the ultimate goal, as is often the case, the central bank's willingness or ability to hit the intermediate target may convey little information about its commitment to the ultimate target, and thus do little for its credibility.

In actual practice, as they have moved away from intermediate targets, inflation-targeting central banks have relied more on variables that provide useful information about the state of the economy, known as *information variables* or *indicator variables*. An information variable is usually chosen to aid in forecasting and planning because historically it has signaled future changes in the economy. Although information variables provide some basis for policy-making, however, they are not treated as policy targets themselves. An example of an information variable used by several inflation-targeting central banks (notably Canada, Sweden, and, recently, New Zealand) is the so-called "monetary conditions index," a weighted combination of interest and exchange rates, which is supposed to help the central bank determine what the future path of inflation is likely to be.

Information variables should be used with care, since there is no guarantee that the information they contain will remain constant over time, particularly if the monetary policy regime is changing. The best approach is to combine the use of information variables with some other means of predicting macroeconomic conditions, such as econometric models.

When Should Deviations from the Target Be Allowed?

Inflation targets are sometimes missed, and some of the misses, far from being accidental, are the result of decisions by the monetary authorities. When, if ever, is it legitimate to miss a target on purpose? When, if ever, should targets be re-set prior to the end of the announced time horizon?

Because inflation targeting is a framework for "constrained discretion," concerns about macroeconomic variables other than inflation sometimes justify missing or changing a previously announced target. The decision about whether to change the target depends pretty much on the type of shock hitting the economy. In general, there is no conflict between output and inflation stabilization when the precipitating shock is an unexpected change in aggregate spending; using monetary policy to offset an aggregate demand shock is nearly always the correct response. However, an aggregate supply shock, such as a sharp increase in oil prices, may cause a conflict between stabilizing output and employment in the short run and stabilizing inflation in the long run. Targeting a price index that excludes the first-round effects of common supply shocks can, as we have seen, ameliorate this conflict to some degree. But a supply shock that is great enough, or that arises from some unanticipated source, may justify missing or changing a previously announced inflation target.

Missing a target need not signal that the entire inflation-targeting strategy should be abandoned, however. So long as the central bank is able to explain that the miss is the result of unforeseen events, the credibility of the central bank with the public need not be compromised. As in the case of the Bundesbank mentioned above, re-setting a target may communicate to the public how the central bank intends to accommodate the un-

foreseen contingency and at the same time define the transition path back
to price stability. Such a strategy, though it will not eliminate the short-run
inflationary effects of supply shocks, may limit those effects and prevent
them from feeding into the trend rate of inflation. Indeed, Svensson
(1997b) has shown formally that gradual adjustment of the medium-
term inflation target toward the long-run inflation goal is a good approach for policy-makers who are concerned about both minimizing
output fluctuations and maintaining low and stable inflation.

When Is the Best Time to Start Implementing Inflation Targets?

To achieve credibility for an inflation-targeting regime, and to ensure political support, it is important to have some initial successes in achieving
inflation targets. We will see that certain periods, or certain stages in the
business cycle, are more propitious than others for the introduction of inflation targeting. It is interesting that inflation targets have most often been
introduced at times when inflation was already low and falling, rather than
(as one might expect) at times when inflation was on the rise and threatening to get out of control. Inevitably, political considerations play an
important role in the design and implementation of inflation targeting.

Communications Issues

As we have seen, one of the benefits of inflation targeting is that it promotes the transparency and accountability of monetary policy. Achieving that benefit, however, requires answering a number of important
questions.

What Should Be Communicated? In What Forum?

Beyond the inflation targets themselves, what information does the inflation-targeting central bank need to communicate to the public? To
maintain credibility in the eyes of the public, the central bank needs to
provide timely information about the economy at large, the bank's monetary policy, and its policy intentions. That has been the practice of most
inflation-targeting central banks. More specifically, the bank should communicate the rationale that underlies the inflation targets chosen and
the policy strategy itself; the current outlook for the economy; and reports and analyses of inflation indicators, including private-sector forecasts and the central bank's own forecasts. It should also provide progress

reports on its success or failure in meeting its targets, with explanations of why a target might have been changed or missed. The credibility of the central bank depends as much on the objectivity and plausibility of its communications as on its record of hitting targets.

Beyond such information, the inflation-targeting central bank has a responsibility to educate the public about, for example, policy tradeoffs and what monetary policy can and cannot do. Encouraging the public to understand and to get involved in the policy-making process will improve the policy-makers' accountability to the public and lead to better economic outcomes. As we mentioned in Chapter 2, for example, the central bank's assessment of the long-run inflationary consequences of a proposed policy might provide a corrective to the urgings of short-sighted politicians.

The central bank has access to many forums for communicating with the public, including speeches, press conferences, testimony before the legislature, statistical releases, and occasional publications. It must also communicate information on a regular schedule in order to forestall the suspicion that the timing may be politically motivated. Consequently the publication of a formal report at specified intervals should be a feature of the central bank's informational campaign. Several inflation-targeting central banks now publish regular "Inflation Reports," or similar documents, which contain detailed assessments of economic conditions and current information on inflation and monetary policy. These reports advance the public's understanding and acceptance of the bank's monetary policies and contribute to its accountability.

To What Degree Should Central Banks Be Held Accountable?

Some observers believe that central banks should be held directly accountable to the public. Others insist that they should be independent of all political pressure. Monetary policy obviously has a significant influence on the welfare of the citizenry and often involves tradeoffs between the interests of various groups in the society, so there is a presumption that close oversight is warranted. On the other hand, there are strong arguments to support the view that monetary policy works better when it is insulated from short-run manipulation. Those who believe that the main sources of myopia in policy-making reside in the executive and legislative branches and who are convinced that central bankers are capable of functioning on their own as disinterested professionals and public servants tend to argue for independence. And there is indeed a worldwide trend toward increased independence for central banks. That trend is supported by academic literature that holds that independent central banks, compared to central banks subordinated to the government, deliver better outcomes for inflation, as well as outcomes for real variables such as output and employment that are no worse than those achieved by less independent central banks (*e.g.,* see Alesina and Summers [1993]).

A compromise is suggested by Debelle and Fischer (1994), who distinguish between *goal independence* and *instrument independence* for the central bank. Under *goal independence,* the central bank is free to set its own policy objectives, including inflation targets. Under *instrument independence,* policy goals are set by the government alone or by the government in consultation with the central bank, but the central bank is solely responsible for the instrument settings (such as the level of short-term interest rates) needed to achieve those goals. Of the two, it seems that instrument independence would be more likely to minimize short-run political interference and maximize central-bank accountability while still leaving the ultimate goals of policy to be determined at least in part by democratic processes.

Inflation targeting is fully compatible with instrument independence for the central bank. This strategy calls for the inflation targets themselves to be set by a political process in which the central bankers consult with the appropriate legislators or ministers. The execution of the policy is then left completely to the central bank, a division of responsibility that reflects its superior technical expertise in implementing monetary policy and the need to insulate the bank from short-run political pressures and arbitrary interventions. The bank's accountability is assured in two ways: first, by comparing inflation outcomes with the targets; and second, by the central bank's obligation to provide the public with convincing rationales for the policy choices it makes. Because inflation responds to policy only after long lags, and because inflation targets are rarely hit exactly, this second means of maintaining accountability is essential under an inflation-targeting regime. It provides another reason for issuing regular, detailed inflation reports to the public.

As we shall see, the degree of independence enjoyed by inflation-targeting central banks varies quite a bit in practice. Some central banks, such as the Bundesbank, command significant goal independence as well as instrument independence. In the United Kingdom (until recently) and Canada, in contrast, the government retains some control over even the instrument settings of monetary policy. The case studies in the chapters that follow will explore the efficacy of various political arrangements and the effect of inflation targets on those arrangements.

Part Two ————————————————————————

CASE STUDIES AND EMPIRICAL EVIDENCE

4

German and Swiss Monetary Targeting: Precursors to Inflation Targeting

OUR CASE STUDIES of monetary-policy strategies in operation begin with Germany and Switzerland, countries long associated with price stability and "hard" currencies. Officially, for the past two decades Germany and Switzerland have classified themselves as "monetary targeters"; that is, their central banks have expressed their monetary-policy objectives at least in part in terms of the growth rate of the money stock (variously defined), rather than primarily in terms of inflation or some other goal variable. Some observers have cited the strong performance of these central banks as evidence in favor of rules-based monetary policies that impose strict limitations on the discretion exercised by the monetary-policy authorities.

However, as we will see, many features of the German and Swiss monetary regimes are features of inflation targeting as well. Those features include not only a basic orientation of monetary policy toward the pursuit of low inflation (and a successful record in achieving it), but many other aspects of central bank operations and strategy used by self-described inflation targeters. Indeed, as suggested by Bernanke and Mishkin (1997), Germany and Switzerland might best be thought of as "hybrid" inflation targeters and monetary targeters, rather than as strict adherents to a money-targeting rule. Thus the experiences of these two countries over more than twenty years should provide useful lessons for practitioners of inflation targeting.

This chapter, like the subsequent case studies, is divided into three main parts. First, we discuss the circumstances surrounding the initial adoption of the monetary-policy regime. Next we describe and analyze the operational framework of monetary policy in the countries being considered, with particular attention to how this framework supports the substantive economic objectives of the policy regime. Finally, we review the historical record of monetary policy under the particular policy regime, concluding with some broad lessons from the policy experience.

Key Features of German and Swiss Monetary Targeting

- Germany and Switzerland are self-described "monetary targeters," and targets for the growth rates of various monetary aggregates are announced each year. However, announced numerical goals for inflation also play a key role in German and Swiss monetary policy (they are used, for example, in deriving the monetary targets), and there is considerable evidence that the inflation goals have ultimate priority in determining policy decisions. Overall, the substantive differences between monetary targeting as practiced by Germany and Switzerland and inflation targeting as practiced by other countries studied in this book are not that great.

- Both countries adopted monetary targeting in order to establish a "nominal anchor" for monetary policy, with the hope of increasing policy flexibility by moderating and "tying down" the public's inflation expectations.

- Monetary targeting, far from being a rigid policy rule, has been quite flexible in practice. Monetary targets are often missed because of central bank concern about other objectives, including output and exchange rates. The convergence of short-run inflation targets with the long-run inflation goal has often been quite gradual, which also permits flexibility regarding short-run objectives.

- The commitment to price stability has been defined in both countries as a target for measured inflation that is greater than zero.

- Germany has settled on the use of a range for its monetary targets, which it views as a source of some short-run policy discretion. Switzerland announces a point target, which it argues does not give the public the false impression that money is controllable over a narrow range.

- Both regimes have demonstrated strong commitment to the communication of strategy to the general public. The monetary targets are used as a framework for explanation, but central bank reports to the public go well beyond the question of whether the target was hit to cover a wide variety of economic issues and developments.

The Adoption of Monetary Targeting in Germany and Switzerland

The decision to adopt monetary targeting in Germany and Switzerland, though prompted by the breakdown of the Bretton Woods fixed-exchange-rate regime in 1973, was a matter of choice by both countries. Neither was under any pressure at the time to reform either its economy in general or its monetary regime. In fact, the breakdown of Bretton Woods was due in part to the commitment of these central banks to price stability and to the concomitant appreciation of their currencies. The loss of the exchange-rate anchor was not the sort of crisis that demanded an immediate response. In fact, it took both countries from two to three years to move to the new regime.

Two main factors led to the adoption of monetary targeting in Germany and Switzerland. The first was a conviction that a nominal anchor was needed for monetary policy and that monetary policy should neither accommodate inflation nor set medium-term output goals. The second was a perception that medium-term inflation expectations had to be locked in to permit the central banks some flexibility in the future. In other words, there was a desire to coordinate the inflation expectations of the public with the policy objectives of the central banks. Over time, the broader proposition emerged that monetary targeting would provide a means of communicating the relationship between current conditions and medium-term goals to the public.

Switzerland and Germany adopted monetary targeting in December 1974; the United States and Canada followed suit with similar targeting approaches in 1975. Although there seems to be a tendency for countries to adopt monetary targets in times of high inflation (Bernanke and Mishkin, 1992, p. 186), the Germans and the Swiss seem to have been most concerned with keeping inflation expectations under control once inflation had begun its downward trend. All four countries set a quantified target for the intended rate of monetary expansion.[1]

The emergence of inflation in the early 1970s drew the attention of monetary policy-makers to the role of money growth in the inflationary process. As early as October 31, 1972, before the first oil shock, the Council of Ministers of the European Community had passed a resolution that called for the member states to

> progressively reduce the growth rate of the [broad] money supply . . . until it equals that of the real [GNP], augmented by the normative price rise deter-

mined in accordance with overall economic aims and after taking account of the structural development of the relationship between money supply and national product. This target is to be reached not later than the end of 1974. (Deutsche Bundesbank, 1972a, p. 24)

This resolution outlined a concept of monetary targeting based on the so-called quantity theory, which states that nominal spending in the economy is determined by changes in the quantity of money. Use of this relationship allowed central banks to consider output as well as inflation in setting targets for monetary policy. Ever since, the quantity theory has been used for target-setting in both Germany and Switzerland. Although the resolution foresaw the need to provide for flexibility in the event of shocks to the relationship between the stock of money and nominal spending (so-called "velocity shocks"), it recommended a point target rather than a target range.

Missing from the EC resolution is any mention of the need to an-nounce the target to the public or any concern about the transparency of policy. We must remember, however, that while the intellectual cur-rent of the time was running toward monetarism, and toward rules rather than discretion, the focus on the role of public expectations and central bank credibility in monetary policy-making had not yet emerged. In adopting their money-targeting policy, Germany and Switzerland do not appear to have been motivated by any desire to increase credibility by "tying the hands" (that is, limiting the discretion) of the central bank. Nor, for that matter, did they make any institutional provision for ensur-ing oversight and accountability. The effective independence of the Swiss and German central banks, and the influence of the political coalitions that supported central bank independence, limited the incentives of the central banks to reduce their range of policy flexibility.

Germany

On December 5, 1974, the Central Bank Council of the Deutsche Bundesbank announced that "from the present perspective it regards a growth of about 8 percent in the central bank money stock over the whole of 1975 as acceptable in the light of its stability goals." (Deutsche Bundesbank, 1974b, December, p. 8). The Bundesbank considered this target to "provide the requisite scope . . . for the desired growth of the real economy" and declared that the target had been chosen "in such a way that no new inflationary strains are likely to arise as a result of mon-etary developments." Since 1973, the Bundesbank had been using the central bank money stock, or CBM, as its primary indicator of monetary developments. (The central bank money stock is defined as currency in circulation plus sight deposits, time deposits with maturity under four years, and savings deposits and savings bonds with maturity under four years, the latter three weighted at their required reserve ratios as of January 1974. The Bundesbank's rationale for this choice of intermediate target variable is discussed in the next section.) Although this was a unilateral announcement on the part of the Bundesbank, the announcement stressed that "in formulating its target for the growth of the central bank money stock [the Bundesbank] found itself in full agreement with the federal government." Coming nearly two years after the demise of the fixed-exchange-rate system of Bretton Woods in March 1973, the Bundesbank's announcement marked the end of a fairly lengthy period during which German monetary policy had been conducted without an explicit nominal anchor. The new approach reflected the Bundesbank's response to the problems that had beset monetary policy during the last years of Bretton Woods and the immediate aftermath.

The Bundesbank had always interpreted its mandate of "safeguarding the currency" under Article 3 of the Bundesbank Act of 1957 as requiring that it strive for price stability in its conduct of monetary policy. During the last years of Bretton Woods, its pursuit of that goal had been imperiled by the flow of massive amounts of capital out of the U.S. dollar into the deutschemark. The flow was also directed into the currencies of countries that were following German monetary policy most closely—namely, Austria, Belgium, the Netherlands, and Switzerland. That flow, which was triggered in part by the sluggish growth and the relatively high inflation that the United States had been experiencing since 1968, repeatedly forced the Bundesbank to tolerate excessively high rates of money growth, despite its domestic objectives.

Upon its release from its exchange intervention obligation following the Bretton Woods collapse in March 1973, the Bundesbank immediately started to reduce the "free liquid reserves" of the country's banking system. Free liquid reserves were defined as excess reserves plus liquid assets that could be converted into CBM at any time. The quantity of these reserves provided a measure of the extent to which the banking sector could expand its balance sheets without facing a shortage of central bank money. Short of imposing reserve requirements on bank loans, reducing the free liquid reserves of the banks to almost zero was seen as the most effective means of controlling the expansion of bank lending, which was the Bundesbank's primary concern. Since the Bundesbank was no longer obliged to buy foreign currency on demand,[2] the balances that the banks maintained abroad had (mostly) lost their quality of being potential central bank money. Within a few weeks the Bundesbank succeeded in reducing free liquid reserves to near zero.

A second step was to deter banks from expanding their balance sheets by increasing the cost of central bank money. On May 30, the Bundesbank decided not to grant Lombard credit until further notice. (Lombard credit is analogous to the Fed's loans via the discount window to U.S. commercial banks. The Bundesbank provides additional funds to commercial banks through what are called rediscount quotas, loans at a subsidized rate known as the discount rate. The interbank interest rate, the market rate at which banks lend to each other, is usually bounded from above by the Lombard rate and from below by the discount rate.) The effect is clearly visible in the movement of the overnight rate in Panel B of Figure 4.1, which shows the history of some basic economic indicators for Germany. This measure was coupled with further increases in the discount rate and reductions in the rediscount quotas over the following months. From late 1973 on, the Bundesbank granted special Lombard credit to limit the volatility in the overnight rate, but still at punitive rates. It was at this stage that growth in the supply of central bank money became the main focus of monetary policy. In a section of the September 1973 *Monthly Report* entitled "Monetary policy through control of the central bank money supply," the Bundesbank stated that it "based its policy on the consideration that the banks' need for central bank money ultimately depends on the scale of the expansion in bank lending," and that it was prepared to make additional central bank money available "only in so far as such [provision] was consistent with its monetary policy target of reducing the inflation-induced excess money supply" (Deutsche Bundesbank, 1973b, September, p. 9).

There were signs that the restrictive policy of the Bundesbank was beginning to slow both inflation, which had peaked at almost 8% in mid-1973, and GDP growth (Panels A and C of Figure 4.1). Then, in October 1973, the first oil crisis broke. The Bundesbank's efforts to bring down inflation were thus jeopardized at the very time output growth was expected to fall drastically. In particular, the Bundesbank was concerned that the oil price increases would quickly lead to a second-round wage-price spiral. Accordingly, by its own account, "the Bundesbank endeavored to keep monetary expansion within relatively strict limits during 1974. Although it did not expressly commit itself—as it did in December 1974—to any quantitative target, it tried to ensure that monetary expansion was not too great, but not too small either" (Deutsche Bundesbank, 1974a, p. 17). Despite the fact that it did not specify a quantitative target, the Bundesbank was determined to communicate its message of restraint as clearly as possible.

> It is of the utmost importance that in the field of price and wage policy management and labor behave in a way appropriate to the new situation. In their decisions management and labor will have to consider the fact that if the oil shortage continues, hardly more goods will be available for distribution next year than in 1973. (Deutsche Bundesbank, 1973b, December, p. 7)

Here the Bundesbank was explaining to the public that policy must be forward-looking and oriented toward inflation expectations. Its justification for a "just right" monetary expansion reflected its concern for real-side effects, a concern which led it to undertake disinflation only gradually.

The announcement of a growth target for central bank money in December 1974 can thus be seen as another step in the gradual reorientation of Germany's monetary policy. It combined the movement toward basing monetary policy on control of the central bank money supply and the perceived need to communicate clearly the objectives of that policy to the public. "Under the influence of the growing weakness of business activity and the first signs of progress in fighting inflation, a change was made in the last quarter of 1974; the target became a slightly faster rate of monetary growth, which was publicly announced towards the end of the year" (Deutsche Bundesbank, 1974a, p. 17).

This announcement is interesting for three reasons. First, although the Bundesbank was mainly concerned with reversing the inflationary trend of the previous five years, its new monetary policy did not ignore real activity as a goal. Second, it speaks of monetary policy as acting in a preemptive manner ("first signs"). Third, it declares that monetary targets were being adopted at a time when both inflation and money growth were expected to slow down, making it easy to meet targets but at the same time nourishing the fear that that very easing might unleash inflationary expectations. As Panel C of Figure 4.1 shows, Germany was entering a short but deep recession, similar to that of 1967. Immediately following the oil crisis in October 1973, GDP growth had started to slow, and by the first quarter of 1975 it had turned negative.

The Bundesbank, in discussing its plan to adhere to the EC resolution quoted above, remarked that

> the formulation of this objective is based on the recognition that the persistent and accelerating decline in the value of money is impossible without a corresponding expansion of the stock of money held by the public and, indeed, that the monetary sphere in its own right not infrequently promotes the inflation of prices and wages. (Deutsche Bundesbank, 1972a, p. 24)

A. CPI and Unavoidable/Normative Inflation

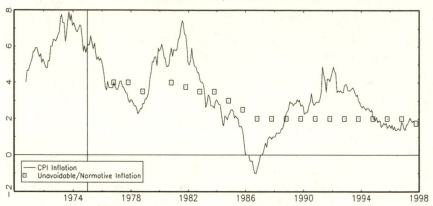

C. GDP Growth and Unemployment Rate

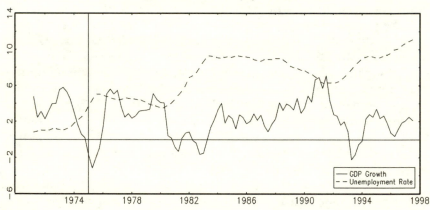

E. Monetary Targets and Outcomes

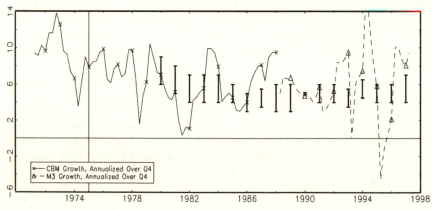

B. Overnight and Long-Term Interest Rates

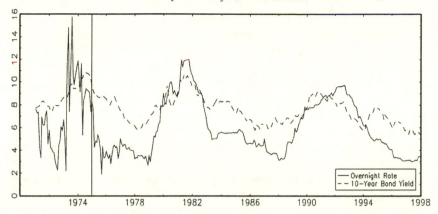

D. Nominal Effective Exchange Rate

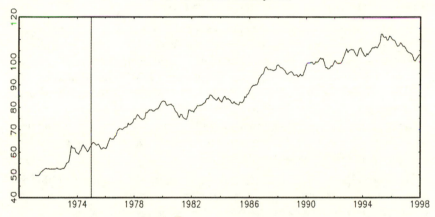

Figure 4.1 German economic indicators. *Sources:* A) Bank for International Settlements database, Deutsche Bundesbank; B) Bank for International Settlements database; C) Main economic indicators of the Organisation for Economic Cooperation and Development; D) Bank for International Settlements database; E) Bank for International Settlements database, Deutsche Bundesbank.

Apparently monetarism was having a significant impact on policy-makers inside the Bundesbank. Still, although the Bundesbank based its annual monetary targets on the quantity theory, it was never dogmatic in doing so. Otmar Issing, the Chief Economist of the Bundesbank, noted (Issing, 1996, p. 120), "One of the secrets of the success of the German policy of money-growth targeting was that . . . it often did not feel bound by monetarist orthodoxy as far as its more technical details were concerned." (Indeed, Issing accepts the characterization of German monetary policy as "pragmatic monetarism" [Issing, 1997, p. 72]). This statement indicates that the Bundesbank makes a link between "technical details" and monetary policy success. The commitment to price stability alone is not enough without the proper design of the operational framework for targeting.

Another impetus for monetary targeting, the coordination of the expectations of economic agents, was a subject of lively interest at the time the Bundesbank announced its first target.

> From the immediately preceding period of fixed exchange rates [trade unions and enterprises] were accustomed to the Bundesbank's monetary policy measures becoming ineffective when they resulted in massive inflows of funds from abroad. As a consequence the Bundesbank initially failed to influence wage and price behavior in the way it wished. In the light of this adverse experience, the Bundesbank, together with the Federal Government and the independent Council of Economic Experts, concluded that it would be useful to explicitly define the 'monetary framework' for the growth of production and prices. (Schlesinger, 1983, p. 6)

Although its statements at the time do not make the point explicitly, one of the Bundesbank's primary concerns appears to have been that public misperceptions might lead to expectations of high inflation. At the beginning of 1975, in view of the apparent weakness in the economy, the Bundesbank continued to ease monetary policy while avoiding any suggestion that its determination to bring down inflation was diminishing. Recent experience had shown that wage-setting behavior in particular had been little affected by the Bundesbank's efforts to lower inflation:

> Wage costs have gone up steadily in the last few months, partly as after-effects of [earlier] settlements . . . which were excessive (not least because management and labor obviously underestimated the prospects of success of the stabilization policy). . . . Despite the low level of business activity and subdued inflation expectations, even in very recent wage negotiations two-figure rises have effectively been agreed. (Deutsche Bundesbank, 1974b, December, p. 6)

The credibility issue arose, then, in association with the Bundesbank's efforts to stop the pass-through of a one-time shock (the oil crisis) to the price level. From this perspective, Germany seems to have adopted monetary targeting, at least in part, in order to create a means of communication with the public with the hope of exerting some leverage on inflation expectations. After central bank money had grown by 6% during 1974, the Bundesbank announced a target growth rate of 8% for 1975:

> An acceleration of money growth was intended to stimulate demand and provide the monetary scope necessary for the desired real growth of the economy. On the other hand, the target was also intended to show that no precipitate action would be taken to ease monetary conditions, in order not to jeopardize further progress towards containing the inflationary tendencies. (Deutsche Bundesbank, 1976a, p. 5)

This explanation was made only after the target had been announced, however—not contemporaneously with the announcement itself.

Switzerland

In many respects Switzerland and Germany followed the same monetary policy during the early 1970s. In both countries, massive capital inflows had caused excessive monetary expansion during the final years of Bretton Woods, and in both countries the central bank had suspended its interventions in early 1973. One of the reasons they experienced such huge capital inflows was the perception that both central banks enjoyed considerable political independence as well as public support for their pursuit of anti-inflationary policies. Finally, at the end of 1974, after a transition period of almost two years, both countries adopted a monetary target as a nominal anchor, replacing the fixed exchange rate.

The General Directorate of the Swiss National Bank "decided, at the beginning of the year [1975], to fix the expansion of official means of payment for 1975. . . . Under [the economic] circumstances, the General Directorate estimated that an expansion by 6% of the money stock M1 . . . would be appropriate" (Swiss National Bank, 1975a, pp. 7-8, translation by authors). With this as a target, the Swiss National Bank intended to provide monetary conditions "that are conducive to furthering tranquillity at the price front without obstructing the broader economic developments" (Swiss National Bank, 1975b, January, p. 3, translation by authors). The announcement of the target was accompanied by little public fanfare or explanation, reflecting a lack of concern over the coordination of expectations and the assumption that the target was simply to guide policy. As in the case of Germany, it appears that the decision to adopt a monetary target was taken unilaterally by the Swiss National Bank but with the support of the Federal Government, though no reference was made to the Government's involvement in the decision.[3] The decision to target a narrow monetary aggregate, in contrast to Germany's choice of a broad measure of money, is discussed in the next section.

As in Germany, the Swiss National Bank's announcement marked the end of a period of almost two years during which monetary policy had been conducted without a nominal anchor. The Swiss experience during the final years of Bretton Woods and the immediate aftermath was, however, even more extreme than that of Germany. Since Switzerland is both a small economy and an important international financial center, the speculative capital inflows into the Swiss franc in 1971 and 1972 as a proportion of the money stock were even larger than in Germany. In the year to December 1971 the monetary base and M1 in Switzerland grew by 18% and 21% respectively, although from August to December the fixed exchange rate had been temporarily suspended. Since most of the expansion was caused by the inflow of funds from abroad, interest rates were impotent as a tool to slow the monetary expansion. One tool that was heavily used to stem the flow was the imposition of minimum reserve requirements, both on liabilities to residents and even more so to nonresidents. In view of the scale of the monetary expansion, the Swiss National Bank went one step further by introducing, in July 1972, a ceiling on the growth of bank credit to persons and companies domiciled in Switzerland. If a bank exceeded the ceiling, it had to pay a certain fraction of the excess amount into a blocked account at the Swiss National Bank.

Despite these and other measures, renewed inflows of speculative capital into the Swiss franc followed the announcement of the unprecedentedly large U.S. trade deficit. On January 23, 1973, the Swiss National Bank was finally forced to suspend its interventions against the dollar, thus freeing itself to cope with the task of controlling monetary expansion. During 1973, the Bank kept both the restrictive reserve requirements and the ceiling on credit growth in place. In July 1973 the ceiling on credit growth for the year ending July 1974 was fixed at 6%. While it is difficult to gauge the stance of monetary policy in view of the multitude of instruments that were being employed, the trends of all the non-interest rate policy measures suggest that the Swiss instrument rate understated just how tight monetary policy was at the time. The movement of the overnight rate shown in the Swiss Economic Indicators (Figure 4.2, Panel B) suggests that monetary policy was kept tight until at least mid-1974.

Movements of the interest rate, however, do not seem to have been very large compared to the movements of the German overnight rate during the same period. One reason that the Swiss National Bank continued to rely on credit restrictions, in addition to its other instruments, was that changes in the interest rate were known to feed through very quickly into the CPI. In Switzerland rent increases were, and still are, tied to increases in mortgage rates (through a legal appeals process available to tenants), and the share of rents in the CPI at that time was 17%. "The authorities nevertheless did supervise the movements of bank liquidity in order to . . . prevent liquidity from contracting too much and causing a sharp rise in interest rates, such a development being considered undesirable mainly because of the effect of rising long-term rates on the trend of prices" (OECD, 1975, p. 33).

The difficulties the Swiss have had with monetary control as a result of peculiarities in their banking and rental markets suggest why some inflation-targeting countries have chosen target series other than the headline CPI. The United Kingdom, for example, targets RPIX inflation, which excludes the first-round effect of interest rates on mortgage rates. The Swiss National Bank, while clearly aware of these difficulties from the start, appears to have felt that having a more clearly understood target series and goal (M1 and later the monetary base, and CPI inflation), and then attributing deviations from target to these factors as they arose, was the better strategy. As we will see, the Bank has consistently chosen simple rules with complicated explanations over complicated rules with simple explanations.

As the Swiss economy began to weaken in the course of 1974, the Bank applied both the reserve requirements and the credit ceiling more flexibly. The credit ceiling in particular was considerably relaxed in January 1975 and was abolished on May 1, 1975. In a situation in which unprecedentedly high interest rates were no longer needed to control the expansion of bank lending without quantitative restrictions, the Bank shifted toward a focus on the control of the money supply. The adoption of monetary targets was thus less gradual than in Germany, partly because of the faster response of the Swiss financial system to monetary impulses. Still, the adoption of the new policy was largely a response to the loss of the nominal anchor during the last years of Bretton Woods. And, as in Germany, monetary targets were adopted at a time when both inflation and money growth were slowing down, making the targets easier to meet.[4]

A. CPI Inflation

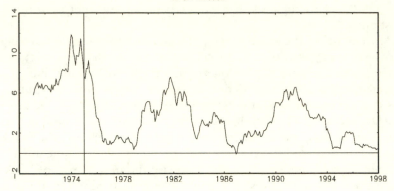

C. GDP Growth and Unemployment Rate

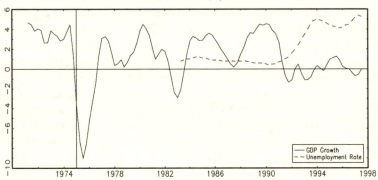

E. AMB and SAMB Growth and Annual Targets 1980-90

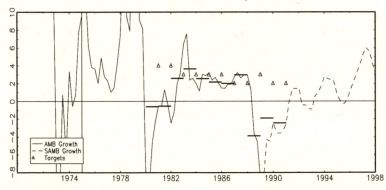

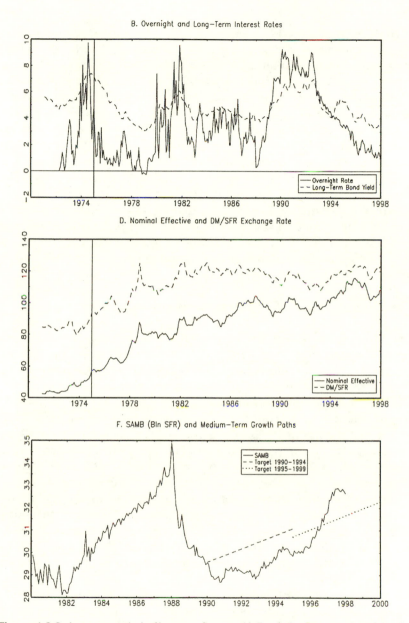

Figure 4.2 Swiss economic indicators. *Sources:* A) Bank for International Settlements database; B) Bank for International Settlements database; C) Main economic indicators of the Organiasation for Economic Cooperation and Development; D) Bank for International Settlements database; E) Bank for International Settlements database, Swiss National Bank; F) Bank for International Settlements database, Swiss National Bank.

At the beginning of 1975, Switzerland was about to enter the worst recession in its postwar history (Figure 4.2, Panel C). The oil shock had
triggered a downturn that must already have been under way. Also, although the strong Swiss franc helped to absorb the inflationary impact of
the shock (Figure 4.2, Panels A and D), that impact posed a serious threat
to the Swiss export sector, which constituted about a third of GNP at the
time. During 1975 exports of merchandise fell by 8% in real terms. Moreover, though subdued growth in real wages supported the Bank's fight
against inflation, it also contributed to a sharp decline in real consumption, which was worsened by a significant outflow of foreign workers. The
money-targeting initiative did nothing to ease the high cost of Switzerland's
disinflation, nor did the Bank suggest that the targeting would provide a
coordinating function for wage- and price-setters that would lower that
cost. The adoption of a target was intended to cap inflation expectations
by indicating a policy commitment, and nothing more.

The Operational Framework in Germany and Switzerland

From 1975 to 1980, both the Bundesbank and the Swiss National Bank
adhered to the strategy of setting and announcing their monetary targets, although they made a number of changes in their procedures along
the way that reflected their experience with those targets. Since 1980,
however, the operational framework of their targeting has displayed a
remarkable degree of continuity. Both banks have coped successfully
with overshootings of their targets, for example. Moreover, both have
made changes in the particular monetary aggregates targeted and in
targeting procedures when they felt circumstances warranted, without
triggering a persistent rise in inflation or inflation expectations.

We now turn to a review of the key features of the operational framework of each country. We then analyze the rationale behind the choice
of the intermediate target variable—narrow money in Switzerland, broad
money in Germany—and the connection between the choice of operational framework and procedures for dealing with deviations from announced targets.

Our historical-institutional analysis in this and the following section
confirms the view of German and Swiss monetary policy-making raised
in Bernanke and Mishkin (1992) and supported by later econometric
studies,[5] that 1) neither country's central bank treats price stability as
the only goal of policy, particularly in the short- and medium-run; and
2) neither central bank views the correlations between money growth

and goal variables to be strong enough to justify strict adherence to the targets or exclusion of other relevant information. In fact, the main function of monetary targeting in both countries has been to provide a framework within which the central bank could convey to the public its long-term commitment to price stability, while retaining some flexibility for shorter-term policy discretion.[6]

Germany

From 1975 until 1987, the Bundesbank announced targets for the growth of central bank money (CBM). Again, CBM is defined as currency in circulation plus sight (that is, demand) deposits, time deposits with maturity under four years, and savings deposits and savings bonds with maturity of less than four years, with the latter three components weighted by their respective required-reserve ratios as of January 1974. (The weights are 16.6%, 12.4%, and 8.2%, respectively.) CBM differs from the monetary base in that the excess balances of banks are excluded and the weights of deposits subject to reserve requirements are based on historical, not current, ratios.

Since 1988, however, the Bundesbank has used the growth rate of M3 rather than CBM as its official target. M3 is defined as the sum of currency in circulation, sight deposits, time deposits with maturity under four years, and savings deposits at three months' notice. Apart from the fact that CBM does not include savings deposits with longer maturities, or savings bonds, the major difference between M3 and CBM is that CBM is a weighted-sum aggregate, while M3 is a simple sum. Because the weights ascribed to the three types of deposits in CBM are fairly small, the only source for large divergences between the growth of the two aggregates is a significant fluctuation in the holdings of currency as compared with deposits. Such a divergence became critical in late 1987 in the face of shifting financial incentives, and again in 1990-91, after German monetary unification.

The Bundesbank has always set its monetary target for the next year at the end of the current year. To derive a monetary target, it uses a quantity equation that states that the amount of nominal transactions in an economy within a given period of time is equal to the amount of the means of payment multiplied by the velocity at which the means of payment changes hands. In rate-of-change form, the quantity equation states that the sum of real output growth and the inflation rate is equal to the sum of money growth and the change in (the appropriately defined) velocity. The Bundesbank derives the target growth rate of the chosen monetary aggregate (either CBM or M3) by estimating the growth of the long-run production potential over the coming year, adding the rate of price change it considers unavoidable (described below), and subtracting the estimated change in trend velocity over the year.[7]

The Bundesbank does not use forecasts of real output growth over the coming year in its target derivation. Instead, it estimates the growth in production potential.[8] This emphasis on potential rather than actual output is consistent with the Bundesbank's public position that it should not engage in policies aimed at short-term stimulation (although the effect of the approach, to a degree, is to create some countercyclicality in interest rates). This approach allows the Bundesbank to claim that it is not making any choice about the business cycle when it sets policy. It also de-emphasizes any public discussion of its forecasting efforts for the real economy, further distancing monetary policy from the considerations of expected fluctuations in output and employment. Thus the quantity approach serves to take certain items off the monetary policy agenda (or at least to de-emphasize them) by limiting the list of the central bank's responsibilities.

A second element in the Bundesbank's procedure for deriving the target growth rate of a given monetary aggregate is the concept of "unavoidable price increases," which measures prices according to the all-items consumer price index (CPI). These goals for inflation, which are set each year before the monetary target is set, specify the intended path for inflation, which in turn drives monetary policy.

> In view of the unfavorable underlying situation, the Bundesbank felt obliged until 1984 to include an "unavoidable" rate of price rises in its calculation. By so doing, it took due account of the fact that price increases which have already entered into the decisions of economic agents cannot be eliminated immediately, but only step by step. On the other hand, this tolerated rise in prices was invariably below the current inflation rate, or the rate forecast for the year ahead. The Bundesbank thereby made it plain that, by adopting an unduly "gradualist" approach to fighting inflation, it did not wish to contribute to strengthening inflation expectations. Once price stability was virtually achieved at the end of 1984, the Bundesbank abandoned the concept of "unavoidable" price increases. Instead, it has since then included . . . a medium-term price assumption of 2 percent. (Deutsche Bundesbank, 1995c, pp. 80-1)

The setting of the annual unavoidable price increase thus embodies four normative judgments by the Bundesbank: First, a medium-term goal for inflation is the principal determinant of policy decisions. Second, the convergence of the medium-term inflation goal with the long-term inflation goal should be gradual, since the costs of moving from one goal to the other cannot be ignored. Third, the medium-term inflation goal should be a number greater than zero. Fourth, if inflation expectations remain contained, there is no need to reverse prior price-level rises.

The target set for 1975 was a point target for CBM growth from December 1974 to December 1975. Since this target turned out to be susceptible to short-term fluctuations in money growth around year-end, the targets for 1976 to 1978 were formulated as point targets for the average growth of CBM relative to the average level of CBM over the previous year.

In 1979, two changes were made. First, with the exception of 1989, all targets have been formulated in terms of a target range of plus or minus 1% or 1.5% around the target derived from the quantity equation.

> In view of the oil price hikes in 1974 and 1979-80, the erratic movements in "real" exchange rates and the weakening of traditional cyclical patterns, it appeared advisable to grant monetary policy from the outset limited room for discretionary maneuver in the form of such target ranges. To ensure that economic agents are adequately informed . . . the central bank must be prepared to define from the start as definitely as possible the overall economic conditions under which it will aim at the top or bottom end of the range. (Schlesinger, 1983, p. 10)

In deciding to express targets in terms of a range rather than as a single point, the Bundesbank gave itself room to respond to economic developments. In fact, the tone of its explanation suggests that it was conferring some discretion on itself rather than buying room for error in a difficult control problem.

The second change made in 1979 was to reformulate the targets as growth rates of the average money stock in the fourth quarter over the average money stock in the fourth quarter of the preceding year. The purpose was to indicate "the direction in which monetary policy is aiming more accurately than an average target does" (Deutsche Bundesbank, 1979b, January, p. 8). Panel E of Figure 4.1 shows quarterly growth rates of CBM (through 1987) and of M3 (thereafter) over the fourth-quarter level of the preceding year and the targets since 1979. (The earlier targets have been omitted from Figure 4.1 because they were not formulated in terms of year-on-year rates.)

The Bundesbank has declared that on occasion it might allow deviations from the announced target path to occur in order to support other economic objectives. As means of supporting short-run policy goals, such deviations would be in addition to those implicit in the setting of a target range and in the establishment of a gradual path for movements in unavoidable inflation. In 1977, for example, signs of weakness in economic activity, combined with a strong appreciation of the deutsche-mark, prompted the Bundesbank to tolerate the overshooting of the target. As the policy statement said at the time:

> However, the fact that the Bundesbank deliberately accepted the risk of a major divergence from its quantitative money target does not imply that it abandoned the more medium-term orientation which has marked its policies since 1975. . . . There may be periods in which the pursuit of an "intermediate target variable," as reflected in the announced growth rate of the central bank money stock, cannot be given priority. (Deutsche Bundesbank, 1978a, p. 22)

The main reason that CBM was chosen as the target aggregate was its perceived advantages in terms of policy transparency and communication with the public. The Bundesbank explained its choice of CBM as follows:

> [CBM] brings out the central bank's responsibility for monetary expansion especially clearly. The money creation of the banking system as a whole and the money creation of the central bank are closely linked through currency in circulation and the banks' obligation to maintain a certain portion of their deposits with the central bank. Central bank money, which comprises these two components, can therefore readily serve as an indicator of both. A rise by a certain rate in central bank money shows not only the size of the money creation of the banking system but also the extent to which the central bank has provided funds for the banks' money creation. (Deutsche Bundesbank, 1976a, p. 12)

The Bundesbank's confidence that it can explain target deviations and re-definitions to the public is reflected in the design of its reporting mechanisms. There is no legal requirement in the Bundesbank Act or in later legislation for the Bundesbank to give a formal account of its policy to any public body. Government oversight is limited to a commitment that "the Deutsche Bundesbank shall advise the Federal Cabinet on monetary policy issues of major importance, and shall furnish it with information upon request" (Act Section 13). The only publications the Bundesbank is required to issue are announcements in the *Federal Gazette* of the setting of interest rates, discount rates, and the like (Act Section 33). According to Act Section 18, the Bundesbank may, at its discretion, publish the monetary and banking statistics it collects.

The Bundesbank makes heavy use of this last opportunity. The Bundesbank's *Monthly Report* is described, on the inside of the front cover, as a response to Section 18 of the Bundesbank Act; but the report does much more than simply report statistics. Every month, after a "Short Commentary" on monetary developments, securities markets, public finance, economic conditions, and the balance of payments, several articles appear. Some of them are on one-time topics (for example, "The State of External Adjustment after German Reunification"), and others are recurring reports (for example, "The Profitability of German Credit Institutions" [annual] and "The Economic Scene in Germany" [quarterly]). In each January issue, the monetary target and its justification are published (between 1989 and 1992, those items were made available in December). The *Annual Report* carries a detailed review of economic (not just monetary) developments during the previous year, lists all movements in monetary policy, and offers commentary on the fiscal policy of the federal government and the *Länder*.[9] With these two publications, along with regularly updated "special publications" such as *The Monetary Policy of the Bundesbank,* no Bundesbank policy decision or its likely effects are left undiscussed.

Despite its commitment to transparency, the Bundesbank imposes certain limits on its accountability. No articles in the *Monthly Report* are signed by the author or authors,[10] and the *Annual Report* has only a brief foreword signed by the Bundesbank President (although all the members of the Central Bank Council are listed on the pages preceding it). Speeches given by the President or by other council members are never reprinted in either document. This practice is somewhat compensated for by the enormously active speaking and publishing schedule engaged in by all council members (not just the President and Chief Economist) and by some senior staffers. Still, the anonymity of the published reports weakens the link between policy and the people who make it.

Another limitation on accountability is that the *Monthly Report* and the *Annual Report* deal only with the current situation and past performance. No forecasts of any economic variable are made public, and neither private-sector forecasts nor even expectations are mentioned. Apparently, the Bundesbank is accountable for its past performance, but not for its plans for the future. In fact, its ability to offer explanations for economic and policy developments after the fact, along with its reliance on potential GDP and normative inflation as the basis for the monetary targets, often enables the Bundesbank to shift responsibility for short-

term economic performance to other factors as it chooses. Nevertheless, those same monetary targets are seen by the Bundesbank as the
main source of accountability and transparency for policy, because they
at least commit the Bundesbank to explaining policy on a regular basis
and with respect to an explicit benchmark.

Switzerland

From 1975 until 1978, the Swiss National Bank announced growth targets for the narrow monetary aggregate M1. In the fall of 1978, after a
trade-weighted appreciation of the Swiss franc of 40% in nominal terms
and 30% in real terms over the previous 12 months, the Bank decided to
shift from a monetary target to an exchange-rate target. It might be said
that the Bank was thereby introducing an implicit "escape clause" into
its targeting commitment.

In the spring of 1979, the Bank returned to money-targeting, "although
this change was not publicly announced" (Schiltknecht 1983, p. 74). From
1980 on, it resumed announcing monetary targets. This time, however,
it chose an even narrower monetary aggregate as its target. From 1980
until 1988, the targets were formulated for the adjusted monetary base
(AMB), defined as the monetary base adjusted for the Bank's end-of-
month accommodation of the liquidity needs of commercial banks. Since
1989, the target variable has been the seasonally adjusted monetary base
(SAMB). In recent years, currency in circulation has constituted roughly
90% of the SAMB, with the deposits of commercial banks at the Swiss
National Bank making up the rest. Consequently SAMB is a narrower
monetary aggregate even than M1. Given the proportionally greater
depth and innovation of the Swiss financial system relative to that of
Germany, the benefit of choosing an aggregate as narrow as SAMB may
be its greater immunity to portfolio shifts, as its demand is largely determined by payments technology. Moreover, given the smaller size and the
greater openness of the Swiss economy, control of a broader aggregate
may have seemed too daunting a challenge.

Until 1990, the Swiss National Bank had announced monetary targets
for the coming year at the end of each calendar year. Then, at the end of
1990, it declared that it would aim "to increase the monetary base to
approach a medium-term expansion path" (Swiss National Bank, 1990c,
December, p. 273), without specifying either the time horizon of the
target or the starting point of the path. As we will see, what the Bank
wanted was greater short-run flexibility than the full-year monetary tar-

get provided. Given the credibility demonstrated by the Bank over the years, long-run inflation expectations would presumably stand unchanged so long as the goal was made clear. Shortly thereafter, the Bank specified that the time horizon of the target was a period of 3 to 5 years. At the end of 1992, it announced that it had chosen the average stock of SAMB during the fourth quarter of 1989 as the basis for the expansion path, thereby providing a means of verifying performance (Swiss National Bank, 1992c, December, p. 312). Apparently the lack of a measurable monetary target for two years did not cause the public to doubt the Bank's underlying commitment. Panel E of Figure 4.2 shows quarterly AMB growth (solid line) and SAMB growth (dashed line) over the corresponding quarter of the preceding year, along with the annual targets from 1980 to 1990 (triangles) and the target outcomes (bold horizontal lines). Panel F of the figure shows the level of SAMB from 1980 on, as well as the first two five-year medium-term growth paths.

Finally, at the end of 1994 ,the Bank announced a new medium-term growth path for SAMB for the period 1995 to 1999, and thus retroactively revealed that the horizon of the first path also had been five years.[11] The implicit and then explicit multi-year horizon of the Bank's monetary and inflation targets is in contrast to the Bundesbank's insistence on one-year targets for both. There is not much evidence that the different choices in target horizons have made much difference in terms of policy or inflation outcomes. However, the multi-year targets have enabled the Swiss National Bank to communicate its plans to the public while at the same time missing fewer targets. Since monetary policy affects inflation only after a lag of 1-2 years or more, and since inflationary shocks can be reversed only gradually, a multi-year target seems to reflect more accurately the realities of policy-making. The main risk of a multi-year target occurs during its final year, if the central bank is locked into a pre-determined and possibly less-than-credible path. We will see that most targeting central banks avoid this box by resetting the target horizon before the end of the target period, or by explicitly rolling the horizon forward.

The manner in which the Swiss National Bank arrives at its monetary targets has been similar to German practice. During the period when its target aggregate was M1, the Bank aimed at lowering the growth rate of M1 to "an average rate of 3 percent over the next [business] cycle," for the reason "that there had been a fairly close relationship between M1 and the consumer price index and that growth rates of M1 had fluctuated around 3 percent during periods of stable prices" (Schiltknecht, 1983, p. 72). The target "was based on the expected and desired economic growth for the year to come and on the assumption about next year's income velocity" (Schiltknecht, 1983, p. 73). After changing to SAMB as the target variable, the Bank considered an annual growth rate of 2%

> to be sufficient for stabilizing the price level in the medium term. The num-
> ber of 2 percent rests on the assumption that (a) the Swiss National Bank
> equates an annual inflation rate of 0-1 percent with price stability and (b)
> the potential growth of the Swiss real GDP is unlikely to be higher than 2
> percent. The nominal potential growth resulting from these assumptions of
> 2-3 percent is thought to increase the demand for base money by 2 percent
> per year. (Rich, 1989, p. 350; translation by authors)

The Bank explains its choice of a greater-than-zero target for measured inflation by referring to the upward bias resulting from incomplete accounting for quality improvements. Again, the inflation goal is specified before the monetary target is set.

Although the Swiss National Bank, unlike the Bundesbank, makes no mention of "unavoidable price increases," the fact that until 1985 its monetary targets were always fixed at numbers higher than 2% (and higher than 3% during the years 1975-78) indicates that it makes some allowance for the inertia of recent inflation when setting its targets. As in Germany, price stability is defined, normatively and operationally, as an inflation rate greater than zero. Moreover, the Bank allows for the gradual pursuit of price stability by accommodating one-time increases in the price level. Like the Bundesbank, it bases its target derivation on estimates of potential growth of GDP, rather than on forecasts of actual growth of GDP, thus downplaying the link between monetary policy and cyclical conditions, at least in the target-setting process.

The Swiss National Bank has always chosen a point target rather than a target band for money growth:

> The decision to abstain from a target band was based on the belief that, from
> a psychological point of view, missing a target band is worse than missing a
> point target. A target band suggests that a central bank is able not only to
> establish a reasonable target but also to control the monetary aggregates
> within a narrow margin. The [Swiss National Bank] never intended to give
> such an impression to the public. (Schiltknecht, 1983, p. 73)

Until 1988, monetary targets were formulated in terms of the average growth of SAMB over the previous year, while in 1989 and 1990 the Bank chose to formulate the targets in terms of the growth rate over the fourth quarter of the previous year. While, in its choice of a point target, the

Swiss National Bank is admitting more explicitly the possibility of control problems than the Bundesbank does, it also engages in extensive explanations of deviations from its targets, analogous to those of the Bundesbank. The advantage of choosing a point target is that it eliminates the damage to credibility caused by missing a target range. The disadvantage is that it leaves less room for maneuver when deviations from the target have to be explained.

Similarly, despite the indexation of Swiss housing sector rents, the Bank focuses on the rate of change of the headline CPI, which forces it to explain when that measure of inflation misrepresents "underlying" inflation, rather than taking the approach of targeting a specially defined price index. Keeping the rule simple complicates explanations and perhaps reduces policy flexibility, but it also makes target misses less damaging to credibility. This strategy assumes the existence of an educated public, or at least shows that the Bank is trying to educate the public.

The Swiss National Bank has repeatedly declared that maintaining price stability is the primary goal of its monetary policy. The Bank "intended, by means of a gradual reduction of monetary growth, to lower inflation, as measured by the CPI, from more than 10 percent in the year of 1973 to zero. The Swiss National Bank's opinion that price level stability constitutes the main goal of monetary policy was also largely undisputed in the public" (Rich, 1985, p. 60; translation by authors). Unlike the Bundesbank's charter, the Swiss National Bank's charter does not limit its mandated goals to price stability. In fact, it includes several potentially conflicting goals. The Bank's commitment to the goal of price stability is evidenced by its behavior and by its credibility, rather than being required by law. In fact, the Swiss public generally has not questioned either the independence of the central bank or its commitment to price stability.[12] The primacy of price stability also finds expression in the Bank's decisions to allow a monetary target to be undershot or overshot when a conflict arises between adhering to the target and maintaining price stability. For example, exchange rate crises, as in 1978, are granted escape-clause status by precedent and common sense, without any explicit statement to that effect.[13]

Accordingly, the Swiss National Bank's original choice of M1, as mentioned earlier, was based on recognition of a "fairly close relationship" between M1 growth and inflation. From 1975 to 1978 it used the monetary base as its instrument to control the growth of M1—a practice made possible by its ability to predict with some accuracy the money multiplier (the ratio of M1 to the monetary base). When the Bank returned to monetary targeting after the 1978-79 interlude, it concluded that the accuracy of its multiplier forecasts had deteriorated. In particular, demand for M1 seemed to be reacting strongly to changes in exchange-rate expectations. The Bank therefore decided to target the monetary base, for these reasons:

> It considered the monetary base to be more stable than the aggregate M1. With hindsight, it is doubtful that this claim was true. But targeting the monetary base turned out to be attractive in another respect: The demand for base money is less sensitive to changes in interest rates and therefore less volatile than the demand for M1. (Rich, 1997, p. 119)[14]

This change in target reflected the Bank's concern about its ability to control M1. According to the evidence available, both aggregates—the monetary base and M1—lead inflation by two to three years (Rich, 1989, pp. 350, 354-5).

The perceived advantages of targeting the monetary base rather than M1 lay in the fact that Switzerland is a small, open economy and in the Swiss franc's importance as a safe-haven currency. In theory, the Swiss National Bank has perfect control over the monetary base. In practice, however, the Bank has repeatedly found itself forced to counteract large and sustained exchange-rate movements, usually appreciations of the Swiss franc, that obliged it to accept large, undesired expansions of the monetary base. That was the case in 1978, when the Bank temporarily abandoned monetary targeting, and again in 1987. Foreign exchange interventions, for example, have an immediate impact on the SAMB, in contrast to their more gradual influence on aggregates such as the CBM. Consequently they immediately force the Bank to present an explanation of why money growth has deviated from target. Announcing a target for the monetary base may serve to communicate that monetary expansions necessitated by excessive fluctuations in the exchange rate are transitory and will be reversed in due course.

The Bank's regular target announcements have served as a communication device, even though no specific timetable for the reversal of target deviations is issued, or even a commitment to meeting the target on average in less than five years. In fact, since the Bank is very forthright in explaining the provisional nature of its targets and the possible need for deviations, it is clear that the primary purpose in the short term of the monetary target is to signal policy intentions and objectives to the public. This is in contrast to the idealized version of an intermediate-targeting regime where meeting the target itself is worth the effort because it moves the central bank efficiently toward its longer-term goals.

Like the Bundesbank, the Swiss National Bank is highly independent. It is also free of governmental oversight and any legislative requirement to give testimony about its performance. It regards public support as its source of legitimacy for the pursuit of its monetary policy. The main vehicle for its appeal for such support is the quarterly publication *Geld, Währung, und Konjunktur* (literal translation, *Money, Currency, and Business Cycle*). Each issue contains a lengthy, data-intensive, "Summary of Monetary and Economic Developments," two to four topical articles, and a one-page "Chronicle of Monetary and Exchange Rate Policy" at the end. The December issue, in addition, begins with a brief (one-to-three-page) statement of "Swiss Monetary Policy in <the coming year>," which contains some evaluation of the previous year's performance and a statement of the intended course of the monetary aggregate in the coming year.[15]

There are several differences, however, between the approaches of the Swiss National Bank and the Bundesbank in reporting on monetary policy. The Swiss National Bank discusses international and real-side developments in detail. That practice reflects its use of many information variables in decision-making and underlines the limitations of its control over outcomes for the Swiss economy. It devotes almost as much space to "The Economic Developments in the Most Important Industrialized Countries" as to the domestic situation, and it puts the international articles first. Moreover, throughout its discussion of economic developments at home and abroad, and even more so in the annual statement about the coming year's monetary policy, it makes forecasts about any number of economic variables and occasionally contrasts its own forecasts with private-sector forecasts.[16]

The Swiss National Bank draws a different line on accountability from that of the Bundesbank. It makes clear that in a small, open, financially innovative economy, the central bank cannot be held responsible for events and conditions beyond its control, but it takes full responsibility for what it can control. In its publications, the Bank requires all topical articles to be signed by the authors, and many policy speeches given by senior officials are reprinted. It puts itself on the line by publishing forecasts and does not associate the publication of its report with any legal statute. The Bank evidently wishes to give the impression that it is voluntarily putting itself in harm's way, while at the same time reminding the public just how harmful that way can be.

Both central banks use monetary targets as a framework for explaining their policy to the public. Their analyses have to do with the whole economy and extend beyond monetary policy narrowly defined. In short, they do not limit themselves to dealing with the question of whether or not a target was met at the prescribed time.

German and Swiss Monetary Policy under Monetary Targeting

Rather than review the entire history of German and Swiss monetary targeting, we start by highlighting events in Germany through the 1970s and 1980s that illustrate the themes discussed above—particularly the treatment of the monetary targets not as rigid rules but as a framework for providing structure and transparency for monetary policy. Then, for each country, we focus on events since the late 1980s. In the case of Germany, the most challenging event was monetary unification. In that instance, the Bundesbank succeeded in handling a one-time inflationary shock of great magnitude, along with politically sensitive developments in the real economy, through flexibility and communication. During this same period, Switzerland experienced a major shift in money demand with serious inflationary consequences, along with the Swiss National Bank's shift from annual targets to five-year growth paths for SAMB. Examination of these events will reveal how the two central banks conducted their money-targeting regimes during the 1990s and will provide a baseline for the inflation targeters we examine in later chapters. The reader is again referred to Figures 4.1 and 4.2, pp. 48 and 54 respectively, which display the paths of inflation, interest rates, nominal exchange rates, GDP growth, unemployment, and monetary growth in both countries.

Germany

During the 1970s and 1980s the Bundesbank either overshot or undershot its annual monetary targets approximately half the time; in most but not all cases, it reversed overshootings. It also responded to movements in variables other than inflation. From the beginning of CBM targeting in 1975, the Bundesbank was aware of the risk that "central bank money is prone to distortions caused by special movements in currency in circulation" (Deutsche Bundesbank, 1976a, p. 11). In 1977, it permitted CBM growth to exceed the target in the face of an appreciating deutschemark and weak economic activity.[17] At that time, only two years after the adoption of the targets, the Bundesbank explained that "there may be periods in which the pursuit of an 'intermediate target variable' . . . cannot be given priority," thereby acknowledging the importance of real-side and foreign-exchange developments in its decision-making (Deutsche Bundesbank, 1978a, p. 2).

In 1981 and early 1982, because of weakness in the deutschemark, CBM grew much more slowly than M3. That trend led to large-scale repatriation of deutschemark notes and an inverted yield curve (short-term interest rates higher than long-term interest rates) that caused portfolio shifts out of currency into high-yielding short-term assets. Accordingly, the monetary target for 1981 of 4% to 7% was undershot (Figure 4.1, Panel E). However, during this period the Bundesbank was pursuing a disinflationary course with some success, so it did not act to bring money growth up to target range.

In 1986 and 1987, a reversal of the situation—namely, a strong mark combined with historically low short-term interest rates—led to CBM growth of 7.7% and then 8%. The Bundesbank tolerated this overshooting in part because of the Plaza Accord, which gave Germany some responsibility for stabilizing G-7 exchange rates. The particularly bad miss for CBM growth prompted the Bundesbank to announce a switch in 1988 to the aggregate M3 as its target, with the following comment:

> The expansion of currency in circulation is in itself of course a significant development which the central bank plainly has to heed. This is, after all, the most liquid form of money . . . and not least the kind of money which the central bank issues itself and which highlights its responsibility for the value of money. On the other hand, especially at times when the growth rates of currency in circulation and deposit money are diverging strongly, there is no reason to stress the weight of currency in circulation unduly. (Deutsche Bundesbank, 1988b, March, pp. 18-21)

The fact that the Bundesbank changed the target variable when CBM grew too fast, but did not do so when it grew too slowly, can be interpreted as an indication of the importance the Bundesbank ascribes to monetary targets as a means of communicating with the public. Allowing the target variable to repeatedly overshoot the target because of factors to which the Bundesbank did not want to react might have led to the public assumption that the Bundesbank's attitude toward monetary control and inflation had changed.[18]

Clarida and Gertler (1997) have argued that the Bundesbank has reacted asymmetrically to target misses, raising interest rates in response to an overshooting of the target but choosing not to lower interest rates in response to an undershooting. In any event, the switch in targets was not accompanied by any other changes in the monetary framework and caused little concern. In short, so long as the underlying inflation goal was met over the medium term, the existence of a monetary target, rather than its precise specification, appeared to be sufficient.

As we noted above, the Bundesbank has tended to pursue disinflation gradually in response to inflationary shocks. Its response to the 1979 oil supply shock was very gradual and was publicly stated to be so. The Bundesbank set the level of "unavoidable" inflation for 1980 at 4%, clearly below the prevailing rate but above the level of inflation acceptable over the longer term. The target level of inflation was brought down in stages and returned to the long-run goal of 2% only in 1984. Even though the underlying intent was clear, each year's target level of "unavoidable" inflation (as well as the monetary target and interest-rate policies determined by that level) was set only a year ahead, permitting the Bundesbank further flexibility to respond to events and to rethink the pace of disinflation. Although what turned out to be four years of inflation reduction is hardly an instance of the Bundesbank's going easy on inflation, it is an illustration of the flexibility and concern for real-side economic effects exhibited by German monetary policy-makers.

The behavior of the Bundesbank in the aftermath of German reunification tells us a great deal about its use of the targeting framework. During the two years prior to its economic and monetary union with the German Democratic Republic (GDR) on July 1, 1990, the Federal Republic of Germany had experienced real GDP growth of about 4% and the first significant decline in unemployment since the late 1970s (Panel C of Figure 4.1). After a prolonged period of falling inflation and historically low interest rates during the mid-1980s, inflation had risen from -1% at the end of 1986 to slightly more than 3% by the end of 1989. The Bundesbank had begun to tighten its monetary policy in mid-1988, raising the repo rate (the rate at which the Bundesbank makes routine short-term loans to the banking system, and at this time its effective policy instrument) in steps from 3.25% in June 1988 to 7.75% in early 1990. The first M3 target of 3% to 6% was overshot in 1988 by 1%, but the 1989 target of around 5% was almost achieved, with M3 growing at 4.7%. That M3 growth rate was certainly not high in view of the prevailing rate of economic growth.

In response to the uncertainties attending German reunification, long-term interest rates had increased sharply from late 1989 to March 1990, with ten-year bond yields rising from around 7% to around 9% in less than six months. Combined with a strong deutschemark, the rise in long-term interest rates enabled the Bundesbank to keep official interest rates unchanged during the months immediately preceding monetary union. It kept the rates unchanged in the immediate aftermath of monetary union as well, even though the effects of expansionary fiscal policy accompanying reunification were beginning to propel GDP growth to record levels.

The Bundesbank's decision to keep official interest rates unchanged for the first few months following monetary union reflected the fact that it was very difficult to assess the inflationary potential of the conversion of GDR marks ("ostmarks") into deutschemarks. The Bundesbank had been opposed to the conversion rate agreed to in the treaty on monetary union (on average, about 1 DM per 1.8 ostmarks) and had been publicly overruled on this point by the federal government.[19] The money stock M3 had increased almost 15% in the wake of monetary union. Interestingly, the rate of conversion set by the treaty turned out to be almost exactly "right." While GDP in the former GDR was estimated to be only around 7% of that of the Federal Republic following reunification, vast government transfers to the east of money from the west were absorbed without causing a major inflationary impetus (see König and Willeke, 1995). During the first few months, the Bundesbank was preoccupied with assessing the portfolio shifts in eastern Germany in response to the introduction of a new currency, a new financial system, and a broad range of assets that had not previously existed there.

So long as the eastern German banks were adjusting to their new institutional structure, and so long as velocity was being destabilized by portfolio shifts, monetary information concerning eastern Germany was hard to interpret. Consequently, the Bundesbank, during the second half of 1990 calculated monetary aggregates separately for eastern and western Germany, basing its calculations on the returns of the banks domiciled in the respective sectors. Although M3 growth in western Germany accelerated in late 1990, the growth rate of 5.6% for the year was well within the target range of 4% to 6%.

During the fall of 1990, the repo rate had approached the Lombard rate, which meant that banks were increasingly using the Lombard facility for their regular liquidity needs and not as the emergency facility it was intended to be. On November 2, 1990, the Bundesbank raised the Lombard rate from 8% to 8.5%, and the discount rate (the Bundesbank's subsidized lending rate) from 6% to 6.5%. Within the next few weeks, however, banks bid up the interest rate (*Mengentender*), and the repo rate rose above the Lombard rate, prompting the Bundesbank to raise the Lombard rate to 9% as of February 1, 1991. With these measures, the Bundesbank was reacting to both the volatile GDP growth rates and the faster M3 growth in the latter part of 1990. Although inflation until then had remained fairly steady, it seems likely that the Bundesbank was expecting inflationary pressures to develop in the near future, given the fiscal expansion, the overstretched capacities in western Germany, and the terms of monetary union.

At the end of 1990, the Bundesbank announced a target range for M3 growth of 4% to 6% for the year 1991, applying a monetary target for the first time to the whole currency area. The target was based on the average all-German M3 stock during the last quarter of 1990. Because that stock was likely to be affected by continuing portfolio shifts in eastern Germany, the target was subject to unusually high uncertainty. Neither of the basic inputs into the quantity equation that generates the Bundesbank's monetary targets—normative inflation and the potential growth rate of the German economy—was changed. (Since the achievement in the mid-1980s of effective price stability in Germany, the Bundesbank has spoken of "normative price increases" rather than "unavoidable inflation" in response to the high inflation of the 1970s and early 1980s.)[20]

> Following German unification, the money targets set by the Bundesbank were decidedly ambitious as they left normative inflation, on which these targets are based, unchanged at 2 percent during this period, even though it was obvious from the outset that this rate could not be achieved in the target periods concerned. (Issing, 1996, p. 123)

This was a statement of policy rather than a forecast. It implied a belief on the part of the Bundesbank that the shock of reunification had not fundamentally altered the basic structure of the German economy. Moreover, it communicated to the public that any price shifts arising from that shock should be treated as a one-time event and should not be incorporated into inflationary expectations.

Clearly this stance required faith in the public's ability to comprehend, and the Bundesbank's ability to explain, the extraordinary nature of the times. It is useful to contrast this adherence to the 2% medium-term inflation goal with the Bundesbank's response to the 1979 oil shock, when "unavoidable inflation" was ratcheted up to 4% and brought back down only slowly. There are two explanations for this difference in policy response: First, since the monetary unification shock was a demand shock rather than a supply shock, the Bundesbank was correct in choosing not to accommodate it; and second, after several years of monetary targeting, the Bundesbank's highly transparent explanations of its monetary policy had trained the public to discern the difference between one-time price-level increases and persistent inflationary pressures. In any event, the Bundesbank was clearly permitting its short-term monetary policy to miss the target in its determination to achieve its longer-term goal.

In February, 1991 long-term interest rates began to fall for the first time since 1988. In hindsight, it is apparent that this was the beginning of a downward trend that continued until the bond-market slump in early 1994. Although the highest inflation rates were still to come, at this point financial markets were apparently convinced that the Bundesbank would succeed in controlling, if not reducing, inflation in the long run. By making it clear that it would not accommodate further price increases in the medium term, the Bundesbank had bought itself the flexibility it needed for short-term easing of monetary policy without inviting misinterpretation. This link between transparency and enhanced flexibility depends on the central bank's ability to make credible its commitment to price stability, but it also indicates how even a credible central bank may increase the transparency of policy through institutional arrangements.

Until mid-August 1991, the Bundesbank left the discount and Lombard rates unchanged, while the repo rate steadily edged up toward the Lombard rate of 9%. CPI inflation in western Germany had remained around 3% during the first half of 1991, while GDP growth had remained vigorous. By contrast, M3 growth was falling, in part because of faster than expected portfolio shifts into longer-term assets in eastern Germany.

These portfolio shifts, along with a sharper-than-expected decline in the production potential of eastern Germany, prompted the Bundesbank for the first time ever to change its monetary target on the occasion of its midyear review. It lowered the target for 1991 by 1%, to a range of 3% to 5%. In this instance, the Bundesbank was able to invoke the implicit escape clause built into its semiannual target review. That process, which requires a clear explanation for any shift in targets, enabled the Bundesbank to justify its action. The discipline of the monetary targeting framework displayed the framework's disadvantages as well; specifically, it is difficult to meet short-run monetary targets when money demand is unstable and the effect of money growth on goal variables is difficult to predict.

On August 16, 1991, as the repo rate approached the Lombard rate again, the Bundesbank raised the Lombard rate from 9% to 9.25% and the discount rate from 6.5% to 7.5%. The discount rate was raised to reduce the subsidy character of banks' rediscount facilities, which until that point the Bundesbank had tolerated as a means of providing liquidity to eastern German banks.

Despite the fact that GDP growth began to slacken during the second half of 1991, M3 growth accelerated. To some extent, that acceleration was a result of the by-then inverted yield curve, which led to a strong growth in time deposits and prompted banks to counter the outflow from savings deposits by offering special savings schemes with attractive terms. This was the first time that the yield curve had become inverted since the early 1980s (and the first time since the Bundesbank had been targeting M3). In this situation, the Bundesbank faced the unusual situation that increases in interest rates were likely to raise M3 growth. This problem was all the more acute since banks' lending to the private sector was growing rapidly despite the high interest rates. This loan growth was probably due, to a large extent, to loan subsidies by the federal government in connection with the restructuring of the eastern German economy and housing sector.

This tendency of the Bundesbank's instrument to work in the "wrong" direction brought the underlying conflict of monetary targeting to the fore: The target must be critically evaluated constantly in relationship to the ultimate goal variable(s). However, if the target is cast aside regularly with reference to changes in that relationship or to special circumstances indicating a role for other intermediate variables, it ceases to serve as a target rather than solely as an indicator.

> Strictly defined, the use of a money growth target means that the central bank not only treats all unexpected fluctuations in money as informative in just this sense, but also, as a quantitative matter, changes its instrument variable in such a way as to restore money growth to the originally designated path. (Friedman and Kuttner, 1996, p. 94)

Despite the acceleration in late 1991, M3 grew by 5.2% during 1991, close to the midpoint of the original target and just slightly above the revised target.

On December 20, 1991, the Bundesbank raised the Lombard and discount rates by another 0.5%, to 9.75% and 8%, respectively, their highest levels since the Second World War (if the special Lombard rates from the early 1970s are disregarded).

> In the light of the sharp monetary expansion, it was essential to prevent permanently higher inflation expectations from arising on account of the adopted wage and fiscal policy stance and the faster pace of inflation—expectations which would have become ever more difficult and costly to restrain. (Deutsche Bundesbank, 1992a, p. 43)

The rhetoric here deserves close attention. Both government policies and union wage demands were being cited for their inflationary effects; that is, their pursuit of transfers beyond available resources. Although the Bundesbank had not been able to override Chancellor Helmut Kohl's desired exchange rate of ostmarks for deutschemarks, or his "solidarity" transfers, the Bundesbank Direktorium (Council of Directors) made it clear in this statement that the Kohl government and not the Bundesbank should be held accountable for the inflationary pressures those measures engendered. The Bundesbank Direktorium was accepting accountability only for limiting the second-round effects of those pressures.

The Bundesbank was also expressing its concern over the persistence of inflationary expectations and the potential cost of lowering them, thereby acknowledging that even for a credible central bank the costs of disinflation, in terms of lost output and employment, may be substantial. Finally, the Bundesbank's emphasis on the ultimate goal—medium-term price stability and inflation expectations—did not lead it to cite measures of private sector expectations directly, as many inflation targeters began doing at this time.

The December 20 increase in the Lombard rate proved to be the last. During the first half of 1992, the repo rate slowly approached the Lombard rate. The repo rate peaked in August at 9.7%, then began to subside as the Bundesbank started to ease monetary policy. The easing was, for the most part, in response to the appreciation of the mark and emerging tensions in the European Monetary System; it also coincided with the rapid slowdown in the growth of German GDP. Although the monetary targets for 1992 and 1993 would not be met, the challenge that reunification had posed to German monetary policy was over.

> Thus in 1992, for example, when the money stock overshot the target by a large margin, the Bundesbank made it clear by the interest rate policy measures it adopted, that it took this sharp monetary expansion seriously. The fact that, for a number of reasons, it still failed in the end to meet the target . . . has therefore ultimately had little impact on the Bundesbank's credibility and its strategy. (Issing, 1996, p. 121)

Monetary policy transparency was explicitly linked to flexibility during reunification, at least according to Bundesbank Chief Economist Issing, and that flexibility was exercised to minimize the real economic and political effects of maintaining long-term price stability.

Since about 1992, however, M3 has continued to prove a problematic intermediate target. The Bundesbank's own explanations for the substantial fluctuations in M3 growth since 1992 (Figure 4.1, Panel E) suggest that the demand for M3 behaves more and more like the demand for a financial asset rather than the demand for a medium of exchange. The Bundesbank, in justifying deviations from the M3 targets, has begun to feature reports on "extended money stock M3," a broader aggregate that includes some forms of money market accounts, but it has given no sign that it is ready to switch target aggregates again (see Deutsche Bundesbank, 1995b, July, p. 28).

The Bundesbank has described itself as "fortunate" that financial relationships in Germany have been more stable than in other major economies that have targeted monetary aggregates. It has attributed this success to the earlier deregulation of financial markets in Germany and to the lack of inflationary or regulatory inducements for financial firms to pursue innovations. The targets continue to serve as a structured framework by which the Bundesbank can explain its monetary policy, even as the targets go unmet for several years at a time.[21]

In 1996, M3 growth exceeded the Bundesbank's target range of 4% to 7%, with much of the difference being attributed to movements in narrow money during the last quarter, when many households took part in the purchase of newly issued Deutsche Telekom stock. It is important to remember, however, that 1996 inflation was at its lowest level since Germany adopted monetary targets (1.4% growth in CPI), and that the Bundesbank cut all three of its instrument interest rates to historical lows, even as M3 growth exceeded the stated target.

In its December 1996 *Monthly Report,* the Bundesbank announced that it would set a target of 5% annualized growth for M3 in both 1997 and 1998. Subsequently, one-year targets for M3 growth were set at 3.5% to 6.5% for 1997 and 3% to 6% for 1998, the latter in response to expectations of continued moderation of inflation. The December 1996 announcement represented the first time since Germany adopted monetary targeting in 1975 that it had announced a target for more than one year. The reason given was to provide policy-makers with flexibility in dealing with the volatility in currency markets that is expected to set in during the run-up to the European Monetary Union (EMU) in 1999. That event makes these the last German monetary targets. Clearly, for these two years domestic price stability was being balanced with other goals, notably the evolving Exchange Rate Mechanism (ERM) parities.

The end game nature of Germany's monetary situation raises a point that affects all inflation targeters with a fixed-term targeting regime. When the end of the targeting regime is tied to a specific event, such as an election or a treaty, it is not clear how much discipline the target will evoke as that event approaches. A central bank could be less strict about target adherence in the early years of the period, making the claim that it will make up for temporary overshootings later. Yet, when this later time arrives, the commitment to return the targeted variable to a level required under the targeting regime will in effect predetermine the path of policy. The central bank is then unable to respond to economic events as they unfold unless it abandons the target.

In addition, the central bank may not be highly accountable for its monetary policy if the targeting regime is unlikely to be kept in place. If the central bank cannot be held accountable, then how can its target commitment be fully credible? This is not to suggest by any means that the Bundesbank will go "soft" on inflation in the run-up to EMU, but rather that it is best if target time horizons can be credibly extended before their expiration. As we will see in the case studies for both Canada and the United Kingdom, there was a need to reassure the public that targets would be maintained past election dates (and changes of political power).

Switzerland

As Panel A of the Swiss Economic Indicators (Figure 4.2) shows, the Swiss monetary strategy kept inflation over the past two decades around 3% per year on average. Yet the graph also shows that "the SNB [Swiss National Bank] *failed to maintain* price stability after it had successfully reduced inflation" (Rich, 1997, p. 115, emphasis in original). While the first inflationary episode under monetary targeting, spanning the years 1979 to 1982, may be explained to a large extent by the second oil shock, the second episode, from 1989 to 1992, cannot be blamed on outside events. In particular, during the latter period the Swiss inflation performance relative to other OECD economies was far less favorable than it was during the former period. Since the events leading to the 1989-92 inflation prompted the Swiss National Bank to switch from monetary targets with a one-year horizon to medium-term growth paths of five years' duration, the most significant change in its framework over twenty years, we will review those events and point out their effect on the Bank's conduct of monetary policy.

The rapid increase of inflation during 1989 and 1990 was the consequence of a complex set of developments. The first, and probably most important, of these arose from the vulnerability of the Swiss economy to the effects of sustained movements of the exchange rate. In early 1987, the Swiss National Bank became concerned about the strength of the Swiss franc, which, after recovering in 1985 from earlier weakness, had gone on rising throughout 1986 at a rate of about 12% in trade-weighted terms (see Figure 4.2, Panel D). So the Bank decided to deviate from the monetary target for 1987 and allow the monetary base to grow at a rate higher than 2% (Figure 4.2, Panel E). Thereupon real short-term interest rates fell to approximately zero%. The Swiss franc showed no signs of weakening, however, and the Bank maintained its looser policy stance through the first three quarters of 1987.

Following the stock-market crash in October 1997, the Swiss National Bank, like other central banks, felt obliged to provide the banking sector with added liquidity, even though that would cause a further deviation from the monetary target for the year. Over the year SAMB grew by 2.9%, nearly a percentage point above the target growth rate. In December 1987, with the economic consequences of the stock-market crash still uncertain, and amidst widespread predictions of a slowdown in economic activity, the Bank raised the monetary target for 1988 to 3% growth. Raising the target was intended to signal to the foreign-exchange market that the current monetary stance was not likely to change soon, with the hope of preventing the Swiss franc from rising further. Combined with the overshooting of the target for the previous year, this change implied that one full year's worth of base money growth, inconsistent with the long-run inflation target, had been injected into the system.

Amidst this uncertainty, the Bank also faced the prospect of a major shift in the demand for SAMB, specifically that portion held as commercial bank deposits at the Bank. Such a shift would be the consequence of two institutional changes in the Swiss financial markets.

The first change was the introduction of the new interbank payment system, known as Swiss Interbank Clearing (SIC). Previously, the Bank had acted as a clearinghouse that produced a net settlement of the commercial banks' accounts at the end of each day. The new payment system replaced this system with real-time settlement, which requires banks to transfer balances from their Swiss National Bank account at the beginning of each day into a special account in which no overdraft is allowed during the course of the day. The Bank publicly admitted that it did not know what effect this system would have on the banks' demand for base money, because the banks first had to gain experience with the system.

The second institutional change was a wide-ranging revision of the commercial banks' liquidity requirements as of the beginning of 1988.

One purpose was to remove the competitive disadvantage the banks faced under the previous liquidity requirements, which required them to hold substantially higher reserves at the Swiss National Bank than they actually needed for clearing purposes. Under the new regulation, the Bank did not expect the reserve requirements under usual circumstances to be binding, even under the assumption that SIC would reduce banks' desired working balances. This meant that the banks' demand for deposits at the Swiss National Bank would be determined by their operating needs. These, however, were impossible for the Swiss National Bank to predict, given the concurrent introduction of SIC.

The Swiss National Bank expected that the predictive properties of SAMB growth for inflation would for a while be significantly impaired. In fact, in its announcement of the target for 1987 (Swiss National Bank, 1986c, December, pp. 207-9), the Bank had discussed the implications of the introduction of SIC in general terms, saying that it would have to "undershoot its longer-term money target of 2% during a certain period by a possibly substantial margin" (p. 208, translation by authors). Furthermore, the Bank explained that during the adjustment of SAMB demand, it would pay increased attention to other indicators, notably M1 and short-term interest rates, although it would not be announcing targets for M1 growth. (As a consequence of the new liquidity requirements, which would come into effect on January 1, 1988, it was expected that the usefulness of M1 as an indicator of future economic conditions was impaired as well.) These developments, and the Bank's response, showed clearly that the Swiss were not targeting money in any strict sense. In fact, when additional information indicated that adhering to the monetary target would cause the inflation objective to be missed, the monetary target was set aside entirely.

The Bank's explanations were again consistent with its commitment to simple rules with complicated explanations. Primarily, the Bank was trying to convey to the public that a one-time rise in money growth and prices (and uncertainty) did not indicate an abrogation of the underlying commitment to price stability. This need to distinguish between the accommodation of a one-time shock and a change in goals, in the hope of preventing the shock from triggering expectations of inflation and wage growth, is a recurring challenge for monetary policy. As seen in the case of German reunification, transparency of policy is an effective tool for making this vital distinction.

As 1988 began, therefore, the Bank faced, all at once, unfavorable developments in the exchange rate, uncertain prospects for economic growth in the near future, and serious problems with its target variable.

Since, in the wake of the stock market crash, a significant economic slow-down worldwide had been generally expected, the SNB decided to continue its expansive monetary policy—in view of the strength of the Swiss franc—during 1988. [The Swiss National Bank] therefore increased the growth target for [SAMB] from 2% to 3% . Because of the fall in [SAMB] demand due to the innovations immediately ahead, the SNB expected to undershoot this target. The target therefore was not intended to serve as a guideline for controlling the money stock. Rather, the SNB meant to communicate to the public with this target its intention to continue the monetary stance of the previous year. (Rich, 1992, p. 77, translation by authors)

The unusual uncertainties surrounding that target should have prompted the Bank to issue a detailed explanation of its plans for the conduct of monetary policy during the upcoming year. Yet, by its own admission, its announcement of the monetary target for 1988 was unusually terse.

When the SNB . . . announced its money target for 1988, it issued a statement that was remarkable for its brevity and vacuity. The statement mentioned the prospect of a shift in money demand, but contained no information whatsoever on the indicators the SNB might use in lieu of the monetary base. The SNB subsequently made up for that mistake and took pains to explain to the public its approach to setting policy. Furthermore, from the end of 1988 onwards, the Bank's policy announcements became much more substantial. (Rich, 1997, pp. 124-5)

Clearly, the Bank regretted its failure to communicate and began again to furnish the public with information beyond mere statements about whether targets were being missed.

As the year 1988 unfolded, it became clear that the Swiss National Bank had guessed wrong regarding all three sources of uncertainty—the exchange rate, prospects for economic growth, and problems with its target variable. Unfortunately for the Bank, what happened in each case worked to intensify the risk of inflation. First and foremost, the decline in the deposits of commercial banks at the Swiss National Bank was much more severe than the Bank had expected. By the end of 1988, those deposits were 57% below their levels in December 1987. At first, the Bank reacted cautiously to the sharp fall in deposits, unable to tell whether it had been induced solely by the institutional changes, or whether it also reflected the onset of the predicted economic downturn. Around the middle of 1988, however, the Bank was convinced, mainly by a sharp fall in short-term interest rates, that it had to contract the supply of liquidity more sharply. Overall, the SAMB fell by 3.9% (calculated as the average of monthly growth rates), undershooting the target by 6.9%.

Second, the widely predicted slowdown in economic activity, both in Switzerland and elsewhere, failed to materialize. Instead, economic growth in all the major economies picked up significantly. The fall in the SAMB masked a brisk growth in the volume of currency in circulation, which expanded by 4.2% during the year. While the Bank at the end of 1987 had expected Swiss real GDP to fall by 1% during 1988, it actually rose by 3% (Figure 4.2, Panel C).

Third, although from mid-1988 on the Bank tightened policy considerably, Swiss short-term interest rates were rising more slowly than German ones, leading to a sharp reversal of the Swiss franc's earlier rise.

The Bank continued to tighten policy sharply during 1989. By that time, however, inflationary pressures had begun to appear, with inflation rising from 2% to 5%. GDP continued to grow, peaking at 4% by the end of the year. SAMB, meanwhile, remained an unreliable indicator, falling by another 2% during 1989, in part in response to the continuing adjustment of the commercial banks' liquidity demand. In contrast to the developments of 1988, however, the 4% shortfall of SAMB growth relative to target in 1989 did not reflect only a technology-induced fall in banks' desired balances at the Swiss National Bank. "[A]bout half the shortfall of approximately four percentage points . . . was caused by the renewed tightening of monetary policy at the beginning of 1989" (Swiss National Bank, 1989c, December, p. 291). The main reason for that tightening was the continuing decline of the Swiss franc, particularly relative to the deutschemark. Since by the end of 1989 the Swiss franc still appeared vulnerable, the Bank decided to add an explicit caveat to the announcement of its monetary target for 1990.

> The sustained weak trends, since mid-1988, of the Swiss franc vis-a-vis the D-mark and the other EMS currencies is particularly undesirable from a monetary policy point of view. The [Swiss National Bank] will not tolerate extreme exchange rate fluctuations and will accordingly adjust its monetary policy if developments in the foreign exchange market warrant this. (Swiss National Bank, 1989c, December, p. 292)

In other words, the Bank granted itself a publicly declared escape clause from its target commitment. Again, transparency enhanced flexibility. Still the Bank announced a target of 2% SAMB growth for 1990.

The Swiss currency continued weak into the first months of 1990, forcing the Bank to exercise its escape clause.

> The [Bank] already realized in the first few months of 1990 that its exchange rate-oriented monetary policy was not in line with the growth target, set at 2 percent, for [SAMB] . . . The [Swiss National Bank] was well aware of the

dangers inherent in its exchange rate-oriented monetary policy. It could not rule out the possibility that an exchange rate-induced curb on money supply expansion would, in the medium term, lead to an unnecessarily strong setback in the Swiss economy. (Swiss National Bank, 1990c, December, p. 272)

In the end, the target for 1990 was undershot by 4.5%.

The undershooting of its targets by such considerable margins for three consecutive years must have been disconcerting to the Bank. The passage from Rich (1992) cited above, together with the caveats attached to the target announcements, reveal the Bank's growing realization that its monetary targets were of diminishing utility as a means of signaling policy direction. On one hand, the target announcements, which were meant to communicate the monetary policy intended over the coming year, were based on an expectation that the relationship between goal and target would hold over a longer time span than the target horizon. On the other hand, as that relationship between SAMB growth and inflation lost its short-run predictive power, the outcomes of SAMB growth, which were intended to indicate to the public how tight or easy recent monetary policy had been, became increasingly uninformative. The Bank thus had to find a way to communicate to the public its growing realization that, while long-run price stability required monetary growth not to exceed 1% on average, short-term deviations from this average rate of growth would be necessary to achieve and maintain price stability in any given year.

The Bank was probably looking for a new, more flexible framework in which to communicate both its intended and its realized stance. Between the end of 1987 and the end of 1990 SAMB had contracted by more than 16% (see Figure 4.2, Panel F). The Bank was convinced that in 1991 demand for SAMB would be well below the level that would be expected under more ordinary cyclical conditions. The very high (by historical standards) short-term nominal interest rates in particular had depressed SAMB demand. As the Bank expected to loosen policy in the near future, it would be doing so in the face of SAMB growth rates that were likely to exceed the medium-term objective of 1% for some time. That growth, moreover, would merely make up for past contraction. The Bank faced the same dilemma that Germany had faced in 1991-92: The target variable and policy were moving in opposite directions. The Bank's hope was to keep the public from interpreting this temporary monetary growth as an overly stimulative policy. In particular, the Bank wanted to avoid a renewed sharp depreciation of the Swiss franc.

The Bank's response to this problem was to announce the replacement of its annual monetary targets with a medium-term growth path for the SAMB in December 1990. Swiss National Bank President Lusser's remarks to the Bank's General Assembly in April 1991 shed some light on the logic behind this decision.

> The effective growth of [SAMB] will presumably exceed the average [growth rate of 1 percent] in some years, and fall short of it in others. It was significantly below the intended average during the past two years. I therefore do not exclude the possibility that [SAMB] will increase in the near future temporarily by more than 1 percent, and only thereafter growth will approach the medium-term growth path . . . The medium-term money target of 1% defines the general direction of monetary policy. It does not, however, necessarily determine the money growth rate which we will aim for in 1991 . . . In particular we are taking the development of the exchange rate of the Swiss franc vis-a-vis the most important currencies into account. The deutschemark/ Swiss franc relation is of particular importance. (Lusser, 1991, p. 168, translation by authors)

The medium-term growth path was to provide the framework in which the Bank could explain current actions and, most importantly, deviations from the medium-term target as necessary steps towards maintaining the price-stability goal over time. The need to explain the relationship between the current position and the medium-term target was the discipline imposed on the short-term discretion of monetary policy required in a small, open economy.

However, the announcement of the medium-term growth path (Swiss National Bank, 1990c, December, pp. 272-274) left a number of issues unaddressed. While the announcement repeated the Bank's commitment to SAMB as "the main indicator of Swiss monetary policy" (p. 273), it also stated

> This aggregate will serve mainly as a medium-term monetary indicator. The [Swiss National Bank] intends to increase the monetary base to approach the medium-term expansion path envisaged. The speed with which it will move towards this path will depend largely on exchange rate developments. (*Ibid.*, pp. 273-4)

The only detail specified in the announcement was the slope of the path—namely, that "a medium-term money supply growth of around 1 percent would be more adequate in future" (*Ibid.*, p. 274).[22] The announcement did not specify the length of the "medium term," the position of actual SAMB relative to the path, or the time horizon within which the Bank expected to bring SAMB back to the path. In short, the announcement contained no specifics about the direction of monetary policy during 1991.

The Bank "preferred to straighten out the loose ends of the new strategy before committing itself to a precise definition of the medium-term target" (Rich, 1997, p. 135). This lag between announcement of a new targeting regime and the provision of specific details reflects a pattern seen in other inflation-targeting countries, such as Sweden and Australia. Apparently, central banks in small, open economies want to make sure that their surroundings are stable before they make a formal commitment. After all, there is little point to announcing a new, more flexible target only to miss it at the outset.

As we have seen, the Swiss National Bank gradually provided the missing details over the next few years. By the end of 1994, for the first time, it provided a chart similar to Panel F of our Figure 4.2. According to this chart, it appears that since the change to medium-term growth paths, the Bank has used the room for maneuver provided by this strategy without deviating too far from its medium-term objective. It is important to put the accumulated credibility of low inflation in postwar Switzerland in perspective. While the record of prior success and the low long-run inflation expectations made this transitional interregnum possible without a dramatic rise in the price level, such credibility could not prevent Swiss monetary policy from running up against the limitations of its control over the economy. Flexibility was required and was used.

Key Lessons from Germany and Switzerland's Experiences

The experience of Germany and Switzerland with monetary targeting suggests two main lessons that are applicable to any targeting regime in which an inflation goal plays a prominent role.

First, it appears that a targeting regime can restrain inflation in the longer run, even when the regime permits target misses in response to short-run considerations. Indeed, the approaches of both countries to monetary targeting represent significant departures from a rigid policy rule in the classical sense.

Second, a key element of a successful targeting regime is a strong commitment to transparency; that is, clarity of policy objectives and approach coupled with clear explanations. The effective use of a target can increase policy transparency by serving as a vehicle for communicating with the public and promoting understanding of what the central bank is trying to achieve.

As we will see in the chapters ahead, these key elements of a successful targeting regime—flexibility and transparency—have played an important role in the policies of all the countries studied in this book.

5

New Zealand: Inflation-Targeting Pioneer

In 1990, New Zealand became the first country to adopt formal inflation targeting. This change in the conduct of monetary policy was part of a wide-ranging economic reform in New Zealand, undertaken by the Labour Government elected in July 1984. The reforms, a response to a long period of poor performance by the New Zealand economy, were remarkably ambitious in scope: The Labour Government tackled fiscal, structural, and trade issues, as well as monetary policy, in the belief that the reforms needed to be mutually consistent and mutually reinforcing in order to succeed. (See Brash [1996a] for an overview of the reform measures.)

The inflation-targeting component of New Zealand's reforms, like many other elements of Labour's policy package, was quite innovative, and sparked considerable analysis and discussion in the academy and in central banking circles. As we will see in this chapter and those that follow, the New Zealand experience in many ways has become a laboratory from which subsequent adopters of inflation targeting have drawn both positive and negative lessons.

Key Features of Inflation Targeting in New Zealand

- Inflation targeting in New Zealand followed legislation that mandated a Policy Targets Agreement (PTA) between the government and the newly independent central bank. Under each PTA, the government and the central bank have agreed on specific numerical targets for inflation.

- Inflation targeting was adopted only after a successful disinflation had been nearly completed.

- The price index on which inflation targets are based is designed to exclude the first-round effects of supply shocks and thus measure "underlying inflation." Statistics New Zealand publishes a consumer price index that excludes the first-round effects of interest-rate changes on the cost of living. This index is further modified by the Reserve Bank of New Zealand, which excludes "significant" first-round impacts from terms-of-trade movements, changes in energy and commodity prices, changes in government charges and indirect taxes, and some other prices as determined on an *ad hoc* basis.

- Although New Zealand's inflation-targeting regime is perhaps the most nearly "rule-like" of any, it still has allowed the central bank considerable flexibility to respond to fluctuations in variables other than inflation, such as employment and real GDP.

- Accountability of the central bank is a key feature of the inflation-targeting regime. Legally, the Governor of the Reserve Bank may be dismissed if the inflation target is breached, although his or her dismissal is not mandatory and so far this provision has not been invoked.

- The inflation target in New Zealand is stated as a range, rather than as a point target, with the midpoint of the range above zero. The long-term goal is also defined as a measured inflation rate above zero.

- Adherence to a relatively narrow target range and a one-year time horizon for targets has resulted in two related problems for New Zealand's policy-makers: (1) a control problem (*i.e.,* difficulty in keeping inflation within the very narrow target range); and (2) an instrument instability problem (*i.e.,* occasional wide swings in interest rates and exchange rates, the instruments of monetary policy).

The Adoption of Inflation Targeting

The current framework for New Zealand monetary policy was set forth by the Reserve Bank of New Zealand Act of 1989. The Act was introduced into Parliament by the government on May 4, 1989, was passed on

December 15, and took effect on February 1, 1990. It requires the Reserve Bank of New Zealand (the central bank) "to formulate and implement monetary policy directed to the economic objective of achieving and maintaining stability in the general level of prices" (Section 8).

Although inflation targeting was the means chosen to achieve price stability, the Act itself does not go beyond stating the need for quantitative performance criteria. Section 9 of the Act requires the Minister of Finance and the Governor of the Reserve Bank to negotiate and make public a Policy Targets Agreement (PTA) that sets out "specific targets by which monetary policy performance, in relation to its statutory objective, can be assessed during the period of the Governor's term" (Lloyd, 1992, p. 211). The first PTA, signed by the Minister of Finance and the Governor on March 2, 1990, specified numerical targets for inflation and the dates by which they were to be achieved.

The passage of the Act was one result of the general sense of crisis about New Zealand's economic performance that had instigated the Labour government's broad package of reforms. Like many other of New Zealand's economic policies, monetary policy did not have a proud record in the 1970s and 1980s:

> New Zealand experienced double-digit inflation for most of the period since the first oil shock. Cumulative inflation (on a CPI basis) between 1974 and 1988 (inclusive) was 480 per cent. A brief, but temporary, fall in inflation to below 5 per cent occurred in the early 1980s, but only as the result of a distortionary wage, price, dividend and interest rate freeze. Throughout the period, monetary policy faced multiple and varying objectives which were seldom clearly specified, and only rarely consistent with achievement of inflation reduction. As a result of this experience, inflation expectations were deeply entrenched in New Zealand society. (Nicholl and Archer, 1992, p. 316)

Following Labour's election and the movement toward policy reform, the Reserve Bank stated that "a firm monetary policy is seen as an essential prerequisite for lower, more stable interest rates and inflation rates over the medium-term" (Reserve Bank of New Zealand, 1985a, August, p. 451). However, at first there was no focused discussion of what the objectives of monetary policy should be. There was some interest in the intermediate targeting of monetary aggregates,[1] but that topic was never pursued. (In recent years the Bank has often asserted that no useful link exists between such aggregates and inflation.)

Over the four years following the 1984 election, a consensus gradually emerged inside the government, and in the Reserve Bank in particular, about the proper objectives of monetary policy, as well as the institutional framework needed to achieve those objectives. A key element of this consensus was the need for increased focus on price stability.

Multiple objectives of monetary policy had been specified in the Reserve Bank Act of 1964, which stated ". . . that the [monetary] policy should be related to the desirability of promoting the highest degree of production, trade and employment and of maintaining a stable internal price level" (Reserve Bank of New Zealand, 1985a, September, p. 512). However, a shift toward a more focused approach was suggested in an article in the September 1987 issue of the Reserve Bank's *Bulletin*. The article stated (p. 104), "The overriding objective of monetary policy is to lower the rate of inflation," and that ". . . an initial objective of government policy has been to reduce inflation to a level comparable with our major trading partners." Left open was the question of what exactly that level was and what the objective of monetary policy would be once it had been achieved. The article concluded that: "Though the direction of the desired movement is clear, the time frame over which this reduction can, or should, be achieved is somewhat less so." (*Ibid.*) In short, the government and the Reserve Bank were slowly shifting to a goal of price stability for monetary policy, however without indicating precisely how they would go about reaching that goal.

The need for clarification became apparent over the following months. During the first quarter of 1988,

> . . . accompanying the growing acceptance that much lower rates of inflation would be achieved, there was an expectation amongst some commentators that policy would be eased once inflation rates of around 5 percent had been achieved or were in prospect . . . Official concern at the growing credence given to this view . . . prompted a more explicit statement [by the Minister of Finance] of the ultimate inflation objective than had previously been formally made . . . that the ultimate goal is to achieve price stability by the early 1990s . . . The Bank shares the Minister's objective. (Redell, 1988, pp. 81-82)

A footnote says that price stability is ". . . likely to be consistent with a small positive measured inflation rate, in the order of 0-2 percent." Thus, two years before the first inflation targets were announced, their final form had effectively been agreed on by the government and the Reserve Bank. Apparently New Zealand's policy-makers realized that some public commitment was necessary to put a cap on inflation expectations. Yet their statement was hardly publicized, and the crucial detail—the likely target range for inflation—was relegated to a footnote.

The recognition of the need for increased independence for the central bank that helped to shape the Reserve Bank Act of 1989 seems to have arisen somewhat later. An article published in the *Bulletin* in 1992 stated:

> In order to improve the prospects for monetary policy to remain—and be seen to remain—on the track to low inflation, and thereby help reduce the costs of disinflation, attention turned to possible institutional arrangements which would improve monetary policy credibility. During 1986, the Government initiated consideration of ways of allowing the Reserve Bank to operate monetary policy more autonomously . . . Nevertheless, [even if independence wasn't seen as the whole answer,] it was at least suggestive that a more autonomous central bank would be helpful, even if neither necessary nor sufficient by itself for achieving and maintaining low inflation. (Lloyd, 1992, p. 208)

Although the link between the autonomy of the central bank and the performance of the economy at large was only beginning to be explored in academic circles, the government clearly felt that the public's uncertainty about monetary policy was a major threat to price stability. Moreover, the Bank, at least at first, believed that a change in institutional arrangements might bring about a decrease in the real economic costs of disinflation.

Lack of central bank autonomy and uncertainty about monetary policy were in fact closely linked in the thinking of the Bank's leadership. The Bank has argued that the costs of inflation result mainly from uncertainty about future inflation, and that to minimize that uncertainty the central bank must be charged with, and held responsible for, achieving price stability.[2] To that end, monetary policy must be both clearly formulated and credible; otherwise, there is nothing to prevent private-sector contracts from being concluded on the basis of inflation expectations that are inconsistent with the objective of price stability. "The Bank must ensure that a credible non-accommodative stance is consistently maintained to influence expectations and wage claims" (Redell, 1988, p. 83). Price stability was considered preferable to a positive, stable inflation rate, since it was ". . . seen as considerably more socially and politically credible over the longer term" than the latter (Redell, 1988, p. 82).

Autonomy for the central bank, together with a focus on price stability, was also argued to promote credibility, transparency, and accountability. A central bank would certainly be more credible if it were both free to set the instruments of policy and also held responsible solely for maintaining price stability, with no incentive to pursue other goals. Transparency and accountability would also be served by the sharpened focus: "Multiple objectives . . . tend to reduce the transparency of monetary policy, and also, therefore, [to] weaken the accountability of both the central bank, and the Government. Given multiple objectives, failure to achieve one objective can too easily be explained by reference to another objective" (Lloyd, 1992, p. 209). The new emphasis on accountability was reflected in the much-discussed provision of the Act that permits (although it does not require) the firing of the Bank's Governor if the goals of the Policy Targets Agreement are not met.

At the time of the signing of the first PTA, in March 1990, the Reserve Bank had succeeded in bringing so-called "underlying" inflation down from almost 17% at the beginning of 1985 to the vicinity of 5%—"although a number of one-off factors meant that only limited progress [on disinflation] was made" during 1989 (Reserve Bank of New Zealand, 1990a, March, p. 6). In this effort the Bank was backed by the Labour government, which had returned to power in August 1987. Thus the decision to announce inflation targets occurred after most of the disinflation (and its recessionary consequences) had already taken place. As we will also see in the case of Canada, the announcement was timed less to promote disinflation than to forestall a rise in inflationary expectations once monetary policy began to ease.

The Reserve Bank responded to the possible revival of inflation during the summer of 1989 with a slight firming of policy, raising short-term interest rates from 13% to 14%. The Bank's forecast, based on data through the first quarter of 1990, indicated that underlying inflation would stay around 5% for the rest of the year and then fall to 1% by the end of 1992. According to that projection, the inflation targets laid down in the first PTA, 3% to 5% by December 1990, would be achieved. During 1989 ". . . the economy moved only slowly out of the recession experienced since late 1987," but Reserve Bank Governor Don Brash remained ". . . confident that the recovery is underway, and that whatever pressure may be necessary to ensure continued progress towards the Government's monetary policy objectives will not stifle the recovery . . ." (Reserve Bank of New Zealand, 1990b, pp. 6-7). The possibility of a recession was taken seriously; the announcement of the targets alone was not held to be enough to change economic behavior.

> It was quite clear from the outset that the mere enactment of the legislation would not be enough to establish monetary policy credibility . . . There did not seem to be a large 'announcement effect' on the passing of the legislation. Ultimately, credibility is derived from results—and particularly from results in relation to publicly advertised intentions. (Nicholl and Archer, 1992, p. 319)

As of 1990, the operational framework for the new regime and, more importantly, the performance of New Zealand's monetary policy under a regime of inflation targeting, remained to be determined.

The Operational Framework

Most of the operational aspects of New Zealand's inflation-targeting framework are governed by the Policy Targets Agreements, which constitute the only legal implementation of the Reserve Bank of New Zealand Act of 1989. The reformers were faced with two unknowns: first, whether domestic institutional change alone could do much to take a small, natural-resource-based, open economy toward macroeconomic stability; and, second, whether it would be possible to enlist and maintain public support for counter-inflationary policies, should these policies work less well at the outset than was hoped. To prepare to deal with those challenges, New Zealand's government and central bank adopted formal, legal means of ensuring flexibility in its new framework for monetary policy. These design choices have made it possible for the Reserve Bank to implement changes in target values and time horizons when such changes appeared necessary, though perhaps at some sacrifice of transparency and credibility.

Initially, the goal of price stability was defined as an annual rate of inflation between zero and 2%. The target was intended to be a true range, with both the floor and the ceiling to be taken seriously, but with no special emphasis on the midpoint. For example, in September 1991, policy was eased to avoid undershooting the range, the idea being to strengthen the public's perception that the bands of the range were "hard" (Nicholl and Archer, 1992, p. 321). Hitting the 0% to 2% target was an extremely ambitious goal, given the narrowness of the range and the fact that the center of the range was so close to zero. In practice, the actual inflation rate has remained near the top of the range for much of the time since targets were adopted, and the public has tended to focus on the 2% ceiling of the target range, rather than on the 1% midpoint or the 0% floor.

Unlike Switzerland, a small, open economy that chose not to adopt a target range in order to avoid conveying the impression that its control of inflation is precise, in New Zealand the central bank initially tried to downplay the likelihood of control problems. However, the reality of the imperfect controllability of inflation could not be avoided, and at the end of 1996 the band was widened, from 0% to 2% to 0% to 3%.

There has been some ambiguity left in the policy framework about the choice of price index for defining the inflation target. Initially, the decision was to define the inflation target in terms of the All Groups, or "headline", CPI

> because it is the most widely known and the best understood index. . . . The above-zero rate of inflation specified [as the target] reflects index number problems, the survey methodology, and the difficulty of adjusting for new goods or for improvements in quality. Effectively, a judgment has been made that 1% CPI inflation is consistent with stability in the general level of prices. (Nicholl and Archer, 1992, p. 317)

However, the first PTA admitted that the headline CPI "is not an entirely suitable measure of [the prices of goods and services currently consumed by households] since it also incorporates prices and servicing costs of investment-related expenditures," most notably prices of existing dwellings. Another problem noted at the time was that increases in interest rates show up directly as increases in the cost of living, as measured by the all-items CPI, so that a policy tightening creates an essentially spurious rise in measured inflation. Still, the PTA concluded that "the CPI will, for practical purposes, be the measure used in setting the targets" (Section 2).[3] In the "Underlying Inflation" section of its August 1991 *Monetary Policy Statement,* the Bank stated that headline CPI "is the basic yardstick against which the Bank should be assessed" (Reserve Bank of New Zealand, 1991c, August, p. 17).

Despite the official role of the headline CPI, however, the Reserve Bank has, in practice, paid greater attention to its measure of "underlying" or "core" inflation; that is, inflation excluding relatively temporary influences on the price level. As will be seen in the chapters to come, while every inflation-targeting central bank has made use of such a measure in one way or another, no single definition of underlying inflation has been universally adopted. This difference arises because the optimal definition of underlying inflation depends to some extent on the structure of the particular economy and the types of economic shocks that it faces. Noting the importance of headline CPI as a "yardstick" in the quotation cited above, the *Monetary Policy Statement* went on to mention the Bank's emphasis in the recent past on controlling underlying inflation. It then continued:

> Unfortunately, because the nature of such shocks [transitory shocks to the price level] cannot be fully specified in advance, and because the impact of shocks can often not be measured precisely, it is not possible to specify a

single, comprehensive definition of "underlying inflation." To some extent, interpretation of the impact and significance of the shocks is a matter of judgment, and hence requires clear explanations by the Bank to support any numerical estimates. (Reserve Bank of New Zealand, 1991c, August, p. 19)

In other words, the measure of underlying inflation developed by the Reserve Bank (and which has been reported regularly alongside headline inflation by the New Zealand press) is somewhat *ad hoc* in its construction. The implied scope for judgment in the target definition is unique to the Reserve Bank of New Zealand among the central banks that we study in this book. Operationally, the first-round effect of interest-rate changes on prices is automatically excluded in a series published by Statistics New Zealand; to this series, the Bank makes additional adjustments that it feels are warranted. The overall effects of these adjustments are not inconsequential; the headline and underlying inflation series have diverged by as much as 2 percentage points and have occasionally moved in opposite directions.

The use of underlying inflation in the targeting procedure is formally recognized by the Policy Targets Agreements. Each of the PTAs has included a list of shocks in response to which the Bank is required to "generally react . . . in a manner which prevents general inflationary pressures [from] emerging" (Section 3).[4] In other words, the PTAs have escape clauses that allow the Reserve Bank to accommodate first-round effects of certain shocks on prices, but that require policy to try to prevent these transitory price changes from being incorporated into wage- and price-setters' expectations and hence into trend inflation ("second-round effects"). The "covered" shocks listed in the PTAs include:

- A movement in interest rates that causes a significant divergence between the change in the CPI and the change in the CPI excluding the interest rates component. This clause, which appears in the third PTA, replaced an earlier clause that specified a significant divergence between the CPI and a price index treating housing costs on an internationally comparable basis.
- Significant changes in the terms of trade (arising from an increase or a decrease in either import or export prices).
- An increase or a decrease in the rate of the goods-and-services tax (GST), or a significant change in other indirect taxes.

- An economic crisis, induced by factors such as a natural disaster or a major livestock epidemic, that is expected to have a significant impact on the price level.
- Changes in government or local-authority tax levies that significantly affect the price level.

As we have noted, the Bank has consistently excluded from its measure of underlying inflation the effect of interest-rate changes on mortgage and credit charges (relying on a price series from Statistics New Zealand). It has also excluded the direct effects of changes in indirect taxes and in government and local authority levies when the impact of such changes on the CPI was judged to be significant (defined as an impact of at least 0.25% in any twelve-month period). Of course, this definition of significance requires some decisions about modeling tax effects, and the Bank has chosen only to respond to those tax changes that were clearly driven by policy decisions.[5] The natural-disaster escape clause has so far not been invoked. The terms-of-trade escape clause, however, has been applied for extended periods in the discretionary manner allowed for in the PTAs: Twice, in 1990-91 and in 1994, oil price changes were excluded from the calculation of underlying inflation, and timber prices were excluded throughout 1993-94.

An important drawback of using adjustments in the target definition to determine which shocks policy should offset and which it should accommodate, as opposed to explaining directly to the public why specific policy actions are being taken or not taken, is that it may reduce the transparency and credibility of policy. It is the Bank itself, after all, that decides whether a given shock has a "significant" impact on the price level. Since outsiders, say in financial markets, cannot reproduce the Bank's judgmental estimates of underlying inflation, an important part of the policy decision process becomes obscured. Potentially, this practice undermines the perceived impartiality of the entire mechanism.[6] This problem seems less likely to arise when the discretion that is exercised is openly discussed and explained, though of course criticisms of particular policy decisions will remain.

There are other concerns as well: The fact that underlying inflation is not defined as a continuous series, but rather as a series whose composition changes at irregular intervals, has led to some confusion. Moreover, the timing of the PTAs themselves—and therefore of the announcement of the inflation target, however defined—is arbitrary. For example, the first PTA lasted only six months, but the most recent is to last indefinitely. Further, given the recent shift to open-ended targets, the PTAs are not tied to either the electoral cycle or to the current parliamentary majority. Nor are they insulated from changes in the electoral cycle or in the make-up of Parliament. A new government could renegotiate with the Bank if it so desired. We will discuss an actual episode of this type below.

On the other hand, attention to some type of underlying inflation series in short-run policy-making appears particularly useful for a small, open economy like that in New Zealand (assuming the judgmental aspects of the series definition are not excessive). Without the terms-of-trade provision in the PTAs (which permits exclusion of the first-round effects of exchange-rate changes on prices), for example, it is hard to see how monetary policy could limit variations in inflation to a narrow range without causing severe disruption in real economic activity. These escape clauses are meant to balance the Reserve Bank's inflation goal with other goals, particularly short-run stabilization of real output and employment, in the face of supply shocks:

> [As a] detailed examination of what has been written about the caveats makes clear, the fundamental rationale for the caveats is that, in certain specified circumstances, the Reserve Bank should be paying attention to consequences for variables such as output and employment rather than concentrating single-mindedly on the inflation rate. (Bryant, 1996, p. 24)

Officially, the Act of 1989 did not mandate objectives other than price stability, and it only admitted supply shocks explicitly as a justification for deviating from the price-stability goal. Five reasons were given for this narrow focus: First, monetary policy affects inflation only in the long run. Second, because monetary policy is only one instrument, it can deal with only one goal at a time. Third, multiple objectives allow policy to change in ways that may appear arbitrary, thereby lowering credibility and raising inflationary expectations. Fourth, to require the Reserve Bank to cooperate with government agencies on objectives such as employment stabilization would compromise its autonomy. Fifth, multiple objectives reduce transparency and accountability, because poor performance on, say, the price stability front might be attributed to the obligation to pursue other goals (*e.g.*, see Lloyd, 1992). Again, the explicit escape clauses were the only exceptions to the single-goal philosophy. However, they have had the effect of increasing short-run policy flexibility and allowing monetary policy to accommodate other goals besides long-run price stability.

Whenever an inflation goal below current inflation levels is to be achieved within a specified time horizon, the required disinflationary trajectory implies a judgment about what real economic costs are acceptable to achieve the reduction in inflation. This is, of course, inherently a political decision, which is why the choice in New Zealand was not left solely to the Reserve Bank, but was embodied in the PTAs. Both the first and the second PTAs envisaged a gradual transition to price stability over the three years following their signing, and both called on the Bank to "publish a projected path for inflation for each of the years until price stability is achieved" (Section 5b).

> The initial Policy Targets Agreement signed in March 1990 called for achievement of 0-2% inflation by December 1992 and maintenance of price stability thereafter. Partly as a result of a view that the output and employment costs of the speed of adjustment implicit in this time frame were too high, the new government elected in October 1990 deferred the target date by one year. (Nicholl and Archer 1992, p. 317)[7]

Clearly, the Reserve Bank of New Zealand under the 1989 Act was designed to operate as a relatively "rule-oriented" central bank. Notice the contrast between the PTA-based framework in New Zealand and the policy framework in Germany: Rather than seeking an agreement with the government, the Bundesbank takes the full responsibility for determining the speed of any necessary disinflation, then justifies the projected disinflation path directly to the public.

In the time since the first Policy Targets Agreement was signed, the Reserve Bank has taken pains to emphasize that the link between the real economy and monetary policy still exists in the short run, and that determining the speed of disinflation is the government's choice (and not the Bank's).[8] In the words of the Reserve Bank's own leadership:

> It should be emphasized, however, that the single price stability objective embodied in the Act does not mean that monetary policy is divorced from consideration of the real economy. At the technical level, the state of the real economy is an important component of any assessment of the strength of inflationary pressures. More importantly, inflation/real economy trade-offs may need to be made on occasion, particularly in the context of a decision about the pace of disinflation. . . . The main trade-offs are essentially political ones, and it is appropriate that they be made clearly at the political level. The framework allows trade-offs in areas such as the pace of disinflation, or the width of target inflation ranges, to be reflected in the PTA with the Governor. The override provision can also be used, if required, to reflect a policy trade-off. (Lloyd 1992, p. 210)[9]

In June 1997, the Reserve Bank changed two aspects of the way in which it expresses its intended stance of monetary policy. The first change was supposed to clarify the net effect on future inflation of changes in the exchange rate, taking monetary policy as given. As discussed in the third section of this chapter, the Reserve Bank had always accorded exchange rate movements a prominent place in its discussions, and had responded to exchange rate fluctuations to some extent by adjusting domestic money-market interest rates. This was a bit confusing, however, because as long as the Reserve Bank had not specified the degree to which it viewed changes in short-term interest rates and the exchange rate as substitutes, it was unclear whether the exchange rate entered policy decisions as a determinant of future inflation or as a goal unto itself. Since both interest rates and exchange rates do affect future inflation, and the former can directly influence the latter as well, the actual impact of any monetary policy move requires taking exchange-rate feedback into account.

In response, beginning in late 1996 the Reserve Bank constructed and explained in several publications the use of a monetary conditions index (MCI) as a means to assess the overall stance of monetary policy. As will be seen in Chapter 6, the Bank of Canada was the first to develop this indicator of monetary policy stance, and the Reserve Bank followed its lead. In New Zealand, the MCI is constructed as a 1:2 weighted average of the trade-weighted exchange rate and the 90-day interest rate. This weighting reflects the relative impact of a move in exchange rates on inflation versus a move in interest rates (*i.e.*, a 2% rise in the exchange rate is estimated to have the same effect on future inflation as a 100 basis point, or one percentage point, rise in the interest rate). This ratio underscores how important the exchange rate is to the New Zealand economy, since other countries which have created such indices have found that it takes 3 or 4 times as much movement in exchange rates to be equivalent to a 1% rise in interest rates. Since June 1997, the Reserve Bank has published a forecast of this MCI to indicate the path of monetary policy for the next three years if conditions remain unchanged.

The second change in the expression of policy had to do with the Reserve Bank's medium-term projections for inflation. Before 1997, these had been derived under the assumption of an unchanged 90-day interest rate (which had served as the *de facto* instrument of monetary policy), as well as changes in the trade-weighted exchange rate in line with the (projected) differential between inflation rates in New Zealand and those of its main trading partners.[10] Occasionally, the inflation forecast derived under these assumptions did not coincide with the midpoint of the target range, meaning that the assumptions on monetary conditions under which the forecast was derived were incompatible with the target, and would therefore have to be changed. In order to avoid this inconsistency between the Reserve Bank's actual behavior and that assumed in its inflation projection, since June 1997, the projection has been generated under the assumption that during the forecast horizon, the Reserve Bank will adjust monetary conditions (as defined by the MCI) such that the inflation projection converges on the target midpoint by the end of the horizon.

Beyond considerations of output and employment stabilization, the Reserve Bank acknowledges that financial stability is also an appropriate short-run objective of monetary policy.[11] "The Bank now has effective independence to implement monetary policy in pursuit of its statutory objective, without limitations on the technique except that the choices made must 'have regard to the efficiency and soundness of the financial system'" (Nicholl and Archer, 1992, p. 316).

In short, New Zealand—although probably the most extreme of all the inflation-targeting countries in its use of formal institutional constraints on monetary policy—is not as constrained or as single-minded in its pursuit of price stability as some would have it.[12]

Never since targets were adopted has the Reserve Bank assigned the status of intermediate target to any variable except the inflation target itself. In this respect New Zealand deviated significantly from the practice of Germany and Switzerland, who at least in their rhetoric have used money-growth targeting as an intermediate step to achieving their inflation goals (see Chapter 4). The reasons for not employing an intermediate target are largely practical ones:

> The judgment to date has been that a target specified in terms of the final inflation objective (suitably defined) is preferable to an intermediate monetary aggregate target, mainly because empirical work had not been able to identify any particular money aggregate which demonstrated a sufficiently close relationship with nominal income growth and inflation. (Lloyd, 1992, p. 213)

Reflecting this judgment, the Reserve Bank has consistently assigned low weight to money (and credit) aggregates even as information variables (variables useful in judging the state of the economy but not used as targets *per se*). In attempting to assess the state of the economy, the Bank, according to its public statements, has instead paid the most attention to the trade-weighted exchange rate and the level and slope of the yield curve (the relationship between bond maturities and bond yields), among other variables:

In building its forecasts of inflation pressures, the Bank has, over the last year or so, taken increasing account of the role of interest rates. Over the years, a better sense has emerged of the strength of the interest rate effect on demand, and hence inflation. . . . Short-term interest rate developments are now playing a greater role in the implementation of policy between formal forecast reviews, alongside the prominent role played by the exchange rate. (Reserve Bank of New Zealand, 1995c, December, p. 8)

As we noted, the Reserve Bank has recently made extensive use of its monetary conditions index. The yield curve (the relationship between interest rates and bond maturities) has also been important in the Bank's analyses. The Bank seems to use the yield curve as a means of assessing the stance or effect of monetary policy, with an inverted yield curve signaling tighter policy, rather than as a way of inferring an implicit, market-based inflation forecast.

In June 1987, well before the target-adoption announcement, the Bank started to conduct quarterly surveys of the expectations of businesses and households concerning a number of economic variables, including inflation, and it has regularly reported on the inflation expectations reported in these and other surveys. Since then, the Reserve Bank has invested a great deal of effort in a survey that covers ten macroeconomic variables and draws the majority of its respondents from the financial and business sectors. Questions and responses from the survey are published in the Bank's *Bulletin*. The Bank attempts to measure uncertainty about future inflation (which it does by measuring the dispersion of reported inflation expectations), as well as the mean level of expected inflation (Fischer and Orr, 1994, p. 162).

All the inflation-related data items and forecasts are assembled and are made available to the public. Section 15 of the Reserve Bank of New Zealand Act of 1989 requires the Bank to produce, at least every six months, a policy statement that (1) reviews the monetary policy of the preceding six months and (2) outlines how monetary policy is to be implemented over the next six months, in a manner consistent with the Bank's stated inflation objective. These *Monetary Policy Statements* are submitted to Parliament and may be discussed by a parliamentary select committee.

They must review the implementation of monetary policy over the period since the last Statement, and detail the policies and means by which monetary policy will be directed towards price stability in the coming periods. The reasons for adopting the specified policies must also be given. The annual report provides a vehicle for accountability and monitoring of the Bank as a whole (not just in terms of monetary policy). This is also tabled in Parliament. The Governor and/or Deputy Governors are questioned by the Parliamentary Select Committee for Finance and Expenditure on both the Monetary Policy Statements and the annual reports. (Lloyd, 1992, p. 214)

In addition to the *Annual Report*, the Reserve Bank publishes the *Reserve Bank of New Zealand Bulletin*, which contains topical articles, reprinted speeches, and official statements. Since the Reserve Bank of New Zealand Act of 1989, most of the articles in the *Bulletin* have been signed, a practice that encourages greater accountability and more open discussion. However, one major limitation on the flow of information is that inflation data are collected and reported on a quarterly basis rather than on a monthly basis. It is not clear whether this unusual (from an international perspective) practice reflects inherent data limitations in the New Zealand context or whether it has the tactical purpose of de-emphasizing short-term "noise" in the inflation rate (and the consequent reactions by the financial markets).

There has been some tendency to regard the Reserve Bank's legal status and degree of independence as similar to those of the Bundesbank or the Federal Reserve System. Actually, the Reserve Bank of New Zealand and its governor face a much different situation than do those other central banks. "This is not independence as the Bundesbank would understand it, since the target is to be set by the government and the Bank is responsible to the government for achieving it. The Bank is an agent, not a principal" (Easton, 1994, p. 86). Put another way, while the German and the New Zealand central banks share a similar goal, similarly defined, the Bundesbank is a trusted (and only informally or voluntarily accountable) institution. The Reserve Bank of New Zealand, however, is an agency of the government and is held regularly to account. This difference in institutional design is neatly captured by Debelle and Fischer's (1994) distinction between "goal independence" (enjoyed by the Bundesbank) and "instrument independence" (the lot of the Reserve Bank). Philosophical as much as practical reasons underlay this design choice:

> The New Zealand reforms were motivated partly by orthodox economics and the desire to apply its precepts to government. However, they were also influenced by the political "New Right," which, on philosophical grounds, sought a smaller role for the public sector than perhaps could be justified from conventional economic theory alone. (Easton 1994, p. 78)

In addition, tighter constraints on the Reserve Bank may have been thought necessary because of the poor performance of New Zealand's

monetary policy in the past and the weaker public support for low inflation. The implication for New Zealand monetary policy in practice is
that there is relatively little exercise of discretion in the short run by the
Bank, except as allowed by the caveats in the PTAs. Moreover, even that
limited discretion must be followed after the fact by formal communications with the government. Accordingly, although those communications
are published in the *Monetary Policy Statement,* and are also conveyed to
the public in an active communication program by the Bank, the relative role played by direct communication with the public is considerably
less in New Zealand than in countries in which the central bank has
greater discretion. In New Zealand, the support of the government for
the Reserve Bank's decisions, rather than the Reserve Bank's explanations to the public, is the principal source of policy flexibility.

New Zealand Monetary Policy under Inflation Targeting

In this section we summarize the history of New Zealand's monetary policy
in the 1990s. We have drawn heavily the Bank's *Monetary Policy Statement,*
the *OECD Economic Reports,* and various newspaper accounts.

Figure 5.1 is a graphical summary of recent macroeconomic developments in New Zealand. Panels A-D of the figure show the paths of inflation, interest rates, GDP growth, unemployment, and the exchange rate
both before and after the commencement of inflation targeting. It is
useful to view the period since New Zealand's adoption of inflation targeting as being made up of three principal episodes.

The first episode, from target adoption in March 1990 to March 1992,
was a period of disinflation and weak real economic performance. It was
characterized by a drop in inflation to within the 0% to 2% range, interest rates that were initially high but later fell rapidly, a gradual depreciation in the exchange rate, negative GDP growth, and rising unemployment.

The second episode, from the second quarter of 1992 through the
first quarter of 1994, was one of recovery. Inflation fluctuated within the
upper half of the 0 to 2% range, interest rates continued to fall, the
exchange rate appreciated, GDP growth rose sharply, and unemployment declined at a moderate pace.

The third episode, spanning the years 1994 to 1997, will engage most
of our attention here. These years saw the greatest challenges that the Reserve Bank had faced since the adoption of inflation targets. The period
following the second quarter of 1994 was one of rising inflation and inter-

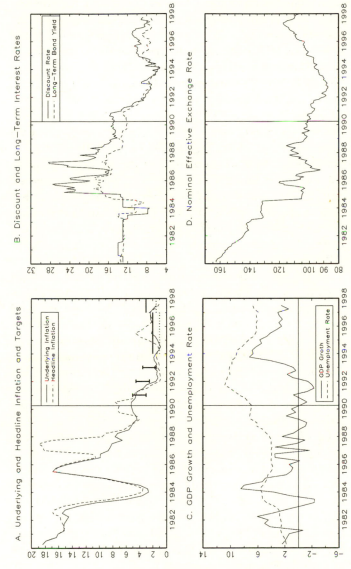

Figure 5.1 New Zealand economic indicators. *Sources:* A) Reserve Bank of New Zealand; B) International Financial Statistics of the International Monetary Fund; C) Reserve Bank of New Zealand, Main economic indicators of the Organisation for Economic Cooperation and Development; D) Bank for International Settlements database.

est rates, continued appreciation of the exchange rate, sustained GDP growth, and rapidly falling unemployment. During that period, the inflation target was breached twice briefly and was reset as the result of an election.

The first episode begins with the first Policy Targets Agreement, signed on March 2, 1990. This PTA stipulated that price stability, defined as annual inflation within the 0 to 2% range, was to be achieved by the year ending December 1992. The PTA also required that each *Monetary Policy Statement* released by the Bank should contain a projected path for inflation over the following five years. The first Monetary Policy Statement, released in April 1990, specified that a 3% to 5% target range be achieved by December 1990, a 1.5% to 3.5% range by December 1991, and a 0 to 2% range by December 1992 and thereafter. At the time the PTA was signed, the Bank was expecting the economy to continue its gradual recovery from the 1988 recession. The December 1989 figure for underlying inflation, excluding the effects of the 2.5% increase in the goods and services tax (GST) effective July 1, 1989, had been 5.3%, and the Bank saw no need to change short-term interest rates in order to achieve the December 1990 range.

Two major surprises presented themselves over the period through January 1991: the oil price shock that followed the Iraqi invasion of Kuwait, and the unexpected continued weakness of the New Zealand economy. In August 1990, the Bank tightened monetary policy somewhat in response to what it called the "fiscal slippage" evident in the budget released in July. In October, it announced that the target range to be achieved by December 1990 would apply to CPI inflation excluding oil prices. The Bank then used that adjustment as an occasion to announce that targets in the future would apply to "underlying" inflation. As it turned out, inflation including oil prices over the year to December 1990 was 4.9%—inside the original target range. By then, however, the target range had been changed to 1.5% to 3.5%.

Following its victory by a large margin in the general election on October 29, 1990, the conservative National Government signed a new PTA with the Bank on December 19. The new agreement extended the planned disinflation process by one year. As we have noted, this extension reflected the government's belief that rapid disinflation had already proved too costly to the real economy. This view was widely held at the time, and prominent figures in the domestic financial sector were outspoken in characterizing the 0% to 2% inflation target range as a dangerous "obsession."[13] Nevertheless, before the election, both the Labour Party and the National Party had urged that the inflation targets be maintained at their original level.[14] These events are indicative of some of the ways in which an inflation target can be manipulated without changing the primary target definition; in particular, the time horizon allowed for achieving the target can be a critical determinant of how tightly the target constrains policy.

The February 1991 *Monetary Policy Statement* set up a new path toward price stability by specifying target ranges for inflation of 2.5% to 4.5% by December 1991, 1.5% to 3.5% by December 1992, and 0 to 2% by December 1993. 9The targets for December 1991 and December 1992, along with the target for December 1990 laid down in the first PTA, are shown as vertical bars in Panel A of Figure 5.1. The target from December 1993 onward is shown by the solid horizontal line for its upper bound and the dotted horizontal line for its midpoint.) Meanwhile, starting in mid-November 1990, the Bank had begun to allow the ninety-day bank bill rate fall substantially in response to lower-than-expected inflationary pressures.[15] The decline in inflationary pressure was attributed to the relatively modest effects of the oil price increases, sluggish domestic growth, and what was seen as the new government's support of the goal of price stability. By mid-January 1991, the ninety-day bank bill rate had fallen to under 11.5%, down from 14.6% in August 1990.

By August 1991, the Bank had expressed its surprise over the speed at which inflation was falling. Growth in wage settlements was low, unit labor costs were essentially unchanged, the exchange rate was stable, and import prices were flat, reflecting the ongoing recession in several major economies. Whereas in its February 1991 *Monetary Policy Statement* the Bank had expected headline inflation to be slightly above the midpoint of the 2.5% to 4.5% range by the next December, in the quarter to June the inflation rate was already down to 2.8%, and the Bank's forecast for the year up to December 1991 was 2%. Likewise, underlying inflation (with mortgage interest rates, oil prices, and indirect taxes and government charges removed) was down to 2.6% by June and was expected to fall below 2.5% by the end of the year. The Bank stated that "this outcome will reflect the firm policy stance maintained throughout [1990], and some imprecision in the process of controlling inflation" (Reserve Bank of New Zealand, 1991c, August, p. 43).

By late September, the Bank started to ease monetary policy sharply "when it became clear that, in the absence of this action, underlying inflation for 1992 was likely to fall below the 1.5 to 3.5% indicative range" (Reserve Bank of New Zealand, 1992c, February, pp. 5-6). In order to emphasize that it was committed to the bottom as well as the top of its target range, the Reserve Bank allowed the ninety-day bank bill rate to fall to 8.8% over the next three months and the exchange rate to depreciate sharply. By October, as the New Zealand dollar reached its lowest level in five years against the currencies of its trading partners, the Bank and the Prime Minister were forced to try to persuade the public that the depreciation would not imperil the achievement of future inflation targets (see, for example *Reuters Financial Service* [1991]). In December 1991, headline and underlying inflation were down to 1% and 1.7%, respectively, roughly 1% below the August forecasts. "The contraction in the domestic economy (which itself was more marked than antici-pated) impacted on inflationary pressures to a greater extent than had been expected" (Reserve Bank of New Zealand, 1992c, February, p. 10). Also, world prices had been lower and the exchange rate had held firm for longer than had been expected. Mostly as a result of the exchange-rate depreciation, the Bank expected underlying inflation to peak at around 3% by early 1993 and then to fall back to 1.2% by the end of that year.

The June 1992 *Monetary Policy Statement,* heralding the beginning of the second episode, stated that "the Bank is now focusing on ensuring that price stability is consolidated, rather than on still trying to achieve significant reductions in inflation" (Reserve Bank of New Zealand, 1992c, June, p. 13). From March 1991 to March 1992, headline inflation and underlying inflation had fallen to 0.8% and 1.3% respectively. With the domestic economy beginning to recover, the Bank saw its task now as to maintain price stability in an environment of moderate growth. The con-tinued favorable outlook for inflation and the reduction in inflation ex-pectations, as documented by the Bank's surveys, had enabled the Bank to ease policy further, allowing the ninety-day bank bill rate to fall to 6.6%. The Bank's forecasts for underlying inflation for the end of 1992 and for 1993 were now at 2% and 1%, respectively, reflecting primarily downward revisions in expected unit labor costs and import prices. The turning point in the exchange rate, in January 1993, was foreshadowed by the Bank's assessment that "over the longer run . . . if the inflation rates of our trading partners . . . remain higher than that in New Zealand, some appreciation of the nominal exchange rate would be entirely con-sistent with the maintenance of price stability" (Reserve Bank of New Zealand, 1992c, June, p. 35).[16]

Unrest in the currency market following the release of the December 1992 Monetary Policy Statement prompted the Bank to increase the ninety-day bank bill rate from 6.4% to 7.8%. Apart from that brief inci-dent, however, the period from mid-1992 to the end of 1993 was a rela-tively placid one. The domestic economy continued its recovery without any notable inflationary pressures, and the ninety-day bank bill rate fell below 5% in December 1993. Inflation expectations remained largely unchanged, and the Bank's inflation forecasts one and two years ahead remained comfortably within the 0 to 2% range. Donald Brash had been reappointed Governor of the Reserve Bank on December 16, 1992, reflecting the Reserve Bank's political strength, while the National Party barely survived the next election with a one-seat majority in Parliament. At the end of 1992, a new PTA signed by the Bank and the National Party specified that the Reserve Bank must maintain underlying inflation within the already-achieved 0 to 2% range.

As the third period in our history of recent New Zealand monetary policy began, continuing domestic expansion and appreciation of the exchange rate had shifted the risk of future inflation from external to domestic sources. With hindsight, it is clear that inflationary pressures started to develop in early 1994. In December 1993, the Bank had noticed signs that the recovery might be stronger than anticipated but still considered it "premature" to tighten policy. Its forecasts of underlying inflation by the end of 1994 and 1995 were at 0.8% and 1.8%, respectively.

A recurring topic in the *Monetary Policy Statement* after early 1994 was the Bank's uncertainty about the level of growth that the economy could sustain without inducing inflation. The structural reforms initiated since 1985, primarily the liberalization of the economy and the opening up of markets to international competition, along with changes in the wage-setting process, were presumed to have made it more difficult for price and wage inflation to develop. Coupled with what seemed to be an increase in the credibility of the monetary-policy framework, the reforms might conceivably have permitted higher non-inflationary growth in the economy. Estimating the non-inflationary rate of growth proved to be difficult, however, as it has in many other countries in recent years.

In line with the optimistic view of New Zealand's growth potential, the Bank permitted the average ninety-day bank bill rate to drop from 5.5% in the December 1993 quarter to 4.9% in the March 1994 quarter. Meanwhile, however, it was determined that real GDP had grown 5% during 1993. Over the second quarter of 1994, monetary policy reversed course and started to tighten in the face of the unexpected strength of the economy; the average ninety-day bank bill rate rose to 6.2% through June. By this point, real GDP was growing at an annual rate of 6% with all sectors expanding rapidly, most notably the construction sector. Despite strong investment over the preceding years, capacity utilization had been on an upward path since late 1991, and employment had grown at an annual rate of 4% since the beginning of the year. By midyear 1994, economists began to worry that a breach of the target range by headline

CPI might raise the public's inflation expectations, even if underlying CPI inflation remained on target.

From June to December, the bill rate rose from 5.5% to 9.5% as monetary policy continued to tighten. The yield curve's slope turned negative once again and the exchange rate appreciated by 4.5% over 1994. At this point, the Bank's assessment was "that the economic upturn may have peaked, and that growth may begin to moderate over the coming year" (Reserve Bank of New Zealand, 1994c, December, p. 15). However, the Bank's forecast of underlying inflation over the next two years came very close to the 2% ceiling, with underlying inflation expected to stay in the vicinity of 1.8% throughout 1995. Headline inflation was expected to peak at 4.2% in the second quarter of the year, mainly as a consequence of rising mortgage rates. A number of private forecasts disagreed with those of the Bank, predicting a target breach in mid-1995. Reporters asked Finance Minister William Birch whether Governor Brash would be dismissed if the target was breached. His response was that the Reserve Bank's forecasts did not offer any grounds for believing that the target would not be met.[17]

In the event, the Reserve Bank's forecast for both GDP growth and inflation in 1995 proved to have been too low. In May, the Bank revised its forecast to predict that underlying inflation would exceed the 2% target ceiling in the second quarter of 1995. In fact, underlying inflation rose above the 0 to 2% range, peaking at 2.2% in the second quarter of 1995. Headline inflation rose even more sharply, to 4.6%, although both measures remained short of the highest private-sector forecasts. But "Mr. Brash said the Bank remained confident the underlying inflation rate would fall back during the third quarter of this year, and therefore planned to take no action on a 'temporary' breach" (Tait, 1995). Governor Brash made it clear that the overshooting would not be reversed so long as there appeared to be no change in the inflation trend, and that he did not anticipate public expectations of inflation to respond unduly to a "temporary" deviation.

Thereafter headline inflation fell rapidly, as the rise in mortgage rates stemming from the monetary tightening during 1994 ceased to have an effect on the CPI calculation. Underlying inflation fell to only 2% in the year to September 1995. Although in June 1994 the Bank had still been expecting underlying inflation to return to 1.2% by June 1996, its December 1995 forecast for the year to September 1996 was 1.7%. A major factor behind the rise in underlying inflation was the continuing boom in the construction sector, particularly in the Auckland area, where construction costs rose by 11.8% over the year to March 1995.

This concentration of inflationary pressures in the nontraded sector made the Bank's monetary policy less effective in slowing prices than it had been in the past, because the exchange rate channel of monetary transmission has weaker and more indirect effects on that sector. Largely for this reason, keeping inflation within the tight target range required a sharp rise in nominal interest rates to more than 9%, and an associated, unusually large, appreciation of the New Zealand dollar. The movement of both the interest rate and the exchange rate shows what can happen when a small, open economy runs an independent monetary policy while its economic cycle is out of phase with the major world economies. It also shows the potential for *instrument instability* (oscillations in the variables controlled by monetary policy), with its attendant economic dislocations.[18] Nevertheless, what New Zealand observers saw was that the country had, for the first time in decades, gone through a period of strong growth without having to face a balance-of-payments or inflation crisis at the end of it.

Governor Brash did take "full responsibility" for the Bank's not having acted sooner to stem inflationary pressures, thereby allowing the target to be breached. Citing the "temporary" nature of the breach, however, he said that he would not resign, and Finance Minister Birch backed him (Hall, 1995). Thus it became clear that the dismissal of the Reserve Bank Governor for a breach of the target was not to be automatic, but was to be left to the judgment of the Board and the Finance Minister. In this respect New Zealand's framework differs from recent proposals for an "optimal central banking contract," as the New Zealand framework has been described, which would not have allowed Governor Brash to escape penalty for exceeding the numerical target set in the policy agreement.

By October 1995 inflation had subsided, but Governor Brash was chastened by the practical problems of keeping inflation within a tightly specified range, given the difficulties of forecasting and the potential for instrument instability. The gap between how finely the Reserve Bank can control inflation and the narrow range to which it was committed became an important political theme for the next year. Indeed, monetary policy in general became a lively political issue in the run-up to the October 1996 elections. Much of the debate centered on whether the target range should be widened, although some minor parties suggested altering the midpoint of the range as well.

In December 1995, the Reserve Bank tightened policy again. Most observers characterized this move as a reaction to the National Party's announcement of tax cuts, to take effect right before the elections nine months later. Finance Minister Birch denied the implication that the

Reserve Bank expected the tax cuts to be inflationary, stating that the size and nature of the tax cuts had been discussed with the Reserve Bank before being presented to Parliament (Birch, 1996).

In any event, the issue in the popular mind had moved from low inflation to high real interest rates. By February 1996, Governor Brash felt it necessary to open a speech to the Auckland Manufacturers' Association with the following remarks:

> Over recent weeks there have been a number of media reports of people calling for the abolition of the Reserve Bank, or the repeal of the Reserve Bank Act, with the claim that the Bank is an anachronism in New Zealand's free-market economy, that its operations result in New Zealanders having to pay interest rates which are among the highest in the world in real terms, and that these interest rates are pushing up the exchange rate to the huge detriment of exporters and those competing with imports. There are variations around this theme, depending upon who is mounting the case, but I think that I accurately reflect the general case. (Brash, 1996b)

While Governor Brash's policies had checked the inflationary trend well enough to justify the government's support, the differential effects of high short-term interest rates on traded and nontraded goods (high interest rates hurt exports and import-competing products more than the nontraded goods sector by strengthening the exchange rate) exacerbated the public's disaffection. Simply meeting the PTA contract was not enough when the PTA itself came under fire, and even though rewriting it was the politicians' responsibility and not the Bank's, the Bank began to suffer the consequences of the unpopularity of its policies.

On April 19, 1996, the Board of the Reserve Bank sent a letter to Finance Minister Birch. Several things had become clear: The target ceiling would be breached again by midyear. Headline inflation would rise, and underlying inflation would rise again, though only temporarily. Also, the issue of dismissing the Governor would have to be dealt with once more, even though again no one felt that policy was too loose or that inflation expectations were rising. However, the fact that the Reserve Bank was running into a control problem for the second time in a year pointed out the difficulties associated with the third PTA. The Board's letter supported Governor Brash's performance—carefully basing the argument on the trend of underlying inflation—and recommended that he continue in his position.

In May, however, the New Zealand First Party—a populist party that was likely, in the November elections,[19] to become a coalition member for the first time—advocated that goals for unemployment and growth be added to monetary policy. In view of the likelihood of an inflation blip and the political uncertainty surrounding monetary policy, long-term bond yields rose; the spread between ten-year bond rates in New Zealand and the United States reached 200 basis points, the highest level since 1992. In response, the Labour Party made a proposal of its own: to widen the inflation band to -1% to 3%.

In June 1996, the Reserve Bank reported that underlying inflation had in fact breached the target ceiling of 2% in the first quarter and forecast that it would reach 2.6% in the third quarter. When historically high real interest rates appeared to be insufficient to maintain inflation within the target range consistently, the feasibility of the target range was questioned more widely. Private-sector economists began to join the opposition parties in advocating a widening of the range, predicting that inflation would remain above 2% through March 1997. The Reserve Bank, among others, feared that widening the range might be interpreted as a weakening of anti-inflationary resolve, which would have harmful effects on credibility and inflation expectations. As we noted above, however, even Governor Brash had come to realize that the control problems posed by a 0 to 2% target range were perhaps too great to be handled.

> Dr. Brash acknowledged that it would be tempting to say that the 0 to 2 percent target range was both too low and too narrow. But . . . "I don't think it is self-evident at all that a wider target would help the real economy," Dr. Brash said. "On the contrary there are some real risks in doing that." The dangers were that widening the range would itself raise inflationary expectations, and that the Reserve Bank itself would be slower to react to inflationary pressures. The width of the target band is only one of the features of the present monetary policy framework to be questioned of late. (Fallow, 1996)

Only successful targeters of long standing, such as Germany and Switzerland, have seemed able to cope with frequent misses of the target ranges without changing their ranges. The premises of the Reserve Bank of New Zealand Act of 1989, the interpretation of inflation targeting as requiring inflation to be tightly controlled quarter to quarter, and the inherent limitations on what New Zealand's monetary policies could accomplish, created pressure for a more activist monetary policy in New Zealand than was originally intended. Further, the stringent requirements of inflation control caused harm to the real economy, notably the export sector, whose competitiveness was harmed by high interest rates and appreciation of the exchange rate.

On October 12, 1996, New Zealand held its first mixed-member proportional representation elections for national Parliament. The outcome was (as expected) indecisive, with no one party getting more than 50% of the vote. The New Zealand First Party, which clearly held the balance in forming a coalition, negotiated with both the Labour Party and the National Party. On October 18, National Party (and caretaker) Finance Minister Birch publicly indicated that the inflation target (its width and its average level) was on the table in negotiations with the New Zealand First Party. The October 16 data release showed underlying inflation remaining above target at 2.3% (headline inflation was 2.4%), but below some private forecasts, which were as high as 2.7%. In the words of one New Zealand business columnist watching the negotiations, "The message: [despite being generally successful,] present Reserve Bank inflation targets are not credible. They could be changed at any time, depending on the whims of whoever wants most to drive about in a ministerial LTD. We are back to politicized monetary policy" (Coote, 1996).

Meanwhile, the Bank found itself on the horns of a familiar dilemma. As capital flowed back into New Zealand after the election, the New Zealand dollar had risen to an eight-year high against the yen and the U.S. dollar. The Bank again was confronted with difficult choices. Despite the above-target inflation rate and the need to rein in inflationary pressures on the nontraded goods sector—and because of the medium-term trend of underlying inflation and the highly unfavorable circumstances for the traded-goods sector—there was good reason not to raise interest rates further. "Unfortunately, in order to keep overall monetary conditions consistent with maintaining price stability, it appears we have to accept rather less interest rate pressure than might be ideal, and rather more exchange pressure than might be ideal," stated the Bank on October 24 (Hall, 1996a). In other words, the Bank was admitting that the control problem of hitting the required narrow target range had forced it into short-run policy trade-offs that it did not want, given the political constraints of the tight target.

Finally, on December 10, a parliamentary coalition between the National Party and the New Zealand First Party was agreed to for a three-year term. Their first substantive announcement was that the inflation target would be modified. The new Policy Targets Agreement, signed by the National Party's Finance Minister Birch and Governor Brash that same day, widened the target range from 0% to 2% to 0% to 3%. The shift underlines the unavoidably political nature of a central bank's accountability under any democratic system: The goals by which monetary policy is evaluated, and, in the New Zealand case, the decision of whether to exercise the option to dismiss the Governor for not attaining the goal, reflect the preferences of the officials who happen to be in office at the moment.

On December 18, Governor Brash described the widening of the inflation target range as a modest change: "We previously aimed at inflation of 1 per cent. It is now 1.5 per cent" (Hall, 1996b). While Governor Brash admitted that this change would allow some easing of policy, he stated that it was already justified by inflation forecasts: "to the extent that increased inflationary expectations lead to higher prices, higher wage settlements and so on, the new inflation target gives much less scope for an easing . . . than might perhaps be assumed" (Tait, 1996). To the extent possible, the Reserve Bank was intent on limiting any damage to its credibility from the modification of the target.

In an address given a month later (Brash, 1997), Governor Brash summarized the meaning of the new PTA, including the amended inflation target. He emphasized that "price stability remains the single objective of monetary policy and constitutes the best way in which the Reserve Bank can contribute to New Zealand's economic development." He noted that the current state of knowledge in monetary economics left unresolved the debate between those who advocate a "low, positive inflation" and those who argue for zero inflation. The Governor continued,

> it is at this stage quite inappropriate to be dogmatic, and in my own view a target which involves doing our utmost to keep measured inflation between 0 and 3 percent is certainly consistent with the intention of the legislation within which monetary policy is operated. . . . Indeed, irrespective of where the mid-point of the target range should be, there may be some advantage in having a slightly wider inflation target than the original 0 to 2 percent target. A number of observers have suggested that a target with a width of only 2 percentage points requires an excessive degree of activism on the part of the central bank. . . . The tension is between, on the one hand, choosing a target range which effectively anchors inflation expectations at a low level but which is so narrow that it provokes excessive policy activism and risks loss of credibility by being frequently exceeded; and on the other, a target range which does a less effective job of anchoring inflation expectations, but which requires less policy activism and protects credibility by being rarely breached. (Brash, 1997)

Key Lessons from New Zealand's Experience

After eight years of inflation targeting, the experience of the Reserve Bank of New Zealand provides several important lessons. First, it suggests that the challenge of bringing down trend inflation and maintaining low inflation expectations is relatively easy compared with that of tightly controlling the course of inflation within a narrow range, especially for a small, open economy. In particular, it indicates that strict adherence to a narrow inflation target range may lead to movements in policy instruments that are greater than the central bank would like, opening the possibility of instrument instability and perhaps macroeconomic instability as well.

Second, the Reserve Bank has found that excessive restrictions on the exercise of its discretion and the manner in which it explains policy—even if in the name of accountability—may create instances in which credibility could be damaged, even when underlying inflation is controlled. This problem is due not only to inflexibility of policy, but also to the focus of the New Zealand policy framework on the formal accountability of the Bank directly to the government. We shall see that credibility and flexibility are enhanced in practice when the central bank also attempts to establish accountability directly to the public, by increasing the transparency of monetary policy and by making the effort to communicate the rationale and objectives of its policy framework.

These cautionary notes do not negate the fact that inflation targeting in New Zealand has, on the whole, been highly successful. This country, which was prone to high, volatile inflation before the inflation-targeting regime was adopted, has emerged as a country with low and stable inflation. Moreover, this has been accomplished as part of an overall package of reforms which has promoted and sustained substantial economic growth and modernization.

6

Canada: Inflation Targets as Tools of Communication

CANADA adopted inflation targeting in 1991, one year after New Zealand. As in New Zealand, the change in policy approach was the result of dissatisfaction among policy-makers with the performance of the economy, particularly on the inflation front. Unlike the case of New Zealand, however, inflation targeting in Canada did not emerge from a legislative mandate, but was developed gradually and somewhat informally. However, over time the new regime has taken on an official quality, with the inflation target being jointly determined and announced by the government and the central bank.

Key Features of Inflation Targeting in Canada

- Inflation targeting in Canada was not the result of formal legislation. However, as in New Zealand, the inflation target in Canada is jointly determined and announced by both the government and the central bank. The Bank of Canada is the entity responsible for meeting the inflation targets, although there are no explicit sanctions for target misses.

- As in New Zealand, inflation targeting was adopted in Canada after substantial progress in reducing the inflation rate was already evident, so that success in achieving the initial targets appeared likely. The likelihood of initial success was also increased by the fact that the horizon for the first targets was set at 22 months from target adoption.

- The CPI inflation rate, as measured by Statistics Canada, has been the official primary target variable in Canada because of its "headline" quality. However, a core inflation rate that excludes energy and food prices has also been used extensively in assessing whether the trend inflation rate is on track for the medium term.

- The inflation target is stated as a range rather than as a point target, with as much emphasis placed on the floor of the range as on the ceiling. The midpoint of the inflation target range, 2%, is above zero, as in all the other cases we examine. Medium-term inflation goals have been set to converge gradually to the long-term goal. Each of these provisions represents a compromise between an exclusive focus on price stability and concern for short-term output and employment goals.

- The Canadian inflation-targeting regime is quite flexible in practice, with real output growth and fluctuations taken into consideration in the conduct of monetary policy. Indeed, in Canada, the inflation target is viewed as a way to help dampen cyclical fluctuations in economic activity.

- Accountability is a central feature of the inflation-targeting regime in Canada, but the central bank is more accountable to the public at large than to the government. Indeed, a central and increasingly important feature of Canada's framework is a strong commitment to transparency and to the communication of monetary-policy strategy to the public.

- In implementing the inflation-targeting regime, the central bank uses a so-called "monetary conditions index," a weighted average of the exchange rate and the short-term interest rate, as both an informational variable and a short-run target.

The Adoption of Inflation Targeting

The adoption of inflation targeting in Canada followed a three-year campaign by the Bank of Canada to promote price stability as the long-term objective of monetary policy. That campaign, beginning with then-Governor John Crow's Hanson Lecture at the University of Alberta in January 1988, "The Work of Canadian Monetary Policy" (Crow, 1988), had spelled out the reasons for the Bank of Canada's disinflationary policy of the late 1980s and early 1990s. It had not, however, been equally clear about what a price-stability goal would mean in practice, either in terms of specific inflation targets or the time frame for achieving those targets (Thiessen, 1995a; Freedman, 1994a and 1995).

On February 26, 1991, formal targets "for reducing inflation and establishing price stability in Canada" through 1995 were announced. The announcement was made jointly by the Minister of Finance, Michael Wilson, of the ruling Conservative Party, and the Governor of the Bank of Canada, John Crow. To maximize publicity and to underscore the government's support of the goal of price stability, the announcement was made on the same day the government released its budget. In March, the Bank issued its *Annual Report, 1990,* which featured remarks by Governor Crow on the appropriateness of price stability as a goal for monetary policy and included an article titled "The Benefits of Price Stability" (Bank of Canada, 1990a). The initiation of the commitment to inflation targeting had been carefully planned to attract public attention and to build public support.

It is interesting that there had been no advance notice to the public of the policy shift to inflation targeting by senior Bank of Canada officials. The *Annual Report, 1990* contained a one-paragraph mention of the adoption of inflation targets tacked onto the end of Governor Crow's annual statement, but no reference to targets earlier in the piece. Nor was there any crisis that might have prompted the abrupt shift in policy (such as the collapse of an exchange-rate peg, or the sudden breakdown of the relationship between an intermediate target and the goal variable). Governor Crow had been appointed to his position four years earlier, and the Conservative Government had been reelected in late 1988, so neither could a change in policy-makers explain the shift.

Before the announcement of specific inflation targets, the Bank's repeated declaration of the price-stability goal by itself appeared to have made little headway against the "momentum" in inflation expectations that had built up (Thiessen, 1991; Freedman, 1994a). In fact, in the "Background Note" released at the time of the adoption of the targets, mention is made of the "unduly pessimistic" outlook for inflation in a number of quarters (Bank of Canada, 1991b, March, p. 11). Evidently, inflation targets were the tactic chosen to reduce inflation expectations and to bring the declared goal of Canadian monetary policy to fruition.

The Bank of Canada apparently decided that February 1991 was a good time to formalize its commitment to price stability. A propitious factor was that year-over-year CPI inflation had dropped to 4.2% in the fourth quarter of 1990 (versus a high of 5.5% in early 1989), and "the pressures from excess demand that were pushing up prices from 1987 through 1989 finally eased during 1990" (Thiessen, 1991, p. 18). Indeed, economic growth was at a cyclical trough. Because the Canadian economy had slowed—and, though it was not realized at the time, had entered a deep recession in 1990—underlying disinflationary pressures were already becoming manifest at the time the targets were introduced. These conditions made it more likely that initial inflation targets could be met.

A negative development motivating target adoption was the large risk premiums that were being built into long-term Canadian interest rates. These premiums reflected a variety of disquieting factors, including rapid growth of government and external debt, political uncertainty, and credibility problems for monetary policy after two decades of inflation. Arresting this increasing uncertainty through whatever devices were available was an important concern of policy-makers.

There were also worries about future shocks to the price level, including the possibility of oil-price increases. Of immediate concern was a new goods and services tax (GST)—an indirect tax similar to a value-added tax, or VAT—which was to take effect at the start of 1991 and was expected to have an impact on the total headline CPI of 1.25 percentage points. A failure of monetary policy to keep the first-round effects of the increase in the indirect tax from triggering a new wage-price spiral would only confirm the public's conviction that inflation would continue.

The current Governor of the Bank of Canada, Gordon Thiessen, has described February 1991 as a period of public uncertainty about inflation, despite the earlier declaration of the price-stability goal (Thiessen 1991, 1995a). Deputy Governor Charles Freedman (1994a) also stated that one of the Bank's primary short-run concerns was to prevent an upward spiral in inflation expectations in the face of these shocks. The Bank went further and seized the opportunity to distinguish between the temporary shocks and the intended path of inflation as an instructional precedent for its targeting framework. As the announcement explained: "These targets are designed to provide a clear indication of the downward path for inflation over the medium term" (Bank of Canada, 1991b, March, p. 5). To underscore this intention, the Bank referred to the targets as "inflation-reduction targets," until the target range stopped dropping in 1995 and the targets became "inflation-control targets." (We have already seen semantic distinctions of this type drawn in the case of Germany, where the Bundesbank used the phrase "unavoidable rate of price increase" during the disinflation phase and then switched to "normative rate of price increase.") Of course, the targets chosen were thought by the Bank to be attainable, the logic being that if declarations of the price-stability goal were not enough, then failure to achieve specific promised reductions in inflation would certainly be detrimental to the credibility of policy and the hope of eventually eliminating inflation (Freedman, 1995).

The Bank set the first target for twenty-two months after the announcement of target adoption, for the stated reason that six-to-eight-quarter lags before the effect of monetary policy became apparent made any earlier target infeasible. Canada may have gone through a period of significant inflation uncertainty as a result of that decision. In the event, inflation actually *undershot* the target range until early 1993. It appears, though, that the public did not regard the inflation target as credible until later, as we will document using data on inflation expectations in Chapter 10. In contrast, New Zealand's and the United Kingdom's target ranges took effect immediately upon adoption, and those countries experienced little problem with target misses until subsequent cyclical upswings.

The Bank of Canada's rationale for its inflation-targeting approach—and for its goal of price stability, rather than just low inflation—was what could be termed a sluggishness, as well as an entrenched upward bias, in the public's inflation expectations. As articulated by Governor Crow (1988) in his Hanson Lecture, "In my view, the notion of a high, yet stable, rate of inflation is simply unrealistic." Offering the hypothetical example of a central bank tolerating 4% inflation, the Governor asserted that a public that sees the central bank as unwilling to reduce inflation from that level would view any shock that moved inflation up (say to 5%) as unlikely to be reversed, and therefore likely to be built into inflation expectations. Inflation expectations get an entrenched bias upward, this argument goes, when there is no clear nominal anchor to keep the goal of price stability in view.

The entrenched upward bias of these expectations is cited repeatedly as an empirical reality of the Canadian economy.[1] For expectations to change, Governor Crow argued, the central bank must demonstrate its willingness to pay the costs of disinflation: "But as lower inflation is achieved, as people are less conditioned by fears of inflation, reducing inflation and preventing its resurgence becomes less difficult" (Crow, 1989, p. 23).[2] While Crow's views help to explain why the announced targets "provide [a path] for *gradual* but progressive reductions of inflation until price stability is reached" (Bank of Canada, 1991b, March, p. 5, emphasis added), this begs the question of why for three years the Bank simply declared its commitment to price stability without naming an explicit nominal anchor. It is likely that the Bank was waiting until the elected government was ready to support fully its commitment to price stability (see, for example, Laidler and Robson [1993]).

It is also possible that the Bank simply went through a prolonged decision-making process that culminated in the opportunity to take advantage of the economic situation of February 1991. The Hanson Lecture itself was ignored in the *Annual Report, 1988*, though it was eventually cited repeatedly in Bank of Canada statements and was followed up by "The Benefits of Price Stability" in the *Annual Report, 1990*. An appreciation for the possible benefits of targeting emerged after an even greater lag: In 1989, Governor Crow stated in a speech reprinted in the *Bank of Canada Review*, "In my experience, if [an inflation] target is suggested it is almost invariably whatever the rate of inflation happens to be at the time. Some target!" (Crow, 1989, p. 22).[3]

In any event, the decision to adopt inflation-reduction targets was made to "buttress" the Bank of Canada's commitment to price stability and to resolve uncertainties about it (Freedman, 1994a). "The targets [were] not meant to signal a shift in monetary policy. . . . All we [were] doing [was] making clear to the public the rate of progress in reducing inflation that monetary policy [was] aiming for" (Thiessen, 1991, p. 19). The Bank of Canada did not suggest that the announcement of targets by itself would bring an immediate payoff in lower inflation expectations; rather, it saw the benefits accruing over a long period of time. Achieving those targets over the medium term would eventually strengthen public confidence in monetary policy, it was thought, and inflation control would be supported by the increased transparency and accountability that the targets would bring to the conduct of monetary policy.

The Operational Framework

When the Canadian inflation-targeting scheme was announced in February 1991, it was in the form of a timetable for reducing inflation, defined by three commitments for inflation levels at later dates. (In fact, as mentioned earlier, Bank of Canada officials originally referred to the targets as "inflation-reduction targets.") The first target range took a midpoint of 3% year-over-year inflation (defined as the change in the CPI) by the end of 1992, twenty-two months after adoption. The second target was a midpoint of 2.5% inflation by the end of June 1994, and the third was a midpoint of 2% inflation eighteen months after that.

The Bank stated at the outset that price stability involved a rate of inflation below 2%: "A good deal of work has already been done in Canada on what stability in the broad level of prices means operationally. This work suggests a rate of increase in consumer prices that is clearly below 2 per cent" (Bank of Canada, 1991b, March, p. 5). There was no mention, however, of targeting zero measured inflation or a constant price level. The Bank wanted to see further research before committing to a precise operational definition of price stability. From the outset of targeting, the Bank made a number of statements indicating that the correct number for price stability would be defined at a later date, and that there would be further reductions in the target until price stability had been achieved. It is interesting that, since later studies by the Bank would estimate the upward bias in inflation measurement of the Canadian CPI to be at most 0.5% per year (Bank of Canada, 1995c, May, p. 4, footnote 1), more than measurement error alone must underlie Canada's reluctance to date to reduce the midpoint of its target inflation range below 2% per year.

On the appointment of Governor Thiessen in December 1993, the new Liberal Government and the Bank extended the 1% to 3% inflation target from the end of 1995 to the end of 1998. The setting of an operational definition of price stability was again put off until more experience was gained about the performance of the economy at low rates of inflation. The Bank specified again that it was not treating the current targets as the equivalent of price stability:

> There were two reasons for the extension—(i) given that it has been a long time since Canada has had such low rates of inflation, it would be helpful to have more experience in operating under such conditions before an appropriate longer-term objective is determined; (ii) some time is needed to enable Canadians to adjust to the improved inflation outlook. (Freedman, 1995, p. 24)[4]

In setting its targets, the Bank attempted to orient both its own policies and the expectations of the public toward a medium-term horizon of one to three years. It accepted, however, that public expectations and their implications for economic behavior (such as patterns of wage-setting) would not be completely altered even after a number of years of targeting.

The medium-term orientation also informed the Bank's choice of target variable. The rate of change in the CPI was chosen as the primary target because of its "headline" quality; it is the most commonly used and understood price measure in Canada. In addition, the CPI comes out monthly, with infrequent delays and without revisions (one alternative price index, the GDP deflator, is frequently revised in Canada). Because the headline CPI includes food and energy prices, however, it tends to be volatile. Consequently, to avoid forced responses to short-run fluctuations, the Bank also uses and reports "core CPI" (which excludes changes in prices of food and energy), asserting that core CPI inflation and headline CPI inflation move together in the medium-to-long term.[5] "How we will react [to a change in inflation] will depend on whether or not a change in measured inflation is associated with a shift in the momentum, or underlying trend, of inflation" (Thiessen, 1994b, p. 81).

There is no fixed procedure by which the Bank is held accountable for performance on either of the two CPI indices over a specified time frame, but repeated deviations from the path set by the targets would certainly be obvious to the government and to the public. Further, the Bank makes a strong effort to communicate to the public its reading of the economy and the rationale for its decisions. It explains the extent to which the changes in the CPI reflect either purely transitory factors or persistent inflationary pressures. The Bank is scrupulous about conveying this message clearly, since its official target, headline CPI inflation, may be sensitive to temporary factors.[6] It takes out the first-round effects of indirect taxes when determining whether a current or future change in inflation exceeds the target range in a manner that justifies a policy response.[7] This practice of distinguishing between the first-round and second-round price effects of shocks is consistent with the Bank's behaving in a preemptive manner against inflationary impulses.

Deputy Governor Charles Freedman's discussion of price developments in 1994 indicates the Bank's attention to special factors in setting policy and in communicating with the public:

> In particular, although the 12 month rate of increase in the total CPI through much of 1994 was virtually zero, the Bank focused on the fact that the reduction in excise taxes on cigarettes in early 1994 accounted for a decline of 1.3 per cent in the total CPI. Operationally, therefore, the emphasis has been placed on the CPI excluding food, energy and the effect of indirect taxes, which has been posting a rate of increase between $1\,^1/_2$ and $1\,^3/_4$ per cent. At mid-1994, the date of the second milestone, the rate of increase of total CPI was at 0.0 per cent while that of the CPI excluding food, energy and the effect of indirect taxes was at 1.8 per cent, near the bottom of the band. (Freedman, 1995, pp. 24-25)

The inflation targets are set in terms of ranges: As initially announced, inflation would be permitted to range from 1% above to 1% below each of these targets. Then, beginning in December 1995, it would be permitted to range between 1% and 3%. In principle, the objective to be targeted was the midpoint of the range. In practice, the Bank never aggressively sought to move inflation from the outer bands toward the midpoints, even when actual inflation lingered at or below the target floor for an extended period. In fact, "in the revised targets more emphasis is placed on the bands than on the midpoints" (Freedman, 1995). The use of a target range is explicitly intended to allow for control problems.[8] The Bank does recognize that a band of 2% width is narrower than what research has shown to be necessary to accommodate control error and unexpected shocks; but it also feels that too wide a band would send the wrong message to the public (Freedman, 1994a).

The Bank also believed that the band would provide sufficient flexibility for monetary policy to deal with supply shocks, beyond those already taken care of by the exclusion of food and energy prices from core inflation and *ad hoc* adjustments to exclude the first-round effects of changes in indirect taxes.[9] No explicit escape clauses were set up for the Bank to invoke should unusually large or unanticipated shocks arise; the response to such extraordinary shocks was left, implicitly, to the Bank's discretion.

Note how loosely defined this target definition appears when compared to the Reserve Bank of New Zealand's highly specified list of exceptions, which in turn must be approved by the elected government. In the actual conduct of policy, however, the Bank of Canada's definition of the inflation target implies an approach very similar to that of New Zealand, reflecting the fact that both are "small" (in an economic sense), open economies largely dependent on exports of natural resources.

Defining the target inflation rate in the way that Canada did has several implications: First, it commits monetary policy in Canada to reversing shifts in the trend inflation rate while allowing price-level shifts in the face of supply shocks; it is not a framework consistent with price-level targeting. Second, it grants the Bank of Canada the freedom to act with reference to the target bands in whatever way it can justify to the public; it does not specify beforehand the circumstances under which the Bank should deviate from its target.

Another aspect of the Bank of Canada's policy framework is that it lends a countercyclical tendency to monetary policy, in that the Bank must respond to aggregate demand-driven price increases *and* decreases that would take inflation out of the target range. While common to all inflation-targeting regimes that put a floor as well as a ceiling on inflation goals, this feature has become more prominent and explicit in the Canadian framework:[10]

> Some people fear that, by focusing monetary policy tightly on inflation control, the monetary authorities may be neglecting economic activity and employment. Nothing could be further from the truth. By keeping inflation within a target range, monetary policy acts as a stabilizer for the economy. When weakening demand threatens to pull inflation below the target range, it will be countered by monetary easing. (Thiessen, 1996b, p. 2)

The link between developments in the real economy and movements in prices is not denied by the Bank of Canada, despite its official focus on inflation goals. Governor Thiessen, in fact, has offered an explanation for inflation distinct from explanations that relate solely to monetary factors:

> Upward pressure on inflation comes about when excessive spending demands in the economy, which are not adequately resisted by monetary policy, persistently exceed the capacity of the economy to produce the goods and services that are being sought. (Thiessen, 1995b, p. 66)

Concern about the trade-off between output and inflation explains the gradual way the Bank moved from an expected inflation rate of 5% at the end of 1991 to a 2% target by the end of 1995. Freedman (1994a) noted that a typical Phillips-curve equation, augmented to allow for the effects of supply shocks, was broadly able to track the decline in inflation in Canada, suggesting that there was no need to resort to explanations involving credibility and changes in expectations to explain the pace of disinflation. However, despite the continuing "output gap" (*i.e.,* a shortfall of output relative to its potential), since that time inflation has not fallen further, as such equations would predict. One reason might be that the Bank's target is now sufficiently credible that the public's inflation expectations have become quite firm at about 2%.

In any event, the Bank repeatedly holds out the hope in public statements that as the expectations of private individuals and firms adapt to the new regime, the cost and time necessary to achieve and maintain inflation goals will drop.[11] It is fair to ask, however, how long Canada (or any other country) must pursue credible disinflationary, and then counterinflationary, policies before results can be expected. Clearly, in the case of Canada, more than four years of inflation targeting, preceded by at least three years of tightening monetary conditions, were not enough to reduce significantly the costs of disinflation.[12]

Accordingly, the Bank of Canada's justification for the pursuit of inflation targets, and from there price stability, does not rest solely on the argument that quantitative goals can help improve credibility; there is also the view that lower inflation will improve the functioning of the real economy within a reasonably short span of time. "In other words, our objective is price stability, but as a means to the end of good economic performance rather than as an end in itself" (Thiessen 1994a, p. 85).[13] It is interesting, though, that Governor Thiessen has also extolled transparency in monetary policy—as fostered by inflation targeting—as having important economic benefits in its own right.

First, [the central bank] can try to reduce the uncertainty of the public and of financial markets about its responses to the various shocks. It can do this by making clear the longer-run goal of monetary policy, the shorter-term operational targets at which it is aiming in taking policy actions, and its own interpretation of economic developments. Moreover, by committing itself to a longer-term goal and sticking to it, as well as by lessening uncertainty about its own responses to shocks, the central bank may be able to lessen the effect of shocks on private sector behavior. (Thiessen, 1995a, p. 42)

No other inflation-targeting central bank has so explicitly made a virtue of transparency for its benefit to the economy as well as for its role in reducing inflation, although all have made efforts in that direction. Note that the benefits Thiessen lists here can stem from any sustainable longer-run goal of a central bank with a consistent operational framework; he makes no explicit mention of either price stability or inflation. Clearly, the Bank of Canada feels that, within such a framework, it can respond effectively to short-run developments without having to compromise its longer-run goals.[14]

From 1982, when M1 was dropped as the Bank of Canada's intermediate target, until 1991, when inflation-reduction targets were announced, the Bank had been searching for a substitute among the various broader monetary and credit aggregates, although "[they had] not found the behavior of any one of them sufficiently reliable to shoulder the burden of acting as a formal target for monetary policy" (Crow, 1990, p. 36). The move to targeting directly a goal of policy (or its forecast), rather than an intermediate variable (such as the money stock) represented a significant paradigm shift for the Bank of Canada. An implication of this change was that the Bank would have to broaden its information-gathering to include any variable containing information about future inflation, and it has since selected a wide range of information variables .

Theory was of only moderate help in selecting the information variables. "In our view, underlying inflation is affected primarily by the level of slack in the economy and by the expected rate of inflation," stated Governor Thiessen (1995a, p. 49). Neither slack nor expectation is a factor that can be observed directly; they can be assessed only in reference to a variety of variables. In practice,

the Bank of Canada has focused closely on estimates of excess demand or supply (or "gaps") in goods and labor markets as key inputs into the inflationary process. It also follows closely such variables as the rate of expansion of money (especially the broader aggregate M2+ . . .), the growth of credit, the rate of increase of total spending and wage settlements as guides to policy action. (Freedman, 1995)

The Bank's May 1995 *Monetary Policy Report,* establishing the format for those that followed, discussed product and labor markets, inflation expectations, commodity prices, and the Canadian dollar exchange rate in the section "Factors at Work on Inflation." Monetary aggregates are not mentioned until later in the *Report,* as the last of "other indicators" listed in the "Outlook" section. For measures of inflation expectations, the Bank considers results from the quarterly survey of the Conference Board of Canada, the forecasts listed in *Consensus Forecasts,* as well as the differential between the returns on thirty-year conventional nominal bonds and real indexed bonds,[15] but it does not conduct its own surveys of expectations.

To aid in assessing the economic situation, the Bank of Canada introduced the concept of a monetary conditions index (MCI) as a short-run operational target.[16] (New Zealand has adopted a similar index; see Chapter 5.) A change in the MCI is defined as the weighted sum of changes in the ninety-day commercial paper interest rate and the trade-weighted exchange rate (for trading partners in the Group of Ten), where the weights are three to one. The three-to-one weighting of interest rates to exchange rates came out of Bank estimates of the six-to-eight-quarter total effect of changes of each variable on aggregate demand. The MCI was arbitrarily based at 100 in January 1987 and then computed backward and forward from that point; because the value of the MCI at a point in time is arbitrary, the Bank correctly stresses that short-run changes in the MCI are more meaningful than the levels themselves.

The main purpose of the MCI is to remind the Bank and the public that there are two key monetary-policy channels of effect on aggregate demand in an open economy, the channel operating through interest rates and the one operating through exchange rates. The MCI is a "short-run operational target . . . most useful over a one- to two-quarter horizon" (Bank of Canada, 1996c, November, p. 21). The MCI does not constitute a nominal anchor in itself, nor does it imply a commitment to intervene to alter exchange rates: "Between quarterly staff projections, the MCI provides the Bank with a continuous reminder that exchange rate changes must be considered when making decisions about interest rate adjustments" (Bank of Canada, 1996c, November, p. 21). Underlining its essentially tactical role in operations, the MCI is considered only briefly in the semiannual *Monetary Policy Report.*

The Bank of Canada's *Annual Report, 1994* was totally redesigned from the 1993 edition to promote openness and transparency. The first item discussed under the heading of monetary policy was the planned introduction of the *Monetary Policy Report.* According to the Bank's own description:

> The new Monetary Policy Report will be designed to bring increased transparency and accountability to monetary policy. It will measure our performance in terms of the Bank's targets for controlling inflation and will examine how current economic circumstances and monetary conditions in Canada are likely to affect future inflation. (Bank of Canada, 1995a, p. 7)

No longer densely printed and formal in appearance, the *Annual Report, 1994* (and all those published since) was printed in large type, with lots of white space and numerous pictures and graphs. The writing became lighter in tone, and the *Report* became more widely distributed. As we discuss further in the next section, these changes may be seen as part of the Bank's efforts at public outreach and education, goals that gained greater attention after Gordon Thiessen succeeded John Crow as Governor. Another factor in the new design may have been the switch in 1995 from "inflation-reduction" to "inflation-control" targets, that is, inflation was now to be stabilized rather than reduced.[17]

In the introduction to the *Annual Report,* Governor Thiessen spoke directly to the reader in an informal manner:

> In carrying out the responsibilities of the Bank, our objective is to promote the economic and financial welfare of Canada. I hope this description of those activities will increase the public's understanding of how the Bank has fulfilled its responsibilities. Communicating what the Bank is up to and why is important if we are going to maintain the confidence of Canadians. This year we have changed the Bank's *Annual Report. . . .* This new style of annual report is designed to provide more information on what the Bank does, thereby providing a better account of our actions. (Bank of Canada, 1995a, p. 5)

This decision was part of a conscious effort to increase the transparency of policy for the general public. When inflation targets were originally adopted, the Bank had stated:

> The Bank of Canada will be reporting regularly on progress relative to the inflation-reduction targets and on its monetary policy actions in speeches, in the extracts from the minutes of meetings of the Board of Directors of the Bank of Canada and of course in the Bank of Canada's Annual Report to the

Minister of Finance. In addition, an analysis of inflation developments relative to the targets will be published periodically in the *Bank of Canada Review.*
(Bank of Canada, 1991b, September, p. 15)

The *Review* switched from monthly to quarterly publication in 1993, however, and the experience of other inflation-targeting countries, particularly the United Kingdom, demonstrated the usefulness of a separate
publication in eliciting and focusing public discussion of monetary
policy.[18] For Canada, this separate publication was to be the *Monetary
Policy Report.*

The semiannual *Monetary Policy Report* varied slightly in structure in
the first issues, but all editions included some discussion of recent developments in inflation, progress in achieving the inflation-control targets,
and the outlook for inflation. The Bank describes the aim of the *Monetary Policy Report* as follows:

> This report reflects the framework used by the Bank in its conduct of policy.
> This framework includes: (I) a clear policy objective; (II) a medium-term
> perspective (given the long lags for the full impact of monetary policy ac-
> tions on the economy); and (III) a recognition that monetary policy works
> through both interest rates and the exchange rate. (Bank of Canada, 1995c,
> May, p. 3)

The *Monetary Policy Report* is designed to be intelligible to the layper-
son, with "technical boxes" explaining various concepts and procedures
(similar to the pedagogical efforts in the United Kingdom's *Inflation Report*). The format is open, and summary bullet points are used in the
margins. Each issue contains fewer than thirty pages, consisting largely
of charts. The *Report* is available on the Internet or by calling a toll-free
number, and a four-page summary is provided for those who do not wish
to read the entire document. Overall, the *Report* represents a major shift
in tone and in target audience from the reporting efforts undertaken in
the early years of inflation targeting in Canada, when the discussion of
inflation was couched in technical language and was bundled together
with other topics in Bank publications.

About the same time, changes were being made in the internal organization of the Bank of Canada. Most prominently (as summarized in
the Annual Report, 1994), "the Board of Directors established a new
senior decision-making authority within the Bank called the 'Governing
Council.' The Council, which [the Governor chairs], is composed of
the Senior Deputy Governor and the four Deputy Governors. A major
decentralization of decision-making is being implemented in the wake

of the Council's establishment" (Bank of Canada, 1995a, p. 8). Since this change, all issues of the *Monetary Policy Report* have carried the note "This is a report of the Governing Council of the Bank of Canada," followed by the names of the six members. This movement to collective responsibility may have been to some extent a reaction to Governor Crow's tendency to become personally identified with the Bank's policy during the early 1990s.[19]

The Bank of Canada remains a relatively independent central bank.[20] In line with its responsibility for the conduct of monetary policy, it has full operational independence in the setting of monetary-policy instruments. For example, the Bank alone determines the setting of policy-controlled short-term interest rates. Nevertheless, the Bank is subject to the "doctrine of dual responsibility," which puts ultimate responsibility for monetary policy in the hands of the Minister of Finance. The Minister can make the Governor follow a particular policy (or move interest rates at a specific time) by issuing a public directive, with which the Governor and the Bank must comply.

No conflict between the Minister and the Bank has ever occurred, however. Because the issuance of a public directive would imply that the Minister had lost confidence in the Governor's ability to carry out the government's monetary policy, such a directive would likely be followed by the Governor's resignation—an action that would have serious repercussions for the government. Such a directive would be used only in extraordinary circumstances, not as a routine measure by the government to influence the conduct of monetary policy.

Indeed, it might be argued that the very existence of the directive power has strengthened the independence of the Bank of Canada, as compared with a system in which the procedures for resolving policy conflicts are not spelled out so explicitly. In general, relations between the Finance Ministry and the Bank have been quite close. The Minister and the Governor meet almost weekly (though not on a required schedule), and the Deputy Minister of Finance holds a non-voting seat on the Bank's Board of Directors. There are a number of other less formal contacts as well.[21]

The Bank's inflation-targeting framework has been exceedingly flexible and has undergone constant refinement, with a marked trend toward greater transparency over time. The targets have changed from "inflation reduction" to "inflation control" at around 2% CPI inflation, although with no commitment to a specific long-run definition of price stability. Moreover, the Bank has assumed added reporting obligations (such as the *Monetary Policy Report*) and adopted new, more transparent operational tactics (for example, the adoption of the MCI and the mid-1994 move to target more explicitly the overnight interest rate within a range of 50 basis points). At the same time, assessment of inflation performance and forecasts of inflation have always been nuanced by reference to developments in the core CPI, indirect taxes, and exchange rates, leaving the criteria for judging success somewhat implicit. Overall, because of Canada's unique institutional arrangements, as well as the Bank of Canada's efforts at communication, the Bank has become more accountable to the public and the financial markets rather than directly to the government. In this respect, Canada's framework is much closer to that of Switzerland and Germany than to that of New Zealand.

Canadian Monetary Policy under Inflation Targeting

We now summarize the main events in Canadian monetary policy since the announcement of inflation targets in February 1991. Our summary is based on accounts in the Bank's *Annual Report* and semiannual *Monetary Policy Report* (since 1995), speeches and articles printed in the Bank of Canada Review, some academic studies, the *OECD Economic Report,* and various newspaper accounts. Figure 6.1 shows the recent histories of inflation, interest rates, the nominal effective exchange rate (henceforth the exchange rate), GDP growth, and unemployment in Canada.

   Some of the sternest challenges faced by the Bank of Canada during this period were political, rather than economic. In general, the targeting framework for monetary policy has received support from the public and has been endorsed by the two governments in power since it was first adopted. However, critics argued that the Bank's success in reducing inflation and maintaining it at a low level had been achieved only at an unacceptably high cost in unemployment. As in Western Europe, which has had similar unemployment problems, it is by no means clear that the level of unemployment reached in Canada was primarily due to monetary policy. Of course, all central banks that have adopted inflation targeting have received criticism from certain quarters. But critics of the Bank of Canada have been particularly vocal in objecting to the Bank's supposed exclusive focus on inflation control and to the low level of its target range. This experience contrasts with that of New Zealand, where there was basic agreement that the monetary reforms, including the adoption of inflation targets, were beneficial, but the control problems of the central bank in meeting a tight inflation target band near zero were the focus of attention. The Canadian experience also contrasts with

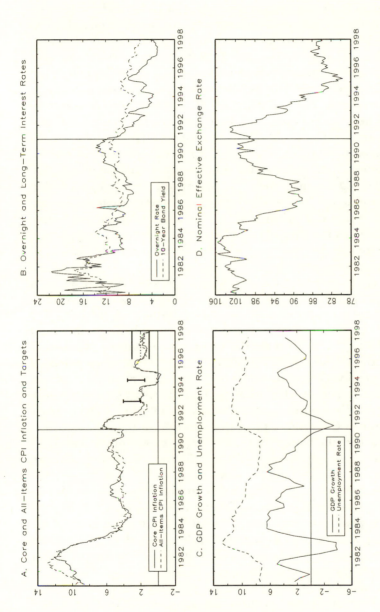

Figure 6.1. Canadian economic indicators. Sources: A) Bank for International Settlements database, Bank of Canada; B) Bank for International Settlements database; C) Main economic indicators of the Organisation for Economic Cooperation and Development; D) Bank for International Settlements database.

that of the United Kingdom, where the central bank, because of its lack of independence, did not control the setting of the monetary-policy instruments and so was not an obvious target for public criticism. Indeed, as we argue in the next chapter, the main challenge in Britain arose from the separation between those accountable for forecasting and assessing inflation performance and those responsible for setting monetary policy.

We focus here on three critical junctures for the Canadian inflation-targeting framework. The first came in 1991 at the time of the adoption of targets, when forces beyond the Bank of Canada's control—in particular developments in world oil markets and Canadian domestic tax policy—created inflationary impulses. The second came in late 1993, when the Liberal Party won in a federal election with a campaign platform that decried the incumbent Conservative Party's "single-minded fight against inflation."[22] The third important event occurred in mid-1996, when the president of the Canadian Economic Association (and a prominent critic of the Bank of Canada) voiced concerns about what he perceived to be the excessive tightness of monetary policy in the face of high and rising unemployment.

In all three instances, the Bank of Canada responded by engaging in substantive public discourse and by redoubling its efforts to improve transparency and communication with the public. In the end, the Bank succeeded in defending its policies without altering its basic commitment to price stability. The fact that the Bank won over a sufficient number of wage- and price-setters in the first instance, the Liberal Government in the second, and the general public in the third, demonstrates the potential of inflation targets—and of the associated transparency and accountability—to foster serious and informed discussion of monetary policy. With the Bank of Canada's competence and responsibilities clearly defined and tracked, the Bank could justify its policies within a clear structure. Meanwhile, critics who argued for different policies were obliged to base their case solely on its economic merits.

The first major challenge to Canada's monetary policy after the announcement of inflation targets on February 26, 1991, was how to cope with upward pressures on inflation that were beginning to emerge at the time. To complicate matters, as we noted earlier, the federal government had just introduced a goods and services tax (GST), accompanied by increases in other indirect taxes by both the federal and provincial governments. The Bank took the line that the price increases caused by the new taxes were identifiable, one-time adjustments that would not have to be offset by monetary policy, *so long as* the private sector did not pass them on through a round of price and wage hikes. The Bank had little incentive to raise interest rates; in fact, it had been trying to ease monetary conditions since the spring of 1990. Further, real GDP growth for 1991 was expected to be weak.

The Bank used the targets as a means of communicating to the public that the one-time price increases should not be incorporated into future inflation or inflation expectations, keeping the threat of a rise in interest rates in the background. Looking back, Governor Crow stated in the *Annual Report, 1991:*

> The fact that the economy was able to absorb the GST and the other indirect tax changes without provoking an inflationary spiral—a process of wages chasing prices, prices increasing further as a result, and so on—has been especially welcome. Certainly, the Bank of Canada has sought to make absolutely clear that monetary policy would not finance such a destructive process. The way that the price effects of the GST have been successfully absorbed has become even more widely recognized with the recent publication of the January 1992 CPI numbers. (Bank of Canada, 1992a, p. 9)

Indeed, because of the tight monetary conditions already established and the sluggishness of the economy, the Bank was able to ease nominal short-term interest rates by 6.5 percentage points between the spring of 1990 and February 1992, a larger drop than the contemporaneous drop in inflation.

The Bank's own analysis of the economic situation at the end of 1991 attributed most of the sluggishness in the Canadian economy to the global slowdown (caused in turn largely by debt overhang in the rest of the Group of Seven) and to low prices for Canadian exports (Bank of Canada, 1992a). In January 1992, the Bank announced that inflation had come in under its expected rate of 5 %.[23] The results were expressed in terms of core CPI (that is, with food and energy prices excluded) rather than in terms of headline CPI, although both were well below target level, having risen only 2.6% and 3.8%, respectively, over 1991. By February 1992, inflation had already dropped below the target level of 2% to 4% for year-end 1992, with core CPI 2.8% higher than a year earlier, despite a depreciating Canadian dollar.

The announcement in May 1991 introducing inflation-indexed (real-return) bonds, with payments of interest and principal linked to the CPI, served as a further indication that the authorities intended to avoid inflationary policies in the future. The introduction of the new bonds was seen, as intended, as an additional incentive for the government and the Bank of Canada to meet the announced inflation targets.[24]

By October 1991, Bank of Canada researchers suggested that Canada had already paid most of the cost of bringing down inflation, as measured by "sacrifice-ratio" calculations (Cozier and Wilkinson, 1991).[25] Some economists immediately voiced their concern, in letters to the press, that the Bank's estimates of the sacrifice ratio were low, possibly by as much as 50 percent.[26] Further, they argued that the unemployment caused by tight monetary policies was likely to be persistent, because of the atrophy of skills and loss of motivation among the unemployed.[27] Their policy recommendation was an easing of monetary policy to prevent this outcome. Significantly, the Bank, in its response, did not deny that the disinflation that had begun before target adoption had involved a cost in terms of output and employment—in fact, it was the release of the Bank's research on sacrifice ratios that prompted this discussion. Nevertheless, various officials did hold out the hope that as inflation expectations adjusted under the targets, the cost of future disinflation would diminish.

So the debate was about the intensity of the Bank's pursuit of low inflation, rather than about the targeting framework *per se,* and the controversy would go on for some time to come. The existence of the inflation targets did help to keep the debate at the level of general principles instead of allowing it to dwell on specific policy actions or on the competence of policy-making.

Much of the discussion during 1991 had to do with the relationship between the Bank's independence and its inflation-targeting framework. In the Conservative Government's proposals for federal reform published in September, the main recommendations regarding the Bank of Canada were to simplify the Bank's legal mandate (replacing the Bank's multiple goals with a focus on price stability) and to make the appointment of the Governor subject to confirmation by the Senate. The Manley Committee in the House of Commons[28] held hearings on those recommendations in late 1991.

The Bank leadership and others testified that a mandate for the Bank to focus on price stability would increase the Bank's accountability, whereas under the existing vague mandate it was possible to defend almost any policy. The Manley Committee concluded, however, that "the problem with a mandate narrowly focused on price stability is that it would tend to enhance the Bank's accountability by reducing unduly the Bank's area of responsibility" (Paragraph 88). In the end, the Committee decided, "The elected government must remain ultimately accountable for the monetary policy followed" (Paragraph 168). Thus the system of dual responsibility and the old legal mandate were maintained.[29]

By September 1992, the Canadian dollar had fallen to 79 U.S. cents from 89 U.S. cents a year earlier, and much of the Bank's attention was devoted to trying to slow down and smooth out this downward trend, as well as the ongoing decline in interest rates. The economy continued to stagnate, but without falling into recession. The *Annual Report, 1992* noted that the Canadian recovery was much slower than the norm of previous business cycles. Headline inflation did meet the target, reading 2.1% in December, while the 1.7% core inflation was below the target range of 2% to 4%. Core inflation would remain between 1.3% and 2% until late 1993.

The second critical juncture for the Bank of Canada's targeting framework came in the summer of 1993, before the November parliamentary election. Given the unpopularity of the ruling majority, and the rising rate of unemployment, Prime Minister Brian Mulroney's Progressive Conservative Party seemed doomed to defeat (although no one at the time foresaw the magnitude of that defeat). The Liberal Party included in its campaign platform a criticism of the Conservative Party's "single-minded fight against inflation."[30] Although the attack focused at first on the Conservative Party's monetary-policy goals, it sparked debate over whether Governor Crow should be appointed to a second seven-year term when the Liberal Party took office. Some private-sector economists warned the Liberal Party leaders through the press that, if Crow was not reappointed, some other measure would have to be taken to reassure financial markets of the new government's commitment to low inflation.[31]

In October 1993, preceding the Liberal Party's victory, Deputy Governor Freedman stated in a speech at an academic conference on monetary policy:

> With the unexpected sluggishness of the economy, the rate of inflation fell faster and further than initially anticipated, and this despite the fact that monetary conditions were easing for most of the period between the announcement of the targets and the first target date, the end of 1992. . . . [Although inflation was 2.1 percent at the end of 1992, versus a lower band of 2 percent,] it would be inappropriate to push up the rate of inflation once it had reached the lower band of the target range, given that the longer-term goal was price stability.[32] (Freedman, 1994a)

This statement underlined the Bank's unwillingness to engage in "fine-tuning" the economy, as well as its readiness to admit forecast errors and to recognize the limitations of its control over inflation. On the other hand, the statement reaffirmed that the boundaries of the target range were to be taken more seriously than the midpoint and gave the impression that, even then, inflation that turned out to be lower than the mid-point of the range would be accepted.[33] As we saw in the case of New Zealand, an emphasis on the "hardness" of the target range may make it more difficult to explain deviations from the range to the public, because the central bank has already specified explicitly the extent of flexibility required. The public can only conclude that the deviation from the range reflects either incompetence or an active decision by the central bank to violate its commitment.

Moreover, a willingness to tolerate inflation rates below the target when inflation is already very low risks economic difficulties, because of the possibility that the output-inflation trade off is more adverse at very low levels of inflation. More recent statements by the Bank of Canada, perhaps in reaction to the economic and political experiences mentioned here, emphasize the advantages of having an effective floor for inflation, as well as a ceiling. Such a floor, if taken seriously, can help to stabilize output fluctuations arising from changes in aggregate demand.

On December 22, 1993, the new Liberal Party government and the Bank made a joint announcement that the 1% to 3% inflation band that was to be reached by year-end 1995 would be extended through 1998. Again, the Bank was careful to indicate that this target represented a medium-term goal, not the achievement of ultimate price stability, however defined. The new Liberal government saw the need to extend the target horizon because the change in the Parliamentary majority had raised fears about its commitment to the target regime. While the government could not guarantee the survival of that commitment beyond the duration of its own majority in the House of Commons, it could at least attempt to create an expectation that the regime would last for the indefinite future.

As we mentioned, the Liberal Party government elected in October 1993 had campaigned against the "single-minded pursuit" of low inflation. John Crow chose not to be considered for a second term as Governor, and Deputy Governor Gordon Thiessen was appointed as his successor, for a seven-year term beginning February 1, 1994. It was on the occasion of Governor Thiessen's appointment that the 1% to 3% target range was extended three more years into the future.[34]

Employment growth finally picked up in 1994, largely in response to a revival of the export trade. Exports were helped by a declining Canadian dollar, particularly against the U.S. dollar; the Canadian dollar had been depreciating for two years before the 1993 election and had only temporarily strengthened on the Liberal majority's reaffirmation of the inflation targets. However, interest rates had risen, reflecting both U.S. rate increases and also concerns over the Canadian fiscal situation and the political power of separatists in Quebec. In the Bank's *Annual Report, 1993* (released in March 1994), John Crow, in his last official act as Governor, called for the reduction of government debt in order to take pressure off interest rates and exchange rates.

Governor Thiessen would make similar statements about fiscal policy in the years that followed, albeit more obliquely at first. In general, inflation-targeting central banks, even independent ones, have a difficult time trying to decide what to say publicly about their government's fiscal policy. The issue is not really avoidable: Even a simple inflation forecast, or an assessment of past monetary policy and inflation performance, entails some attitude on the central bank's part toward the government's fiscal stance and its likely effects. Yet a central bank that appears to be shifting responsibility for economic outcomes onto the other macroeconomic policy lever, or that takes an (actual or perceived) ideological stand on budgetary politics, could well undermine its own political legitimacy. Like all the central banks we consider in this book, the Bank of Canada tended to limit its discussion of fiscal matters to statements about the fiscal stance broadly, its effect on the exchange rate risk premiums on interest rates, and general encomiums to the ideal of long-run fiscal balance.

Over 1994, core CPI inflation adjusted for the effects of changes in indirect taxes had fluctuated between 1.5% and 2%, well within the target band. Headline CPI inflation, as well as core inflation adjusted for the tax changes, had dropped to as low as zero because of a reduction in the excise tax on tobacco in early 1994. Again, the Bank made judicious use of core versus headline CPI to distinguish one-time price shifts from trend inflation. By so doing, it largely avoided confusion and minimized the pass-through of first-round effects to wage and price inflation. Indeed, in February 1995 headline CPI jumped from zero to 1.8% after the first-round effects of the tax reduction on tobacco had been dropped from the calculations. Since the Bank had already stressed the one-time nature of the earlier price drop (and the stability of core inflation), it felt no need to react to this price rise when it occurred (see, for example, Bank of Canada [1995c, May]).

Meeting the announced target (and therefore maintaining a positive inflation rate rather than driving inflation even closer to zero) bolstered the Bank's standing by demonstrating its competence and its reasonableness in its pursuit of price stability. In the *Annual Report, 1994*, Governor Thiessen spoke of the third successive year of "maintenance of a low level of inflation . . . after two decades of high and unpredictable inflation" and remarked on "the progress that has been made towards price stability" (Bank of Canada, 1995a, p. 5).

When the first *Monetary Policy Report* was issued in May 1995, the Bank stated in the four-page summary that "core inflation has been consistently within the Bank's inflation-control targets band since early 1993." Year-over-year core inflation had risen to 2.7% by that month (its highest level since the end of 1991) but had then declined, while headline inflation had peaked at 2.9%. After lowering interest rates on three occasions during the summer of 1994, the Bank tightened toward the end of the year. First, it raised the overnight interest rate in November and early December 1994, in response to rising U.S. rates and evidence of a domestic expansion. Later, in January and February 1995, it raised rates five times in an effort to stabilize financial markets in the face of a rapid depreciation of the Canadian dollar that followed the general crisis of confidence associated with the Mexican devaluation. By March 1995, monetary conditions as measured by the MCI were 2% tighter, reflecting a rebound in the Canadian dollar. Demand for exports was expected to remain strong through the end of the year, while domestic aggregate demand declined in response to the higher interest rates and government fiscal restraint. The Canadian economy had grown more strongly than expected in 1994, at a rate of 5.6%.

Inflation remained in the upper half of the 1% to 3% target band through October, largely because the Canadian dollar had reversed course and begun to depreciate again.[35] The Bank accepted that fact and turned to other concerns. "Throughout the rest of the second quarter [1995], it became increasingly apparent that the economy was not expanding as expected and that an easing of monetary conditions was warranted" (Bank of Canada, 1995c, November, p. 4).[36] Apparently the Bank was willing to admit having made a forecasting error and to link its monetary-policy decisions to real economic developments so long as the inflation target was met. It can be argued that the Bank was able to do so only after having invested in credibility-building disinflation and in educating the public to understand that a good monetary policy must be a forward-looking policy.

The Bank cut interest rates 25 basis points in early May and then lowered interest rates twice in June, while the Canadian dollar was depreciating. It then cut rates twice again, in July and in August, while the dollar was appreciating. The Bank expected inflation to remain high within the target band until 1996, when "added downward pressure coming from greater-than-expected excess slack in the economy" would bring it into the lower half of the band (Bank of Canada, 1995c, November, p. 4). Interest rates were cut on October 31, 1995, the day after the Quebec referendum on sovereignty failed to pass; in December, headline inflation declined to 1.7%, heading into the lower half of the target band and prompting another cut in the overnight interest rate.

When output remained further below potential than the Bank had forecast through the first two quarters of 1996, monetary easing continued. The overnight rate was cut on January 25 and again on January 31, following a reduction in the U.S. federal funds rate. Rates were cut once again in March, and once in April. Since October 1995, the MCI had declined the equivalent of 200 basis points to its lowest level since 1994 (Bank of Canada, 1995c, November, p. 43). However, inflation expectations appeared to be unaffected by the loosening of policy and remained at historical lows; for example, the Canadian Conference Board *Survey of Forecasters* and *Consensus Forecasts* both displayed downward trends in two-year-ahead inflation expectations, from around 4% in the first half of 1990 to 2% in the second half of 1995. The differential between Canadian "real bonds" and thirty-year conventional bonds was 3.25%, on par with the smallest differential recorded since the bonds were first issued in 1991.

Most significantly, the Canadian-U.S. short-term interest-rate differential turned negative (with Canadian rates dipping below those of the U.S.), while the Canadian dollar remained firm, raising hopes at the Bank that Canada's inflation-targeting regime had become such a source of counterinflationary credibility that the interest rates in the two countries might be decoupling. The positive news on inflation and inflation expectations gave the Bank some scope to increase its attention to the needs of the real economy. The Bank kept this change of emphasis within the inflation-targeting framework by beginning to emphasize how seriously it takes the floor on its inflation target, as well as the ceiling; and by pointing out the potentially stabilizing effect on real output of keeping inflation from dropping too low, as well as rising too high.[37]

The third critical juncture for Canadian monetary policy occurred in the summer of 1996. This time, the problem was the continuing stagnation of Canadian GDP and employment. Criticisms of the Bank's policies were delivered by Pierre Fortin, the newly elected president of the Canadian Economics Association. On June 1, 1996, Fortin delivered a presidential address titled "The Great Canadian Slump" (Fortin, 1996a) to the annual meeting of the Association. He characterized Canadian economic performance since 1990 as

a long slide in economic activity and employment . . . [with the] accompanying employment and output losses still accumulating, but . . . they surpass the losses experienced by other industrial countries since 1990. The last decade of this century will arguably be remembered as the decade of The Great Canadian Slump. (*Ibid.,* p. 761)

After considering and dismissing a number of possible structural explanations for Canada's economic performance, Fortin argued that the depression of domestic demand was largely attributable to interest-sensitive consumer durables and business fixed-investment demand. "This gives us the clue to the true cause of the great slump of the 1990s: old-fashioned monetary and fiscal contraction. I argue that monetary policy has been the leader, and that fiscal policy was *induced* by the monetary contraction" (*Ibid.,* p. 770).

In Section IV of his address, "Monetary Policy and the Slump," Fortin cited Bank of Canada statements affirming its control over short-term interest rates and then posed a question:

> The only serious question is why the Bank of Canada has kept the short-term real interest rate differential with the United States so large for so long in the 1990s. The answer to this question has two parts: first, since 1989 the central bank has focused exclusively on the goal of zero inflation; second, contrary to expectations, achieving this objective has forced it to impose permanently higher unemployment through higher interest rates. (*Ibid.,* pp. 774-5)

Elaborating on the first part of his answer, Fortin emphasized the Bank's exclusive focus on inflation, its "religious" zeal in doing so, and its excessive independence from popular preferences and political control (pp. 775-77). He based the second part of his answer on the argument of Akerlof, Dickens, and Perry (1996), that low inflation inhibits real wage adjustment when (whether for reasons of "fairness" or simple money illusion) workers strongly resist nominal wage cuts (see Chapter 2).[38] Applying the argument to the Canadian context, Fortin suggested that

> the zero constraint [on nominal wage change] can take a large macroeconomic bite when the median wage change itself is around zero, as was observed over 1992-4. . . . But if inflation is to fall to a very low level, such as the 1.4 per cent of 1992-6 in Canada, and is to stay there, the proportion of wage earners that are pushed against the wall of resistance to wage cuts must increase sharply. The long-run marginal unemployment cost of lower inflation in this range is not zero, but is positive and increasing. (*Ibid.,* p. 779)

He went on to say that the Bank of Canada has misjudged the output-inflation trade off at low inflation rates and "has displayed a strong deflationary bias that has not reflected the true state of knowledge on the benefits of zero inflation, the true preferences of the Canadian population, and the spirit and letter of the Bank of Canada Act, which reflects those preferences by asking for a reasonable balance between the inflation and unemployment objectives" (*Ibid.*, p. 781).

Fortin acknowledged that "the Bank of Canada has made every effort at explaining this strategy through public speeches, appearances in Parliament, research papers, *Annual Reports,* and, more recently, *Monetary Policy Reports.* But it is also true that these attempts have more often been exercises in advocacy of a controversial and extreme policy orientation than genuine dialogue with the public" (*Ibid.*, p. 781). His two primary policy recommendations were to make the Bank of Canada more like the U.S. Federal Reserve System (as he described it), with five governors holding staggered terms, and to raise the midpoint of the inflation target by 1%, to 3%.

In the press discussion that ensued (informed by Fortin's own summary of his arguments for mass readership), the permanent costs and the transitional costs of achieving low inflation were repeatedly confused.[39] The Canadian-U.S. interest rate differential had dropped along with interest rates elsewhere, suggesting that the Bank of Canada had proved successful in containing inflation. Moreover, it appears that the Bank of Canada had eased monetary conditions because of the risk that the slack in the real economy might cause inflation to drop below the target range. Whether the Canadian economy had borne too great a cost in lost output during the transition process than can be justified by the benefits of lower inflation— despite the Bank of Canada's acknowledgments of the cost of disinflation and conscious gradualism documented above—is an issue that certainly merits discussion, although in the end the conclusion may depend on difficult-to-resolve debates about the long-run benefits of low inflation.

At the time, however, with the record of the Canadian inflation-targeting framework's goals, actions, and results available for all to see, discussion was limited to the costs and benefits of low inflation and did not touch on ideology or competence. Consequently, participants were obliged to take a stand (as Fortin did) on the proper goal of monetary policy. The Bank responded by repeating its rationale for the existing 1% to 3% inflation target. In a speech to the Ecole des Hautes Etudes Commerciales in Montreal on October 9, 1996, Governor Thiessen put the debate in just those terms while addressing Fortin's argument (without mentioning him by name):

A distinction should be made here between *reducing* inflation and *maintaining* it at a low level. Reducing inflation requires a downward adjustment in inflation expectations and may entail transition costs, which is not the case with simply maintaining low inflation. It is generally agreed that the gains achieved by reducing inflation exceed transition costs when inflation is high. Where opinions are more divided is on the question of how far inflation should be reduced. Some fear that if inflation falls below a certain threshold, the economy will be deprived of a lubricant. . . . I must say that this argument assumes a degree of money illusion that I find difficult to reconcile with the observed behavior of wages in inflationary periods. . . . Recent experience will provide us with more useful information in [the wage behavior during periods of slow wage growth]. We have therefore undertaken new research on this question. . . . Since this research is just getting under way, I will confine myself here to reporting that our preliminary examination of the major wage agreements concluded between 1992 and 1994 does not lend evident support to the thesis of inflation as lubricant. (Thiessen, 1996b, p. 3)

Governor Thiessen's remarks prompt three observations: First, the costs of disinflation are once again forthrightly acknowledged; second, the argument for inflation reduction is made on the basis of empirical claims, with the Bank assuming the burden of having to provide supporting (or opposing) research; and third, the discussion is centered on the appropriate level of inflation to target and the pace at which that level should be reached, not on what the goals of monetary policy should be. Later in his remarks, Thiessen attributed the stalling of the expansion in 1995 to increased interest-rate risk premiums, arising from international market fluctuations and political uncertainties about Canada. "In such a context [of high interest rates], the benefits of low inflation were slow to be felt" (*Ibid.,* p. 7). Referring to the easing of monetary conditions since that time and the decline in the Canadian-U.S. interest-rate differential, he stated, "It shows that keeping inflation down is a low-interest-rate policy and not, as some critics have often claimed, a high-interest-rate policy" (Ibid.).

A month later, Thiessen gave a speech titled "Does Canada Need More Inflation to Grease the Wheels of the Economy?,"[40] in which he responded even more directly to the Fortin argument. He began by alluding to

some ideas you have probably heard about recently. . . . The suggestion is that the Bank, with its focus on bringing inflation down, is largely responsible for Canada's sluggish pace of economic expansion and stubbornly high unemployment in the 1990s. . . . Moreover, in this view, a monetary policy that emphasizes price stability will somehow always be too tight to allow the economy to achieve its full potential in the future. (Thiessen 1996a, p. 63)

He then asserted that what had slowed the Canadian economy in the early 1990s was the combination of externally induced high interest rates and widespread structural change (in response to globalization and technological innovations), and that the economy was poised to pick up over the long term. Next the Governor made explicit his view of the relationship between maintaining low inflation and economic growth:

> In fact, when the Bank takes actions to hold inflation inside the target range of 1 to 3 per cent, monetary policy operates as an important stabilizer that helps to maintain sustainable growth in the economy. When economic activity is expanding at an unsustainable pace . . . the Bank will tighten monetary conditions to cool things off. But the Bank will respond with equal concern, by relaxing monetary conditions when the economy is sluggish and there is a risk that the trend of inflation will fall below the target range. (*Ibid.*, p. 67)

Having stressed the distinction between disinflating and maintaining low inflation, Thiessen then reiterated his belief that the process of wage setting in a low-inflation environment would be flexible enough to allow for occasional wage reductions in industries that required it. He thus responded to the view that zero inflation would be costly to the economy because of downward nominal wage rigidity.[41]

The purpose of our extended treatment of this third critical juncture in Canadian monetary policy since the adoption of inflation targets is not to support one side of the argument or the other, but rather to emphasize the form the argument took. The existence of the inflation-targeting framework channeled debate into a substantive discussion about appropriate target levels, with all sides having to declare their assumptions and estimates of costs and benefits while working from the record of what the goal had been and how well it had been met.

It is interesting that, although Fortin's argument provided a means of attacking the Bank's policies that was potentially far better grounded than the arguments used in the 1993 elections, the run-up to the 1997 elections did not include criticism of the Bank of Canada as a major issue. What this difference indicates most of all is that the failure of political accountability claimed by Fortin in "The Great Canadian Slump" address did not exist. A key element of this accountability was the sustained effort by the Bank to communicate its policies and their rationale to the public. Indeed, the Bank won support through its response, its responsiveness, and its record.

Key Lessons from the Canadian Experience

Three observations based on the Canadian experience are worth stressing. First, the Bank of Canada has been successful both in keeping inflation low and in preventing one-time shocks to the price level (including
supply shocks, indirect tax changes, and currency depreciation) from
feeding into the trend inflation rate. This success was made possible both
by the cooperation of the Bank with the Ministry of Finance and by the
great emphasis on accountability to the public. Indeed, it is likely that
the Bank's efforts to increase the transparency of its policies helped the
public to distinguish between one-time shocks to the price level and
movements in trend inflation, reducing the risk of "pass-through" of one-
time shocks.

Second, inflation targeting has worked to keep inflation low and stable
in Canada even though the inflation-targeting regime is actually quite
flexible (for example, target misses do not imply any automatic sanctions against the Bank). That flexibility has allowed the Bank of Canada
some room to deviate from the inflation targets when unforeseen shocks
to the economy occur. Again, the commitment to communication and
transparency has helped to permit this flexibility.

Finally, inflation targeting in Canada has probably dampened rather
than amplified the business cycle, because the floor of the target range
has been taken as seriously as the ceiling. Indeed, at times, the Bank of
Canada has been able to justify easing of monetary conditions in the
face of a weak economy by appealing to the inflation targets, with the
confidence that this easing would not lead to expectations of higher
inflation in the future. Because of the flexibility of the targeting framework, and the attention to the floor of the target range as well as the
ceiling, inflation targeting has not obliged the Bank to foreswear all responsibility for stabilization of the real economy.

7

United Kingdom: The Central Bank as Counterinflationary Conscience

THE United Kingdom followed Canada in adopting inflation targeting, but under quite different circumstances. Canada came to inflation targeting gradually, through a process of experimentation and discussion. In contrast, British adoption of the inflation-targeting approach was provoked by a crisis, namely the foreign-exchange crisis of September 1992, which resulted in the floating and depreciation of the pound. Inflation targeting was adopted in Britain largely as a means of restoring the credibility of monetary policy lost in the speculative crisis and to provide an alternative nominal anchor.

The institutional arrangements in the United Kingdom were also significantly different from those in Canada, which had important effects on the operation of the new policy regime. Unlike the relatively independent Bank of Canada, the Bank of England did not have unilateral authority to manipulate the instruments of monetary policy. To a significant extent, the Bank exerted its influence over policy through its analyses and its public exhortations; in doing so, it functioned as the government's "counterinflationary conscience." Our analysis of this case suggests that the system of divided responsibility, in which the Chancellor of the Exchequer controlled the instruments of policy but the Bank of England had primary responsibility for assessing the outlook for inflation, had a substantial influence on the effectiveness of monetary policy in Britain between the introduction of targets in October 1992 and the granting of independence to the Bank of England in May 1997.

Key Features of Inflation Targeting in the United Kingdom

- The United Kingdom adopted inflation targets in the aftermath of a foreign exchange rate crisis, in order to strengthen the credibility of monetary policy and restore a nominal anchor. Like the other countries examined in this study, the United Kingdom's adoption of targets also followed a period of successful disinflation, which made hitting the initial targets relatively easy.

- Monetary policy in the United Kingdom under inflation targeting remains relatively flexible, an approach more akin to that of Canada or Germany than to that of New Zealand, where the central bank has somewhat less discretion in the short run. In particular, monetary policy in the United Kingdom has responded to fluctuations in output and employment.

- The inflation target in the United Kingdom is defined in terms of the annual change in the retail price index excluding mortgage interest payments, or RPIX. Attention is also paid to the price index RPIY, which is RPIX less the first-round effects of indirect taxes. Both RPIX and RPIY include food and energy prices, so that the target index has in practice been a compromise between headline inflation and a measure of "core" or "underlying" inflation. The agency reponsible for producing these two indexes (the Office for National Statistics) differs from the agency that assesses whether the target has been met (the Bank of England).

- Initially, the United Kingdom set a target range for inflation. Since May 1997 the target has been expressed as a point, but with "thresholds" on either side. If inflation breaches a target threshold, the Bank of England is required to provide a formal explanation to the government.

- Before the Bank of England achieved independence following the May 1997 election, it had little independent control over the instruments of monetary policy; control was exercised instead by the Chancellor of the Exchequer. Under the pre-1997 targeting regime, the activities of the Bank were substantially limited to forecasting inflation and assessing past inflation performance. Rather than being a fully active policymaker, to a considerable degree the Bank functioned as the Chancellor's "counterinflationary conscience."

- In part because of its weak position before May 1997, the Bank focused its inflation-targeting efforts on communicating to the public its monetary-policy strategy and its commitment to price stability. In doing so, it relied heavily on publications such as the *Inflation Report,* an innovation that has been emulated by other inflation-targeting countries.

The Adoption of Inflation Targeting

The Chancellor of the Exchequer, Norman Lamont, announced an inflation target for the United Kingdom at a Conservative Party conference on October 8, 1992.[1] Three weeks later, at his annual Mansion House Speech to the City (Lamont, 1992), the Chancellor "invited" the Governor of the Bank of England to publish a quarterly *Inflation Report* that would detail the progress being made in achieving that target, an invitation the Governor accepted.

The adoption of a target was in reaction to the exit of sterling from the European Exchange Rate Mechanism (ERM) three weeks earlier, following a series of speculative attacks. (Black Wednesday, as the day of the exchange-rate crisis was known, had seen the pound devalued by more than 10%.) The Chancellor's purpose was to reestablish the credibility of the government's commitment to price stability, which had apparently grown stronger during the pound's two years in the ERM, as measured by interest-rate differentials with Germany and spreads in the U.K. yield curve. Unfortunately, the United Kingdom had a history of adopting and then abandoning a series of monetary regimes during the post-Bretton Woods period; hence there appeared to be considerable potential for damage to the credibility of British monetary policy.

Prior to the Chancellor's announcement, there had been no public discussion by either the Treasury or the Bank of England about setting inflation targets. So long as the pound was part of the ERM, of course, such talk would have been irrelevant, because maintenance of the parity committed the United Kingdom to matching the Bundesbank's interest rates and inflation performance. As the exchange-rate crisis approached, moreover, it would have been dangerous to reveal the existence of a fallback plan. Accordingly, the announcement of an inflation target of 1% to 4% per year in October 1992, unaccompanied by any explanation of how that target was to be monitored and achieved, had a certain amount of shock value. Perhaps plunging ahead in this abrupt fashion was seen as a means of underlining the commitment.

The Chancellor announced the new policy at a partisan, though public, forum, and he committed the nation to the target only "through the end of the present parliament," that is, May 1997. In other words, this new policy was one of the ruling Conservative majority and could not be guaranteed to survive beyond the life of that majority. It was implied, of course, that if the policy proved successful, it might win support from the public and from opposition parties and thus be continued beyond the term of the current government.

The timing of the target adoption was auspicious. The U.K. economy was just beginning to rebound after faltering through 1990, 1991, and the first half of 1992. Since the exit from the ERM had been accompanied by a 1% cut in interest rates, as well as by the currency devaluation, there was no need for any further short-term stimulus. Moreover, the drop in interest rates lowered the interest on flexible-rate mortgages, which make up almost a fifth of the headline RPI (retail price index), a lightning rod for press coverage. The direct inflationary effect of the devaluation was believed by both private and public forecasters to be 12 to 18 months down the road. Finally, unemployment was still rising at the time, putting downward pressure on wage settlements, and the Chancellor was committed to budget cuts whose major target would be public-sector pay.

In short, the United Kingdom adopted inflation targets at a time when it was most likely to meet them, at least for the first couple of years. The timing of and motivation for target adoption were in many ways analogous to that of New Zealand and Canada. As in both those cases, the primary concern was to lock in previous reductions in inflation in the face of a one-time price-level rise (here, from the devaluation). Following the dramatic crisis and the currency devaluation, of course, the United Kingdom's situation was more urgent than the situation faced by those earlier inflation targeters.

To understand the arguments underlying the United Kingdom's new monetary framework, it is useful to examine their origins in the experience of U.K. monetary policy since the Conservative Party came to power in 1979. The previous Labour government had begun publishing monetary targets in July 1976, in accordance with an IMF support arrangement. Its commitment to those targets, however, was doubtful at best, as suggested by its reliance on incomes policies (wage-price controls) to constrain inflation, and on taxes on high-interest bank deposits (the "corset") to reduce the growth of M3, its target aggregate. The incomes policies collapsed in the "winter of discontent" of 1978-79. On taking office, the Conservative government was faced with inflation that was rising rapidly from levels already above 10%. In addition, the public sector borrowing requirement (PSBR), at 5% of GDP, was high already at the onset of the 1980-81 recession.

From the beginning of the Thatcher majorities, the government was aware of the urgent need to restore credibility to economic policy. In the government's first budget, presented in March 1980, the Chancellor, Sir Geoffrey Howe, announced the Medium-Term Financial Strategy

(MTFS), a five-year plan of annual targets for M3 growth (M3 is a broad measure of the money stock) and for the public sector borrowing requirement. A gradual reduction in the borrowing requirement was seen as a prerequisite for giving credence to the deceleration in M3 growth, which, it was hoped, would lead to disinflation. The government succeeded, by means of very tight monetary policy throughout 1980 and 1981, in reducing headline inflation from 22% in early 1980 to below 4% in mid-1983. Nevertheless, the first two targets for M3 were overshot by wide margins.

The unexpectedly high rate of M3 growth resulted from a set of measures announced as part of the Medium-Term Financial Strategy, measures that abolished the corset and allowed banks to engage in mortgage lending. Those rule changes led to fierce competition between banks and building societies (analogous to savings and loans in the United States) for deposits. The government was aware that the high rates of M3 growth were giving false signals about the tightness of monetary policy, as indicated (for example) by the decline in the growth rate of the monetary base (M0) from about 12% in early 1980 to -2% in early 1982.

Faced with the dilemma of either continuing to overshoot the M3 targets, having to reset the targets, or changing the target aggregate, any of which might damage the credibility of the whole Medium-Term Financial Strategy, the government opted to reset the targets. This episode exemplifies a pattern that would recur in the United Kingdom over the next 12 years, namely the tendency for conflict to arise between adherence to the announced intermediate target of the day and the maintenance of price stability. As we shall see, the inflation-targeting regime, by offering a medium-term goal for policy rather than an intermediate target, provided a clearer framework within which a degree of flexibility in policy could be employed and explained.

The government had formally announced that targets for M3 growth would be in place until 1986. As an immediate consequence of this episode, however, the targets for M3 were gradually de-emphasized, and growth in the narrower aggregate M0 came to be considered the most important indicator of the stance of monetary policy. In the 1984, 1985, and 1986 budgets, targets for both M0 and M3 were announced; thereafter, for M0 only. More importantly, monetary policy-makers made efforts to qualify the commitment to monetary targets to avoid potential damage should the monetary aggregates again issue wrong signals. In a speech given in October 1984, the Governor of the Bank of England, Robin Leigh-Pemberton stated:

> Because of the variability in short-run monetary relationships, monetary tar-
> gets have to be operated pragmatically. The course of the monetary target
> aggregates of itself thus provides only a first approximation to the overall
> assessment of monetary conditions, and to the appropriate policy reaction
> . . . It is not in any sense to diminish the importance of such targets—they
> provide a continuing and essential constraint against purely discretionary
> policy: they give policy its backbone. The existence of targets places the
> onus on the authorities to explain why they are ignoring the signals given
> by diverging money growth, or why they are making course corrections by
> changing target indicators or target ranges. (Leigh-Pemberton, 1984, p.
> 476)

Monetary targets, it appears, served at this point primarily to enhance
the accountability of the government's commitment to price stability
by providing a means of communication. In the absence of a primary
monetary objective, however, let alone an explicit medium-term goal,
there was no baseline against which to evaluate the performance of
policy.

By then it was recognized that, if the authorities chose to miss the
targets repeatedly, while at the same time not specifying the ultimate
policy goals, the clarity and transparency of monetary policy would be
greatly diminished. One possibility was to choose a target other than
money growth. In the same speech, under the heading "Alternative Targets," Governor Leigh-Pemberton discussed nominal-GDP targeting and
exchange-rate targeting as alternative strategies. He noted that nominal-GDP targeting would not only suffer from the delay with which GDP
data become available, but would also require policy to act in a publicly
forward-looking manner (which the Governor implied was impractical).
He went on:

> Unfortunately forecasts have a somewhat dubious status; indeed cynics see
> them as potentially offering undue scope for wishful thinking. So, reliance
> on forecasts could be thought to undermine the role of the intermediate
> target as a constraint on the authorities and a protection against systemati-
> cally inflationary policies. (Leigh-Pemberton, 1984, p. 476)

The contrast with current thinking on the role of forecasts and forward-
looking monetary policy, especially in light of the Bank of England's
views, is striking. The problems associated with communicating a policy
based on the Bank's forecasts were at this stage seen as more severe than
the risk that the money-income relationship, on which the money-growth
targets were based, might become unstable. In short, there was more

fear of giving the impression of excessive political control of policy than of revealing limited ability to control economic outcomes.

Monetary targets were further de-emphasized in the spring of 1987, when Chancellor Lawson embarked on a policy of "shadowing the DM" by keeping sterling in a narrow band at around 3.00 deutschemarks per pound. At the time the United Kingdom was in the midst of a boom, with GDP growing at 5.3% and 4.8% during 1986 and 1987, respectively. Headline inflation was, however, still subdued, at 3.4% and 4.1%, respectively, in those two years. Broad money was growing rapidly: M3 at 18% and 23%, and M4 at 15% and 18% in 1986 and 1987, respectively. But the narrow aggregate M0, the preferred indicator and target variable, failed to give any early indication of the inflationary pressures that would develop during 1988 and 1989. During 1986, M0 grew at 5.2% and during 1987 at 4.3%, well inside the announced target ranges. The Bank's instrument interest rate, the bank lending rate, was cut from 9% to 7.5% between December 1987 and May 1988. Although these cuts probably would not have occurred without the exchange-rate target, it is questionable whether monetary policy would have tightened before the spring of 1988 under strict adherence to the M0 target either.

Then, with inflationary pressures becoming rapidly apparent, monetary policy tightened sharply. The base rate doubled over the 16 months from June 1988 to October 1989, from 7.5% to 15%, where it remained for the following 12 months. However, it was too late to prevent headline inflation from rising to a peak of 10.9% in September 1990. By that time the United Kingdom was in deep recession, with real GDP falling by 2% during 1990. Monetary targets, which had failed to prevent another boom-bust cycle, were abandoned in all but form when on October 8, 1990, the United Kingdom joined the European Exchange Rate Mechanism (ERM).

The ERM was supposed to deliver what monetary targets had failed to provide, namely, credibility and predictability for British monetary policy. There appears never to have been any question, however, that ERM membership would be subordinate to the achievement of domestic price stability, should the two come into conflict. In a speech delivered on the day of sterling's joining the ERM, Governor Leigh-Pemberton said, "Perhaps the key point is that, by putting an effective floor on sterling's exchange rate, we have introduced an extra discipline—a discipline for policy-makers and for both sides of industry and commerce. . . . [T]he ERM is *not* a panacea. Its benefits will have to be worked for, most of all by maintaining a *firm anti-inflation policy*." (Leigh-Pemberton 1990, p. 483, emphasis in the original)

The priority of domestic price stability as the objective of monetary policy was stated even more forcefully in the Governor's Mansion House speech on October 31, 1991:

> The commitment of the authorities to maintaining the value of the currency is an essential ingredient of a stable policy. And this makes it vital that we have a credible medium-term nominal framework. The way in which this nominal framework is expressed in terms of intermediate targets will vary with circumstances. In times of substantial innovation in financial markets monetary aggregates may not provide a clear picture; and it may then be more helpful to express our objective in terms of some other variable, such as nominal GDP or the exchange rate. But, in any event, of much greater importance is the credibility of the policy stance itself—the belief that the authorities will not take gambles with inflation. Inflationary expectations—and inflation itself—should then converge on the ultimate goal of price stability. (Leigh-Pemberton, 1991, p. 496)

In contrast to the Governor's 1984 speech, the language of this speech clearly put the focus of policy on inflation expectations, and accordingly on a wide range of information, on looking forward, and on the medium term. To some extent this change may have reflected the diffusion of developments in macroeconomics during the intervening period. For example, in the academic literature, "rational expectations" models of inflation, which emphasize forward-looking behavior, had replaced a more mechanistic monetarism.

In September 1992 the foreign-exchange crisis forced the government to choose between attempting a prolonged and expensive defense of the exchange rate and leaving the ERM; the government opted for the latter despite the potential damage to credibility. The unwillingness of the U.K. monetary policy-makers to raise interest rates to defend the currency beyond Black Wednesday suggests that their commitment to the ERM was not very strong.

Thus, the United Kingdom's adoption of an inflation target in 1992 incorporated two elements of continuity and one of change with respect to the period of ERM membership. First, achieving price stability remained a key objective of monetary policy. However, the explicitness with which that goal was stated, and its primacy among policy goals, had increased during the 1990s. By the time the pound exited the ERM, the government had made clear that it wished to be released not from policy discipline, but from the problems arising from asynchronous German and British business cycles. Second, to achieve that objective, credibility with the public had to be fostered through improved means of communicating the intentions and performance of monetary policy.

The main element of change for the United Kingdom, having abandoned both monetary and exchange-rate targets, was the strategic decision not to employ any intermediate target variable in the setting of policy. In fact, Chancellor Lamont, in his speech announcing the inflation-targeting policy, made clear that money-growth and exchange-rate measures would be monitored but would not determine policy.[2] A speech delivered by Governor Leigh-Pemberton, on November 11, 1992, made the point again:

> Experience leads us to believe that monetary policy cannot be conducted with reference to a single target variable. The overriding objective of monetary policy is price stability. Therefore policy must be conducted with reference to our expectations of future inflation . . . Consequently, policymakers should make use of every possible variable, with the importance attached to any given variable at any point in time dependent on its value as a guide to prospective inflation. (Leigh-Pemberton, 1992, p. 447)

Thus, targeting inflation directly was seen as the only practical way to achieve the goal. This conclusion, however, left open the question of how to make the new policy credible, especially after the exit from the restraint of the ERM. The Governor continued: "But in such an eclectic framework it is possible for the underlying rationale of policy to be lost in a welter of statistical confusion. That is why we have opted for a policy of openness" (*Ibid.*).

The belief that sustained efforts to communicate with the public—and not just the announcement of a goal—are required for policy credibility, is at the core of the United Kingdom's inflation-targeting framework. Nevertheless, while the framework emphasized accountability, it did not forfeit flexibility, even in principle. The idea that monetary policy must retain some flexibility to deal with macroeconomic events as they occur probably reflected less a deep-seated conviction than the reality that, ultimately, the responsibility for monetary policy-making rests with the elected government. As we noted in our discussion of New Zealand, the extent to which inflation targeting is treated as a rule is best seen as a design choice.[3]

The Operational Framework

The target variable in the United Kingdom is the annual change in the retail price index excluding mortgage interest payments (RPIX). RPIX inflation was to remain in a range of 1% to 4% at least until the next election, with the expectation that it would have settled in the lower half of that range by that time (that is, it would be 2.5% or less).[4] The long-term intended average for RPIX inflation is 2.5% or less. RPIX is meant to capture underlying inflation and is usually reported along with RPIY, which is RPIX altered to exclude the first-round effect of indirect taxes. The effects of commodity price shocks, including oil shocks, are included in the target; thus, the targeted inflation measure is closer to headline inflation than in the New Zealand and Canadian cases. As we have seen, in all inflation targets other than headline inflation, there is some trade-off between transparency (because headline CPI is what people are accustomed to) and flexibility (because various types of price changes are excluded from the definition of the target, permitting some discretion regarding to which types of shocks the central bank must respond).

RPIX has proved to be an effective measure, with the financial press and the public adapting to it over time. There was some consideration of a switch to RPIY in 1995, but that tactic was decided to be too risky, as the public might feel that targets (and the shocks that monetary policy was committed to offset) were being changed too often. Indeed, to discourage the perception of excessive manipulation, the Office for National Statistics, an agency separate from the Bank, was made responsible for calculating the various inflation series.

The use of a target range, set by the Chancellor, was interpreted by many as a way of setting a clear limit on the amount of discretionary policy that would be permitted. Later interpretations by the Bank and the U.K. Treasury, however, indicated that the band was never intended as a target range strictly speaking, but was rather an admission of imperfect control of inflation.[5] However, as of this writing, the official position of the Treasury and the Bank is that there is no longer a target range, but a point target of 2.5% to be met into the indefinite future. This change was first made explicit in Chancellor Kenneth Clarke's Mansion House Speech to the City on June 14, 1995.[6] In reality, the endpoint of such a time horizon is likely to correspond to the lifetime of any parliamentary majority, as it did in New Zealand when that country changed its target range after the October 1996 election. Unlike New Zealand, however, the United Kingdom now makes no explicit commitment to remain within a range. Arguably the United Kingdom's point target allows some flexibility to policy by permitting some short-run deviations from target without causing the public to focus unduly on whether the official target range has been breached.

Another issue inherent in the United Kingdom's targeting framework was whether the endpoint of the target period should be tied to a specific event: in this case, the end of the Parliament then sitting. Unless the commitment to inflation targeting is open-ended, there is uncertainty about whether the targeting regime will continue to exist beyond the longest target horizon. As a result, doubts may arise about the country's will to meet the targets as the end of the period approaches and as pressures increase to let bygones be bygones. As we noted in our discussion of German monetary targets in the run-up to European Monetary Union (EMU), such doubts are likely to arise for any targeting framework that is not renewed far ahead of its announced (or politically determined) endpoint. However, just as the Liberal majority in Canada extended the 1995 targets to 1998 shortly after taking office in 1993, the British Labour Party made clear that it would extend the inflation target of 2.5% or less for the duration of its tenure in office, should it win the election in May 1997. This early commitment helped to remove a potential source of uncertainty and strengthened the credibility of policy.[7] In contrast, in the New Zealand elections of October 1996, there was no way to separate the time horizon of the targets from the political process.

Actually, the real target of the Bank of England's policy is not current RPIX inflation but the *expectation* of RPIX inflation. Success in meeting the target is judged by whether the Bank's own inflation forecast over the succeeding two years falls within the intended range. This way of assessing success is consistent with the forward-looking perspective inherent in inflation targeting, and with the belief that it takes about two years for monetary policy to influence inflation. Indeed, at the time of the Chancellor's initial announcement of the adoption of targets, he was criticized by market observers for focusing on RPIX inflation *per se,* rather than its expectation.

From the first *Inflation Report* onward, the Bank has reported private-sector inflation forecasts, in addition to its own inflation forecasts. In recent issues of the *Inflation Report,* the Bank has also paid close attention to the variance among forecasts, a measure of inflation uncertainty.[8] In its emphasis on variability and uncertainty, the Bank has communicated to the press and the public that a forward-looking monetary policy must balance risks rather than pretend to exercise tight control.

The Bank of England appears to be working from a standard policy feedback framework in line with the Chancellor's and the Governor's initial speeches—that is, one in which many pieces of information are gathered and weighed. M0 and M4 (narrow and broad money) figures must be reported, with "monitoring ranges" announced for them. However, there is an explicit understanding that when information obtained from monetary aggregates is in conflict with RPIX forecasts, the RPIX forecasts will be accepted. Exchange rates and housing prices have often been cited as indicators to be used in policy decisions, but there has been no explicit ranking of the usefulness of such alternative indicators. The Bank acknowledges that its lack of success with money and exchange rate-targeting has made it hesitant to rely on any one indicator or relationship.

The stated goal of the United Kingdom's inflation targets is price stability, "namely that the rate of inflation anticipated by economic agents is unimportant to savings, investment, and other economic decisions" (Leigh-Pemberton, 1992, p. 446). As in many other countries, a target of zero inflation was dismissed as unduly restrictive given the failure of standard price indexes to capture fully the extent of quality change (although the Bank of England points out that RPIX is rebased far more frequently than in many other countries, so there would be less substitution bias for the United Kingdom's price index). Consequently, as we have noted, price stability is operationally defined as growth in RPIX of 2.5% per year or less. The choice of this figure was primarily a pragmatic decision, with the likelihood that if the 2.5% goal was achieved and maintained, a lower goal, say of 2%, would then be set. No consideration of other goals, such as exchange-rate stability or smoothing of the business cycle, is explicitly acknowledged within the targeting framework.

Like every other central bank, however, the Bank of England remains committed in fact to trading off disinflation when necessary against its real-side costs and its effects on the financial system. This reality is best illustrated by excerpts from Governor Leigh-Pemberton's November 1992 speech, "The Case for Price Stability," reprinted in the Bank of England's *Quarterly Bulletin*. In that speech the Governor states, "The overriding objective of monetary policy is price stability" (p. 447). In the preceding paragraph, however, the Governor explains why other factors had been permitted to override that objective and prompted the pound's exit from the ERM:

> It [the ERM] certainly offered a very visible sign of our commitment to price stability . . . [but] there was a real risk of these disinflationary forces doing quite unnecessary damage to the real economy. Although we would have achieved price stability very quickly—indeed there is reason to believe we might have reached that position during 1993—there was a real danger that the deflation which was already apparent in certain sectors of the economy (notably asset markets) would have become much more widespread. It was

not necessary to compress the transition phase to price stability into such a short time span and could well have been counterproductive in the longer term.[9] (*Ibid.*)

The tradeoff between price stability and other objectives is apparent even when the choices are less stark than in the period prior to the 1992 crisis. Why else would the achievement of price stability be pursued gradually, as outlined by the Bank and the Chancellor for the path from the September 1992 RPIX rate of 3.6%? Clearly, a gap exists between the claims and reality of inflation as a sole goal even under inflation targeting.[10] In various speeches in recent years, Governor Eddie George has stressed that the Bank aims to stabilize the business cycle (and thereby at least partially to induce exchange rate stability) within the target constraint.

Only three weeks after the decision to adopt inflation targeting, Chancellor Lamont and the Bank of England worked out their joint implementation of the policy. The Bank would produce its own inflation forecast each quarter, beginning with February 1993, and that forecast would be the main yardstick used to measure success or failure. As mentioned above, the role of this forecast in accountability for policy becomes quite complicated. One complication arises when the government's interest-rate decisions are inconsistent with the implications of the Bank's forecasts. Nevertheless, the speed with which the commitment to publish inflation forecasts was undertaken underlines just how central communication efforts are to the operation of the United Kingdom's inflation targets—and how the announcement of the targets themselves was never thought to be enough on its own.

In tracking progress toward the inflation target, the Bank of England, in its *Inflation Report*, details past performance of the U.K. economy, compares actual inflation outcomes (both RPIX and its components) with prior forecasts by the Bank, identifies the factors that are presenting the greatest danger to price stability, and forecasts the likelihood that inflation will in two years' time be within the target range. In the words of Governor Leigh-Pemberton (1992, p. 447), "Our aim will be to produce a wholly objective and comprehensive analysis of inflationary trends and pressures, which will put the Bank's professional competence on the line." From the third issue (August 1993) onward, the *Inflation Report* has followed a six-part format covering inflation, money and interest rates, demand and supply, the labor market, pricing behavior, and prospects for inflation. In addition, the *Quarterly Bulletin* publishes policy speeches and relevant research, with the authors of the research articles regularly identified.

The clarity with which the Bank presented its views, and the need for the Chancellor to react explicitly to those views, were meant to serve as a check on the government's monetary policy stance between elections. Following the issuance of the third *Inflation Report* in August 1993, it was decided that the Bank would send the *Report* to the Treasury only after its contents had been finalized and printed. Thus, the Treasury would have no chance to edit or even suggest changes. This arrangement indicated the government's acceptance of the Bank's distinct voice.

The *Inflation Report* is best seen in the context of the Bank's traditional role as adviser to the Chancellor on monetary policy. Even after the adoption of inflation targeting, the Bank continued to provide advice and information, just as it did at the time of Chancellor Lamont's decision to implement inflation targeting. What was innovative was that the Bank began to report to the public independently of its regular meetings with the Treasury staff and with the Chancellor. At the same time, the Treasury, which reports directly to the Chancellor, has been publishing its own monthly monetary report since December 1992. This publication, which antedated the *Inflation Report* and was issued more frequently, tracked the growth of broad (M4) and narrow (M0) money in the monitoring ranges set by the Chancellor and kept readers apprised of movements in the foreign-exchange and asset markets, particularly U.K. housing. In granting this mandate to the Treasury, the Chancellor committed U.K. monetary policy to the monitoring of a set of indicators compiled by his own staff, even if the Bank of England was emphasizing other variables and computing other numbers. Thus the Bank, despite the prominence of its *Inflation Report,* did not enjoy a monopoly on providing monetary-policy advice.

The emphasis on explaining policy to the public, especially when differences arise between the Chancellor's and the Bank's points of view, was buttressed by three additional institutional changes. First, in February 1993, the monthly meeting between the Chancellor and the Governor to set monetary policy was formalized. Second, starting in November 1993, the decision on when to put into effect any interest-rate changes decided on by the Chancellor at the monthly meeting was to be left to the Bank's discretion, so long as they were made effective before the next meeting. Combined with the Bank's commitment to issue a press release explaining the reason for any interest-rate change once it had been made, this discretion gave the markets a great deal of information about the Bank's view of the Chancellor's decision. Third, and most significant, beginning in April 1994, the minutes of the monthly meetings between Chancellor and Governor were released two weeks after the next meeting (replacing a thirty-year lag with a six-week lag).

In a very real sense, throughout this entire period the Bank had operated as the government's institutional "counterinflationary conscience." There was an underlying tension in this role because the Bank remained under the control of the Chancellor, who also controlled the instruments of monetary policy. The Bank's use of public forums and other venues to communicate its forecasts, its analyses, and even its explicit monetary-policy recommendations had the effect of increasing the cost for the government of going against the Bank's assessment, presumably serving the cause of price stability. Unfortunately, since the Chancellor did not have a symmetric requirement to report the reasoning behind his policy decisions, beyond what he chose to reveal at the monthly meetings, disputes whose origins may have lain in policy preferences or in differences in competence could degenerate into competitions over forecast accuracy, as we will see in the next section.

The standing given the Bank by the monthly minutes did not, however, provide monetary policy with accountability beyond that bestowed by elections. It was the Bank, not the financial markets or the general public, that was passing judgment in the *Inflation Report*; but any punishment or reward for that judgment (beyond market reactions) had to wait until the next election. Even under the new Monetary Policy Committee of the Bank, which has set U.K. monetary policy since May 1997, ultimate responsibility for the goals of policy rests with the parliamentary majority at the next elections.[11] Nor did these forums for the Bank provide real clarity about policy intentions and goals, since the Chancellor could override the Bank's recommendations with only limited public explanation.

British Monetary Policy under Inflation Targeting

In this section we summarize both the macroeconomic outcomes and the interactions between the Treasury and the Bank at critical junctures since the adoption of inflation targets. We draw on various issues of the Bank's quarterly *Inflation Report* and on the Minutes of the Monthly Monetary Meetings between the Chancellor and the Governor. Figure 7.1 tracks the path of inflation, interest rates, the nominal effective exchange rate (henceforth the "exchange rate"), GDP growth, and unemployment in the United Kingdom both before and after inflation targeting was introduced.

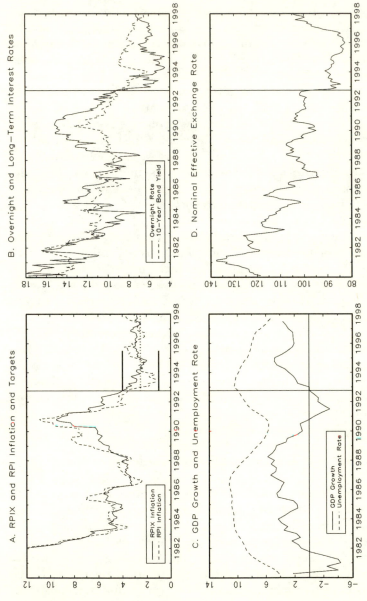

Figure 7.1. United Kingdom economic indicators. Sources: A) Bank for International Settlements database; B) Bank of England; C) Main Economic Indicators of the Organisation for Economic Cooperation and Development; D) Bank for International Settlements database.

The period from October 1992 (when sterling left the ERM) to the end of 1993 marked the end of recession and the beginning of recovery in the British economy. GDP growth turned positive in the first quarter of 1993, and the unemployment rate peaked at 10.6% in December 1992 (Figure 7.1, Panel C). Throughout 1993, output growth accelerated and the unemployment rate declined. With some brief interruptions, RPIX inflation continued its downward trend and reached the midpoint of the designated target range of 2.5% for the first time in November 1993 (Panel A). The exchange rate bottomed out in February 1993 and then rose through the rest of the year (Panel D).

Two major themes in the discussion of medium-term inflation forecasts in the first two issues of the *Inflation Report* (February and May 1993) were the depreciation of sterling and the government's growing budget deficit, each of which had the potential to raise inflation. The official interest rate (the base rate) had been reduced from 10% in August 1992 to 6% in January 1993 (Panel B), reflecting the government's desire to escape from German monetary tightness. Not surprisingly, in the five months following the United Kingdom's exit from the ERM, sterling had depreciated by 14.5%, as measured by the Bank of England's exchange-rate index. On the fiscal side, the Bank mentioned fears of possible future monetization of government debt as a source of increased inflation expectations. The Bank did not, however, call for immediate fiscal action or directly criticize the government's fiscal policy. Despite these concerns and the recovering economy, the Bank's inflation projections in these first two issues continued to fall at all the horizons discussed.

In the May 1993 *Inflation Report,* the Bank stated its belief that the government would hold inflation below 4% over the following eighteen months. This was not an endorsement of the government's monetary policy, for not only had the Chancellor committed to being within the inflation range (that is, below 4%) in two years, but he had also stated that he would have inflation in the lower half of that range (below 2.5%) by 1997. The Bank linked the possibility of inflation above target to the government's policy decisions, rather than to economic conditions outside of the government's control. The Bank also expressed concern about the effects of the exchange rate on prices, noting that the 5% appreciation of sterling (trade-weighted) since February permitted some optimism but not much, as surveys and financial market interest rates continued to indicate a lack of medium-to-long-run credibility for the inflation targets. The Bank also emphasized that the main uncertainty about the inflation forecast, most of it on the upside, stemmed from uncertainty about the likely course of domestic wages and profits. Following these concerns about inflation to their logical conclusion, three weeks later Governor George of the Bank gave a speech explicitly warning against a rate cut. The Bank apparently feared that with the imminent change in chancellors (from Norman Lamont to Kenneth Clarke) and submission of the budget, a decision to ease would be made in compensation for various fiscal measures. At the time, however, rates were not cut.

Six months later, in the November *Inflation Report,* the Bank touched on the same themes even more sharply. There was a slight probability, according to the Bank, that inflation would exceed the target in the near term. Moreover, the Bank said it foresaw the potential for a nominal wage push if headline inflation rose to the upper limit of the 4% target range. Again, the Bank was responding to a political situation in which many Conservative Party backbenchers and commentators were expecting a cut in interest rates. The government had agreed to certain spending cuts and an extension of the value-added tax (VAT) to domestic fuel and power starting in April 1994, while news about real economic developments was generally not good. This time Chancellor Clarke did lower rates by 0.5%, without further fiscal tightening to compensate for the reduction.

What made this conflict between the Bank and Chancellor particularly interesting was that the Bank had already offered an out for the Chancellor in the May and November issues of the *Inflation Report.* The Bank attributed 0.4% of the projected rise in inflation during 1994 to the change in the VAT, which it accepted as a deficit reduction; further, the Bank reminded readers that if RPIY (which excludes the first-round effect of taxes) rather than RPIX were considered, inflation would be on target, albeit near the top of the range and with upside risks. For some reason, the Chancellor chose not to take advantage of the proffered defense.

Though unexercised in this episode, this sort of definitional tactic raises a real dilemma for the maintenance of policy accountability. If indirect taxes are to be excluded from consideration, why did the Chancellor and the Bank choose to target RPIX rather than RPIY in the first place? If the government had in fact switched to RPIY after the Bank had "allowed" (that is, refrained from criticizing) the move, how could the financial markets and the electorate have been sure that this was just a one-time event? And if the wage spiral the Bank worried about had materialized, would this switch have been beside the point, or would it have allowed a shift of blame to the unions' lack of sophistication? On the basis of this case, it would appear that the people who define and measure the target inflation series should be kept separate from the people who assess success in achieving the targets. The United Kingdom's framework might be compared with New Zealand's on this score: New Zealand's central bank—partly because of the country's small size—retains some amount of discretion over the short-run definition of the target inflation series and, on a few occasions, has exercised it.

Around the beginning of 1994, with the performance of inflation better than expected, the Chancellor eased monetary policy further. Inflationary pressures remained subdued, as the lagged effect on prices of the earlier depreciation was offset by a reduction in unit labor costs related to continued weak employment. It was apparent at the time that pass-through of the one-time drop in the exchange rate upon the exit from the ERM had been averted—a major success for the new monetary regime.[12] This achievement was even more impressive than the Bank of Canada's success at preventing pass-through from the 1991 tax increase, given that it followed a presumptive blow to Britain's credibility upon the country's exit from the ERM. The base rate, which had been reduced from 6% to 5.5% in November 1993, was cut another 25 basis points to 5.25% in February 1994. These reductions occurred despite projections in every *Inflation Report* from August 1993 on that inflation was likely to rise. Indeed, inflation did not start to rise until the end of 1994.

When assessing the quality of its past forecasts, the Bank pointed to specific sources of error, such as unexpectedly slow earnings growth and a squeeze in retail margins. The Chancellor, having given no explicit forecast, did not have to rationalize his interpretation of the data. Herein lay a basic ambiguity of the British arrangement: There was no way to know for sure whether the divergence between the Bank's opinion and the Chancellor's policies was the result of different assessments of the economic situation or differing assessments of the importance of achieving the inflation target in the short run. Indeed, in general, so long as elected officials are not required to give their own forecasts to be compared with those of the central bank, they have the option of concealing what may be a weaker commitment to the inflation goal.

Throughout 1994, GDP grew vigorously, with fourth-quarter real GDP exceeding the previous year's value by 4%. For the first ten months of the year RPIX inflation was trending downward, reaching a 27-year low of 2% in September and October, before rising to 2.5% in December. The unemployment rate continued to fall during the year, to around 9%. Sterling (according to the Bank's index) had peaked at the end of 1993 and trended slightly downward during 1994.

During the summer of 1994, it became clear to the Bank that the economy was rebounding more strongly than expected, and the *Inflation Report* began to cite evidence of inflationary pressures, such as rising wholesale prices. Despite good inflation numbers (both RPIY and RPIX inflation at the time were below 2.5% and falling), the Chancellor, on the advice of the Governor, raised the base rate on September 12, and again on December 7, by 0.5% each time. Unlike the tightening in 1988, these increases were preemptive—a fact that was widely noted in the press.[13] The ability to tie current policies to expected future conditions, thereby taking into account the lags with which policy affects the economy, is a clear advantage of having an explicit medium-term objective for policy.

The discussions between Chancellor Clarke and Governor George during the months leading up to the September 1994 tightening of policy provide some insight into the role played by the Bank's medium-term inflation forecasts in the policy process. During their meeting on July 28, the Governor pointed out that, on the basis of the Bank's latest forecast,

> he did see a risk to the inflation objective in 1996, implying a need to tighten policy in some degree before very long. . . . He was not, on the current best guess, forecasting a strong upturn in inflation, and there was, as always, a significant margin of error around that best guess. But the best guess for mid-1996 was already slightly above the mid-point of the target range, and there was an uncomfortable sense that the upside risks to the medium-term forecast might, this time, be somewhat greater than the downside risks. (Bank of England, 1994a, July 28, p. 5)

The Chancellor, however, remarked that "there was a danger of trying to set a game plan too far in advance and not looking at the actual evidence as it unfolded. . . . The forecasts suggested inflation might be even lower in the next few months" (*Ibid.*, p. 6). Although they agreed not to raise interest rates at the time, that decision cast doubt on the extent to which monetary policy decisions were indeed based on the Bank's medium-term forecast. While the existence of target commitments and the Bank's open statements of opinion moved the U.K. government toward a more forward-looking monetary policy, the government could not be forced to adopt the policy that the Bank considered optimal. Again, the government's private forecast—even if driven as a politically motivated markdown from the Bank's formal analysis—became the actual target. Moreover, because neither the estimate itself nor the reasoning behind it was shared with the public, the government forecast could not serve the function of a publicly announced target, nor could policy be fully transparent.[14]

During 1995, GDP growth decelerated, from 4% between the fourth quarter of 1993 and the fourth quarter of 1994, to 2% by the last quarter of 1995. The unemployment rate continued its gradual decline, however, reaching 8% at year's end. RPIX inflation rose to 2.8% in January, and for the rest of the year fluctuated between 2.6% and 3.1% without exhibiting a clear trend. Early in 1995, it became apparent that output growth, though below the pace of 1994, might still be high relative to the growth in the economy's productive potential; this observation contributed to the Bank and the Chancellor's belief that the inflation outlook was in danger of worsening. Consequently, on February 2, the base rate was raised 0.5%, to 6.75%. Despite this preemptive tightening of policy, the exchange rate fell over the next three months; by May 4, the Bank of England's sterling index was down 4.7% from February 2. The depreciation aggravated the worrisome discrepancy between the rates of recovery in the tradables and nontradables sectors. The "dual economy" of this period could be seen in the contrast between 10% growth in exports during 1994, and flat retail sales and falling earnings growth in the service industries during early 1995.

As a consequence of the depreciation and the resulting increase in import prices, the Bank's RPIX inflation projection in May 1995 was revised upward by nearly 1% throughout 1996 from the February forecast. RPIX inflation reached almost 4% in the first half of 1996 before falling to around 2.5% in early 1997.[15] The possible consequences of the currency depreciation for the inflation outlook dominated the monthly meetings on April 5 and May 5.

It was against the background of this upward revision of the Bank's inflation forecast and the "dual economy" problem that in their meeting on May 5, 1995, the Chancellor overruled the Governor's advice to raise interest rates. That refusal provides a stark example of the conflict that arose from the Bank of England's subordinate status. Indeed, at the end of that day's monthly meeting with Governor George, Chancellor Clarke immediately summoned the press and announced that he was leaving interest rates unchanged. Since, contrary to custom, the Governor was not present to echo the Chancellor's post-meeting statement, and Clarke mentioned details of the discussion (including some of George's reasons for concluding that inflation was a real threat) rather than waiting for release of the minutes six weeks later, it was clear that Clarke was overruling the Bank.[16] Clarke cited his skepticism about the growth forecasts but seemed to be as intent on revealing the conflict as on explaining it (Chote, Coggan, and Peston, 1995).

Perhaps the Chancellor's candor was in response to the new influence achieved by the Bank through the inflation-targeting framework: He may have felt that the best defense was a bold offense. In any event, the conflict would have become evident with the release of the Bank's May *Inflation Report* a week later. The Bank's central estimate was for 3% inflation in two years' time, indicating that, contrary to the government's pledge, inflation would be in the upper half of the target range at the end of the current Parliament. Furthermore, the Bank added that the risks to its forecast were almost uniformly on the upside and were "large." The Bank noted that sterling was currently depreciating as it had in the fall of 1992, but that, unlike the situation then, wage demands and pressure on productive capacity were also high.

Upon taking office, Chancellor Clarke had made a commitment to Governor George that he would not censor the *Inflation Report* at any time, but he reserved the right to disagree with the Bank's views. What seems to have emerged was a system in which the Chancellor had to make explicit his independence from the Bank's position when a disagreement arose, and to make at least some modest effort to justify rejecting the Bank's inflation forecast. That system may have had a salutary effect on the overall tendency of policy to resist inflation; however, because of the "game" it set up between the Chancellor and the Bank, it may also have undermined public trust in the competence and objectivity of forecasting and policy-making.

Over the following months, it became apparent that, in this instance, the Chancellor had guessed right. First-quarter GDP growth was revised downward, new numbers on housing and manufacturing came in below expectations, and a rally in the global bond market (in anticipation of an expected drop in U.S. interest rates) supported the pound. In a September 1995 account of the discussions between the Chancellor and the Governor that had taken place since May, Governor George declared that "we still think that the chances are against achieving the inflation target over the next 18 months or so without some further [base rate] rise," but he conceded that "we are not in fact pressing for one—and have not been doing so since before the summer break" (George, 1995a).

So should the Bank be taken to task for being less accurate in forecasting than the Chancellor in this one instance? Since Chancellor Clarke's forecast of May 1995 remained private, it again proved impossible to determine whether he disagreed with the Bank because he was skeptical of its forecasts, or simply because he was willing to risk greater inflation to achieve higher growth. Would a point-by-point rebuttal of the *Inflation Report* have been worth the damage it might have done to public perceptions of the Bank's forecasting role? A record of forecast performance clearly affects accountability; equally clearly, however, reducing the monetary policy debate to a forecasting competition is undesirable. Tension appears to be inevitable as long as the forecasts and the policy decisions come from different sources.

The minutes of the meetings provide no clear answers to these questions, but they do sharpen the issues. The minutes give the impression that the Governor and the Chancellor never discussed the reasoning behind the Bank's medium-term forecast itself; instead, the discussion centered on whether the data feeding into that forecast reflected an underlying trend or were influenced by transitory developments. The minutes of the discussion during the June 7, 1995, meeting state that "while one strength of the policy process was that all the new evidence was examined each month for its implications for inflation, it was important not to read too much into one month's data which could prove to be erratic" (Bank of England, 1995a, June 7, p. 8). Such considerations might justify less attention to the Bank's medium-term forecast.

On June 14, 1995, in his Mansion House Speech to the City,[17] Chancellor Clarke extended the inflation target beyond the latest possible date for the next general election. He did admit, however, that inflation might rise temporarily above 4%, the ceiling of the target range, in the following two years; he also created some confusion about whether "meeting the target" meant being below the 4% ceiling or below the 2.5% target set by him and his predecessor for the end of the current Parliament. Governor George (1995b), in his speech to the same audience, referred only to the 2.5% target and called it achievable. Inflation expectations at a ten-year horizon, as derived from government-bond yields, rose in response to these remarks, from 4.36% in early May to 4.94% in late July, a movement that began to be reversed only in late 1996.

To develop its inflation outlook for the second half of 1995, the Bank weighted the upside risks resulting from the delayed effects of the sterling depreciation against the downside risks resulting from signs of a slowdown in output growth and a buildup in inventories. Domestic inflation pressures remained weak, with inflation in tradables continuing to outpace inflation in nontradables. Moreover, in its November *Inflation Report* the Bank noted that during the current cycle real wage growth had been much more subdued than expected. Still, RPIX inflation, at 3.1% for the year to September, was forecast to peak at about 3.5% during the first half of 1996. Substantial downward revisions of GDP figures for the first three quarters of 1995 followed, however, as well as an unexpectedly low RPIX inflation rate of 2.9% in the year to November. These signs of economic slackening set the stage on December 13 for the first of four successive quarter-point cuts in the base rate.

The hoped-for "soft landing" of the U.K. economy materialized in 1996. GDP growth picked up toward the end of the year; in the third quarter, GDP was up 2.4% over its level for the third quarter of 1995. The unemployment rate continued its gradual decline, dropping to 6.7% by December 1996. From October 1995 to September 1996, RPIX inflation fluctuated between 2.8% and 3% and then rose to 3.3% in October and November. From January to the end of September, sterling strengthened gradually, then rose briskly during the last three months of the year, appreciating by 11.6% in that period.

Receding cost pressures and weak manufacturing output data, as well as GDP growth of 0.5% for the last quarter of 1995, prompted the next two quarter-point base-rate cuts, which occurred on January 18 and March 8, 1996. At their March 8 meeting, the Chancellor and the Governor agreed that demand and output were likely to pick up later in the year and through 1997, and that there was a possibility that the latest rate cut would have to be reversed at some point. Again, the Bank granted the Chancellor what amounted to an escape clause—or at least a justification of future policy reversals as deemed necessary—by supporting the Chancellor's interpretation of the economy. In May 1995, a similar defense had been offered but not used; this time the option was exercised.

The Bank's assessment did not change during the spring of 1996, and its medium-term inflation projection published in the May *Inflation Report* was essentially unchanged from the previous one. The projection of RPIX inflation in two years remained at 2.5%, with the risks biased downward over the short term but upward over the medium term because of uncertainties concerning the strength of the expected pickup in activity. Following the June 5 meeting, despite the Governor's opposition, the Chancellor announced another quarter-point cut in the base rate, arguing that the cut "was sufficiently small not to cause any significant inflationary risk, while reducing the downside risks to the recovery. If consumer demand started growing too strongly, and put the inflation target at risk, the rates could be raised when this became evident" (Bank of England, 1996a, June 5, p. 9). Again, there appears to have been some tension between the Bank's forward-looking approach based on its projections and the Chancellor's tendency to emphasize the current economic situation and the latest data. With the election approaching, the Chancellor (an elected official) may have been willing to take greater inflation risks than before on behalf of stimulating economic growth in the short run.

The Bank, in the August *Inflation Report,* was unusually frank about the consequences of the June base-rate cut it had opposed. Citing as evidence "lower interest rates since May, the new Treasury forecasts for taxes and public spending, and the slightly better-than-expected gross export performance in the first half of the year" (Bank of England, 1996b, August, p. 45), the Bank predicted that inflation would rise above 2.5%. Consistent with that prediction, from the August meeting on, the Governor pressed for a rate increase; but it was only on October 30, 1996, that the Chancellor agreed to raise the base rate by a quarter point, to 6%. Some members of the financial press speculated that the decision to increase the base rate at that time might have been intended to avert the need for further rate increases as the general elections (which had to be held by May 1997 at the latest) approached.[18]

This continuing split between the agency that made the inflation forecasts and the agency that made the policy decisions, and the bias it imparted to inflation expectations, might be regarded as the basic limitation of the otherwise largely successful inflation-targeting regime in the United Kingdom. The problems arising from the division of responsibility probably contributed to the decision on May 6, 1997, by the new Labour Government, to grant operational independence to the Bank of England. On that day, the new Chancellor of the Exchequer, Gordon Brown, called a news conference and announced that he has moving up his scheduled monthly meeting with the Governor of the Bank of England; it was expected that he would also announce an interest-rate hike, long sought by the Bank, to deal with mounting inflation. (RPIX inflation was forecast to be 2.9% by the end of 1997.) He did announce a quarter-point hike in the base rate, the main monetary-policy instrument. But then he made the surprise announcement that the Bank of England would henceforth have control of the base rate and of short-term exchange-rate intervention.

One important factor in the decision to grant the Bank of England operational independence was the Bank's generally successful performance in providing forecasts and policy advice, as measured against a clear and public baseline. Another factor cited by Chancellor Brown was the increased accountability that an independent bank would bring to the inflation-targeting framework—a change that would make monetary policy more responsive to political oversight. When monetary-policy goals are publicly stated, as they are in the United Kingdom's inflation-targeting regime, they cannot diverge from the interests of society for extended periods of time, although they can be insulated from short-run political considerations.

In the new regime, decision-making power is vested in a newly created Monetary Policy Committee. Beginning in June 1997, meetings of that Committee replaced the Chancellor-Governor meetings. The Committee consists of nine members: the Governor and two Deputy Governors (one for monetary policy, one for financial matters), two other Bank Executive Directors, and four members appointed by the government (all well-known academic or financial economists). Members serve three-year renewable terms, which are eventually to be staggered.

The elected government retains a "national interest" control over monetary policy that allows it to overrule the Bank's interest rate decisions or pursuit of the inflation target when it deems such action necessary. The government did not specify ahead of time any formal process for implementing the escape clause or the conditions under which the clause would be invoked.

On June 12, just prior to the first meeting of the Monetary Policy Committee, Chancellor Brown told the Committee to pursue a target of 2.5% for underlying inflation. The target range was replaced by a 1% "threshold" on either side of the target. "The thresholds' function is to define the points at which I shall expect an explanatory letter from you [the Committee]," the Chancellor stated. In the letter, the Bank is required to explain why inflation has moved so far from the target, what policy actions it will take to deal with it, when inflation is expected to be back on target, and how this meets its monetary-policy objectives. The Chancellor retains the ability to tell the Bank how quickly the miss is to be rectified (see Chote [1997]).

This mandated response to a target miss is intended to provide the public with the relevant information. The government is not committed to "punish" the Bank for misses by dismissing the Governor, nor indeed to any pre-specified course of action. Thus the government's control over the Bank of England is more like the control exerted by the Canadian Parliament over the Bank of Canada than the control exerted by the New Zealand government on its central bank. As in all the cases we consider (except those of the Bundesbank and the Swiss National Bank), however, the numerical value of the inflation target and the targeting horizon remain under the Cabinet's control. That is, the Bank was not granted goal independence.

Again, this change in framework is likely to increase the transparency and accountability of monetary policy and decrease public uncertainty by tying policy decisions to the forecasts and explanations published in the *Inflation Report*. It may also strengthen the credibility of the United Kingdom's commitment to its inflation targets, because deviations from target now require the government to overrule the Bank publicly or to reset the target, whereas under the old regime the government could attribute deviations from the target to disagreements over short-run forecasts.

Key Lessons from the United Kingdom's Experience

The United Kingdom's experience provides some particularly interesting lessons for inflation targeting. Until May 1997, inflation targeting in Britain was conducted under a system in which the government, not the central bank, controlled the monetary-policy instruments. As a result, it was not at all clear what motivated a decision to move or not to move interest rates: Was it differences in forecasts between the Chancellor and the Governor, or differences in commitment to the announced inflation goals? Also unclear was which agency was accountable for whether inflation met its target: Was it the agency that made public forecasts (the Bank of England) or the agency that set the monetary-policy instruments (the Chancellor of the Exchequer)? This lack of clarity created much confusion about the degree of commitment to inflation targets and strongly suggested that short-run political considerations were influencing monetary policy.

Even so, British inflation targeting before May 1997 produced lower and more stable rates of inflation than the United Kingdom had enjoyed in years. The success of inflation targeting in the United Kingdom can be attributed to the Bank of England's focus on transparency and its reliable explanations of monetary-policy strategy. Perhaps because for many years its position was weaker than that of other central banks, the Bank devised innovative ways of communicating with the public, especially through its *Inflation Report*. Indeed, its achievements in that direction have been emulated by many other central banks committed to inflation targeting.

8

Sweden: Searching for a Nominal Anchor

LIKE the United Kingdom, Sweden adopted inflation targeting after being forced to abandon its exchange-rate peg. Sweden's defense of its fixed exchange rate against a series of speculative attacks was more dogged than that of the British; at one point the central bank raised overnight interest rates at 500% in order to stem an attack. This reluctance to abandon the peg no doubt reflected the influence of Sweden's long and almost unbroken record of exchange-rate targeting (although with frequent devaluations) during the twentieth century. Eventually, though, as in the United Kingdom, the economic costs of shadowing Germany's monetary policy became too heavy to sustain, and Sweden devalued the krona. Unwilling to do without a nominal anchor for any extended period of time, Sweden, again like the United Kingdom, found an alternative strategy in inflation targeting. Both Sweden's monetary history and its size in the world economy differ from those of Great Britain, however—factors that help to explain why Sweden made different choices in designing its targeting framework.

Key Features of Inflation Targeting in Sweden

- Despite its long history of keeping monetary policy in service to an exchange-rate peg, for the most part Sweden implemented inflation targeting in a flexible manner, more akin to the approaches of Canada and the United Kingdom than to that of New Zealand. For example, the introduction of inflation targets was intentionally delayed to increase the flexibility of monetary policy in the face of domestic financial fragility and recession.

- This philosophy of flexibility did not extend to all aspects of the Swedish framework, however. Some of the more rigid aspects of the Swedish strategy, such as the targeting of headline rather than core inflation (see below), increased the burden on the Riksbank to give persuasive public explanations of its policy decisions, and also raised the possibility of instrument instability, à la New Zealand.

- Sweden targets inflation in the headline CPI rather than using a modified price index that excludes the effects of certain shocks. Sweden's choice may have reflected the importance of headline inflation in the context of the corporatist wage-setting arrangements of that country. Nonetheless, measures of "underlying" or trend inflation have played a greater role in the Riksbank's decisions and explanations in recent years, so that in this respect Sweden is converging towards the norm among inflation targeters.

- Sweden's inflation target is expressed as a fairly narrow range, usually 2% in width. The use of a band is justified as a way of accommodating inevitable errors in controlling inflation. The target floor for measured inflation has been 1% per annum. As in Canada, the emphasis on the need for a floor as well as a ceiling reflected concerns about the risks to the financial system from deflation, as well as Sweden's positive experience with a price-level floor during the Great Depression.

- The government maintains legal control of the Riksbank, but the Riksbank sets the inflation target and the instrument interest rates in practice. The government's ultimate control has avoided issues of divided accountability, as arose, for example, during the pre-1997 period in the United Kingdom.

- Sweden, like other inflation targeters discussed in this book, publishes a regular *Inflation Report*. The *Report*'s pedagogic strengths, breadth of distribution, and economic sophistication have increased steadily over time. At times the *Report* has provided the Riksbank with a bully pulpit from which to exert pressure on fiscal policy-makers to control Sweden's budget deficits.

The Adoption of Inflation Targeting

On January 15, 1993, the Governing Board of the Riksbank issued a state-ment that the objective for monetary policy was to "limit the annual in-crease in the consumer price index from 1995 onwards to 2%, with a tolerance up or down of 1 percentage point." The Board also announced that in both 1993 and 1994 "monetary policy would aim to prevent infla-tionary impulses connected with the depreciation of the krona from lead-ing to an increase in the underlying rate of inflation" (Sveriges Riksbank, 1994a, 1, p. 6). Coming only two months after the floating of the krona on November 19, 1992, the Board's statement reflected the urgency of finding a new nominal anchor to replace the one lost in the currency-market turbulence of the fall of 1992. The decision to adopt an inflation target was supported by all the governing parties, which are represented on the Riksbank's Governing Board.[1]

Except for the years 1914 to 1922 and 1931 to 1933, Swedish mon-etary policy since 1873 had been conducted with a fixed exchange rate as nominal anchor, first under the gold standard and later under the Bretton Woods system.[2] From March 1973 to August 1977, Sweden par-ticipated in the "snake," the bloc float of the currencies of the Scandina-vian countries and of some EC members. In August 1977, the Riksbank began to peg the krona to a trade-weighted basket of currencies, initially within an unannounced band of 2.25% around the central value. On September 14, 1981, and on October 8, 1982 the Riksbank devalued the krona by 10% and 16% respectively (see Panel D of Figure 8.1).

During the next ten years, no further devaluations occurred. Follow-ing some unrest in foreign-exchange markets in the spring of 1985 (the interest-rate effects of which can be seen in Figure 8.1, Panel B), the Riksbank reaffirmed its commitment to maintain the peg and narrowed the width of the exchange-rate band to 1.5%. It was thought that a nar-rower band would convey greater commitment and thus help to stabi-lize the krona in foreign exchange markets. However, the signaling value of a narrower band comes at a cost in that it reduces the flexibility of policy and is more difficult to maintain, especially for a very open economy like Sweden's. Indeed, many of the ERM's members could not maintain their bands of plus or minus 2.25% after September 1992.

Early in 1988, the Riksbank, noting the risks of inflation caused by a buoyant domestic economy and the associated pressures on the exchange rate, started to tighten monetary policy. GDP growth had been high since the mid-1980s and unemployment was below 2%, low even by Swedish

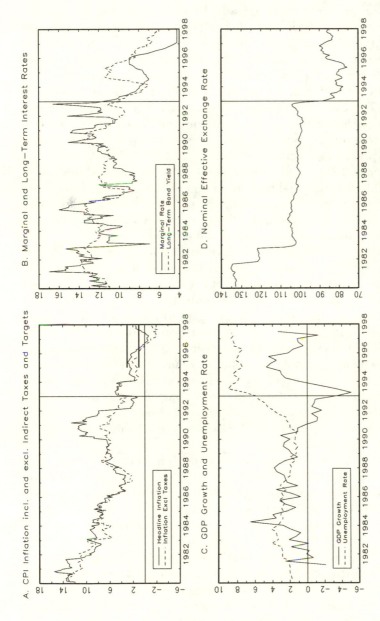

Figure 8.1. Swedish economic indicators. Sources: A) Bank for International Settlements database, Sveriges Riksbank; B) Bank for International Settlements database; C) Main Economic Indicators of the Organisation for Economic Cooperation and Development; D) Bank for International Settlements database.

standards (see Panel C of Figure 8.1). Measures taken earlier in the 1980s to liberalize the Swedish financial markets, coupled with preferential tax treatment of interest payments, had fueled borrowing by both private households and businesses. The expanded stock of debt raised the possibility that the interest-rate increases necessary to defend the exchange rate would have a stronger effect on the real economy than had earlier tightenings of monetary policy. Consequently, the disparity between domestic goals and the policies required to maintain the peg was widening. The United Kingdom—with an even more liberalized financial system and less synchronization with the continental business cycle—experienced a similar conflict in its attempts to maintain its peg, as we saw in the preceding chapter.

In February 1990, and again in October, the Riksbank found itself forced to raise the Marginal Rate (its main policy instrument) sharply in order to arrest large currency outflows and defend the exchange-rate peg. At that time, increases in interest rates had an even greater potential to slow economic activity, because the tax-deductible component of interest payments had been reduced from 47% to 40% as of January 1, 1990, and to 30% as of January 1, 1991. (The effect of these measures on headline inflation is visible in Figure 8.1, Panel A.) Combined with the rise in interest rates, the reduced tax deductions implied that interest payments after tax on household mortgages had more than doubled between 1989 and 1991, making a contraction of the economy within the next one to two years appear increasingly likely. Presumably the intent of the change in the tax code was to reduce the incentives that had given rise to high levels of private-sector indebtedness and inflationary pressure; but by the time the change was enacted, it was too late. The incompatibility of maintaining the peg and choosing monetary policies appropriate to the state of the domestic economy was becoming manifest.

Confidence in the krona improved markedly in December 1990, when the Swedish Parliament authorized the government to apply for European Community membership. The yield on ten-year Swedish government bonds fell rapidly throughout 1991, reflecting the economy's movement into recession and the prospect of closer economic and monetary integration with the EC. The Riksbank's decision on May 17, 1991, to unilaterally peg the krona to the ECU (as opposed to the trade-weighted basket of currencies used previously) was followed by further declines in both short-term and long-term interest rates.[3] The changes over time in the definition of the exchange-rate target, in response to changing circumstances, illustrate how a degree of flexibility may be introduced even

into supposedly inflexible monetary regimes. The change in the definition of the exchange-rate target also served as a way of communicating
with the public by underlining the government's commitment to economic integration with the European Community. The interest-rate differential for ten-year bonds vis-à-vis Germany fell from above 4% in September 1990 to below 1.5% by September 1991, indicating the increased
credibility of that commitment.

Toward the end of 1991, however, public doubts about the compatibility of the exchange-rate policy with domestic policy objectives began
to surface. In particular, the tight monetary policy in Germany following
that country's reunification required high short-term interest rates
throughout the European Monetary System, as well as in countries (such
as Sweden) that pegged their currencies to the ECU. Yet high interest
rates were clearly not the best medicine for Sweden. The country had
been in recession for the entire year of 1991, unemployment was rising
quickly, and inflation was on a downward trend from an already low level.
In addition, the Swedish financial sector was plagued by extremely high
levels of loan defaults, the result of the combination of monetary tightening, earlier over-expansion of credit, and ill-advised changes in regulatory policies. Matters were made worse by the Finnish central bank's
decision, on November 15, 1991, to devalue the markka vis-à-vis the ECU
by 12.3%, thus increasing market pressure on the krona.

The Riksbank was nevertheless determined to defend the krona's peg.
In response to large currency outflows throughout November, at the
beginning of December the Riksbank raised the Marginal Rate by 6% to
17.5%. The Riksbank argued that

> [a] marked increase in short interest rates can effectively break negative ex-
> pectations and thereby turn a currency outflow into an inflow. This can be
> followed by a relatively rapid return to lower interest rates. Just a cautious
> interest rate increase in connection with exchange rate uncertainty runs the
> risk of not breaking expectations. (Sveriges Riksbank, 1992a, 1, p. 10)

No sustained return to lower interest rates proved possible, however,
and the prospect of interest-rate increases strengthened fears of a financial crisis. This dynamic of credit booms followed by financial fragility,
which often arises when a tightening of monetary policy fails to stave off
a depreciation, is one of the inherent disadvantages of maintaining a
fixed exchange rate. During 1992, Sweden remained in recession, unemployment rose further, the state of the financial sector turned peril-
ous, and government finances deteriorated sharply.[4] Applying the same
logic as in December 1991, the Riksbank hoped that by raising interest

rates briefly but vigorously, it would be able to defend the peg at acceptable economic cost. On September 8, it announced that as of September 10 it would raise the Marginal Rate from 16% to 24%. On September 10, it announced that it would actually raise the Marginal Rate to 75%. On September 13, it briefly lowered the Marginal Rate to 20%. On "Black Wednesday," September 16, it raised the Marginal Rate to 500% and kept it there for the rest of the week. After the French referendum on the Maastricht Treaty on September 20, the Riksbank lowered the Marginal Rate to 50%, and over the next six weeks the rate gradually came down to 11.5%. Sweden had managed to maintain its ECU peg even though the United Kingdom and Italy had been forced to exit the ERM.

The successful defense of the krona was not to be repeated, however. On November 12, Sweden's National Debt Office announced an unexpectedly large borrowing requirement, and the subsequent issue of treasury bills was not fully placed. These events focused attention on the fact that the Riksbank's successful defense of the krona had not solved any of the economy's underlying problems. A new crisis began: During the following week, the equivalent of 158 billion krona in foreign currency left the country. This time, however, the Riksbank did not resort to interest-rate increases. Instead, on November 19, 1992, it decided to abandon its exchange-rate peg and float the krona.

Immediately following that decision, the Riksbank emphasized that it still considered price stability to be the ultimate goal of its monetary policy. In fact, it made that goal much more explicit than in previous discussions of policy.

> Instead of raising the marginal rate to 20%, as announced earlier [on November 19], the level was set at 12.5% or 1 percentage point higher than before. In this way the Riksbank indicated that the change to a flexible exchange rate did not imply any change in the ultimate monetary policy objective; also under the new regime the Riksbank would strive for long-term price stability. (Sveriges Riksbank, 1993a, 1, p. 12)

During the weeks that followed, the Riksbank undertook to devise a new framework in which to conduct monetary policy. It was agreed that domestic factors would replace the exchange rate as the main determinant of monetary policy, and that a broader set of information variables would be used in policy planning and assessment. Although the Riksbank did not define "price stability," the phrase was clearly not intended to imply a goal of zero measured inflation or a commitment to reversing past price rises. Moreover, low inflation was evidently not the only goal of concern to Swedish policy-makers. If it had been, they could have simply maintained the ECU peg irrespective of cost to domestic activity and the financial sector. Finally, the Riksbank intended to communicate to the public the practical limits of monetary control of the economy, as indicated by its use of the word "strive" in the quotation above.

In the eighteen months following the Riksbank's pegging of the krona to the ECU, a significant reduction in inflation had already been achieved, and the Riksbank wanted to preserve that gain. Moreover, the Riksbank wanted to avoid giving the impression of being without a guide to monetary policy and an anchor for expectations, at least for any length of time. Nonetheless, like the United Kingdom, during the period of the peg Sweden had not engaged in any extended public or even private discussions of alternatives to exchange-rate targeting, for fear that such discussions, if leaked, would further imperil the commitment to the peg.

> It appeared that the Riksbank had no contingency plan for the new situation. Riksbank staff and a few invited academics were quickly summoned by the Governor to produce, under considerable time pressure, a set of position papers . . . Studies of monetary policy in Canada, New Zealand, and Switzerland were included . . . , which proved to indicate in what direction the new monetary policy would turn. (Svensson, 1995, pp. 69-70)[5]

The adoption of an inflation target was thus not a carefully considered or long-planned shift in policy. Rather, it was a forced reaction to the loss of a long-standing nominal anchor for monetary policy. The Riksbank, having had very little experience with the conduct of monetary policy under a flexible exchange rate, chose to draw on the recent experience of other open economies in similar situations.

From the reading of contemporary documents, it appears that there had been two main motives behind the decision to adopt an inflation target. First, after the loss of the fixed exchange rate, and the associated loss of policy credibility (given the extraordinary earlier efforts that the Riksbank had made in the krona's defense), the Riksbank needed a medium to communicate its ongoing commitment to price stability. Second, experience during the previous years suggested that a framework was necessary that would permit greater short-term flexibility of monetary policy to address domestic goals and respond to various macroeconomic shocks.

Regarding the first motive, there can be no doubt that the circumstances under which the peg had collapsed had had a detrimental effect on the credibility of Swedish monetary policy. At the same time, the economic situation required a significantly easier stance of monetary policy than had been maintained during the end of the krona's peg to the ECU. The dilemma, then, was that an easing of monetary policy on the heels of the devaluation (which in itself had contributed to an easing of monetary policy) would risk raising long-run and short-run inflation expectations.

> In the absence of a . . . restriction on interest rate policy (with no intermediate target as a guide), after the krona's fall outside observers had greater difficulty in assessing the probable direction of monetary policy and the goals that would be established . . . Weak economic activity and high unemployment, in Sweden as well as abroad, nourished expectations that the long-term inflation objective might be relegated in favor of a markedly expansionary monetary policy. (Sveriges Riksbank, 1994a, 1, p. 5)

With no obvious, reliable intermediate target to adopt, a strategy of announcing a numerical range for the ultimate goal of policy seemed to be the most promising means for anchoring expectations and communicating the intentions of the policy-makers.[6] Conducting monetary policy without an explicit target was not considered a viable option, a view supported not only by the experiences of Canada and New Zealand (of which the Riksbank of course was aware), but also by the Swedish public's own largely unbroken experience of having a nominal anchor for monetary policy.

Regarding the second motive, the need for greater short-term policy flexibility: During the early 1990s, a conflict had evolved between the external and domestic demands on monetary policy in Sweden. In particular, as we have mentioned, while tight monetary policy to support the krona-ECU peg may have been compatible with price stability in the long run, as the Riksbank repeatedly asserted, in the shorter run it probably contributed significantly to the 1991-93 recession. The budget deficit that resulted from these cyclical factors, and that was worsened by the costs of supporting the fragile banking system, showed signs of becoming unsustainable. Both the problems of the financial sector and the related fiscal deficits were of concern to the Riksbank. More broadly, the Riksbank was prepared to pursue multiple policy objectives in the short run despite its commitment to long-run price stability, and it needed a framework that would permit that flexibility.

The Riksbank viewed the new framework as involving more than a change in monetary policy. It emphasized that credibility demanded that fiscal imbalances be addressed as well:

> For [an inflation target] to be meaningful, however, it is necessary that the conditions that will make it credible exist . . . Consequently, other economic policies must be compatible with the price stability target. An important factor of uncertainty in this respect is the development of the government budget . . . Over a period of time, demand in the Swedish economy has been supported by means of public expenditure, at the same time as interest rates were high because of lack of confidence in economic policy and the fixed exchange rate. If a consolidation of the budget is achieved, this would create the conditions for lower interest rates. As a stimulant for the economy, lower interest rates—a less restrictive monetary policy—would be more effective than the fiscal policy pursued to date. (Hörngren, 1992, pp. 73-4)

In sum, the Swedish adoption of an inflation target had two objectives: first, to allow monetary policy to be directed toward domestic objectives, including short-run output stabilization; and second, simultaneously to reduce the public's concerns about both the long-term orientation of monetary policy and the possibility that unsustainable fiscal deficits would eventually be monetized.

The pursuit of multiple objectives was in seeming contrast to Sweden's successful experience with a price-*level* target in the 1930s—the only true example of a price-level target for monetary policy in the twentieth century, so far as we are aware. But that contrast is more apparent than real. The achievement of the Swedish price-level target of the 1930s was to provide a floor for prices in the face of worldwide deflation and depression, and the main benefit of this policy was to avoid the negative effects on output and employment that followed from sharply declining prices. A similar benefit of inflation targeting (as stressed, for example, by the Canadians) is that a properly managed inflation-targeting regime avoids deflation as well as excessive inflation.

By the time the inflation target was adopted in January 1993, the Swedish economy was in deep recession. Real GDP had fallen over 1992 by 4%, unemployment had reached 7% and was continuing to rise toward unprecedented levels, and the central government's budget deficit had grown to more than 11% of GDP. Inflation, which had been falling steadily since early 1990, however, was down to a historically low rate of 3% per year. While the 14% depreciation of the krona (vis-à-vis both the DM and the ECU) over the last few months of 1992 would inevitably have some inflationary impact, the recession was sufficiently deep that a reversal of the downward trend of inflation seemed unlikely. When the inflation target was announced, therefore, it appeared probable that it would be achieved without further drastic policy measures. However, to enhance its flexibility, the Riksbank provided an escape clause by saying that the target would not have to be met until more normal economic conditions prevailed. Somewhat surprisingly, the fact that Sweden chose to set the target for a period commencing after the pass-through effects of the devaluation were likely to be completed did not lead to the explicit provision of an escape clause for similar shocks in the future (as was the case, for example, in New Zealand). Conceivably, however, the use of this *de facto* escape clause may have provided the Riksbank and the Swedish government with a precedent on which to draw, should circumstances warrant.

Pronounced political division over monetary policy arose following the floating of the krona. The governing liberal-conservative coalition supported the Riksbank's policy of cautious interest-rate cuts; but the Social Democrats, though supposedly supporting the adoption of the inflation target, were advocating a much more aggressive monetary expansion.[7] Especially odd, from a political standpoint, was that the target of 2% CPI inflation (the midpoint of the 1% to 3% range) was set for 1995 onwards—a period commencing after the next general election, which was due to be held no later than September 1994. Thus there must have been some public confusion about the force of the government's commitment to the target, although given the recession and the slowdown in inflation, it did seem likely that the target would be achieved.

The evident ability of inflation-targeting commitments to survive beyond the current government is interesting. In the cases of the United Kingdom and Canada, we saw that once inflation targets had been made public and some effort had been invested in achieving them, succeeding governments seemed to have little choice but to extend the policy. Thus announcements of inflation targets appear to carry some real weight with the public, independent of which party is in control of the government.

The Operational Framework

Apart from the Governing Board's initial announcement on January 15, 1993, no official document has been published that outlines the operational details of Sweden's inflation-targeting framework. This omission gives rise to certain ambiguities about the new framework, including the duration of the commitment. In general, Sweden has not emphasized transparency of policy to the degree that some other inflation targeters have. It sometimes seems to take the view that policy flexibility is better maintained by being less than fully open with the public. As discussed in Chapter 3, while this tradeoff between flexibility and transparency does exist in the short run in some instances, the evidence suggests that in the longer run, flexibility and transparency tend to be mutually reinforcing.

According to the target announcement, the objective of monetary policy was "to limit the annual increase in the consumer price index from 1995 onwards to 2%" (Sveriges Riksbank, 1994a, 1, p. 6). As with all other inflation targeters, the operational definition of price stability is a measured inflation rate above zero (the initial target range was set as 1% to 3%). Given the extreme fragility of the Swedish financial system at the time, it was clear that the Riksbank intended to prevent deflation, which would have weakened the system further. No mention was made of items that would be excluded from the target CPI, nor of any circumstances in which the definition of the target price index might be modified. This omission is surprising in view of, for example, the strong potential impact of changes in indirect taxes on the Swedish CPI. As can be seen by comparing the evolution of all-items CPI inflation and inflation in the CPI excluding indirect taxes and subsidies (the solid and dashed lines, respectively, in Panel A of Figure 8.1), the first-round effects of such tax changes can be quite large. Similarly, the effects of the (presumably) one-time devaluation of the krona in November 1992 on oil and food imports would have required a response by this definition of the target price index. The Riksbank avoided responding to the effects of the devaluation, as well as to the interest-rate increases mentioned earlier, by delaying the commencement of the targeting period, a more *ad hoc* approach than simply excluding those factors from the target index.

In any event, this apparent lack of interest in discriminating core inflation from headline CPI inflation differentiates the initial Swedish framework from those of other major inflation-targeting regimes. The contrast with New Zealand in this respect is especially striking. As we pointed out in the study of New Zealand (Chapter 5), a narrow definition of inflation (excluding many types of inflationary shocks) compensates only partially for the potentially destabilizing short-run effects of monetary policy on a small, open economy. Sweden's decision to target a broad or headline measure of inflation, rather than a modified index designed to measure core inflation, suggests either a willingness to be especially flexible in adherence to the targets in the face of shocks, or a high tolerance for risk on the part of the policy-makers.

Perhaps the targeting of headline CPI in Sweden reflected the central role that that measure plays in collective bargaining and wage-in-

dexing in that country. It would seem, however, given the public's awareness of indexing and inflation issues in the wage-bargaining context,
that educating wage- and price-setters to understand a core inflation target would not have been a difficult task. Policy-makers discussed these
pros and cons actively, and over time began to bring underlying inflation into the public discussion.[8] For example, the December 1997 *Inflation Report* presented a forecast of CPI inflation excluding indirect taxes,
subsidies, and interest costs for owner-occupied housing, in a manner
similar to the reporting practices of other inflation targeters.

Another ambiguous aspect of the target formulation was that for some
time it was unclear whether the 2% target from 1995 onward referred to
monthly inflation rates (as measured on an annualized basis) during
1995 and later, or to the full-year inflation rate from December 1994 to
December 1995. "Only recently did Riksbank officials clarify that the
target did not apply to 12-month inflation rates of individual months
during 1995" (Svensson, 1995, p. 82). So, like other inflation targeters,
the Riksbank built in some flexibility by establishing a longer time horizon for its targets. Moreover, it was decided that success at hitting targets
was not to be based on the most recent calendar year, but instead on the
most recent four quarters.[9]

Further, once the target was attained, the target horizon was to become open-ended. By clarifying the period over which the target was to
be achieved, in line with the practices of other inflation-targeting countries, the Riksbank could have increased its accountability and the transparency of policy. The reasons for leaving this commitment vague at the
outset are unclear; the effect was to leave the public guessing whether
headline inflation above 3% in early 1995 should be considered as a
target miss. Nor was it made clear what would happen in the event of a
target breach. However, as in the current British framework, the Riksbank
is required to publish explanations, at least once a year, of any deviations
from the band.

According to the Riksbank's clarification, then, the policy framework
called for a period of three years during which inflation was to be steered
into the target band of 1% to 3%. The leadership of the Riksbank chose
a narrow target range rather than a point target, despite their recent
experience with the difficulties of observing a narrow target band for
the exchange rate, because they sensed the need to reestablish credibility after the loss of the ECU peg. As we discussed in Chapter 3, there is a
tradeoff implicit in the choice of the width of the target range: The narrower the target range, the more likely the public is to take seriously the
central bank's commitment to the inflation goal, all else equal. On the

other hand, a narrow range reduces policy flexibility, increases the risk of inadvertently missing the range, and may raise the possibility of instrument instability (as interest rates are adjusted sharply in attempts to keep inflation within the desired bounds). Again, Sweden did set its target range floor at 1%, putting some space above zero inflation in light of ongoing problems in the financial sector.

According to the January 1993 announcement, the reason for having an initial period without Canadian-style guidelines for the inflation transition path was to increase short-term flexibility—in particular, to free monetary policy from having to counteract the first-round effects of the November 1992 devaluation. Instead, policy was merely required to prevent the devaluation effects from increasing "the underlying rate of inflation," much as in other inflation-targeting countries. Once again, the delay in implementing the targets amounted to the invocation of an escape clause. However, given the absence from the framework of some measure of underlying inflation, this escape clause could, in effect, never be used again. The implicit contradiction between the use of an escape clause and the absence of a measure of underlying inflation in the targeting procedure became a recurring burden for the Riksbank to justify: If it is acceptable to have an escape clause that permits the authorities to ignore shocks that do not affect core inflation, then it would seem that the appropriate target is a measure of core inflation, not headline inflation.

The Riksbank stressed that it would not employ any one intermediate target in the new framework:

> This decision has to do with the lack of a variable which can be presumed to meet the criteria of controllability and a stable relationship with price formation. . . . Monetary policy control in Sweden, as in most other countries with a flexible exchange rate, starts instead from attempts to form a comprehensive picture of economic development and the course of inflation by studying several indicators of future activity and future inflation. (Sveriges Riksbank, 1994a, 1, pp. 6-7.)

The information variables that the Riksbank adopted included monetary and credit aggregates, the exchange rate, interest rates (in the form of a yield spread, or combined with the exchange rate as a monetary conditions index), wages, and some goods prices (such as import prices and commodity prices). This use of many types of information in formulating policy is consistent with the view that the current inflation forecast itself should be treated both as the intermediate target and as the basis for explaining policy decisions.[10]

Since the Riksbank's Governing Board is to some extent an arm of Parliament, parliamentary supervision of monetary policy seems assured. Four of the Board members, including the Chairman, are appointed by the governing party (or parties), and the other three by the opposition. The members serve for the duration of the Parliament. Although the appointment of outsiders is possible, most of the appointees are themselves members of Parliament. The Governor is chosen by the Board members for a term of five years and can be dismissed by them at any time. By all the standard legal measures, the Riksbank is one of the least independent central banks in Europe. In practice, however, the Riksbank does exercise reasonable autonomy, and even has responsibility for exchange rate intervention (unlike most European central banks).

Before the krona was floated, a government-appointed committee had been working on proposals for reforming the Riksbank. It presented its report to the government in March 1993. The report recommended a legislated price stability goal and a more independent status for the Riksbank. However, faced with opposition by the Social Democrat parliamentary faction, and the far more pressing need to decide on and to implement a new monetary framework, the government chose not to submit the proposal to Parliament.[11] A similarly ill-timed juxtaposition of proposals occurred in Canada, with the need for a new nominal anchor crowding out plans for formally increasing the independence of the central bank. However, in Sweden, as in Canada, the inflation-targeting regime *de facto* increased operational independence of the central bank. In 1997, the legislative initiative to increase the Riksbank's legal independence was revived and survived a first parliamentary reading.[12]

Since, as we noted, the Riksbank is in some respects an arm of the government, there is no explicit oversight mechanism for monetary policy in Sweden. Accountability presumably is ensured through parliamentary elections, since the performance of monetary policy helps to determine the electoral fate of the government. Nevertheless, many economists (including ourselves) regard the Swedish arrangement as a poor second-best to a fully instrument-independent central bank.

The Riksbank reports to the public on monetary policy through inflation reports (titled *Inflation and Inflation Expectations in Sweden* until November 1995, *Inflation Report* thereafter), which it published three times a year from June 1993 to December 1995, and four times a year since then. Since its first issue, the format has undergone a number of changes. In its present form, the *Report* surveys various measures of inflation. It also covers measures of current inflationary pressures (*e.g.,* capacity utilization rates), developments in important sectors and in the labor market, fiscal policy, and monetary aggregates. A section on inflation expectations reports the results of surveys of households and firms (at a one-year horizon), bond investors (at two-year and five-year horizons) and, since October 1994, of money-market agents, purchasing managers, and employer and employee organizations (at horizons of one, two, and five years). Because of the centralized, corporatist wage-bargaining arrangements in Sweden, it may be easier to obtain accurate measures of inflation expectations there than in other countries. This section of the report also lists some financial-market indicators of inflation expectations, such as movements in implied forward interest-rate curves and interest-rate differentials vis-à-vis Germany. In addition, the *Inflation Report,* like the reports published by other inflation-targeting central banks, carries frequent explanations of the economic significance of the matters discussed, aimed at educating the public.

Until June 1995, the *Inflation Report* was published by the Riksbank's Economics Department and signed by its head, not by the Governor or the Governing Board. The implied distance between the professional assessment of the inflation situation and the political forces affecting the Riksbank may have increased the credibility of that assessment, though at some cost in accountability. Since November 1995, however, the *Inflation Report* has been published by the Riksbank and signed by the Governor. In its Foreword, it states that "the Governing Board has discussed the future design of monetary policy in the light of the inflation analysis." This may be seen as an attempt to avoid the sort of separation between policy analysis and policy responsibility that had occurred in the United Kingdom. In theory, of course, there is still room for open disagreement over policy, should the politically appointed Governing Board choose to overrule the Governor.

The Riksbank, much like the Bundesbank, did not initially publish an inflation forecast of its own. Only since June 1995 has the *Inflation Report* contained statements to the effect that the Riksbank expects inflation during the next two years to be within or outside the target range, and whether in the upper or lower half of it. In terms of concreteness, the Riksbank was thus at the opposite end of the spectrum from the Reserve Bank of New Zealand, with the Bank of England and the Bank of Canada somewhere in between. As with the targeting of the headline CPI, in this area the practice of the Riksbank has shifted over time toward the norm established by other inflation targeters. As of December 1997, the Riksbank had begun publishing its inflation forecast in graphical form, in the manner of the Bank of England.

As we mentioned earlier, so far the most ambitious effort at reform of the Riksbank was the report of the government-appointed Riksbank Committee, which was presented to the government in early March 1993.[13] It contained three main proposals: (1) to have Parliament formulate a statutory objective for the Riksbank by the Swedish Parliament, (2) to change the rules for the appointment and composition of the Governing Board, with the aim of distancing the Board from Parliament, and (3) (in an expert report appended to the Committee's report) to impose stringent performance conditions (enforced by threat of dismissal) on either the members of the Governing Board or on the Governor.

Though the Committee report was not proposed as legislation, it is worth considering briefly, both because of the effect it has had on the Swedish public debate and the view it takes on the link between inflation targeting and central bank independence. The formulation of a statutory objective for the Riksbank was seen as a move toward a more independent role for the Riksbank. "Greater independence for the Riksbank presupposes . . . that an objective for its activities is laid down by [Parliament]. This gives monetary and exchange-rate policy a democratic foundation." The Committee further proposed that the Riksbank's objective

> should be . . . price stability. A specific target in the form of a quantified rate of inflation should not be enacted. The objective is taken to refer to the development of inflation in the medium- and the long-term.

The goal of price stability was to be given an operational definition that could be varied over time with changing circumstances, that would not be unduly binding in the shorter term, and that had as its main purpose the anchoring of long-run inflation expectations. The proposal went further in stating that the pursuit of price stability was not to be seen in isolation from the pursuit of other objectives.

> Neither does the objective of price stability imply that monetary policy is not to take other objectives into account. In so far as other objectives can be promoted without prejudice to the goal of price stability, the Riksbank should support general economic policy and contribute to the attainment of its other objectives.

Again, this distinction between long-run commitment to price stability and short-run inflexibility, between inflation targeting as a framework and as a rule, has been followed in design and in practice to a greater or lesser degree by all countries discussed here (note the similarity in language to the Bundesbank's charter, for example). This Commission report, though it was not adopted, is widely known in Sweden and is consistent with the current vision of the Riksbank's objective and role.

Swedish Monetary Policy under Inflation Targeting

We turn now to developments in Swedish monetary policy since the target adoption in January 1993. As the panels in Figure 8.1 suggest, the period since then can be divided into three episodes. The first, which spans the period from target adoption until April 1994, is characterized by falling inflation, a rebound in GDP growth, and falling short-term interest rates. The second episode covers the period from May 1994 until the end of 1995. During that time inflation increased, reaching the upper half of the target range of 1% to 3%; GDP growth was strong; and short-term interest rates rose. During the third episode, from the beginning of 1996 to the end of 1997, the pattern of 1994-1995 was reversed: Inflation fell rapidly, breaching the lower bound of the target range; GDP growth slowed down; and short-term interest rates fell sharply.

Annualized CPI inflation rose significantly in January 1993, to 4.8%, from 2% in December 1992. The increase was due mostly to a swift pass-through of the effects of the November 1992 devaluation on import prices. The inflation rate rose gradually to a peak of 5.2% in April. The yield on ten-year government bonds increased slightly during the first half of January, but following the target announcement, it resumed the decline that had begun following the devaluation of the krona. Well aware of the degree of uncertainty among market participants over future monetary policy at this time, the Riksbank pursued a policy of cautious interest-rate cuts. Expectations for inflation in 1994 were above 4%, based apparently on the belief that the Riksbank would lower interest rates aggressively to fight the recession. Indeed, soon after the Riksbank reduced the Marginal Rate from 10.5% to 9.75% on February 5, it was forced to intervene in the money market to prevent short-term interest rates from falling below 9%. The krona continued to depreciate during the first quarter of 1993, possibly in response to the gridlock in Parliament over what to do about the government budget deficit, which was rising to record levels.

From April 1993 through the end of the year, inflation fell (with the exception of a brief upward blip in October and November). The yield on ten-year government bonds declined from above 10% in January to 7.25% in December, reducing the yield differential vis-à-vis Germany from more than 3% in January to slightly above 1% at year's end—that is, to levels lower than had ever been achieved under the ECU peg. The Riksbank continued its policy of cautious easing by cutting the Marginal Rate in eight quarter-percent steps, to 7.75%. By November, inflation expectations at the two-year horizon obtained from a survey of bond investors had declined to 3%, while inflation expectations at the five-year horizon were still above 4%. Around the end of 1993, there were signs that GDP growth was turning positive again, led by growth in exports. The devaluation, together with falling unit labor costs in the wake of the massive job shedding during the recession, had improved the competitiveness of Sweden's export sector. By year's end, the krona had depreciated from its November 1992 level by 24% in trade-weighted terms.

Headline inflation fell to 1.9% in January 1994, down from 5% in November 1993 and from 4.1% in December, as the direct impact of the devaluation receded. Inflation remained at this new, low level through April. The yield on ten-year government bonds bottomed out at 7% in January 1994. During the downturn in the international bond market from February to August 1994, however, the ten-year yield rose from 7.0% to 11.4%, and the differential between Swedish and German ten-year yields widened from just above 1% to over 4%. From January through May, motivated by domestic real factors and the financial situation, the Riksbank continued to cut the Marginal Rate, in three quarter-percent steps, to 7%. The inflation target did not officially take hold until the end of 1995, but the announcement of the target framework had apparently succeeded in locking in inflation expectations at the low levels achieved prior to the devaluation of the krona. Equally gratifying was the absence of any significant pass-through of the one-time inflationary shock from the devaluation. As in the United Kingdom, Sweden's switch from an exchange-rate target to an inflation target provided the flexibility to loosen policy in accord with domestic (rather than German) needs, with no apparent cost in terms of inflation—despite the widely held expectation that exiting the ERM would be a major blow to the credibility of monetary policy.

Estimates of inflation expectations obtained from polling professional forecasters stayed mostly unchanged during the first half of 1994, at 2% for the year 1994 and 3% for 1995, within the target range. Headline inflation rose in May 1994 to 2.3%, from 1.8% in April. The signals from the real side of the economy were mixed: Although exports and private consumption rose during the first quarter, investment was still falling. The Riksbank concluded in its *Inflation Report,* published in mid-June, that "economic growth to date in 1994 seems to be weak," and that inflationary impulses from the labor market were weak as well (Sveriges Riksbank, 1994b, June, p. 16). Absent clear signs of emerging inflationary pressures, the Riksbank claimed that the rise in long-term yields "may have to do with factors that do not represent increased inflation expectations," citing for example changes in bond investment strategies and the still unresolved problem of the government budget deficit (Sveriges Riksbank, 1994b, June, p. 36). This view was supported by the fact that the krona appreciated markedly during the first half of the year. More importantly, the Riksbank's explanation emphasized to the public the limits of monetary policy's control over the economy. The Riksbank also revealed that, despite the fact that the official target was defined in terms of headline inflation, not all movements in inflation would produce the same reaction from monetary policy.

Shortly after the publication of the June *Inflation Report,* it became clear that the outlook for inflation was less benign than first thought. Headline inflation rose to 2.9% in July and fell only to 2.7% in September. Measures of underlying inflation showed a pronounced rise during the spring, revealing that the price increases were broadly based and were occurring in all major sectors of the economy. Furthermore, as a result of the reduction in production capacity that had taken place during the recession, together with the vigorous growth in export demand following the krona's depreciation, the remaining production capacity was almost fully utilized. By this time, measures of capacity utilization—key indicators of inflationary pressures—were at their highest levels since 1989. Inflation expectations among professional forecasters for the year 1994 jumped from 2% to 3% during the summer, while inflation expectations among bond investors had risen to 3.4% and 4.2% at the two-year and five-year horizons respectively. Meanwhile, the government's need to borrow had remained stable, but at a very high level. On August 11 these developments prompted the Riksbank to raise the repo rate (which had as of June 1 replaced the Marginal Rate as the Riksbank's policy instrument) from 6.92% to 7.20%, reversing the downward trend in short-term interest rates that had prevailed since the November 1992 devaluation.

The parliamentary elections on September 18, 1994, brought the government into the control of the Social Democrats, as had been widely expected. During the weeks before the elections, that party had made clear that they would neither alter the inflation target nor replace the Riksbank's Governor, Urban Bäckström. After forming a minority government, the Social Democrats appointed the last Social Democrat finance minister, Kjell-Olof Feldt, who had retired from politics and was not a member of Parliament, as chairman of the Governing Board, further signaling that they would abstain from exerting direct political pressure on monetary policy. Although the original announcement of inflation targets had stated that they would apply indefinitely from 1995 forward, the decision of the new government to leave the targets unchanged was an important confirmation of that principle. As in Canada and the United Kingdom, the switch from a right-majority to a left-majority in the Parliament after the adoption of inflation targets did not result in a change of the targets, but actually strengthened the public's sense that the government had a long-term commitment to price stability. Importantly, this continuity of policy was observed in countries in which the choice of monetary policy objectives was clearly the prerogative of the government, with no legal or procedural barriers to making a change. Apparently, a public announcement of inflation targets can act as a powerful constraint on the priorities of an elected government, without further need for "binding (the government's) hands."

With the elections out of the way, the Riksbank stepped up its criticism of fiscal policy. In the *Inflation Report* published in mid-October, the Riksbank stated:

> The inflation expectations and the associated weak exchange rate and high long term interest rates, are a consequence of the central government borrowing requirement being very high . . . [A] consolidation of central government finance is essential for achieving a sustainable development of central government debt. Conditions would then be created for lower inflation expectations, a fall in long interest rates and an appreciation of the krona. (Sveriges Riksbank, 1994b, October, p. 8)

Inflation expectations, and therefore long-term interest rates, remained vulnerable to the high government budget deficits during 1993 and 1994. The existence of the inflation target enabled the Riksbank to delineate those aspects of policy for which it was responsible and gave it a platform from which to appraise (and criticize) those policies for which it was not.

After a gradual decline during the third quarter of 1994, headline inflation began to rise in November 1994, peaking at 3.4% in April 1995. The yield on ten-year government bonds fluctuated until April between 11% and 12%, and the differential vis-à-vis the yield on German government bonds widened to above 4% during March and April. According to surveys published in the February 1995 and June 1995 issues of the *Inflation Report,* inflation at the horizons of one, two, and three years was expected to be between 3.5% and 4%. Clearly the public did not expect that the inflation target would be met, or that inflation would decline during the rest of the year. The Riksbank had raised the repo rate on October 27 and again on December 13, 1994, to 7.6%. These actions were followed by a rapid succession of rate increases during February through April 1995, with the repo rate topping out at 8.5%. Despite the rise in short-term interest rates, the krona depreciated sharply during the first quarter of 1995.

During the summer of 1995, the outlook began to improve. Headline inflation had peaked in April, and by July it had fallen back into the upper half of the target range. The ten-year government bond yield and the interest-rate differential with Germany had peaked in April as well, at 11.4% and 4.7% respectively. The krona had not depreciated any further since March and started to appreciate in June. On July 5, the Riksbank raised the repo rate to 8.91%, and left it unchanged for the rest of the year. By the time that the Riksbank had published its November *Inflation Report,* the effects of the tighter stance of monetary policy were becoming visible. Measures of underlying inflation had been on a steady downward path since April. Private consumption had not increased, and industrial capacity utilization had been mostly unchanged since late 1994, in part because a healthy increase in industrial investment had increased productive capacity. The state of government finances had improved markedly during 1995, and the ongoing fiscal tightening was expected to have a further dampening effect on private consumption. The stance of monetary policy was supported by the appreciation of the krona by about 10% since June. Based on these developments, the Riksbank's own assessment of likely CPI inflation during 1996 was between 2.5% and 3%.

By the end of 1995, inflation expectations obtained from all the surveys considered by the Riksbank had fallen below 3% at the one-, two-, and five-year horizons. By January 1996, headline inflation was down to 2%. The yield on 10-year government bonds had decreased since April by 3.2% to 8.2%, narrowing the differential vis-à-vis German government bonds to 2.5%. The improvements in the outlook for inflation over the previous six months prompted the Riksbank to lower the repo rate in four steps by 80 basis points to 8.05% during January and February. Implied forward interest rates in late February showed that investors expected short-term interest rates to fall to 7.25% until the end of the year. Implied forward rates at the ten-year horizon, however, had risen by almost 150 basis points since the first repo rate cut in January, indicating yet another dip in the public's faith in the commitment to price stability.

In its March 1996 *Inflation Report,* the Riksbank expressed confidence that inflationary pressures had receded. First, both domestic and international economic activity had slowed down during the second half of 1995. Second, inflation during 1995 had turned out to be considerably lower than had been expected at the end of 1994. This led the Riksbank to conclude that

> . . . the fact that unexpectedly strong growth in 1995 was accompanied by relatively limited inflation and that inflation expectations have been subdued indicate that earlier patterns of inflation are being broken up. But it remains to adapt wage formation so that employment can rise at the same time as the development of wage costs is compatible with price stability. (Sveriges Riksbank, 1996b, March, p. 10)

Like the Bundesbank, the Riksbank had to confront centralized wage-setting mechanisms, as well as the government's tenuous fiscal policy, in its attempt to hold down inflation expectations. The Riksbank took the position that the rate of wage increase does not necessarily determine the rate of price increase. Thus, even though the Riksbank noted the risks to inflation resulting from high wage settlements, it stated that it considered the conditions for "inflation developing in line with the inflation target . . . to be good" (Sveriges Riksbank, 1996b, March, p. 10).

Inflation continued to fall during the second and third quarters of 1996, at a rate considerably faster than expected. In April headline inflation stood at 1.3%. In its *Inflation Report* published at the beginning of June, the Riksbank attributed the lower-than-expected inflation figure mostly to lower import prices and lower mortgage rates. The continued appreciation of the krona also had the effect of reducing foreign demand for Swedish exports, contributing to a marked slowdown in GDP growth during the first half of 1996. The yield on ten-year government bonds remained largely unchanged during the first half of 1996, at between 8% and 8.5%, indicating that the drop in inflation was seen as largely cyclical and transitory. During the months from March to May the Riksbank had cut the repo rate further by 155 basis points to 6.5%. Inflation expectations one and two years ahead had fallen to 2% to 2.5%. The Riksbank considered it "probable . . . that in the latter part of 1996 inflation (measured with the CPI) will tend to move up... but that the rate during the main part of the year will be below 2%" (Sveriges Riksbank, 1996b, June, p. 19). In contrast to its optimism in the March *Inflation Report,* however, the Riksbank now emphasized the downside risks to inflation resulting from the possibility of a prolonged international slowdown and from labor-market weakness.

It appears that the Riksbank had been surprised by the rapid fall in inflation during the summer and fall of 1996. By September, headline inflation had fallen below the bottom of the target range, to 0.2%. By October the Riksbank had cut the repo rate by another 185 basis points, to 4.65%, while the yield on ten-year government bonds fell below 8%. GDP growth remained stable at a low level through the second and third quarters. In October, despite a rise in the average industrial wage of 6% in the 1996 pay round, Sweden saw its first deflation since 1959, with headline CPI dropping 0.1% year-over-year. The Riksbank and the government pointed to the one-time effects of a reduction in the value-added tax on food (from 21% to 12%) and a reduction in home mortgage interest rates; despite the absence of an official measure of core inflation, the authorities made a point of noting that inflation exclusive of those effects was still between 1.5% and 2%, and therefore fell within the target range. Finance Minister Erik Asbrink stated that the government considered economic developments "extremely positive . . . . It is not deflation in the sense that we are on the brink of an economic downturn. On the contrary, there are increasingly strong signs that we are on the verge of an economic upswing" (McIver, 1996). Swedish monetary policy-makers would not let a target breach determine their policy so long as the underlying rate of inflation remained subdued, even though their stated target commitment was to the headline CPI inflation rate.

In the December 1996 *Inflation Report,* following another month of CPI deflation, the Riksbank admitted that "[i]nflation in 1996 will be below the inflation target's lower tolerance limit. The low rate of inflation is mainly a consequence of increasing confidence in economic policy, and this has brought interest rates down and strengthened the exchange rate" (Sveriges Riksbank, 1996b, December, p. 4). The missed forecast was taken as a sign of unexpected gains in the framework's credibility. Later in the *Report,* while acknowledging the disinflationary consequences of output below the economy's potential, the Riksbank expanded on this hopeful interpretation:

> There are, moreover, other signs of more permanent changes in price formation. Together with the low inflation and decreased inflation expectations in recent years, it seems that increased domestic and international competition has altered price behaviour. Such changes appear to be particularly marked in trade in everyday goods and clothes . . . . In an economy where inflation is stable and low, relative price shifts within and between product groups are more transparent. This leads to tighter competition and less possibility of automatically passing on costs to consumer prices. (Sveriges Riksbank, 1996b, December, p. 7)

The Riksbank did allow that the passage of time and the collection of additional data were required before such a judgment could be strongly supported. In light of high wage increases in the industrial sector as well as the rising unemployment level in Sweden, it also noted that "wage formation has not yet been adapted to the low-inflation economy" (Sveriges Riksbank, 1996b, December, p. 11).[14] There was no question that inflation expectations had declined, but also no indication that inflation was turning into deflation. The survey of household expectations put two-year-ahead CPI inflation at 1.5%, and the expected five-year-ahead rate at 2%, both consistent with the announced inflation target.

Of particular interest is the Riksbank's statement about how monetary policy should react to inflation below both forecasts and the "tolerance interval" of around 2%. In a chapter titled "Monetary Policy Conclusions" in the December 1996 *Inflation Report,* the Riksbank emphasized the close connection between the lag in the effect of monetary policy on inflation and the need to make assessments of future inflation when setting current policy. In particular, the response to a substantive change in the behavior of inflation, which may have been created by the adoption of inflation targets, had to be cautious.

> Effects of monetary policy on demand and inflation can also be difficult to foresee in that historical relationships may have been changed by the move to a flexible exchange rate and a price stability target. The economy may also move onto new paths that could not be predicted when the monetary policy was constructed. If the economic trend seems to be running counter to the inflation target, the monetary stance is adapted so that inflation gradually comes into line with the target. In such a situation, an ambition to keep inflation in line with the target even in the very short run could require more drastic, perhaps unreasonable, monetary policy measures that might lead to destabilising effects. (Sveriges Riksbank, 1996b, December, p. 26)

Unlike the Reserve Bank of New Zealand, the Riksbank treated target breaches as less of a problem than the sharp movements in monetary-policy instruments that would be necessary to prevent such breaches. At the time the passage quoted above was written, Swedish headline CPI inflation had been below the 1% to 3% target for six months. Those breaches did not cause a collapse of credibility, as can be seen from the inflation expectations data, so the Riksbank's exercise of policy flexibility appeared to be costless, at least in the short run.

It might have been argued that the Riksbank was treating its inflation targets asymmetrically, responding less strongly to targets undershot than to targets overshot, much in the same way that the Bundesbank has sometimes treated its money-growth targets. Yet the Riksbank's emphasis on the need for gradualism and its concern for "destabilizing effects," juxtaposed with the detailed description of longer-term expectations within the target range, make that interpretation unlikely to be correct. Moreover, whether the Bundesbank responded to target misses in money growth has depended largely on the inflation situation; the Bundesbank has shown little asymmetry in responding to inflation rates above and below the desired level. Sweden's policy should be seen instead as another instance in which transparency and communication (including remarks about forward-looking indicators and underlying inflation, despite the fact that the official target was the headline CPI) have enhanced the flexibility of policy.

The link between flexibility in responding to target misses and transparency in explaining the economic forecast was underlined in remarks by Riksbank Deputy Governor Lars Heikensten at a conference in January 1997. After summarizing the combination of factors (appreciation of the krona, decreased mortgage interest rates, and so on) that had led to headline CPI deflation, Heikensten explained why no monetary-policy move was forthcoming to bring inflation back into the target range:

> It is because of temporary effects that the average level of inflation in 1996 is outside the Riksbank's target interval. As a rule, the interval surrounding the target figure should suffice to absorb changes of this type in the composition of inflation. That this was not the case in 1996 had to do with the marked reappraisal of the situation in Sweden. (Heikensten, 1997, p. 2)

Here the Riksbank was regarding the target range as a source of built-in flexibility. However, when faced with the choice of responding to temporary factors or missing a range that had proved to be too narrow, the Riksbank allowed the target to be missed. Deputy Governor Heikensten's statement also underscored the limits of monetary control; in particular, the Riksbank appears to have taken the view that changes in inflationary expectations, even salutary ones linked to the adoption of a new monetary framework, are to some degree exogenous and hence uncontrollable.

Thus, monetary policy-makers in Sweden have chosen not to take too much credit for changes in inflation and inflation expectations. Heikensten extended his view about what monetary policy can and cannot do by reminding his audience:

> It was not until the [government] budget outcome started to turn that we could reap the positive effect on bond rates, etc. . . . . In view of the political

> debate, there may be cause to underscore fiscal policy's importance for monetary policy. A tighter fiscal policy normally implies a better situation for inflation; it makes it easier for the Riksbank to fulfill the inflation target in conjunction with low interest rates. In addition, a fiscal policy which lacks credibility creates problems for monetary policy—as was the case during much of the period 1990-95. The radical lowering of interest rates during 1996 is something for which our thanks are very much due to fiscal policy. (Heikensten, 1997, p. 3)

The importance of all these developments, both within and outside the control of the Riksbank, was primarily their implication for the inflation forecast. As long as the inflation forecast remained within the desired bounds, there was no need to respond to the realization of lower-than-target inflation. As Heikensten put it, "Figures for 'yesterday's' inflation are therefore relevant only in so far as they say something about the future. . . . In the main, however, [the last six months' figures] have reflected the strength of transient effects" (*Ibid.*, p. 5).

During January and February 1997, year-over-year headline CPI inflation continued to decline, while underlying inflation (excluding house mortgage rates and the effects of changes in indirect taxes and subsidies) remained unchanged at 1%. In the March 1997 *Inflation Report*, the Riksbank continued to attribute much of the unexpectedly low inflation to a "lower inflation propensity" in the Swedish economy, but it also acknowledged that "registered inflation as measured with the CPI has been affected by transitory factors to a greater extent than expected" (Sveriges Riksbank, 1997b, March, p. 4). Of equal concern to the Riksbank, as measured by the number of pages devoted to the topic, was the continuing sluggishness of employment growth through the 1990s. Analysis of the Beveridge curve for the Swedish economy (the relationship between total unemployment and unfilled job vacancies) indicated that the process of matching jobs and workers in the labor market was becoming less and less effective. The discussion was as much to show why such unemployment was not due to monetary policy as to clarify this issue of public debate.

> In general, however, the pattern in recent years suggests that Sweden is now experiencing the problems of persistently high unemployment that the rest of Western Europe has been facing in recent decades. . . . Diminishing labour market efficiency implies that unemployment acts as less of a restraint on wage formation and the high unemployment becomes still more permanent. This could be one reason why 1995 settlements gave wage increases around 6 per cent even though unemployment was rising. (Sveriges Riksbank, 1997b, March, p. 13).

If unemployment in Sweden was no longer much related either to monetary policy or the level of inflation, the Riksbank argued, then rising unemployment should not be used as a justification for easing monetary policy.

Pressures for a response to the unemployment problem, however, were implicitly acknowledged with repeated references in the March *Inflation Report* to how far the repo rate had already been lowered (*e.g.*, "In the course of 1996 the repo rate was lowered a total of 4.81 percentage points" [p. 7]). The authors of the *Inflation Report* reminded Swedes that for a small, open economy, the actual effect of monetary policy was in the combination of inflation and exchange rate:

> The somewhat higher real short-term interest rate in the early part of 1997 has thus been countered by a weaker real exchange rate. Since the December report, the overall monetary conditions—the impact of interest and exchange rates on demand—have become somewhat more expansionary. (Sveriges Riksbank, 1997b, March, p. 19)[15]

For all the explanations and justifications, however, months of below-target inflation had begun to take a toll. In most surveys of inflation expectations cited by the Riksbank, one- and two-year ahead inflation expectations were below the 2% target. The Riksbank attempted to address the fact that, in 1997, transitional factors would continue to keep headline inflation below underlying inflation and below the target.

These observations led to the conclusion that the Riksbank's "main scenario and its underlying assumptions do not preclude somewhat more stimulatory monetary conditions because inflation *in 1998* is expected to be somewhat under 2 per cent" (Sveriges Riksbank, 1997b, March, p. 5; our emphasis). The Riksbank's looking ahead to 1998 raises a key point: While Swedish monetary policy would ease in response to below-target inflation, letting the target floor stabilize output and prices as we saw in Canada, it would do so only to the extent that current conditions presaged below-target inflation in the future. The Riksbank would not ease policy in response to low inflation if the low rate was due entirely to transitory factors; similarly, monetary policy would not ease in response to mounting unemployment if the predictive relationship between unemployment and inflation no longer held. This strategy should not be interpreted as saying that the Riksbank was unconcerned about real outcomes or about maintaining inflation above the floor of the target range; it does indicate a recognition that the lags of monetary policy imply the need for forward-looking policies.

Through mid-1997, headline CPI inflation fluctuated between 0.0% and 0.2%, and underlying inflation stayed between 1% and 1.5% (by various measures). Both rates were in line with Riksbank forecasts. The many months during which headline inflation had remained below target without inducing a monetary-policy response or sanctions from the government (or, for that matter, without leading to protests from the public or the financial markets) represented a *de facto* shift of policy toward targeting underlying rather than headline inflation. The need to respond only to trend inflation (and not to transitory inflation shocks) in order to carry out a forward-looking policy compelled Swedish policy-makers to match their practice to that of other inflation-targeting countries, despite the differences in declarations. Continuing in this direction, the Riksbank discussed in great detail various measures of underlying inflation in its June 1997 *Inflation Report*. It also warned of the transitory effects that government proposals for tax changes in the Spring Economic Bill were likely to have on headline inflation, preparing the public for the likelihood that monetary policy would not respond to those effects (Sveriges Riksbank, 1997b, June, p. 28).

The prolonged divergence of underlying inflation from headline inflation, which seemed to indicate that one-time inflationary shocks were not being passed through to increases in wages and prices, prompted the Riksbank to ask, "Has the inflation process changed?" Using Phillips-curve estimation, Riksbank researchers analyzed whether the break in household inflation expectations that appeared in their surveys translated into a change in the inflation process.[16] The researchers found that when demand was represented by indicators of an output gap, inflation tended to be overpredicted for the years after 1993; however, "when demand is represented instead by unemployment, the relationship no longer overestimates inflation in the period after 1993" (Sveriges Riksbank, 1997b, June, p. 9). As we mentioned in Chapter 6, Canada also experienced a period of unexpectedly low (below-target-range) rates of both underlying inflation and headline CPI inflation in the 1990s. However, since in Canada low inflation was accompanied by recession (rather than by the combination of GDP growth and rising unemployment experienced in Sweden and in Europe generally), the Bank of Canada took the low inflation as evidence that practices of wage- and price-formation were slow to change, despite the downward shift in inflation expectations.

Key Lessons from Sweden's Experience

Sweden's experience illustrates many of the recurring themes concerning the relationship of flexibility and transparency in the inflation-targeting framework. As in all the other countries studied here, Sweden's adoption of inflation targets was no indication that the central bank was unconcerned about output, employment, and financial stability in the short run. On the contrary, its concern for these aspects of the economy was demonstrated by the long transition from the exchange-rate peg to the inflation target, which effectively served as an escape clause. (Indeed, as with the United Kingdom, if low inflation had been the only goal of Sweden's policy, there would have been little barrier to that country maintaining its ECU peg, or setting it at a different parity.) The replacement of an exchange-rate-based policy that was in direct conflict with domestic economic goals with a more flexible inflation-targeting regime apparently did not damage the Riksbank's credibility, despite the crisis that resulted in the loss of the exchange-rate peg.

The evolution of Sweden's definition of the inflation target demonstrates another aspect of the relationship between transparency and flexibility. From the outset, the Riksbank and the government stated that headline CPI inflation would be targeted, probably reflecting the role of the headline CPI in national wage bargaining. It may have also been a concession to those who felt that a strong, transparent commitment to price stability, perhaps even to a price-level target, was necessary to offset the credibility losses arising from the loss of the peg. Despite its stated intentions, however, the Riksbank did not respond to repeated short-term movements in headline inflation, a policy that amounted to adoption of an underlying or core inflation target. In other words, when faced with the choice, the Riksbank could not bring itself to sacrifice important elements of flexibility to achieve maximum transparency. Instead, Sweden's practice was like that of other inflation targeters, who regularly ignore "special" or "transitory" influences on current inflation rates, so long as they do not affect the forecast of future inflation.

The recognition of these realities by the Riksbank probably accounts for the increased visibility and completeness of the *Inflation Report*, as well as other efforts to inform and educate the public. As in all the other countries we have studied, the transparency achieved by better communication was viewed as an important benefit for policy. In particular, the Riksbank was able to convey that a narrow target definition in the short

run did not conflict with the pursuit of a long-run goal for trend inflation. In this respect, the Riksbank now most resembles the Bank of
Canada, which constantly compares developments in headline inflation
and core inflation, targeting and responding to core inflation in the
short run but asking to be judged on the performance of headline inflation in the long run.

9

Three Small Open Economies: Israel, Australia, and Spain

INFLATION targeting has spread beyond its original proponents to a diverse set of countries. In this chapter, we examine the experiences of three small, open economies: Israel, Australia, and Spain. All three adopted inflation targeting after extended disinflations and even longer histories of inflation. Though they differ along many dimensions, including their degree of development and of integration with the major industrial economies, these countries responded to the challenges of the new policy approach in similar ways. Each achieved historically low inflation rates, while at the same time exhibiting fiscal restraint and managing the transition from exchange-rate pegs to the more flexible approach. Their success supports the view that inflation targeting is a viable strategy in a wide range of economic contexts.

Key Features of Inflation Targeting in Israel, Australia, and Spain

- In all three cases, the transition to inflation targeting was gradual, with no sharp shift in regimes as in New Zealand and the United Kingdom. The precise timing of the Australian move to inflation targeting is particularly difficult to pinpoint. As the policy frameworks of these countries became better defined, however, policy transparency increased, and inflation expectations stabilized.

- All three countries adopted inflation targeting as a means of balancing the uncertainties of their external economic environment, particularly the behavior of the exchange rate, with the need to anchor the public's inflation expectations. Israel and Spain gradually de-emphasized strict exchange-rate bands

---

in favor of a policy that responds to exchange-rate changes only when they are deemed likely to affect domestic prices. Australia chose a "thick point" inflation target rather than a target range and has paid relatively less attention to the behavior of the exchange rate.

- Israel and Spain have chosen to target inflation as measured by the all-items "headline" CPI. Australia's reference inflation series is an "underlying" inflation series that excludes many volatile prices.

- Like all the other countries we have discussed, these three countries chose an inflation goal greater than zero, both at the outset and over the longer term. In Israel, although further disinflation is planned, even a target in the range of 8% to 10% inflation has served to anchor inflation expectations. Once again, there appears to be nothing special about zero inflation as a nominal anchor.

- In Israel, responsibility for setting the inflation target has lain primarily with the Finance Minister, in consultation with the Bank of Israel. Spain took the opposite tack, giving the Banco de España the price stability mandate required by the Maastricht treaty. In Australia, the adoption of inflation targets was a unilateral decision by the central bank.

- Israel and Australia made more explicit statements of the central bank's responsibility for the short-run real effects of monetary policy than did any of the countries considered in the previous chapters. However, none of these three countries instituted explicit escape clauses of the New Zealand sort. Instead, all three adopted a gradualist approach to bringing inflation back to target following a macroeconomic shock.

- Since all three countries have sizable public sectors and pervasive indexation of wages to inflation, the central banks expressed concern about the ability of the wage-bargaining mechanisms to adjust to a low-inflation environment. Unlike the central banks of Canada and New Zealand, which were optimistic from the start, the central banks of these three countries took for granted that wage structures would be slow to change. These three central banks also frequently spoke in support of fiscal consolidation. In emphasizing the importance of labor market flexibility and fiscal policy for macroeconomic outcomes, the monetary authorities attempted to give clear signals to the public about what monetary policy could and could not be expected to achieve.

- To maintain transparency of policy, all three central banks have published regular reports on monetary policy and inflation, provided public testimonies, and encouraged public discussions along the lines of those in other inflation-targeting countries. Their decision to do so is a reminder that a commitment to inflation targeting leads naturally to a commitment to greater public disclosure and explanations. None of the three countries had had such a tradition in the past.

- Both Israel and Spain experienced a brief conflict between their surviving (though looser) exchange-rate targets and their domestic inflation goals. They chose not to respond to short-term exchange-rate fluctuations, however, and managed to keep both inflation expectations and interest rates stable. Australia faced a similar potential for conflict when current inflation and forecast inflation diverged in 1995 in response to a short-run price rise. Keeping its focus on the inflation target, however, the Australian Reserve Bank explained why it chose not to react to the increase. Again, these episodes illustrate that transparency tends to enhance the flexibility and effectiveness of monetary policy in the long run.

ISRAEL

Israel's Adoption of an Inflation Target

On December 17, 1991, the Ministry of Finance and the Bank of Israel jointly announced that CPI inflation would be kept between 14% and 15% during 1992. In each year since, an inflation target has been announced for the following year.[1] The Finance Minister has had primary responsibility for setting the target, usually in consultation with the Bank of Israel.

Israel is unique among the inflation-targeting countries we have studied in at least two ways. First, it is the only country that began targeting inflation when its inflation rate was at double-digit levels.[2] Second, it is the only one of those countries that sets official targets for both inflation and the exchange rate. Reliance on the exchange rate as a guide to policy has diminished over time, however, as the credibility of the Bank of Israel's commitment to price stability has improved and as inflation has begun to come under control.

Israel's movement toward inflation targeting began at a time of macroeconomic crisis. In 1985, under extreme fiscal pressure from the costs of the war in Lebanon and its extensive social safety net, the country was on the verge of hyperinflation. The fiscal deficit was running at an unsustainable rate of 14% of GDP, and (public and private) debt obligations to foreigners were at 80% of GDP.

In July 1985, under the leadership of Bank of Israel Governor Michael Bruno,[3] Israel adopted a major economic stabilization program. In addition to steps designed to control the budget deficit, the government announced an exchange-rate target to serve as a nominal anchor for prices. For the first year, the shekel's exchange rate was fixed against the U.S. dollar; thereafter it was fixed against a currency basket consisting of the currencies of the G5 countries.

The program was remarkably successful. Within a few months, inflation had fallen from annual rates of about 400% to 20%. Moreover, that gain held: Until 1990, inflation in Israel remained in the vicinity of 16% to 18% per year.

But even that rate of inflation was too high to be consistent with a fixed exchange rate for the shekel. As Israeli prices rose, the fixed value of the shekel implied a steady real appreciation of the exchange rate and a loss of competitiveness for the Israeli export sector. Moreover, in order to maintain the fixed exchange rate, the central bank had to intervene frequently in the foreign exchange market, leading to wide swings both in interest rates and in foreign reserves. Occasional devaluations of the shekel, as in January 1987, failed to fully resolve the problem of exchange-rate management, since the real exchange rate remained highly variable and difficult to predict, with consequent damage to trade.

In January 1989, the government decided to let the exchange rate fluctuate within narrow bands, with provisions for intermittent devaluations of the central parity as well. Initially the width of the exchange-rate band was set at 3% on either side of the target; that tolerance was increased to 5% in March 1990. Devaluations of the central parity occurred in June 1989, March 1990, September 1990, and April 1991.

Although the introduction of the bands around the central parity drastically reduced real-exchange rate variability,[4] the periodic realignments of the exchange rate had undesirable side effects, most notably recurrent speculative attacks against the shekel:

> [T]he band was shifted upwards by 6 to 10% every six to eight months. Not only did the new system fail to stop the speculative capital movements, but after March 1991 these even intensified, once it had become clear that under an exchange rate band discrete changes in the exchange rate could still occur. (Ben-Bassat, 1995, p. 21)

Increasingly, monetary policy makers were diverted from inflation control and other macroeconomic objectives by the need to respond to speculative attacks on the shekel. Something had to be done. In December 1991,

> after standing firm against another major speculative attack, through a considerable rise in short-term interest rates, the authorities relaxed the fixity of the central parity rate. Instead, they announced an upward crawl of this rate at a pre-announced pace . . . [U]pon implementing the shift to a crawling band regime the authorities had to determine the upward slope of the band. It was decided that the slope of the pre-announced rate of crawl of the central parity for a given year would be approximately equal to the difference between the authorities' inflation target for that year and a forecast of the average inflation rate for Israel's main trading partners. This is how the *inflation target* became a goal of policy. (Bufman *et al.*, 1995, pp. 172-73, emphasis in the original)

The decision to relate the exchange-rate target to an inflation target was made jointly by the Finance Ministry and the Bank of Israel. It was not considered a major political step at the time. In fact, the inflation target was mentioned only in the second-to-last paragraph of the press release announcing the introduction of a "crawling band" for the exchange rate.

The adoption of an inflation target did not mean that a lost nominal anchor was being replaced (as in the United Kingdom or Sweden), nor was it intended to lock in disinflationary gains (as in New Zealand and Canada). Rather, it seems to have been an attempt to loosen the straitjacket imposed by the fixed-exchange-rate regime on monetary policy once the peg had lowered inflation and had bestowed some credibility on the central bank.

> [I]t is safe to assert that the *explicit inflation target* was not embraced by policymakers because of its own virtues, but rather as an important input to the choice of a specific upward slope for the crawling exchange rate band. It

is perhaps for this reason that the introduction of an explicit inflation target for 1992 was not even noticed by large segments of the public (including economists) in Israel . . . [T]here was no clear perception of the degree of *commitment* by the authorities vis-à-vis the target. It was only gradually, over the years, that the inflation target began to have a life of its own. (*Ibid.*, p. 173, emphasis in the original)

Paying attention to both the exchange rate and inflation was an attempt to balance macroeconomic objectives. In an economy as small and open as Israel's, the exchange rate is a variable that cannot be ignored by monetary policy. We have seen the political and operational difficulties the Reserve Bank of New Zealand encountered when it was perceived as being unconcerned with the exchange rate. Israeli policy-makers apparently decided that exchange-rate stability was too important an objective for the exchange-rate bands to be abandoned altogether. However, the persistence of inflation in the low double-digit range was also a concern; the inflation targets were an attempt to deal with that problem. For the first time, the authorities specified the pace at which progress was to be made in lowering the rate of inflation. At the same time, they hoped that the inflation targets, together with a gradual approach to disinflation, would protect the economy from excessive real costs.

> It was felt that the stability provided by this system, along with the favourable aggregate supply conditions, would allow for gradual reduction of the inflation target and the slope of the exchange rate crawl, perhaps at little or no cost in terms of real output loss . . . [T]here is little public support for an active program to reduce inflation to single-digit Western levels, if such a program is likely to incur real costs in the short run. (Offenbacher, 1996, pp. 61, 63)

Unfortunately, the evidence reveals that disinflation *does* generate real costs, in terms of lost output and jobs, in the short run (see Chapter 10).

Recognizing the political problems associated with disinflation and its burdens, the Bank of Israel chose to take a more open approach with the public rather than trying to conceal its disinflationary intentions. Its hope was that openness and persuasion might encourage more forward-looking behavior on the part of wage- and price-setters and perhaps prompt a movement away from the widespread indexation of contracts. There was little international experience to go on at the time: The only experiments with inflation targeting were of less than two years' duration in New Zealand, and of ten months in Canada. The Bank's decision to link its exchange-rate policy to inflation targets was thus a daring and creative step.

In summary, the Israeli monetary authorities announced an inflation target after some central-bank credibility had been achieved (following the 1985 stabilization), but at a time when further progress toward price stability had stalled. The persistence of double-digit inflation, combined with the commitment to a fixed exchange rate, placed too heavy a burden on both monetary policy and the export sector. The announcement of an inflation target in conjunction with the move toward controlled devaluation of the shekel was meant to discourage speculative attacks and to focus on inflation control. At the same time, it provided the monetary authorities with a framework in which to communicate the intended rate of disinflation to the public. Thus, almost accidentally, the Israeli monetary authorities had found a new, coherent approach to making policy.

The Operational Framework of Israel's Inflation Targeting

The Israeli monetary authorities chose to use all-items CPI in defining the inflation target. Prices of volatile items such as fruit and vegetables are not excluded from that index, nor are mortgage interest costs or the price of apartments. The rationale is that items whose prices are volatile make up about 40% of the CPI, and that indexation of financial and wage contracts to the all-items CPI is still widespread. Moreover, prices and wages have traditionally been linked to the all-items "headline" CPI in Israel. In its policy-making, the Bank of Israel probably puts as much weight on the headline CPI (as opposed to core or underlying inflation measures) as any central bank covered in our study. However, "[d]espite the fact that the CPI was chosen as the target, it does not serve on its own to determine monetary policy, and the three volatile components and underlying inflation are also taken into consideration" (Ben-Bassat, 1995, p. 43). It is interesting that a core-CPI measure of inflation that excludes the prices of housing, fruits, and vegetables was lower than headline CPI inflation in five of the six years following 1992 and was less volatile as well.

Each year Israel announces its inflation target for the following year (in some cases, as late as December). Since monetary policy actions in most countries affect inflation with lags ranging from six months to more than two years,

> it is difficult to determine whether the target indeed reflected a strong commitment by policy-makers, or just a 'realistic' forecast of inflation to be used to calculate the rate of crawl of the central parity exchange rate. This ambi-

guity as to whether the inflation target is really a 'policy target'—meaning
that the authorities are expected to take definitive policy measures to achieve
the target—or a reasonable inflation 'forecast' has accompanied the policy
since its inception. (Bufman *et al.*, 1995, p. 174)

Evidence has recently been presented that changes in the Bank of Israel's
instrument interest rate and in M1 (narrow money) affect inflation relatively quickly, with the main effects occurring within two quarters. If that
evidence is correct, then even short-horizon inflation targets might be
achievable by monetary policy in Israel.[5] In any event, the announcement of the inflation target for 1997 suggested that the target horizon
might be extended to a multi-year framework. "Recently the government
adopted a more rigorous long-term strategy and decided to complete
the disinflation process by the year 2001, with an inflation rate equal to
the level prevailing in the OECD countries" (Frenkel, 1996, p. 53). Starting with the announcement of the 1998 target, this was embodied in a
government commitment to reduce inflation gradually, acknowledging
the lags of monetary policy's effect.[6]

The inflation target for 1992 was formulated as a narrow range, only
1% wide, and the targets for 1993 and 1994 were formulated as point
targets. However, since 1995 targets have been formulated as broader
ranges, with a width of 2% (1996) or 3% (1995 and 1997).

> Setting a band for the inflation target is essential, because the link between
> policy tools and inflation is not stable . . . In the short term, moreover, the
> economy is affected by various shocks—principally on the supply side—which
> also contribute to deviations from the target. In view of these considerations,
> it is evident that setting a specific point cannot be credible. At the same time,
> there is a danger that the public will ascribe credibility only to the upper
> limit of the band, so it should be relatively narrow. (Ben-Bassat, 1995, p. 45)

As we found in earlier case studies, the use of a target range encourages financial markets and the public to focus on the limits of the band
(especially the upper limit), rather than on the central goal. The Israelis
would have preferred to use a point target for inflation, like the Swiss
and the British, but they feared that their control over inflation was too
imprecise to make such a commitment credible.

The practice of announcing targets only for the year ahead has led to
extreme gradualism in the pace of disinflation. As we have mentioned, it
was felt that gradualism was necessary to maintain public support for the
goal of price stability in the face of the real costs entailed by disinflation.
The first target, of 14% to 15% inflation for 1992, was followed by tar-

gets of 10% for 1993, 8% for 1994, 8% to 11% for 1995, 8% to 10% for 1996, 7% to 10% for 1997, and 7% to 10% for 1998.

The setting of the target every year is the result of a decision-making process that takes into account both political and economic factors. The timing of the announcement itself has varied, a practice that probably reduces transparency and increases uncertainty: The 1994 target (a point) was announced as early as July 1993, reflecting a spirit of optimism, while the 1997 target (a range) was announced as late as possible in 1996 (on December 27), reflecting political pressures on the Finance Ministry, and through it on the Bank of Israel.

The method by which the path for the exchange rate is set makes clear that this variable functions to some degree as an intermediate target. Indeed, there are interesting parallels between the determination of the exchange rate path in Israel and of the monetary targets in Germany. As we saw in Chapter 4, Germany's monetary targets are derived in a process that begins with an inflation objective. This objective is linked to assumptions on the rate of growth of potential output and the trend in velocity through the quantity equation (an identity which states that money growth plus the trend in velocity must equal output growth plus inflation), to find the warranted rate of money growth. Similarly, the exchange rate path in Israel (the "rate of crawl" of the peg) is determined by the inflation target plus assumptions on the likely rates of inflation abroad, linked through the purchasing power parity relationship (which states that the depreciation of the Israeli exchange rate must equal the difference between Israeli and foreign inflation rates).[7] At the same time, Israeli monetary policy-makers consider many other factors besides the value of the shekel, just as monetary policy-makers in Germany respond to developments other than those reflected in the growth of the money stock.

A difference in the Israeli and German policy frameworks is that stabilization of the exchange rate in Israel has some independent utility in the eyes of the policy-makers, whereas there are no direct consequences of missing the monetary target in Germany. In particular, the exchange rate affects patterns of trade, and there is the danger of speculative runs if the exchange rate wanders too far from its target. Thus the exchange-rate commitment in Israel may constitute a stronger constraint on policy than are the monetary targets in Germany. Ultimately, however, in Israel as in Germany, monetary policy is driven primarily by the inflation target, which both determines the setting of the intermediate targets and imposes a long-run constraint on policy choices. As in Germany, Israeli policy-makers have become increasingly willing to subordinate the intermediate target (the exchange rate, in Israel) to the inflation objective, and to use information beyond the intermediate target that is relevant to hitting the inflation goal.

Israel's ability to downplay the exchange rate in favor of an approach that targets the "full-information" forecast of inflation (in the sense of Svensson [1997a]) is particularly striking for a country that completed an exchange-rate-based stabilization only a decade before, with the attendant emphasis on exchange-rate stability that such an approach brings. As we have seen, however, the transition from the crawling peg being the sole guide for monetary policy to its being subordinated to the inflation target has been quite gradual since inflation targets became effective in 1992. A consensus has emerged that, as the disinflation proceeds, the exchange-rate targets will be emphasized less and less.

> It can be argued that with the passage of time the Israeli economy moved more and more toward enhanced exchange rate flexibility, and shifted to inflation targets as anchors. A natural continuation of this process would allow for an even larger degree of exchange rate flexibility, *e.g.* in the context of a wider exchange rate band than the one at the present time. (Bufman *et al.,* 1995, p. 189)

The Bank of Israel monitors a variety of inflation series and measures of inflation expectations, which it derives from the comparison of yields on indexed and non-indexed Treasury securities with similar maturities. "The Treasury currently issues non-indexed securities with maturities of up to three years and there is a fairly active secondary market for both non-indexed and indexed securities maturing at various frequencies up to two years" (Offenbacher, 1996, pp. 64-5). The sophistication and depth of the Israeli financial markets enable the Bank of Israel to gather forward-looking private sector information and to conduct sterilized intervention in foreign exchange markets. That may be one reason why Israel has been able to adopt inflation targets despite its borderline status as a developing country in other respects. The Bank of Israel uses various other indicators in forecasting inflation, including asset prices, M1 growth, and indicators of the state of the real economy.

The Bank has not published an official inflation report until very recently (March 1998). It has, however, published a 10-page document every three months titled "Recent Economic Developments," which reports on a broad range of indicators of the state of the economy. This document's seven sections correspond to those of the Bank's *Annual Reports*: main developments, the principal industries, the labor market, foreign trade and the balance of payments, prices, government finances, and money and capital markets. This publication reviews economic developments but does not contain any forecasts or discussions of the effect of those developments on monetary policy. It is likely that this limited reporting over the first years of Israel's inflation-targeting regime increased the public's uncertainty about the Bank's efforts to conduct policy in a forward-looking manner.

The Bank of Israel Law of 1954 specifies several monetary-policy goals, including "(1) the stabilisation of the value of the currency in Israel and outside Israel; (2) a high level of production, employment, national income and capital investments in Israel."[8] Asked whether it was time to review the law, Bank of Israel Governor Jacob Frenkel said:

> Yes, I believe the time has come to review it. At present the law sets us multiple objectives—to increase the standard of living and achieve price stability. The time has come when the objectives should reflect the reality that monetary policy has a comparative advantage in affecting inflation. I would recommend the adoption of Maastricht-style language, where the setting of price stability is the overriding objective. (Frenkel, 1996, pp. 56-7)

The Bank of Israel enjoys a high degree of independence, particularly in the day-to-day conduct of policy. The Governor is appointed for a renewable five-year term of office (as compared to a maximum four-year electoral cycle if a governing coalition survives). The Governor consults with an Advisory Council and an Advisory Committee, which have no managerial authority but serve solely (as their names suggest) in an advisory capacity. Since the adoption of the economic stabilization program in 1985, the Bank has been barred from financing the government deficit. The Governor also acts as economic advisor to the government.

The Finance Minister, acting as a representative of the government, and with the advice and cooperation of the central bank, sets the inflation targets and holds the Bank responsible for meeting them. This is the same procedure followed in Canada, New Zealand, Sweden, and (relatively recently) the United Kingdom. Governor Frenkel has expressed approval of this arrangement: "When set by the government, [the inflation targets] become an integral part of the overall policy objectives for the economy" (Frenkel, 1996, p. 53).

However, the active participation of the Bank of Israel in the government's decision-making process has raised questions about whether this division of responsibility, which is clear in principle, is quite so clear in practice. During the transitional period, when it was sometimes less than evident whether the exchange rate or the inflation target would take precedence, this ambiguity had a certain logic. As in all countries with independent central banks, responsibility for exchange-rate policy in Israel is shared by the Finance Ministry and the central bank, with the decisions about short-run intervention left largely to the Bank. The inflation targets for 1993 and 1994 also were set jointly by the Ministry of Finance and the Bank of Israel, reflecting the close relationship between inflation targets and exchange-rate policy. After the 1994 overshooting of the inflation target, however, target-setting became a politically charged and economically significant decision, especially since it would require a commitment to a path for disinflation; hence, the government began to take a leading role. Regarding the target for 1996, "differences of opinion as to the proper target and as to the role of monetary policy in achieving the target led to the Finance Minister announcing it without the concurrence of the Bank of Israel" (Offenbacher, 1996, p. 63). The target for 1998 (set in July 1997) was discussed by the entire Cabinet, with the lead of the Finance Minister. These developments have settled the question of which entity should set the target, and be held accountable for that decision. One Israeli official summarized the matter as follows:

> A necessary, but not sufficient, condition for improving credibility is for the Ministry of Finance and the Bank to work out an institutional program by which the cabinet formally decides on the ultimate goal of monetary policy and assigns both responsibility and tools to the Bank of Israel for attaining it. (*Ibid.*, p. 64)

Even so, accountability is complicated by the need for constant discipline in fiscal matters on the part of the elected government. In the absence of such discipline, the ability of monetary policy-makers to control inflation without resorting to painfully restrictive measures is undercut. This tension between fiscal policy and monetary policy is common when the focus of monetary policy is on price stability, while the focus of fiscal policy is on other matters. It appears that inflation targeting in Israel, as in Canada and New Zealand, has at least forced the government to acknowledge the effects of government spending on inflation and inflation expectations.

Israel's Experience under Inflation Targeting

Israel's experience with inflation targeting has, on the whole, been successful. (See Figure 9.1 for a history of key macroeconomic indicators for Israel.) With the exception of the large (6%) overshooting of the

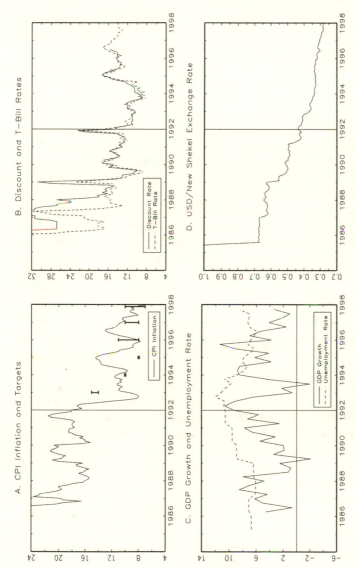

Figure 9.1. Israeli economic indicators. Sources: A) International Financial Statistics of the International Monetary Fund, Bank of Israel; B) International Financial Statistics of the International Monetary Fund; C) International Financial Statistics of the International Monetary Fund; D) International Financial Statistics of the International Monetary Fund

target in 1994, since 1992 the inflation targets have either been met or have been exceeded by less than 1%, and inflation has averaged 10.6% annually. Recent inflation rates have been in the single digits. Even after the target miss in 1994, neither inflation nor inflation expectations appear to have gotten out of control. Nor has the reduced attention to the exchange rate, and the resulting increased flexibility of policy, created problems; indeed, the incidence of speculative attacks on the shekel has declined. Further, the shekel has been consistently hitting the lower (stronger) end of its crawling band, even following repeated widenings of the band and a reduction in the slope of the band's lower boundary (which implies a lower expected inflation differential between Israel and the G-5). In short, Israeli inflation targeting provides a striking example of how monetary policy can be made more flexible with no apparent loss of credibility and effectiveness.

The critical point for the Israeli inflation targeting strategy occurred in 1994. As of 1993, the relative importance of the exchange-rate target and the inflation target was still ambiguous. For example, in that year the Bank of Israel imposed a 3% devaluation of the shekel in order to offset the effects of a reduction in export subsidies, citing its concern for private-sector competitiveness as the reason for its action. Meanwhile, the announcement of the inflation target was buried at the end of a series of announcements relating to changes in the exchange-rate band.

The wording of the inflation target announcement for 1994, however, was far more explicit than in previous years and set an ambitious point target for inflation of 8%. Moreover, for the first time ever, it was clearly the inflation target that determined the exchange-rate target, as the slope of the exchange-rate band was reduced to make it consistent with the inflation objective. Policy-makers also began to respond strongly to the inflation target: The Bank of Israel's instrument interest rate reached a low of 13% in August 1994 but then was raised steadily as it became clear that the inflation target was going to be overshot. By February 1995, the instrument interest rate stood at 18%.

The inflation target of 8% for 1994 was badly overshot, by 6.5%. More important than the target miss, however, was the fact that the Bank sharply tightened monetary policy in response to the higher inflation, despite the fact that the exchange rate was almost precisely on target (at its central parity). Thus, when the two objectives came into conflict, the Bank of Israel made it clear that achieving the inflation target took precedence over maintaining the exchange-rate peg. The Bank's key measure of private-sector inflation expectations—the difference between nominal and indexed government bonds—peaked in November 1994 at an expected inflation rate of 15%, in line with actual inflation. However, perhaps reflecting the Bank's growing anti-inflation credibility, inflation expectations fell swiftly as the Bank moved aggressively on interest rates.

The power of the exchange rate to determine monetary policy was further weakened in 1995 when the exchange-rate band was widened to 14%, at the same time that restrictions on international capital flows were reduced or eliminated. These steps were taken despite a worrisome fiscal expansion that was occurring at the time. The fiscal deficit overshot its target in 1995 (a deficit of 3.2% of GDP versus a target of 2.75%, exclusive of interest payments on the government debt) and missed even more dramatically in 1996 (4.6% versus 2.5%). Reflecting that movement, unemployment fell from 11.2% in 1992 to 6.7% in 1996 despite massive Russian immigration, and the current account deficit increased as the shekel depreciated more slowly than expected.[9] Lax fiscal policy no doubt contributed to a sharp rise in inflation expectations (as measured by the interest-rate differential between nominal and indexed bonds), which peaked again at 15% in July 1996.

Despite these enormous pressures, monetary policy held the line. Interest rates rose, and economic growth slowed in the second half of 1996. By year's end, inflation had overshot its target by only 0.6% (the ceiling of the target range was 10%), and inflation expectations fell in line. The short but consistent record of the Bank's counter-inflationary commitment appears to have limited the damage of an overheated economy without the need for drastic measures, even as the commitment to the exchange rate was being loosened.

Because the fiscal deficit overshootings in 1995 and 1996 were the results of intense political pressures from a variety of sources, there was little support in the cabinet for ambitious inflation goals in the following years. It seemed likely that fiscal policy would be highly expansionary and probably inflationary in 1997, in accordance with a familiar pattern in Israel. As we have mentioned, the Finance Ministry postponed its announcement of the 1997 inflation target until the very end of 1996 and made no secret of the fact that the delay had been caused by a conflict between the Ministry and the Bank over the target. The inflation target of 7% to 10% finally announced by the Finance Ministry was a compromise: Though it held the line on inflation, it required no further disinflation.

Despite this compromise, the existence of the inflation target and the government's commitment to (ultimate) price stability had positive effects. Clearly, with the inflation-targeting regime in place, the Israeli government could not announce a significantly higher inflation target in 1997 than in 1996—let alone forego a target altogether—without draw-

ing attention to its violation of the commitment to stabilize prices. Strenu-
ous political negotiations brought the 1997 deficit down to its target of
2.8% of GDP.

Progress against inflation continued in 1997. The shekel, again, was
repeatedly driven to the strong end of its exchange-rate band; at last it
was announced that the band would be widened from 14% to 28% in
1997, and then to 30% in 1998, while the lower (strong) band's rate of
depreciation would be reduced from 6% to 4%.[10] Monetary credibility
was clearly high and rising. Meanwhile, because of the extremely wide
bands around the central parity, the exchange-rate target was losing some
of its significance as a constraint on monetary policy.

Disinflation is often accompanied by recession, and the Israeli
economy had clearly begun to slow in 1997. In the face of concerns about
rising unemployment, the inflation target was kept unchanged for 1998,
again forgoing the commitment to further disinflation. This time, however, the inflation target was announced in August 1997 and was clearly
the reference point for all other economic policies. As of this writing, in
mid-1998, inflation in Israel is running below the 7% floor of the target
range. It will be interesting to see if the Bank of Israel follows the Canadian example in treating the floor of the target range as being of equal
importance as the ceiling of the range.

By 1998, Israel had completed the transition from the fixed exchange
rate on which it based its stabilization in 1985 to the more flexible and
forward-looking strategy of inflation targeting as practiced in other countries. The potential conflict between the exchange rate and the inflation
targets had been managed without incident but had certainly slowed the
Bank's efforts to win support for further disinflation. In particular, the
explicit recognition of the exchange-rate bands prior to the granting of
primacy to the inflation target gave interest groups such as exporters an
opportunity to comment on monetary policy. The final move toward
putting primary emphasis on inflation thus provided some political insulation for the Bank of Israel, although the Bank has certainly remained
accountable to the government for the effects of its policies.

AUSTRALIA

Australia's Adoption of an Inflation Target

On September 26, 1994, the Governor of the Reserve Bank of Australia
declared, "In our opinion, underlying inflation of 2 to 3 per cent is a
reasonable goal for monetary policy." He continued:

These figures, incidentally, are not intended to define a (narrow) range; rather, they are indicative of where we would like to see the average rate over a run of years. Such a rate . . . is similar to the informal goals of the US Federal Reserve and the Bundesbank, and not dramatically different from the more formal targets in the United Kingdom, Canada and New Zealand. (Fraser, 1994c, p. 21)

The fact that this statement was made in a speech given by then-Governor Fraser to a conference of economists meeting in a holiday resort illustrates the informal character of the Reserve Bank's move toward an inflation target. The lag between a shift of policy toward a strategy focused on inflation control and the formal announcement of an inflation target was not unique to Australia; similar lags occurred in New Zealand and Canada. However, the adoption of an inflation target in Australia was more gradual and incremental than in any of the other countries we have discussed.

Australia's adoption of an inflation target was a unilateral decision on the part of the Reserve Bank; it was not prompted by a change in the legislated mandate of the Bank, as had been the case in New Zealand and Spain. Nor was there any attempt to present the adoption of an inflation target as a joint policy of the government and the central bank, either in the form of a joint declaration, as in Canada and Israel, or as a directive by the government, as in the United Kingdom. Possibly the Governor did not regard the inflation target as a significant departure from the Bank's previous interpretation of its mandate: Section 10 of the Reserve Bank Act of 1959 stipulates only that the objectives of monetary policy are "the stability of the currency of Australia; the maintenance of full employment in Australia; and the economic prosperity and welfare of the people of Australia." In his 1994 speech, Governor Fraser underlined the continuity of policy after the adoption of the inflation target ("Personally, I am quite comfortable with those multiple objectives" [*Ibid.*, p. 19].)

The fact that for a substantial period of time the Reserve Bank chose not to assume the accountability associated with a public commitment to explicit targets makes it hard to identify the precise starting date of inflation targeting in Australia. Unlike several of the other countries we have considered, there was no sudden loss of a nominal anchor that would have forced the Reserve Bank to look for a new strategy. Targeting of money growth (specifically, of the broad aggregate M3) had been abandoned in 1985, and Australia had survived the 1980s without any sense of monetary crisis.

The Reserve Bank's own view is that it has had an inflation target since early 1993.[11] While conceding that there is some ambiguity, we prefer to date the beginning of inflation targeting in Australia as September 1994, with Governor Fraser's statement. That date is consistent with our view that inflation targeting begins with the public announcement of a numerical goal for a specified measure of inflation and a specific horizon. This is not just an academic question, since we would like to be able to distinguish whether the complete inflation-targeting framework, or simply the desire to strengthen control of inflation (which was present in Australia prior to September 1994), is necessary for achieving the maximum benefit. The Australian experience suggests that explicit adoption of the inflation-targeting framework is helpful; as we will see, the response of financial markets to the Reserve Bank's policy moves improved following its actions to increase transparency between 1993 and early 1995.

Monetary-policy actions in Australia resembled those of New Zealand quite closely from at least the latter part of the 1980s, suggesting that economic conditions and policy objectives were quite similar in those two closely related economies. Like New Zealand, Australia considered its inflation rate to be a problem during the late 1980s. For example, between February 1988 and November 1989, the Reserve Bank raised its instrument interest rate, the Cash Rate, from 10% to 18%, despite little change in headline inflation and a decline in underlying inflation. Evidently, the Reserve Bank considered the inflation rate, about 7% at the time, to be unsatisfactory. In a speech given three years later, then-Deputy Governor (subsequently Governor) Macfarlane remarked, "Policy was conscious of the need to capitalize on the 'once-in-a-decade' opportunity to reduce inflation" (Macfarlane, 1992, p. 15). As in New Zealand, though perhaps not to the same degree, there had been a feeling among policy-makers in Australia in the 1980s that years of lax policy and the resultant high rates of inflation and inflation expectations had to be reversed.[12]

However, while New Zealand imposed formal inflation targets at the end of 1989, the Reserve Bank of Australia made no public commitment to a numerical target for inflation. Instead, over subsequent years it tried to convey to the public that the Australian disinflation, which was largely completed by the end of 1991, was the result of a permanent shift in policy objectives and not just a side effect of the 1990-91 recession. In the words of Deputy Governor Macfarlane:

> In our Annual Report released [in August 1992], and its predecessor in 1991, we pointed out that monetary policy in this cycle had developed a more medium-term anti-inflationary focus. It is a difficult story to tell because it is

about a change in emphasis, rather than the abandonment of one policy approach and the embrace of a totally different one . . . The Bank has put out numerous articles, speeches and reports highlighting the costs of inflation, and the opportunities available for a return to low inflation. (Macfarlane, 1992, p. 14)

This effort to build public support for price stability without adopting a new framework for policy is reminiscent of the Bank of Canada's statements in the years between Governor Crow's Hanson lecture and the adoption of inflation targets in 1991 (see Chapter 6).

By early 1993, a number of operational aspects of what was to become Australia's inflation-targeting regime were already in place. In a speech given on March 31, 1993, Governor Fraser said that in his view "if the rate of inflation in *underlying* terms could be held to an average of 2 to 3 percent over a period of years, that would be a good outcome" (Fraser, 1993, p. 2, emphasis in the original). Yet in the same speech, he said:

To my knowledge, no country has reduced its inflation by incantation, rather than by creating slack in the economy. My reading of the evidence is that Australia reduced inflation at least as effectively (in terms of the trade-off between inflation and lost output) as countries like New Zealand, which have an inflation target . . . An inflation target of the narrow '0 to 2 percent' variety would, I believe, do us more harm than good. In particular, such targets are apt to bias policy responses to shocks which impinge on prices. Such shocks are probably best absorbed by changes in *both* prices and activity but if the authorities are bound to a narrow inflation target then virtually all of the shock has to impact on activity. (Fraser, 1993, pp. 3-4, emphasis in the original)

The last two sentences reveal why, at this stage, the policy-makers in the Reserve Bank were unwilling to follow the route of their counterparts in New Zealand and Canada. In their view, the constraint arising from an explicit numerical inflation target would impose inflexibility on policy and would harm the real economy. Further, unlike the cases of New Zealand and Canada prior to target adoption, in Australia the central bank issued no public statements stressing the positive benefits of formal targets; for example, it did not declare that a change in the policy framework might alter the patterns of wage- and price-setting or reduce the output and employment costs of further disinflation.

The concern that an inflation target would limit the Reserve Bank's flexibility seems to have diminished over the following 18 months, however, leading up to the Governor's September 1994 speech. More importantly, it is likely that economic circumstances prompted the Reserve Bank to be more specific about its commitment to maintaining price stability than it had been in the past. While it became clear in early 1994 that the Australian economy was rebounding strongly from the 1990-91 recession, the bond-market downturn over the first half of 1994 sent 10-year government-bond yields from 6.4% to 9.6%. That was twice the increase in long-term yields in the United States, and 1% more than that in New Zealand, suggesting that the Reserve Bank's commitment to price stability was not fully credible among financial market participants. The view that inflation targeting might help to anchor inflation expectations gained increasing credibility.

In his September speech, as we have noted, the Governor declared underlying inflation of 2% to 3% to be "a reasonable goal" for the Reserve Bank's monetary policy. He also discussed in some detail the issues involved in choosing appropriate measures of inflation, as well as the use of indicators and the Reserve Bank's own inflation forecasts in the policy process. Despite Australia's "impressive" inflation record over the previous three years, the Governor cautioned that "we will need to sustain low rates of inflation through the upswing of the current cycle to build real credibility" (Fraser, 1994c, p. 23). While the speech left ambiguous how the Reserve Bank's performance was to be evaluated in the absence of a more clearly defined target horizon, the Bank had nevertheless committed itself to a numerical target for inflation.

The language the Reserve Bank used to describe its inflation target became gradually more specific. In a speech given on March 30, 1995, Governor Fraser mentioned an average underlying inflation of 2% to 3% "over a run of years" as "the Reserve Bank's objective" (Fraser, 1995, p. 22). The word "target" first appears in a statement given by the Governor to the House of Representatives Standing Committee on Banking, Finance and Public Administration on October 19, 1995:

> Like other central banks, we have an inflation objective or 'target' to help guide monetary policy. This is to hold underlying inflation to 2-3 percent on average over a run of years. As we have explained on many occasions, this does not mean that underlying inflation should be between 2 and 3 percent every year; rather, it means that over the cycle the average rate of inflation should be '2 point something.' (Reserve Bank, 1995, November, p. 7)

The time horizon to be used in evaluating the Reserve Bank's performance was now tied to "the cycle," which was not further specified.

In summary, the adoption of an inflation target in Australia was a unilateral decision by the Reserve Bank made after a disinflation had been completed. The adoption of the target was neither prompted by nor accompanied by a change in the Reserve Bank's statute, nor was it subject to any agreement between government and the Reserve Bank. Rather, it was part of a gradual reorientation of monetary policy toward recognizing price stability as its primary goal. The Reserve Bank committed itself to a target at a time when public uncertainty about its commitment threatened to unleash inflation expectations and to damage the price stability that had already been achieved.

The Operational Framework of Australia's Inflation Targeting

To understand the Australian variant of inflation targeting, we might best compare it with the experience of other small, open economies, such as New Zealand, Israel, and Spain. Like those countries, Australia faced the prospect of having its economy buffeted by shocks to the external sector and to the terms of trade. Like them, Australia faced a business cycle driven as much by a large trading partner (the United States) as by domestic factors. Again like these other economies, Australia was trying to consolidate the inflation gains it had made in recent years following a long period in which its commitment to price stability had been perceived as weak.

In sharp contrast to New Zealand's targeting framework, however, the Reserve Bank of Australia emphasized flexibility in all aspects of its operations, from the definition of target to the recognition of its discretion in responding to shocks.[13] The closest analogy may be the Swiss monetary targeting framework (Chapter 4). Like the Swiss National Bank, the Reserve Bank of Australia emphasized the difficulties involved in meeting an exact inflation target range over a short period of time. The Australian target is for a "thick point" target of "around 2-3% over the medium term" (Stevens and Debelle, 1995, p. 82). The inflation rate to which the target refers is in "underlying terms" for the rate of increase in consumer prices. Given the relative independence of the Reserve Bank to set its instruments, and the relatively non-specific commitment to its targets, the overall tone of Australian policy is very similar to the "disciplined discretion" of the Swiss National Bank:

> [The 2% to 3% target] is not a range within which the Bank feels inflation must, or necessarily can, be maintained at all times and under any circumstances. Such a narrow band would in our view be much too ambitious, given the difficulties of short-term forecasting and control of inflation . . .

Given some cyclical variation in inflation and the occurrence of myriad minor shocks affecting prices, some deviations will almost certainly occur. (*Ibid.*)

The Reserve Bank denies that it can specify in advance the conditions under which it would have to deviate from its target (unlike the Reserve Bank of New Zealand), or even that it can be held to its target in the shorter term. As some of the designers of the Australian policy framework state, "This does not represent, in our view, a lesser degree of commitment to 'price stability' as a long-term objective for monetary policy. It reflects, instead, a measure of caution about what Australian monetary policy can claim to be capable of achieving over short periods" (Stevens and Debelle, 1995, p. 82). The Reserve Bank of Australia appears to have drawn much the same interpretation of the New Zealand experience as we did in Chapter 5, that an excessively inflexible pursuit of a strict inflation target in the short term is likely to produce instability in policy and in the economy.

Regarding Australia's choice of a "thick point" rather than a target range, Grenville (1997, p. 147) states

Considering the regular terms-of-trade shocks which Australia experienced, and looking at the history of cyclical fluctuations in inflation in Australia (going back to the period of price stability in the 1950s and 1960s), it was clear that these variations were greater than the 2 per cent in the New Zealand specification.[14]

A striking similarity between the Australian and Swiss monetary frameworks is that Australia managed to acquire a Swiss-like degree of policy discretion and still improve its inflation performance, despite having nothing like the long Swiss record of price stability to draw on.[15]

The Australian target itself, as we have noted, is open-ended (for "a run of years") rather than for a specific horizon. The target has always been set above zero measured inflation. Measurement error, however, has not been featured as an explanation for choosing a target greater than zero. Rather, as in many other countries that have adopted above-zero inflation targets, the rationale has been concern over whether the benefits of continued disinflation for the real economy outweigh the costs when the inflation rate is already very low.[16] Announcement of a relatively low target for inflation in Australia apparently proved sufficient to anchor inflation expectations, with debates over the ultimate amount of disinflation left safely to the future.

The Reserve Bank of Australia does share one operational aspect with New Zealand, in that the target "underlying CPI" series is specifically defined, with many exemptions. The series excludes movements in the prices of fruit and vegetables, petrol, mortgage interest, public-sector goods and services, and "other volatile prices."[17] Since the Reserve Bank of Australia, unlike the Reserve Bank of New Zealand, is not subject to a "hard" band on its target, making the definition of the target series so specific seems a bit incongruous. The Reserve Bank of Australia's practice is closer to the Swiss example of "simple rules, complicated explanations." For example, with regard to the role of the mortgage interest rate in the target series, ". . . there is a need for the Bank to explain clearly what these interest rate effects are, why it abstracts from them for policy purposes, and that there is a requirement that price and wage setters distinguish between headline and underlying inflation rates in their own decisions" (Stevens and Debelle, 1995, p. 84). Where accountability cannot be a mechanical comparison of performance of a series to some standard, because rigid pursuit of that standard is itself harmful, the burden of making clear explanations to the public increases.

The indefinite (medium-term) time horizon for achieving the target implies that the Reserve Bank is concerned about the longer-term average of inflation; there will be no reversals of short-term overshootings or undershootings of inflation in the Australian framework. It appears that the Reserve Bank intends to respond to shocks to the economy as it deems necessary in the short term, without recourse to the "escape clauses" of the New Zealand framework, or even to the required explanations for breaches of the target range in the approach recently adopted by the United Kingdom. Indeed, the Reserve Bank has been more explicit than any other central bank we have discussed in responding to short-run fluctuations in output and employment. As Governor Fraser noted, there never was strong support for making price stability the sole goal of monetary policy:

> There was also a feeling that, taken literally, [shifting to a single goal of price stability] made the task of monetary policy too simple—or simplistic . . . The Bank understood that, for the most part, there would be no conflict between activity and price objectives (and, in fact, activity would be a principal forward indicator of inflation); when there was a conflict (in the case of a supply-side shock, or when a structural reduction in inflation was needed), this could not be resolved by the simplistic expedient of giving an absolute overriding priority to prices. (Grenville, 1997, p. 149)

Once again, this pragmatic tone is reminiscent of the Swiss approach.

As with all the inflation targeters we have considered, Australia's concern for real-side goals is embodied primarily in the gradual adjustment of inflation following a shock to the price level. The Reserve Bank has not specified a time limit for reaching its inflation goal following an unexpected shift in inflation. "[I]n the event of an unanticipated change in inflation . . . there is a commitment to adjust policy settings in such a way as to achieve a return to the 2-3 per cent level as quickly as feasible. What is feasible cannot be predicted in advance—it depends upon the nature of the event, and is a function of, among other things, the slope of the short-run Phillips curve [that is, the unemployment cost of each point of disinflation]" (Stevens and Debelle, 1995, p. 84).

In making its forecast of inflation, the Reserve Bank pays close attention to measures of real economic activity, such as changes in employment, changes in spending, and the like. It also takes into account private-sector inflation expectations and forecasts, as well as current wage settlements. Interestingly, and in contrast to Spain and Israel, the Reserve Bank is not usually responsive to short-term fluctuations in the exchange rate. This attitude is consistent with the Bank's belief that many (though not all) movements of the exchange rate reflect shifts in the terms of trade (that is, the relative price of Australian goods), rather than changes in inflation expectations or business cycles. The assumption is not unreasonable, given Australia's orientation toward commodity exports.

However, the difference between the Australian approach to the exchange rate and that of New Zealand and Canada, two other commodity exporters, is quite marked. Canada and, more recently, New Zealand have adopted as operating guides to policy a "monetary conditions index," or MCI, which combines changes in domestic interest rates and changes in exchange rates (Chapters 5 and 6). Thus monetary policy in Canada and New Zealand reacts fairly vigorously to changes in the exchange rate. To the extent that shifts in the exchange rate do in fact represent changes in the terms of trade, monetary policy should not offset them, as an MCI requires. Clearly, Australia believes itself to be facing a different external environment from that faced by Canada and New Zealand. Whether that belief is correct is ultimately an empirical question; still, it is surprising that such apparently similar economies would differ on this key point. The strengths and weaknesses of using an MCI in the context of inflation targeting are topics worthy of further research.

The primary vehicle for reports on the state of the economy, speeches given by the Governor and Deputy Governors, and occasional research articles is the Reserve Bank's monthly *Bulletin*. Except for the speeches, all articles published in the *Bulletin* are unsigned. Well before 1993, the Reserve Bank was already publishing in every third issue of the *Bulletin* a report titled "The Economy and Financial Markets," divided into sections on "The International Economy" and "The Australian Economy." The latter section included discussions of developments in prices and costs, as well as other measures of economic activity. Since 1993, the Bank has continued to publish a quarterly report on the economy in the *Bulletin,* but the format has changed substantially. That report, which since January 1995 has been called the "Quarterly Report on the Economy and Financial Markets" (henceforth Quarterly Report), usually consists of a section on financial market developments as well as sections on the international economy and the domestic economy. The section on the domestic economy continues to discuss a variety of matters but now includes information on inflation trends and prospects, wholesale prices and margins, labor costs, and inflation expectations. The Financial Markets section deals with developments in international bond and equity markets, monetary policy and short-term interest rates, developments in the banking sector, and foreign-exchange markets.

The shift toward inflation targeting during 1993 and 1994 was accompanied by increased emphasis in the Quarterly Report on forecasts of inflation, from both outside and inside the Reserve Bank, and on current developments in monetary policy. Consumers' one-year-ahead expectations of inflation from the Melbourne Institute Survey were already being published before 1993. Since 1994, the Consensus Forecasts, which reflect the opinions of private-sector forecasting professionals, are discussed as well.[18] Following the first of three consecutive increases in the Cash rate on August 17, 1994 (that is, beginning with the October 1994 issue), the Quarterly Report has explained changes in monetary policy as well. Finally, since April 1995 the Quarterly Report has published the Reserve Bank's official inflation outlook, though in relatively vague terms reminiscent of the Swedish Riksbank's references (before December 1997) to the position of inflation relative to its target.

The Bank also engages in more formal reporting. Since 1991, the Bank's *Annual Report,* which is presented in the budget session of Parliament, has been subject to a hearing by the House of Representatives Standing Committee on Banking, Finance and Public Administration (although at first the Committee seems to have made little use of this opportunity, as reported by Fraser [1993]). When Governor Macfarlane was appointed to succeed Fraser on August 14, 1996, the Treasurer and the Governor-designate released a "Statement on the Conduct of Monetary Policy." In it, the parties agreed that the Governor (designate) will support the release by the Bank of specific statements on monetary policy and the role it is playing in achieving the Bank's objectives. It is intended that these statements will include information on the outlook for inflation and will be released at roughly six monthly intervals. (Reserve Bank of Australia, 1996, September, pp. 2-3)

Accordingly, since May 1997, the Bank has provided the *Semi-Annual Statement on Monetary Policy*. The *Statement* is, in effect, the official inflation report of the Reserve Bank. Though similar in structure to the Quarterly Report, it is much more detailed, about four times as long, and replete with pedagogic devices, such as boxes explaining economic concepts and measurements, as well as numerous historical comparisons of the current state of the economy with previous business cycles. Like the Quarterly Report, the *Statement* starts with an in-depth discussion of the economic situation abroad. The section on domestic economic activity covers developments in households, business, and rural sectors, the balance of payments, and the labor market. Conditions in the credit markets, financial intermediaries, and monetary aggregates are the subject of a section on the financial sector. The *Statement* concludes with a section on inflation trends and prospects. Several measures of inflation, import and producer prices, deflators, and trends in labor costs are surveyed, as are numerous measures of inflation expectations. The Reserve Bank's own inflation outlook is more fully covered here than in the Quarterly Report, in that the factors shaping the outlook, as well as the upside and downside risks, are explained in some detail. However, the *Statement,* like the Quarterly Report, does not provide a quantitative inflation forecast. Instead, it provides only a general assessment of where inflation is likely to be relative to the target over a horizon that is not very clearly specified.

An important aspect of the *Statement* is that it contains a strong endorsement by the government of the inflation target and emphasizes the independence of the Reserve Bank to conduct monetary policy in pursuit of the target. This show of support, together with the prominence accorded the now twice-yearly formal appearances before the Parliamentary Committee, has added legitimacy to the monetary policy framework in Australia.

Australia's Experience under Inflation Targeting

In Australia, as in New Zealand, the critical episode in monetary policy since 1993 was the tightening of monetary policy in 1994, and the rise in inflation that followed in 1995.

Macroeconomic conditions in Australia and New Zealand were remarkably similar during the early 1990s (compare the panels in Figure 9.2 to their counterparts in Figure 5.1). GDP growth rates and the increases in unemployment rates in the two countries between 1990 and 1992 were almost identical, and after 1990 the rates of both headline inflation and underlying inflation in the two countries had moved closely together as well. Also similar were financial market indicators (such as the nominal exchange rate and long-term interest rates) and monetary policy, as reflected in short-term interest rates.

By the end of 1993 Australia's recovery from the 1991 recession had gained ground, with real GDP growth accelerating toward 4%, in line with the Reserve Bank's expectations. As the unemployment rate remained in the vicinity of 11% throughout 1993, the Reserve Bank's assessment was that real growth of 4% would have to be sustained to restore unemployment to a more acceptable level. Given the amount of slack in the economy, the only risk of inflation at this stage came from external factors: The Australian dollar had fallen by 20% in trade-weighted terms over the two years to September 1993, to the point that "the Reserve Bank intervened heavily in the foreign exchange market at the time, and also considered raising interest rates to support the exchange rate" (Fraser, 1994b, p. 21). In the event, the Australian dollar recovered, and the Reserve Bank held its instrument Cash Rate stable at 4.75%.

The data available at the beginning of 1994 indicated that the recovery was increasingly broad-based, and although there was still slack in the economy, the rate of unemployment was expected to fall during 1994. According to the January 1994 Quarterly Report, the depreciation of the Australian dollar before September 1993 was "the main source of inflationary pressure on the cost side" (Reserve Bank of Australia, 1994, January, p. 8), while growth in labor costs remained subdued. The Reserve Bank's benign view of the prospects for inflation was shared by the markets in early 1994. The yields of 90-day bills had edged down to 4.8%, and futures prices for those bills indicated that no tightening was expected over the coming months. Yields on 10-year government bonds fell to 6.4% in January.

Then, following the U.S. Federal Reserve's tightening move on February 4, 1994, the assessment of future inflation in the bond market changed quite suddenly and dramatically. During February and March, Australian 10-year bond yields rose from 6.4% to 8%. The Reserve Bank did not share the financial markets' view that the risks of higher infla-

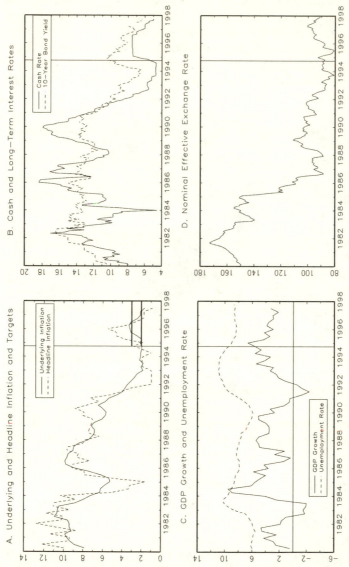

Figure 9.2. Australian economic indicators. Sources: A) Main Economic Indicators of the Organisation for Economic Cooperation and Development, Reserve Bank of Australia; B) Main economic indicators of the Organisation for Economic Cooperation and Development, Reserve Bank of Australia; C) Main Economic Indicators of the Organisation for Economic Cooperation and Development; D) Bank for International Settlements database.

tion had increased. In a speech on March 30, 1994, Governor Fraser listed several reasons why low inflation could be expected to persist, even though growth was accelerating a bit above 4% (Fraser, 1994a). One of the reasons he gave—the closer integration with world markets of the Australian economy following the reform measures of the 1980s— is reminiscent of views expressed at about the same time by the Reserve Bank of New Zealand, that earlier structural reforms might have raised the sustainable growth rate of the economy.

By early July, however, the Reserve Bank began to prepare the ground for a tightening of policy, while at the same time defending its current policy stance. Its outlook had changed neither with respect to output growth, which was still expected to be in the 4% to 5% range over the next 12 months, nor with respect to inflation, which was forecast to remain in the 2% to 3% range over the same horizon. "The economy is not about to burst out of its current 4 to 5 percent growth range, and there are few signs that wage or other cost increases are accelerating. Indeed, there is every reason to believe that current growth and inflation rates will be sustained in 1994/95" (Fraser, 1994b, p. 22). However the financial markets clearly disagreed with that assessment, with 10-year bond yields having risen by 3.2% between February 3 and June 30, compared to 1.6% in the United States and, significantly, only 2.1% in New Zealand.

> The higher-than-average rise in bond yields in Australia appears to reflect judgments by the market that the already fast-growing Australian economy could be pushed even faster by rising commodity prices, generating inflationary pressures which, in the eyes of the market, the authorities would be slow to respond to. While the stronger outlook for Australia and the world economy suggests that bond yields should be higher today than they were, say, a year ago, the authorities in Australia have indicated that they do not share the judgment about the outlook for inflation which is implicit in the rise in Australian bond yields. (Reserve Bank of Australia, 1994, July, p. 15)

The yields on 90-day bills had risen to 5.8% by late June, and the yield implied by prices for September futures on 90-day bills had risen to 6.4%, reflecting the market's expectation that a tightening of monetary policy was about to occur. The absence of either a clearly formulated inflation target or an exact statement of how the Reserve Bank expected inflation to develop contributed to uncertainty about the future course of inflation.

On August 17 the Reserve Bank finally began to tighten policy, raising the Cash Rate by 0.75% to 5.5%. "Although the timing of the move has been influenced by the latest rise in U.S. interest rates, the move itself is driven by the marked turnaround in Australia's domestic economic conditions" (Reserve Bank of Australia, 1994, September, p. 23).

In its October 1994 Quarterly Report, the Reserve Bank noted that "cyclical price pressures can be expected to increase as spare capacity in the economy is taken up" (Reserve Bank of Australia, 1994, October, p. 1), but again it gave no indication of where it expected inflation to go. Real GDP had grown by 4.3% in the year to June, while underlying inflation had remained steady at 1.9% over the same period. Unemployment had been falling since November 1993, from 11% to 9.5%. There had been little market reaction following the August 17 Cash Rate hike, which had been widely anticipated. Yet by the time of the October Report, 90-day bill yields had risen from 5.7% to 6.4% "as markets began to price in the possibility of a further tightening of policy" (*Ibid.*, p. 11). Ten-year bond yields, which had fallen to 9.2% following the August 17 move, had risen to 10.3% by the end of September, bringing the rise since February 3 close to 4%.

The watershed came in the fourth quarter of 1994, as the Reserve Bank raised the Cash Rate twice, on October 24 and on December 14, by 1% each time, to 7.5%. In its statement following the December 14 rise, the Reserve Bank acknowledged that

> This further tightening has occurred rather sooner than some might have expected, basically because of evidence that the economy overall has been growing more strongly than earlier thought . . . To date, price and wage increases remain well contained. In underlying terms, consumer prices are increasing by about 2 percent . . . Looking ahead, however, this reassuring situation could not be expected to continue at current rates of growth. (Reserve Bank of Australia, 1995, January, p. 27)

Both tightenings had been anticipated, as reflected in the rise in the yield of the 90-day bills above the Cash Rate well before the Reserve Bank's moves. Ten-year government bond yields held steady around 10%. However, the Reserve Bank's inflation outlook in the aftermath of the tightenings, as reflected in the January 1995 Quarterly Report, remained opaque.

In its April 1995 Quarterly Report, the Reserve Bank finally furnished its forecast of inflation over the coming year. That practice has persisted. Although there were tentative signs that the Cash Rate increases had had some moderating effect on economic activity, and although underlying inflation had remained around 2%, developments in the financial markets continued to be inauspicious. Ten-year bond yields fluctuated between 10% and 10.5%, and the Australian dollar fell 11% over the first quarter relative to the currencies of its trading partners. The Reserve Bank conceded that the fall in the Australian dollar

> [in] part also clearly reflected concerns specific to Australia. Other currencies which often move in tandem with the Australian dollar—namely, the New Zealand dollar and the Canadian dollar—were stronger during the quarter; in both cases, they were underpinned by further rises in official interest rates .... Of more direct relevance to Australia, [bond] yields in Canada and New Zealand fell sharply to 8.5 percent and 7.9 percent respectively. (Reserve Bank of Australia, 1995, April, p. 17)

The retreat of the Australian dollar was in no small measure due to the deterioration of the current account, which in turn reflected the strong growth in domestic demand during 1994. At any rate, the Reserve Bank expressed the concern that "the underlying rate of inflation is expected to move upwards—and could rise above 3 percent—during 1995" (*Ibid.*, p. 15).

These developments posed a challenge to the Reserve Bank's policy strategy. The advantage of the Reserve Bank's "soft" approach to inflation targeting was that, so long as the rise of underlying inflation above 3% was considered temporary, it need not elicit a policy response.

> Prospective developments on inflation owe more to the inherent dynamics of the business cycle than they do to any loss of resolve on the part of the authorities to maintain low inflation. This cyclical variation in inflation, as well as the fairly wide margin of uncertainty around forecasts of inflation, are among the reasons why the Bank has eschewed a narrow, hard-edged inflation target, preferring instead to focus on keeping the average rate of underlying inflation to 2 to 3 percent over a run of years. Monetary policy will continue to be directed towards maintaining that outcome. (*Ibid.*, pp. 15-16)

The problem inherent in this approach, however, was how to convince the public that there was no need to tighten policy further, even as GDP growth continued high and the exchange rate was weakening rapidly. Possibly, by this point, the Reserve Bank also saw a link between the superior performance of the Canadian and New Zealand currencies and bond markets and the greater emphasis those countries had put on communicating the stance of their monetary policy.

The expected rise in underlying inflation set in during the next two quarters. Underlying inflation rose from 1.9% (measured year-on-year) in March to 2.5% in June and 3.1% in September. By that time, however, the Reserve Bank had apparently been successful in convincing the public of the temporary nature of the increase; its shift to a more open policy, closer in spirit to that of other inflation targeters, appeared to be having an effect. Yields on 10-year government bonds began to fall, from just below 10% at the end of March to 9% by the end of June, and to 8.5% by the end of September. The fall in long-term interest rates came amid increasing signs that the policy tightening during 1994 was slowing real GDP growth to below 5%. By late June, 90-day bill yields had fallen to 7.5%, the same as the prevailing level of the Cash Rate, indicating that for the first time in over a year the markets did not expect any further tightening of policy. Furthermore, after stabilizing during the second quarter, the exchange rate regained during the third quarter almost the entire ground that it had lost during the first, suggesting that the current account deficit had peaked.

The gradual downward trend in the financial markets' inflation expectations, as reflected in long-term yields, differences between the yields of indexed and non-indexed bonds, and surveys of private sector forecasters, continued into 1996. The decline in bond yields came to a temporary halt in February, largely in response to developments abroad, in particular the assessment that the U.S. interest rate cycle had bottomed out. Between January 18 and April 9, 1996, Australian 10-year bond yields rose by 85 basis points, to 9%. Significantly, however, in contrast to early 1994, this time Australian bond yields rose less than yields in New Zealand. Moreover, in April, for the first time since 1990, the differential between Australian and New Zealand bond yields closed, and from June onward Australian yields fell below those in New Zealand.

The Reserve Bank predicted (accurately, as it turned out) in its January 1996 Quarterly Report that underlying inflation would rise beyond its September 1995 value of 3.1% before moving back toward the 2% to 3% range in the second half of 1996. Despite this, and despite the trend in inflation expectations, the Cash Rate was kept at 7.5% for the first half of 1996. The main source of concern for the Reserve Bank was the high rate (5% to 6%) at which wages were rising.

> Clearly, these [wage increases] will have to come down as they are inconsistent with the low-inflationary world we now live in. A stronger exchange rate, or some squeezing of profit margins, would help to cushion final product prices temporarily from higher labour costs, but on-going wage increases of 5 percent or more would not be consistent with holding inflation to an average of between 2 and 3 percent. (Macfarlane, 1995, p. 13)

The Reserve Bank made clear that it would accept the present wage increases as "bygones" and would not try to reverse them by tightening policy further. However the Bank was equally clear that it was determined to prevent such wage increases from becoming the norm.

As wage growth moderated to around 4% by July, and the June figure showed that underlying inflation, at 3.1%, had peaked in the previous quarter, the Reserve Bank reduced the Cash Rate by half a percentage point, to 7%. Four more reductions of 50 basis points each would follow over the next twelve months. Underlying inflation passed through the 2% to 3% target range in September before falling below the "thick point" in June 1997 to 1.7%. Throughout 1996, GDP growth remained moderate at 2.8% percent, and the unemployment rate remained around 8.5%, unchanged from its level in mid-1995. With another brief interruption in early 1997, yields on Australian government bonds continued their downward trend, falling below 7% in July 1997. By the end of that month, the yield differential between Australian and U.S. 10-year government bonds had narrowed to 35 basis points, while New Zealand bonds bore yields 30 basis points higher than Australian bonds.

Overall, Australia's approach to inflation targeting moved toward international norms rather slowly, with little emphasis at first on communication, transparency, and accountability. Increasingly, though, the Reserve Bank became more explicit about its forecasts and its objectives. That movement appears to have paid off in terms of controlling inflation expectations, particularly as reflected in bond markets, and in helping to maintain a low and stable rate of inflation.

SPAIN

Spain's Adoption of an Inflation Target

The Governor of the Banco de España announced an inflation target for Spain in his address to the Spanish Parliamentary Committee on Economic Affairs on November 28, 1994.[19] The announcement was made in compliance with the Law on the Autonomy of the Banco de España, which had been adopted on January 1 of that year and had come into force on June 2. The adoption of an inflation target had been a unilateral decision by the Governing Council of the Bank, in accordance with Article 7 (2) of the Law, which states, "The Bank shall define and implement monetary policy with the primary objective of achieving price stability," and with Article 8, which states, "The Bank shall formulate monetary policy by establishing, as appropriate, intermediate objectives for rates of growth of monetary aggregates or for interest rates, or by using other procedures as it deems necessary."[20]

In a narrow sense, the adoption of an inflation target was a direct consequence of the enactment of the Law. In a broader sense, however, three developments had led to the target adoption. First, the Spanish government, as a signatory to the Maastricht Treaty on European Union, was obliged to grant the Bank autonomy at some point prior to European Monetary Union (EMU). The Law, however, went beyond granting independence of the Bank from government influence as required under the Maastricht Treaty; it laid down, in the articles cited above, the Bank's responsibility to define a framework in which to pursue its objectives—in particular, price stability. Second, the Spanish peseta had remained inside the Exchange Rate Mechanism (ERM) of the European Monetary System, despite successive devaluations following the September 1992 crisis. The widening of the bands for currency fluctuations inside the ERM to 15% following the July 1993 crisis, however, had prevented the ERM commitment from functioning as a nominal anchor, as it had done since the peseta's entry into the ERM in June 1989. Thus, some new means of anchoring the price level and expectations appeared necessary. Finally, there was mounting evidence of instability in the relationship between nominal income and liquid assets held by the public (given the Spanish acronym "ALP"), the broad monetary aggregate for which the Bank had set annual monetary targets since 1984. As in many other countries, instability in the relationship between money aggregates and income created pressure to replace an approach based on the use of money growth as an intermediate target with an approach that used more complete information to target the goal variable directly.

Since 1978, the Bank had been setting targets for the growth rate of the monetary aggregate ALP. Instability in the demand for ALP, due in part to the rapid development of the Spanish financial sector in the mid-1980s, led the Bank to choose successively broader target ranges for the growth of this aggregate, thereby rendering the targeting procedure nearly meaningless. Despite the peseta's entry into the ERM in June 1989, the Bank continued to set annual targets for the growth of ALP. However, any conflict between adherence to the monetary targets and the exchange-rate peg was to be resolved in favor of the latter, effectively reducing ALP to an information variable rather than a target.

> [O]rderly movements in interest rates, consistent with exchange rate stability, were the priority of monetary policy. Only in the medium run, and in so far as the exchange rate offered sufficient scope, were monetary policy mea-

sures adopted to aim at approaching the target path for ALP. In this setting, the period 1989-93 saw the domestic and external strands of monetary policy pose considerable conflicts and dilemmas regarding the objectives to pursue. (Ortega and Bonilla, 1995, p. 52)

So, as in the case of Israel after its stabilization, maintenance of the exchange-rate peg became a dominant concern of Spanish monetary policy-makers after 1989.

The exchange rate remained a policy objective after 1994, although, as noted, the much wider bands around the central parity reduced the degree to which the exchange rate constrained policy. The introduction of the inflation target, as in Israel, provided an alternative nominal anchor. Article 11 of the Law defined exchange-rate policy as the domain of the government, with the proviso that it "must be compatible with the objective of price stability." Without a specified inflation numerical target and time horizon, however, the meaning of "compatibility" remained unclear. That put a limit on the Bank's accountability.

At the time the target was adopted, the recovery of the Spanish economy from the 1993 recession (which had been induced by high European interest rates after German reunification) was gathering momentum. Real GDP growth, above 2% during 1994, was rising (see Figure 9.3, Panel C). CPI inflation had reached a low point at 4% in March 1993 from a high of 8% in 1989; between 1989 and 1995 it fluctuated between 4% and 5% without moving further downward (Figure 9.3, Panel A). The peseta had been devalued three times between September 1992 and May 1993, and between January 1993 and July 1994 short-term interest rates had been cut almost in half, from 14% to 7.35% (Figure 9.3, Panels B and D). Clearly, however, the commitment to price stability had some credibility, since the Spanish inflation rate did not rise following those devaluations, nor did inflation expectations escalate.

Nonetheless, the Bank was clearly concerned that inflationary expectations might rise soon, a development that would threaten its medium-term objective of a significant reduction in inflation. In particular, it worried that the slight improvement in CPI inflation during the closing months of 1994 might be swamped by a rise in VAT and excise duties, which was to take effect January 1, 1995. As in Canada, the announcement of an inflation target was timed to convey the one-time nature of the effect of the VAT increase on inflation to prevent an increase in inflation expectations. If there were no reaction by wage- and price-setters to the rise in inflation, a response that would mitigate the longer-term effects of the increase in the VAT, there would accordingly be no

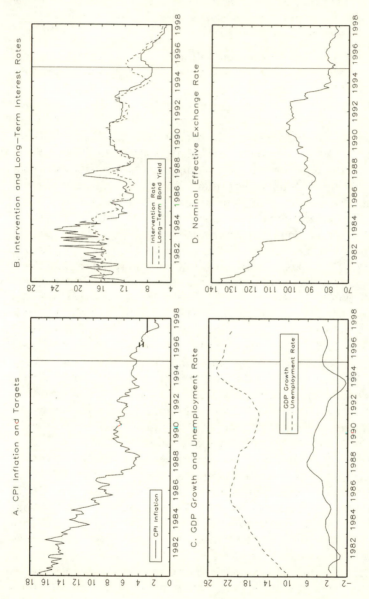

Figure 9.3. Spanish economic indicators. Sources: A) Bank for International Settlements database, Banco de España; B) Bank for International Settlements database; C) Main Economic Indicators of the Organisation for Economic Cooperation and Development; D) Bank for International Settlements database.

need for the Bank to tighten monetary policy. At the same time, the Bank professed uncertainty as to how effective the new framework would be in keeping inflation from rising.

> [T]he widely satisfactory result of direct inflation-targeting strategies in other countries had only been observable during the downward phase of the cycle, there being no experience of their effectiveness in controlling inflation in an economic upturn. As the Spanish economy was in a process of recovery, it was not known to what extent the introduction of [an inflation target] could adequately confront the inflationary risks proper to the foreseeable firming of economic activity. (Banco de España, 1995a, p. 17)

Of course, as we saw in Chapter 4 (Germany and Switzerland), Chapter 7 (United Kingdom), and Chapter 8 (Sweden), there were abundant precedents for central banks to announce inflation targets not only in the face of looming one-time shocks to the price-level, but even when the intended next move in interest rates was downward. What Spain shared with the other targeters was the difficult decision of whether to adopt targets during a slackening of inflation, when they were sure to be met; or whether instead to adopt them at a time when their ability to constrain expectations and the second- and third-round effects of a shock to the price level would be put almost immediately to the test.

The arguments in support of adopting an inflation target were consistent with the Law's stipulation that price stability be the primary objective of monetary policy. The Bank was charged with the task of formulating the most suitable framework for achieving that objective. In view of the increasingly unreliable relationship between the money aggregates and income, further reliance on monetary targets was seen as harmful to the transparency of policy and decreasing operational utility. By contrast, "the setting of direct objectives in terms of prices involves binding the [operational] objective of monetary policy to the statutory objective, which may help to increase the transparency and credibility of the central bank's actions" (Ortega and Bonilla, 1995, p. 50). The Bank was clearly aware that it was forsaking an intermediate target, and that the exchange-rate commitment, though relevant, was not going to replace it. Rather, the inflation forecast would be the guide to policy, and thus the anchor for expectations.

To summarize, Spain adopted inflation targeting in response to institutional changes in the status of the Bank, in turn brought about by the government's determination to comply with the Maastricht Treaty. Adoption of an inflation target came after the exchange-rate commitment had ceased to be a binding constraint on monetary policy, and after monetary targeting had become unreliable as a guide to achieving price stability. The new approach was also adopted at a time when the Bank was concerned that inflation expectations were about to pick up, in response both to the recovery of the Spanish economy and to the first-round effects of an increase in indirect taxes on inflation. In short, other than the Maastricht commitments, the motivation for target adoption was analogous in nearly all respects to that in New Zealand, Canada, the United Kingdom, and Sweden.

The Operational Framework of Spain's Inflation Targeting

The November 1994 announcement of the inflation target specified that the medium-term objective of monetary policy was "a gradual and stable reduction in the inflation rate, measured in terms of consumer prices, to less than 3% over the course of the next three years" (Banco de España, 1995b, January, p. 12). The measure of inflation chosen was the 12-month percentage change in the all-items CPI, which includes volatile components, interest-rate effects, tax effects, and the like. In practice this means that, as in Israel, the Bank has chosen a simple target definition with the likelihood that complicated explanations of deviations from the target will be needed. In introducing the target, however, the Bank observed that factors out of its control, such as fiscal policy and aggressive wage-setting, might affect inflation outcomes.[21]

By 1997, the announcement that inflation was to be below 3% had come to mean that 3% was to be treated as a strict ceiling for inflation— a requirement that, if taken literally, would leave little scope for policy flexibility or control error. The "hard" upper limit creates a difficult dilemma for the Bank: If the policy-makers try to avoid overshootings by targeting inflation at a level below the ceiling, they are being less than honest with the public about their intentions. But if they try to meet the target, they are likely to overshoot the ceiling with some frequency.

The Bank did not confront these issues immediately. Citing the VAT increase effective January 1, 1995, the Bank chose not to set any target for 1995 (a tactic that was employed by Canada and Sweden in their transitions to inflation targeting). But even a target pushed into the future requires that a transition path from current levels of inflation be specified. The Bank suggested that

> By early 1996, once the impact of VAT has been absorbed, the 12-month growth rate of the CPI should be in a range of 3.5% to 4%. From this posi-

tion it could advance more rapidly towards the medium-term objective. (Banco de España, 1995b, January, p. 12)

In January 1995 inflation was 4.3%, so if there was no significant pass-through to inflation from the VAT increase, those levels looked attainable. Even though the Bank was proposing to lower the inflation rate by less than 1.5%, apparently it still regarded a gradual approach as desirable. In December 1996 the Bank extended the target horizon into 1998:

> The specific objective is to place the twelve-month rate of [CPI inflation] close to 2% in the course of 1998. To attain this goal, the twelve-month rate of inflation should, at end-1997, be running at close to 2.5%, making it possible thereafter to converge progressively towards the medium-term target set. (Banco de España, 1997b, January, p. 7)

As we have mentioned, Spain's inflation target seems to differ from those of New Zealand, Canada, and the United Kingdom in that it coexists with an exchange-rate target, reflecting Spain's membership in the ERM. That distinction is more apparent than real, however. While the exchange-rate commitment was not made subordinate to the inflation target at the start, it quickly took on a secondary role (as in the case of Israel). Spain's membership in the ERM does not immediately provide an intermediate target for monetary policy, given the width of the ERM bands. If Spain follows the convergence criteria for inflation laid down in the Maastricht Treaty, as it has through the time of this writing, it is hard to imagine that the exchange rate could wander outside the 15% band. As we will see, so far there has been only one instance in which the inflation target and the exchange-rate goal have come into conflict.

The subordination of the exchange rate to the inflation target is consistent with the emerging consensus in Europe:

> [R]ecent years have taught that exchange rate stability, which is a key objective both per se and because of its contribution to nominal stability, can but be attained in a stable manner as a consequence of economic policies that are consistent overall with [the objective of price stability]. (Banco de España, 1994a, p. 20)

Spain's monetary policy strategy is in any case finite, as control of monetary policy will be handed over to the European Central Bank in January 1999 (*de facto* in May 1998, when the official parities are set). We will return to the implications of inflation targeting for the European Central Bank in Chapter 12. For Spain, given the finite time until EMU, and the lags of monetary policy, the only Bank actions likely to matter have already been taken as of this writing. So its inflation targeting can already be pronounced successful in keeping inflation expectations on a downward path through the 1990s. That achievement is impressive, because in 1995 it was not evident that Spain would make it into the first round of EMU; so it was necessary that the strategy work.

The Bank uses various sources of information in addition to the CPI and its components. It draws on producer prices, prices of agricultural products, import prices, wages, unit labor costs, and corporate profit margins. It also considers various measures of aggregate demand, including a measure of the impact of fiscal policy on inflation. By the Bank's own description, the forecast continues to include subjective evaluation, but an ALP growth rate of less than 8% is still used as a primary benchmark, a remnant of the earlier money-growth targeting.[22] In fact, Spain is the only inflation targeter to identify explicitly a primary indicator for its inflation forecast, whether monetary or other. The money-market overnight interest rate is the operational target for changes in monetary policy, but the actual instrument used by the Bank is its so-called "intervention" interest rate, the rate on 10-day repos. These practices are similar to those used prior to the shift from targeting ALP to targeting inflation.

Details of the Bank's communication and accountability are covered by Article 10 of the Law. Paragraph 1 requires that

> At least once a year, and whenever significant changes occur, the Bank shall make public the general objectives of the monetary policy that it has set and the procedures that it plans to use in its implementation.

Paragraph 2 stipulates that

> The Bank shall regularly inform parliament and the government of its objectives and the implementation of monetary policy, and must report, as relevant, on the obstacles to the maintenance of price stability it encounters.

The Governor, beginning with the November 1994 address in which he announced the inflation target, has appeared annually before the Spanish Parliamentary Committee on Economic Affairs to describe the monetary-policy objectives for the coming year. That degree of formal legislative accountability is relatively substantial by European standards for a legally independent central bank (compared, for example, with the practice in Germany and Switzerland). On the other hand, the Bank clearly has more independence in setting its inflation targets than the Bank of England or the Swedish Riksbank; in this regard it is more like the Bundesbank or the Bank of Canada.

The Governor's annual address is reprinted in the January issue of the Bank's monthly *Boletín Económico* (which appears quarterly in English as the *Economic Bulletin*). Both the *Annual Report* and the monthly *Bulletin* have been upgraded in the extent and accessibility of their coverage of monetary policy. Moreover, although not required by the Law, the Bank has published an *Inflation Report* (in both Spanish and English) every six months since March 1995. The *Inflation Report* follows a four-part format, beginning with an overview. The second part discusses developments in the CPI and its components, with particular emphasis on a "core-CPI"-type series called "services and non-energy processed goods index," or IPSEBENE by its Spanish acronym. The attention given to this series, despite the official commitment to targeting the headline CPI inflation rate, does not seem to have confused the public. Developments in producer prices, agricultural product prices, import prices, and various sectoral deflators are reported as well. The third part of the *Report* covers external factors as well as the components of aggregate demand; supply-side developments, including measures of capacity utilization and labor-market tightness; and monetary and financial indicators such as interest rates and interest-rate differentials between Spain and other countries.

The only part of the *Report* that contains any forward-looking information at all is the fourth, titled "Monetary Policy and the Inflation Outlook." However, even this part presents no precise forecasts for any variables. Instead, the Bank's views are summarized by a one-sentence, qualitative statement regarding the efforts that will be required to meet the inflation target, much in the manner of Australia and of Sweden prior to December 1997. This statement is followed by a detailed discussion (again without numbers) of the upward and downward risks to the inflation outlook. Also absent are any statements of the lag with which monetary policy is expected to affect inflation. Given the brief time in which the Bank's activities are likely to have an impact on the Spanish economy, and the possibility that the Bank will disclaim responsibility for future outcomes once the transition to the euro begins, this last omission is surprising. The absence of both an explicit inflation forecast and a timeline for inflation reduction complicates any outside monitoring of the Bank's current policy actions.[23]

As mentioned above, Article 7 (2) of the Law specifies:

The Bank shall define and implement monetary policy with the primary objective of achieving price stability. Without prejudice to this objective, monetary policy shall support the general economic policy of the government.

The Preamble of the Law points out that "the new law balances the provisions of the Treaty on European Union with the mandates of our Constitution." It continues:

> Article 7, for example, which defines the objectives towards which monetary policy should be directed, sets price stability as a priority objective, which is an essential, though admittedly not the sole, element of the "economic stability" referred to in article 40 of the Constitution.

This passage suggests that, as in all other inflation-targeting countries, real economic developments, and in particular the costs of disinflation in terms of lost output and jobs, are not to be ignored.

The basic thrust of the Law is to guarantee the autonomy of monetary policy from government interference. The Governing Council of the Bank, which is the policy-setting body, consists, according to Article 20, of ten members, eight of whom are allowed to vote on matters of monetary policy: the Governor, the Deputy Governor, and six elected council members. Articles 24 and 25 specify that the Governor is to be appointed by the government for one non-renewable six-year term, and that the Deputy Governor is to be appointed by the government, following a proposal by the Governor, for a simultaneous six-year non-renewable term. The six elected council members are appointed by the government "following a proposal by the Economy and Finance minister, after consultation with the governor of the Bank" for a four-year term and may be reappointed once. These eight members of the Governing Council can be dismissed by the government

> due to permanent incapacity to perform their functions, serious lack of compliance with their obligations, incompatibility [*i.e.*, conflicts of interest] that may have arisen during the term of office, or prosecution for deliberate crimes. (Article 25 [4.d])

No specific performance clauses of the sort contained in the Reserve Bank of New Zealand Act are included.

Spain's Experience under Inflation Targeting

Since inflation targets were adopted in Spain, inflation has reached its lowest level in recent decades (Figure 9.3, Panel A). As of the summer of 1997, Spain's inflation rate had met the Maastricht convergence criterion. The Bank has steadily lowered its instrument interest rate since December 1995, and long-term financial-market interest rates have followed that rate and the inflation rate downward (Figure 9.3, Panel B). While unemployment has remained extraordinarily high, economic growth has recovered despite concerted fiscal consolidation and declining inflation (Panel C). By August 1997, Spain's headline inflation was 1.8% (measured year-on-year), well below the stated "Upper Limit Target" for 1997 of 3%. That target was later modified by the statement "The twelve-month rate of inflation, should, at the end of 1997, be close to 2.5%" (Banco de España, 1997c, September, p. 6). Although the inflation rate had risen slightly from its low of 1.5% in May, as of this writing it was still below the announced target for 1998 of 2%, with little reason to expect any upward trend.

The only real challenge to the brief inflation-targeting regime in Spain occurred early, in the one instance so far in which the domestic inflation objective and the exchange-rate objective came into potential conflict. In March 1995, in the aftermath of the Mexican crisis (which began in December 1994), speculative pressures on the peseta became strong enough to force a devaluation of its ERM parity, despite the 15% bands on the exchange rate (Panel D of Figure 9.3). Spain was facing a dual challenge in that it had to limit the pass-through of both a one-time shock to the exchange rate and a rise in indirect taxes. In the event, the Bank felt that the inflation target was not in serious danger of being breached, and short-term interest rates were not raised significantly to defend the parity.

The challenge to the new framework turned out to be more hypothetical than real, because the peseta proved resilient. Within a year, the currency had returned to its level prior to the realignment of its ERM central parity in March. "It . . . thus completely turned around the heavy depreciation it underwent in the opening months of 1995, dispelling the inflationary risks arising from such a slide in the peseta" (Banco de España, 1996c, March, p. 7). By mid-April of 1995, the peseta began to appreciate against the deutschemark. From September to December 1995, a period long enough after the devaluation for its effects on prices to be felt, inflation averaged 4.35%, including the effects of the indirect tax increase. The maximum monthly inflation rate, 5.2%, occurred in April. By February 1996, when the effects of the indirect tax increase had largely died down, headline CPI inflation dropped to 3.7%, well within the declared target range. As we saw in the case of Israel (and in the exit from the ERM of the United Kingdom and Sweden), backing off from an inappropriate exchange-rate commitment can apparently be done without damaging the central bank's inflation-fighting credibility. The drop in inflation even showed up sufficiently in private-sector expectations (as measured by wage bargains and yield curves) that the Bank was able to cut its intervention rate twice, each time by 25 basis points, on December 22, 1995, and on January 12, 1996.

The Bank did not try to grab credit for these developments, or even to claim that there were no risks to the forecast. Indeed, in a warning repeated in various forms in every *Inflation Report* thus far, the Bank stated:

> In this connection, the effectiveness of the macroeconomic policy design should not rest exclusively on the anti-inflationary discipline of monetary policy. To continue lowering the inflation rate, it is essential to dispel uncertainty over the fiscal consolidation process, eliminate income- and price-indexing mechanisms and further the liberalisation of the economy . . . The fiscal policy stance should pay particular heed to avoiding those effects that may translate into inflationary pressures. (*Ibid.,* p. 7)

In defining the limits of what monetary policy could and could not do, and in emphasizing the role of sound fiscal policy in fighting inflation, the Bank of Spain was following the pattern of similar declarations by the Bank of Canada, the Reserve Bank of New Zealand, and the post-reunification Bundesbank. In Spain those declarations apparently had a salutary effect in that they helped to force the government to address the implications for inflation of their fiscal moves.

The Bank cut its interest rate by a further 50 basis points to 8.25% on March 13. At the same time it announced a new medium-term objective of monetary policy "which consist[ed] of placing the inflation rate steadily below 3% during 1997" (*Ibid,* p. 28).

The Bank continued to loosen policy during the remainder of 1996, as inflation headed downward toward the target level. Understanding these tactics required some recognition by the public that the Bank's policy was preemptive in nature and that the Bank was already looking beyond current developments. While the Bank did not specify the horizon at which it expected its current changes in interest rates to be effective, it did tie its actions to ongoing changes in the economic environment:

> The fall in the Banco de España intervention rate initiated in December 1995 was able to continue after the release of the last Inflation Report [March 1996] thanks to two factors: first the perceptible improvement in inflation, which can be seen in other price indicators; and further, the climate of confidence progressively established as the new government's economic policy commitment to give priority to attaining the convergence criteria laid down by the Treaty on European Union . . . became patent. There were three suc-

cessive cuts in the basic rate in April, May and June this year (the first for half a point, the other two for a quarter of a point) . . . (Banco de España, 1996c, September, pp. 5-6)

Although the Bank stated its target in terms of headline CPI inflation, it continued to monitor measures of "underlying" inflation, including the IPSEBENE series, wholesale producer prices, import unit values, and even various GDP deflators. In paying attention both to the headline series (used in indexing and featured in public discussion) and the less well-known measures of inflation trends, the Bank is following the practice of central banks in all inflation-targeting countries. In using the headline series as its official target, the Bank differs from central banks that focus more closely on measures of "core" inflation. In this regard, Spain follows the practice of Sweden; perhaps the common thread is the large public sector and the use of wage contracts indexed to the headline CPI in both countries. Unlike the Riksbank, however, the Bank of Spain has made calls for the eventual eradication of indexing.

As inflation in Spain declined to unusually low levels, it began to appear that further reductions would be quite difficult because of the downward "stickiness" of inflation and inflation expectations. In September 1996, the Bank stated,

> This has visibly been the case both in consumer expectations, drawn from the corresponding confidence surveys, and in the inflation forecasts released by the markets. The inadequate solidification of inflation expectations has fed through to wage settlements . . . The stabilising of average wage growth at levels between 3.5% and 4% does not seem compatible with inflation rates below 3%. (*Ibid.*, pp. 26-7)

The phenomenon of sticky downward wage expectations as inflation approached new lows was a critical point of debate in Canada as well (Chapter 6). The Bank clearly could have chosen to disinflate further regardless of the stickiness of wage and price expectations, and in doing so might have achieved the Maastricht inflation criterion more quickly. Concern about exacerbating the already high unemployment rate was the likely reason that the Bank did not proceed more aggressively.

Progress on inflation, however, continued to be made. A new target announcement stipulated that inflation should be brought close to 2.5% by the end of 1997, rather than remaining at 3% throughout the year. The shift to 2.5% as a *de facto* point target at year's end, in place of the 3% ceiling, was not, however, emphasized by the Bank. Overall, there has been relatively less attention to quantitative measurement of performance and accountability by the Bank. The change in target is an interesting example of re-setting targets when circumstances are favorable, rather than the more common practice of re-setting targets when conditions are adverse.

As confidence increased that the lower inflation target would be met, the instrument interest rate was lowered again, in four steps, to 5.75% by March 1997. CPI inflation had dropped from 3.7% in August 1996 to 2.5% in February 1997. Core inflation, as measured by the IPSEBENE index, fell to 2.3% in February. Again, the Bank emphasized that various conditions influencing the inflation forecast, not past inflation performance *per se*, had enabled it to cut the interest rates:

> Fresh scope to continue lowering interest rates, used cautiously by the Banco de España so as to uphold its commitment to sustain a climate of macroeconomic stability, was offered by a series of factors. These were, namely: the results emerging on the budget outturn; the gradual recovery in demand; the measures unveiled to improve the economy's competitiveness and make aggregate supply more flexible; the behaviour of the monetary and financial aggregates; and finally the aforementioned headway in reducing the inflation rate. (Banco de España, 1997c, March, p. 6)

Notable for its absence is any direct mention of the performance of the peseta as a motivating factor in the interest-rate cuts. While the Bank did cite the stability of the peseta against the deutschemark later in the report, it has generally taken the view that if inflation performance is good, the peseta will be strong.

Later, in discussing elements of uncertainty to the inflation forecast, the Bank noted "The considerable depreciation of the peseta against the dollar and the odd European currency in recent months is an additional factor that may bear negatively on import prices in 1997" (*Ibid.,* p. 8). Since the rate against the deutschemark remained steady, however, and the excess of Spanish inflation over the Maastricht reference value for inflation (the average of the three lowest annual inflation rates of ERM member countries) declined, the depreciation was not treated as a major concern.

In fact, while the Bank allowed that demand for the U.S. dollar, as well as doubts about European monetary integration in the run-up to EMU, could lead to some downward pressure on the peseta, it insisted that the inflation target would be the ultimate determinant of policy.

> Changing market sentiment is no doubt one of the factors that may most closely influence monetary policy implementation during 1997. But the monetary authorities' decisions will be primarily determined by the foresee-

able course of inflation and its conditioning factors . . . Not only has the inflation rate moved ahead of schedule to the medium-term target set in 1995, but it is also reasonably likely that the new medium-term objective set in the monetary programming exercise for 1997 [to 2% CPI inflation in 1998] . . . will prove attainable. Attesting to this are the various indicators of inflation expectations, which in recent months have gradually begun to converge and progressively adjusted downwards. (*Ibid.*, p. 29)

The inflation forecast is what drives monetary policy in Spain, and the exchange rate is taken into consideration only insofar as it influences that forecast. Moreover, the inflation targets themselves are re-evaluated and changed in a forward-looking manner as it becomes clear whether they are likely to be achieved. Despite the seeming constraint of the ERM, the Bank of Spain has been pursuing a paradigmatic inflation-targeting strategy both in what motivates its monetary-policy moves and in how it justifies those moves to the public.

As we noted at the outset of this section, the Bank's inflation-targeting strategy proved a success. Inflation reached 1.8% in August 1997, assuring that the target of 2.5% by the end of 1997 would be met comfortably. Perhaps more important, as of July 1997, Spain had come into compliance with the Maastricht inflation convergence criterion. The Bank's instrument interest rate was cut by 25 basis points twice more, in April and May, cuts that were reflected across the entire term structure of interest rates (Banco de España, 1997c, September, p. 7). The Bank gave credit for falling rates not just to monetary policy but also to ". . . a fiscal policy aimed at reducing the budget deficit and . . . a package of liberalising measures designed to heighten market efficiency and flexibility" (*Ibid.*, p. 8).

Without making any direct reference to the fact that monetary-policy moves made in late 1997 or later would be only felt after EMU took place (on January 1, 1999), the Bank began to shift responsibility for economic outcomes:

[T]he move to EMU involves a progressive reduction of the scope for monetary policy autonomy. The prospect of convergence in monetary conditions between participants in the EMU project constrains the contribution Spanish monetary policy may make to stabilizing expenditure and containing financing flows. Rather, a greater onus will be placed on fiscal policy as a regulator of domestic demand in the task of entrenching the macroeconomic stability attained. (*Ibid.*, p. 9)

Thus the communications channels established in Spain under inflation targeting have been found useful in educating the public about the changes to come when Spain joins the EMU, in particular the changes in the conduct of and accountability for monetary policy. Even when monetary autonomy decreases, transparency can reduce uncertainty and maximize whatever flexibility remains.

Key Lessons from Israel, Australia, and Spain

Israel, Australia, and Spain, as small open economies, must be acutely aware of the international value of their currencies. Nevertheless, their experiences, as reported in this chapter, illustrate the advantages of using inflation targeting rather than exchange-rate targeting. If the exchange-rate band is narrow, exchange-rate targeting puts very tight constraints on monetary policy, raises the threat of speculative attacks, and makes the domestic economy exceedingly vulnerable to macroeconomic shocks and policy decisions emanating from abroad. If the exchange-rate band is wide, then targeting the exchange rate may be an inadequate means of establishing a nominal anchor and of little guidance to policymakers. Inflation targeting puts the primary focus of monetary policy on domestic economic conditions, while also providing conditions consistent with long-run stability of the exchange rate.

Israel and Spain both increased policy flexibility by shifting from an emphasis on the exchange rate toward inflation targeting. Moreover, they appear to have experienced no costs in loss of credibility, higher inflation or inflation expectations, or even exchange-rate instability. Australia has gone even further in de-emphasizing the importance of the exchange rate for monetary policy. It pays little attention to exchange-rate fluctuations, even when making inflation forecasts. In all three countries, long-term interest rates remained steady or dropped even as policy was released from the exchange-rate constraint, indicating that monetary policy can be made more flexible without losing anti-inflation credibility.

The decisions made about the operational design of inflation targeting in these three countries conformed in large measure to what we have termed the "emerging best practice." In particular, all three countries followed in the general trend toward greater flexibility (for example, longer target horizons and less attention to transitory changes in prices). All three central banks substantially increased their communication with the government and with the public, thereby enhancing both accountability and public understanding of what monetary policy could reasonably be held accountable for. That augmented communication was particularly useful in laying out for the public the consequences of changing fiscal policies (all three countries underwent fiscal consolidations during this period), and changing exchange-rate regimes.

As in the other countries we have examined, increased transparency and accountability in these three economies has had beneficial effects on public discussion of monetary policy. For example, the debate on monetary policy in the Israeli cabinet has become focused more on the rate of future disinflation than on short-term employment trends. In general, inflation targeting in the Swiss style, which emphasizes long-run evaluations of the results of a relatively flexible monetary policy, seems to have worked well in these countries.

Israel, Australia, and Spain, countries with relatively poor records on price stability and significant fiscal and structural problems, were able to maintain low rates of inflation after adopting inflation targeting. Their economic performance is strong evidence that the combination of transparency and flexibility associated with modern inflation-targeting regimes can work well in a wide variety of economic contexts.

10

Inflation Targeting: How Successful Has It Been?

DOES the adoption of an inflation-targeting framework for monetary policy affect the rate of inflation in the adopting country? Does adoption of inflation targeting alter the private sector's inflation expectations and, if so, how quickly? What effect does inflation targeting have on the real economy, in particular on the output and employment costs of disinflation? Theoretical arguments about the need for a nominal anchor and for policy transparency may help to justify a move toward inflation targeting, but it is equally important to know how well this approach has worked in actual applications.

The question of whether inflation targeting has been effective in a particular country amounts to asking whether the country obtained economic benefits that it would otherwise not have enjoyed. Since we cannot know what would have occurred in a given country had inflation targeting not been adopted, answering this question is difficult and necessarily somewhat speculative. Nevertheless, in this chapter we make a start in the empirical evaluation of inflation targeting by bringing to bear a variety of types of evidence from a number of countries, including some countries that adopted inflation targeting within our sample period and some that did not.

The inflation-targeting countries we will consider in our analyses are New Zealand, Canada, the United Kingdom, and Sweden. These are the OECD countries that have engaged in inflation targeting for at least four years. One general approach that we will use in this chapter is to compare each country's economic performance after target adoption with its performance prior to adoption. Since none of these countries has been through a complete business cycle since adoption, however, and since they did not all adopt targeting under similar circumstances (two replaced an exchange-rate peg, and two installed a nominal anchor where previously there had been none), such a comparison has obvious limitations.

As an alternative approach, we also use a "control group" strategy, in which we compare various aspects of economic performance in an inflation-targeting country with the analogous developments in a country which is broadly similar, but which did not adopt inflation targeting during the period we examine. For Canada and New Zealand, our comparison country is Australia (in our empirical work utilizing the controls, we use data from the period before 1994, when Australia joined the ranks of inflation targeters). All three of these countries are small, open, resource-exporting economies tied closely to the U.S. business cycle. We compare Sweden and the United Kingdom with Italy, each of which is a European industrial economy forced to abandon its exchange rate peg by speculative attacks in 1992.[1] Finally, we compare the effects of monetary policy under inflation targeting to the effects seen in the two targeters (though of money, not of inflation) of long standing, Germany and Switzerland, and also to the effects observed in the United States, a low-inflation country that however has not yet announced a numerical inflation goal.

Even a cursory look at the data for the four inflation-targeting countries in our study suggests that inflation targeting has been a success, at least in its own terms: Inflation was within or below the target range for all the targeting countries, and noticeably below the average inflation levels of the 1970s and 1980s. Yet, while the reduction of inflation in these countries represents a genuine achievement, it is not clear whether it was the result of forces that were already in place before inflation targeting was adopted or whether the adoption of targeting contributed to the process. Moreover, we would like to know how inflation targeting affected other important macroeconomic variables, such as output and interest rates, during the disinflation processes. In this chapter, we present three sets of tests of the effectiveness of inflation targeting.

In the first test, using so-called sacrifice ratios and Phillips-curve equations, we examine whether disinflation in the inflation-targeting countries has been achieved at a lower economic cost than would otherwise be expected, or whether inflation has declined to a greater extent than can be attributed to normal cyclical factors, domestic and international.

In the second test, we look at private-sector inflation expectations, as inferred from surveys of forecasters and from interest-rate differentials, to see whether they have declined after targeting beyond the degree associated with a drop in inflation.

Finally, in the third test we use simulations from a simple forecasting model to determine whether the interactions among inflation, monetary policy, and real GDP have changed following the adoption of inflation targeting.

We use three tests because there are several distinct issues to address and because the limits of the sample size (the small number of inflation-targeting countries and the limited span of time since the adoption of inflation targeting) caution us against relying on any one piece of evidence. Our approach differs from that of comparative empirical assessments of inflation targeting, which tend to focus on just one measure, usually the expectations of the financial markets.[2] By using three different tests and data from a variety of targeting and non-targeting countries, we hope to be able to provide some reasonably robust evidence on the effects and effectiveness of inflation targeting.

To foreshadow the results, we find that inflation targeting appears to have been successful in reducing both inflation and (with a lag) private-sector inflation expectations. It may also have contributed to the maintenance of price stability, once achieved, particularly by preventing one-time shocks to inflation from permanently affecting the inflation rate. Unfortunately, however, we find essentially no evidence that the adoption of inflation targets has reduced the real output and employment costs of disinflation, at least not during the early stages of the new approach.

Does Inflation Targeting Make Disinflation Less Costly?

We look first at the response of inflation to the business cycle. We consider two related measures: so-called "sacrifice ratios" and forecasts based on estimated Phillips curves.

Evidence from Sacrifice Ratios

Sacrifice ratios are measures of the loss of output or employment that an economy must sustain in order to achieve a reduction in inflation. A sacrifice ratio is usually calculated as the number of "point-years" of reduced growth in output or in increased unemployment that a country must accept in order to achieve a one-percentage-point reduction in the inflation rate.

Several hypotheses have been advanced about the determinants of sacrifice ratios. For example, it has been suggested that if a disinflationary policy is clearly stated in advance, and if the central bank's commitment to the policy is credible to the public, then the sacrifice ratio will be lower. Disinflation might be less costly under a credible policy because the public's expectations should adjust more quickly, leading to a more rapid re-setting of prices and wages. Since one of the objectives of inflation targeting is to increase the central bank's credibility, it will be interesting to see whether the introduction of inflation targeting does indeed result in lower sacrifice ratios.

In studying the effect of inflation targeting on sacrifice ratios, we need to control for other potential determinants of the real economic losses resulting from disinflation. For example, it seems plausible that the cost of reducing inflation by one percentage point will be smaller when the inflation rate is high than when it is low. At low rates of inflation, wage- and price-setters are less concerned about the effects of inflation, and hence may be less aware of, or less likely to respond to, changes in the central bank's policies. Thus a greater short-run loss of output or a greater increase in unemployment may be necessary to induce changes in wages and prices. Conversely, if the inflation rate is high, or if the disinflation is a large one, we would expect a faster and more pronounced response by wage-setters and price-setters, leading perhaps to a smaller output loss per point of disinflation achieved. For similar reasons, the output effects of a disinflation might well depend on the speed with which the disinflation takes place. Our analysis will control for the size and speed of the disinflation, as well as the initial level of inflation.

To compute the sacrifice ratios for the countries under consideration, we follow the methodology of Ball (1994), using quarterly data throughout. Ball focuses on output loss rather than on employment loss. First he defines the path of *trend inflation* for each country as a centered nine-quarter moving average of annual inflation rates. He then identifies peaks (troughs) in trend inflation as quarters in which trend inflation is higher (lower) than in both the preceding four quarters and the subsequent four quarters. We will follow Ball's definition of a *disinflation* as an episode that starts at an inflation peak and ends at an inflation trough, with an annual inflation rate at the trough at least two percentage points lower than at the peak.

Having identified periods of disinflation for each country, Ball next estimates the associated loss in output. To do so, he assumes that output is at its trend level at the inflation peak and four quarters after the inflation trough (thus allowing for the possibility that output has recovered only after a lag from an episode of disinflation). He then calculates trend output for the whole period by drawing a straight line between real GDP (in logarithms) at the inflation peak and real GDP four quarters after the inflation trough. The numerator of the sacrifice ratio—that is, the output loss during the disinflation—is computed as the difference between trend real GDP and the real actually observed GDP. The denominator is the change in trend inflation over the disinflationary episode.

In commenting on Ball's paper, Friedman (1994) and Cecchetti (1994) level a number of criticisms at his methodology. Friedman raises the question of whether the sacrifice should be measured as output foregone, or instead as the increase in unemployment, and questions Ball's approach to the measurement of trend output. Since our goal here is to compare sacrifice ratios both across time and across countries, however, we are primarily interested in the relative magnitude of the ratios. In this sense, consistent mismeasurement would not significantly affect the results. Cecchetti notes that Ball's interpretation of the output loss as being due to demand contractions only, which leads him largely to ignore the potential effects of supply shocks, affects the results critically. We will return to this question later before we present results based on estimated Phillips curves.

In applying Ball's methodology, we use data on real GDP from the OECD Main Economic Indicators and all-item CPI series from the Bank for International Settlements (BIS). We compute quarterly inflation as the percentage change of the CPI in the last month of the quarter over the corresponding month of the previous year.[4] For each of the nine countries in our sample, we identify two completed disinflations, following each of the two oil shocks (in 1973 and 1979); and for all the countries except Germany and Switzerland, we identify a third completed disinflation during the early 1990s, which gives us a total of twenty-five disinflationary episodes from which we compute sacrifice ratios. As a check, we compared our results with those of Ball where possible (in particular, for the first two disinflations for seven countries in our sample for which Ball also reports sacrifice ratios based on quarterly data). The mean of Ball's sacrifice ratios for these episodes is 1.59, while that of the comparable episodes in our sample is 1.35. The correlation between the two sets of ratios is 0.71, indicating reasonable consistency between our results and Ball's.[5]

With the estimated sacrifice ratios in hand, we consider whether the countries that adopted inflation targets did in fact lower their costs of disinflation, relative both to their own past and to comparable countries that did not adopt inflation targets. The regression reported in Table 10.1 attempts to explain variation in the sacrifice ratio by the initial level of inflation (to check whether, at lower initial inflation levels, disinflation is more costly); the total amount of disinflation in the episode (to test whether a larger disinflation induces a smaller cost per point of disinflation); and the length of the disinflationary episode (to determine whether quicker disinflations are more credible and therefore less costly). Our results, based on the sample of 25 sacrifice ratios, confirm the importance of initial inflation and the length of the disinflationary episode for determining the sacrifice ratio, in that the estimated coefficients on these two variables are statistically significant and of the expected sign.

Using the estimated coefficients listed in Table 10.1, as well as the level of inflation for each country at the beginning of its latest disinflation, the reduction in inflation, and the length of the disinflation, we compute the value of the sacrifice ratio we would predict based on our regression results. For three of the four inflation targeters in our sample (all except Sweden), we find that the actual sacrifice ratio experienced after the introduction of inflation targeting was not only *higher* than the average sacrifice ratio of previous disinflations in that country, but higher than that forecast by the regression in Table 10.1. For Italy, one of our non-targeting comparison countries, as well as for the United States, we obtain the same pattern as for most of the inflation targeters, in that the actual sacrifice ratio in the early 1990s is higher than both the past average and the predicted value. For Australia, however, the actual sacrifice ratio during the latest disinflation was lower than forecast, although higher than the past average sacrifice ratio. Finally, the sacrifice ratios for Germany and Switzerland (from an earlier period) are lower than both the predicted values and their own past sacrifice ratios. Disinflation under inflation targeting—or at least the first disinflation under targeting—does not appear to be less costly than it would have been absent inflation targeting. The finding of no "credibility bonus" (in terms of lower sacrifice ratios) from inflation targeting is reminiscent of recent findings that changes in monetary institutions (such as increased central bank independence) do not appear to generate a credibility bonus (see, for example, Debelle and Fischer [1994] and Posen [1995a]).

Probably the most controversial aspect of Ball's methodology, as we have mentioned, is that all deviations of output from potential during his disinflations are being attributed to policy-induced demand contraction. Indeed, as King and Watson (1994) point out, measures of the sacrifice ratio are often sensitive to the specific assumption by which the policy-induced part of the output contraction is being identified. If, for example, some productivity-enhancing innovation (a positive supply shock) occurred during a disinflation (as defined above), Ball's measure of output lost due to contractionary monetary policy would understate the true cost of the disinflation, leading to too low an estimate of

TABLE 10.1

Sacrifice Ratios and Their Determinants

Results from regressing a sample of 25 sacrifice ratios (3 for each country except for Germany and Switzerland) on a constant, inflation at the beginning of the disinflation, change in inflation during the disinflation, and the length (in quarters) of the disinflation. T statistics in parentheses.

Constant	2.16 (2.80)
Initial Inflation	-0.17 (2.98)
Change in Inflation	-0.01 (0.07)
Length of Disinflation	0.09 (2.06)
Adjusted R-Square	0.56

Sacrifice Ratios for the Latest Completed Disinflation

	New Zealand	Canada	Australia	U.K.	Sweden	Italy	U.S.	Germany	Switzerland
Disinflation	86Q3-92Q4	90Q3-93Q4	89Q2-93Q1	90Q1-93Q4	90Q4-93Q1	90Q2-93Q4	90Q1-94Q4	80Q4-87Q1	82Q1-87Q1
Initial Inflation	15.38%	5.25%	7.62%	8.64%	9.55%	6.42%	5.13%	5.87%	5.93%
Change in Inflation	14.25%	4.16%	6.22%	6.48%	6.43%	2.05%	2.43%	5.75%	4.82%
Sacrifice Ratio	2.05	3.04	1.87	2.19	0.53	2.58	3.77	2.47	2.15
Predicted Sacr Ratio	1.67	2.34	2.12	1.95	1.32	2.28	2.99	3.19	2.78
Past Avg. Sacr Ratio	0.98	1.06	0.28	0.55	0.93	0.34	1.52	4.46	2.34

the sacrifice ratio. A potential avenue for avoiding this problem, when asking whether target adoption has changed the terms of the output-inflation tradeoff, is to consider forecasts of inflation, and then to compare the inflation rates realized following target adoption to the rates that would be expected based on information available prior to target adoption. This is the approach that we consider next.

Inflation Forecasts from Estimated Phillips Curves

To determine whether inflation-targeting countries saw inflation drop more than macroeconomic conditions would have predicted, we forecast inflation for each country from an estimated Phillips curve, in the manner of Gordon (1985) and Fuhrer (1995). Specifically, for each country in our sample, we regress quarterly inflation on lags of itself, a measure of resource utilization, and two measures of price pressures from supply-side factors: the lagged change in the nominal effective exchange rate, and the lagged change in a U.S. dollar-denominated commodity price index. The measures of supply pressures were included only if they improved the fit, as measured by the adjusted R^2.[6] Using these regressions, which are estimated using data up to the date of target adoption, we construct 8-quarter forecasts of inflation. This exercise is intended to determine whether inflation in the inflation-targeting countries dropped beyond the extent we would attribute to normal cyclical factors, domestic and international. As a byproduct, the regression may also help us judge whether introducing inflation targeting induced observable changes in wage- and price-setting structures.[7]

The regression is estimated over the period 1971:2 (the second quarter of 1971) to the time of target adoption for each of the four inflation targeters in our sample. For Australia, the sample for the estimation is the same as that for New Zealand. (Note that even the out-of-sample forecasts for Australia end before its adoption of inflation targeting, by our dating, so that Australia may be treated as a control country). For Italy, the sample period is the same as for the United Kingdom; that is, until the lira's exit from the ERM in the third quarter of 1992. For the United States, Germany, and Switzerland, the regression is estimated up to German economic reunification in 1990:2, allowing comparison with the putatively credible commitment to low inflation in the United States as well as with nominal targeters of long standing.

Table 10.2 reports results from the regressions and the inflation forecasts. As a check of the robustness of the results with respect to the num-

TABLE 10.2
Forecasting Inflation from Phillips Curves

Results from regressing quarterly inflation (annualized) on its own lags, a utilization measure, changes in the nominal effective exchange rate and in commodity prices prior to the adoption of inflation targets (prior to 1990Q3 for the U.S., Germany and Switzerland; prior to 1990Q1 for Australia; prior to 1992Q4 for Italy), and from forecasting inflation out of sample over 8 quarters following target adoption (or equivalent).

	New Zealand	Canada	Australia	U.K.
Utilization Measure	Unemp Rate	Unemp Rate	Unemp Rate	Unemp Rate
Sample	71Q2-89Q4	71Q2-90Q4	71Q2-89Q4	71Q2-92Q3
Forecast Horizon	90Q1-91Q4	91Q1-92Q4	90Q1-91Q4	92Q4-94Q3

A. Basic Specification, Four Lags of Each Variable Included

	New Zealand	Canada	Australia	U.K.
Adj R Square	0.66	0.62	0.63	0.56

Sum of coefficients on all lags (joint significance of all lags) of variable:

	New Zealand	Canada	Australia	U.K.
Inflation	0.60 (8.57)*	0.90 (24.02)*	0.83 (25.54)*	0.63 (7.41)*
Utilization Measure	-0.08 (3.12)*	-0.06 (2.33)	-0.06 (1.88)	-0.14 (3.84)*
Exchange Rate	-0.08 (4.16)*			
Commodity Prices		0.01 (0.98)		
Parameter Stability (5% Critical Value)	0.44 (1.73)	1.63 (1.67)	0.40 (1.70)	0.35 (1.74)
Avg Forecast Error	0.69	-0.84	0.87	1.89

B. Parsimonious Specification

	New Zealand	Canada	Australia	U.K.
Adj R Square	0.65	0.63	0.64	0.53

Sum of coefficients on all lags (joint significance of all lags) of variable:

	New Zealand	Canada	Australia	U.K.
Inflation	0.53 (4, 7.78)*	0.88 (3, 33.76)*	0.75 (1, 109.95)*	0.48 (1, 26.79)*
Utilization Measure	-0.11 (4, 3.32)*	-0.07 (3, 4.96)*	-0.06 (1, 4.49)*	-0.17 (1, 13.75)*
Exchange Rate	-0.01 (3, 4.63)*			
Commodity Prices				
Parameter Stability (5% Critical Value)	0.39 (1.73)	1.67* (1.66)	0.42 (1.70)	0.46 (1.74)
Avg Forecast Error	0.25	-0.51	2.81	2.39

Table 10.2 continued

Sweden Output Gap 71Q2-92Q4 93Q1-94Q4	*Italy* Unemp Rate 71Q2-92Q3 92Q4-94Q3	*U.S.* Unemp Rate 71Q2-90Q2 90Q3-92Q2	*Germany* Unemp Rate 71Q2-90Q2 90Q3-92Q2	*Switzerland* Output Gap 71Q2-90Q2 90Q3-92Q2
0.23	0.71	0.67	0.57	0.42
0.66 (5.50)*	0.78 (18.22)*	0.92 (21.43)*	-0.01 (0.24)	0.49 (3.61)*
0.11 (1.61)	-0.13 (4.22)*	-0.07 (2.89)*	-0.14 (6.24)*	0.13 (5.64)*
	0.02 (3.25)*	-0.01 (3.29)*	-0.15 (3.00)*	0.01 (2.47)
0.08 (2.50)	0.01 (0.77)	0.03 (1.70)	0.04 (3.24)*	
1.01 (1.80)	0.48 (1.89)	0.68 (1.69)	0.72 (1.69)	0.52 (1.68)
0.12	0.29	-0.54	-1.78	-0.11
N/A	0.68	0.64	0.58	0.40
	0.65 (1, 57.31)*	0.89 (3, 29.06)*		0.39 (3, 3.47)*
	-0.15 (2, 9.99)*	-0.09 (2, 4.29)*	-0.14 (3, 30.91)*	0.15 (4, 5.49)*
	-0.05 (4, 4.87)*	0.01 (2, 6.43)*	-0.15 (4, 3.65)*	0.01 (3, 3.86)*
		0.02 (1, 3.55)*	0.04 (4, 3.31)*	
	0.57 (1.88)	0.51 (1.69)	0.73 (1.69)	0.57 (1.68)
	2.88	0.13	-1.78	-0.14

ber of lags included, for each country we report results from two different specifications. The first specification includes four lags of each variable in order to guarantee a reasonably good fit. The second specification is more parsimonious: We obtain the lag structure in this case by sequentially reducing the number of lags of each variable until the t statistic of the last lag included was significant at the 5% level.[8] The adjusted R^2's indicate a good fit of both regressions for all countries except Sweden. Also, for Sweden the lags of the output gap are jointly insignificant, which is why we do not report a parsimonious specification for that country. For each regression and for each of the variables included in the regression, we report the sum of the coefficients on all lags of that variable, as well as their joint significance (that is, the F-statistic from testing the exclusion of all lags of that variable; 5% critical values are between 2.50 and 2.53). The sum of the coefficients captures the cumulative response of inflation to a unit change in the variable considered.

The fact that the nominal exchange rate and commodity price inflation apparently do not have a significant impact on inflation in a number of countries is rather surprising, particularly for open economies with sizeable raw materials production, such as Canada and Australia. The exchange rate appears significant in half of the regressions; commodity-price inflation appears significant in only two out of eight. A peculiar result from the German regression is the insignificant impact of past inflation on the current rate of inflation. This last result, however, is not robust with respect to the choice of utilization measure.[9]

Our main interest in these Phillips curve regressions, however, is in identifying possible changes in the relationship between inflation and unemployment or output following the adoption of inflation targets. To help do this, we turn now to parameter instability tests and out-of-sample forecasts generated from the Phillips curves.

In Table 10.2, we report results from re-estimating the regressions from 1971:2 through 1996:4[10] and testing for parameter instability; if the adoption of inflation targets induces changes in wage-setting and price-setting behavior, then we should observe instability in the Phillips curve around the time of target adoption. For three of the four inflation targeters, the hypothesis of parameter stability in the Phillips curve at the time of target adoption is never rejected at the 5% level—that is, it does not appear that the Phillips curve was materially shifted by the introduction of inflation targeting in these countries. Only for Canada do we find some evidence of parameter instability. For neither Germany nor Switzerland, the two targeters of long standing, nor for the other comparison countries in our sample, is there evidence of parameter instability around this time. The results from these tests for parameter instability for all nine countries are robust with respect to the choice of utilization measure and the choice of lag length.

Although, with the exception of Canada, there is no evidence for parameter instability following target adoption, it is nevertheless interesting to ask whether inflation was below the values predicted by the Phillips curve during this period. To do so, we perform out-of-sample forecasts of inflation over a horizon of eight quarters, using actual values of all variables except inflation itself, for which we use past forecasted values. We interpret the resulting forecasts as representing the course inflation would have been expected to take in each country, given the actual realized values of all other variables during the forecast horizon. These counterfactual paths of inflation can be compared to the actual paths, to help us assess the degree to which inflation targeting made a difference.

A technical issue that must be addressed is how to judge whether differences between actual values and forecast values of inflation are due to chance, or instead are large enough to be statistically and economically meaningful. Answering this question requires an analysis of the distribution of the forecast errors for inflation. Since the forecasts are out-of-sample, the distribution of the forecast errors is a nonlinear function of the estimated parameters.[11] Also, because the forecasts are conditional ones, their distributions also depend on the actual values of the remaining variables in the regression.

We address the measurement of the distribution of forecast errors as follows. We need to construct an approximate estimate of the uncertainty surrounding the forecast at each quarterly horizon from 1 to 8. To do so, we compute 15 forecasts of eight quarters' length for each country, beginning at dates at least eight quarters prior to the adoption of inflation targets (so as not to overlap with the post-adoption period). We use these pre-adoption forecasts only for estimating the standard deviation of the forecast error. In particular, we first estimate the Phillips curve regression for each country in the sample ending 23 quarters prior to adoption, then forecast inflation over the period from adoption minus 22 quarters to adoption minus 15 quarters. Next we estimate the Phillips curve until adoption minus 22 quarters; then we forecast inflation from adoption minus 21 quarters to adoption minus 14 quarters; and so on. In this fashion we constructed 15 different forecasts. We then estimate the root mean squared error (RMSE) at each quarterly horizon, 1-8, as the empirical standard deviation of the 15 different forecast errors at each corresponding horizon.[12]

The results of these forecasts are shown graphically in Figure 10.1, where the vertical line represents the onset of forecasting, the dashed line is the forecast of inflation, the two bold lines are one-RMSE bands generated as described, and the simple line is the actual course of inflation.[13] In Table 10.2 we report the average forecast error from forecasting inflation over 8 quarters following target adoption, expressed in points of annual inflation. (Likewise, in Figure 10.1 quarterly inflation has been expressed at annualized rates on the axes to facilitate interpretation). A positive forecast error implies that actual inflation was, on average, below what we would predict from the regression results.

For three of the four inflation targeters, actual inflation during the eight quarters following target adoption shows no sign of persistent deviations from the forecast, and stays well within the one-RMSE band. The average over-prediction for New Zealand is 0.69, and that for Sweden 0.12, while for Canada actual inflation exceeds the forecast on average by 0.84%. For the United Kingdom, however, there is stronger evidence that inflation is lower than would be expected, being below forecast in 7 out of 8 quarters, and outside the error band in 3 out of 8 quarters. On average, actual inflation is below forecast by 1.9%.

Consistent with the results from the parameter instability tests, for none of the other five countries is there much evidence of a change in the behavior of inflation, conditional on the behavior of other macroeconomic variables, after the adoption of inflation targeting. In Australia, inflation is almost consistently below forecast (0.87% on average), but mostly inside the error band. In Italy, inflation is more often below than above the forecast (0.29% on average), but again mostly within the error band. Inflation in the United States is well above forecast in the third quarter of 1990. Thereafter, actual inflation is always inside the error band and very close to its forecast, leading to an under-prediction by 0.54% on average. After the demand shock of economic reunification in Germany, inflation exceeds the predicted values in all but one quarter, twice (in the third quarters of 1990 and 1991) by far more than one RMSE, resulting in an under-prediction of actual inflation of 1.78% on average. Yet, by the end of the forecast horizon, German inflation has returned to its predicted value, which we interpret as being consistent with a successful price-stability commitment based on targeting of a nominal anchor. Likewise, the upsurge of inflation in Switzerland during 1989-90 was reversed during the next two years, almost exactly in line with the predictions. On average, inflation exceeds the forecast by only 0.11%.[14]

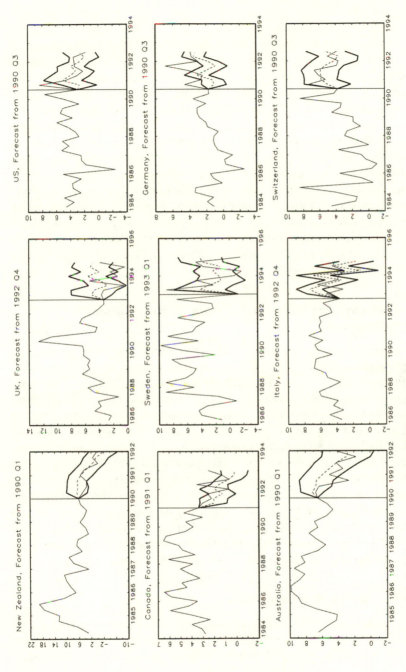

Figure 10.1. Inflation forecasts from Phillips Curves.

Summary

Our Phillips-curve and sacrifice-ratio results together suggest that the adoption of inflation targeting in the four inflation-targeting countries studied here did not significantly alter the real economic costs of achieving disinflation. Therefore we presume that the underlying wage- and price-setting structures did not change either. Given their desire to move inflation down, the inflation targeters got only small, if any, extra disinflationary effect beyond the business cycle they experienced (or induced) or, for that matter, beyond the disinflation experienced by countries without inflation targets. Based on the German and Swiss experiences, moreover, it seems that even a credible targeter of long standing does not see these benefits. In other words, it appears, unfortunately, that the only way to achieve disinflation is the hard way: by accepting possibly significant short-run losses in output (and employment) in exchange for the longer-run economic benefits of price stability. The use of inflation targeting as a framework for monetary policy does not change that basic fact.

Does Adoption of Inflation Targeting Reduce Inflation Expectations?

The second kind of evidence relevant to assessing the effect of inflation targeting concerns the public's inflation expectations. To see whether the adoption of inflation targeting caused a decline in expected inflation, we look both at consensus forecasts of inflation in each country and at changes in interest differentials relative to the United States or Germany at both a long and short maturity. The questions of interest are whether adoption of an inflation target confers greater credibility in the form of either less uncertainty about policy or lower risk premiums on government debt. Even if the structures in the economy that determine the response of inflation to the business cycle (wage-setting institutions, for example) are initially unresponsive to the adoption of inflation targeting, as the evidence described in the first part of the chapter suggests, it still might be the case that expectations of future inflation (as reflected, for example, in financial markets) would change when the policy regime changes.

Evidence from Surveys of Expectations

The panels of Figure 10.2 show actual CPI inflation rates for each country, as well as consensus private-sector forecasts for inflation by the end of each year since 1990.[15] A square denotes the consensus forecast of

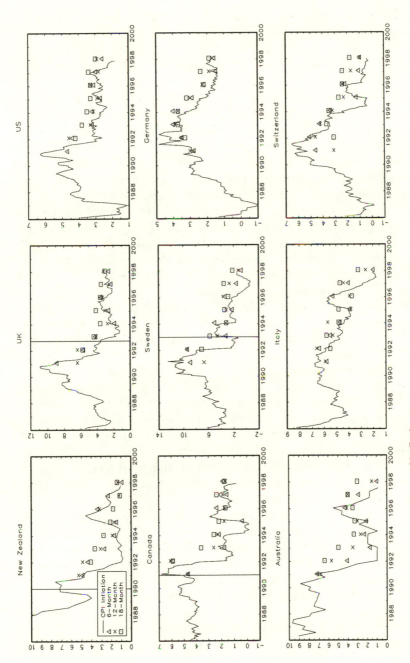

Figure 10.2. Consensus forecasts of inflation.

inflation made 18 months prior (an asterisk 12 months prior, a triangle 6 months prior) to the date at which the symbol appears, forecasting inflation at that specific time. Using Figure 10.2, we can analyze the response of inflation expectations, as measured by forecasts, for each country in our study.

In New Zealand, the first country to adopt inflation targeting, the forecasts at all three horizons show a continuous downward trend (with the exception of the 6-month and 12-month forecast in 1995). Yet for the first four years for which targets were announced, inflation expectations were either at the upper end of the target range or above the range; this was the case even though actual inflation was within or below target at the end of 1991, 1992, and 1993. It was only in mid-1993 that the 18-month forecast fell within the official target range. Thus expectations did not adjust instantaneously by any means. However, over time, the New Zealand targeting regime seems to have acquired credibility: in mid-1995, even though headline inflation was 3% above the target range, the 18-month forecast for inflation at the end of 1996 was still at 1.1% and has remained inside the band since then.

In Canada, not unexpectedly, the forecasts of 1991 inflation made prior to target adoption predicted a rise in inflation; interestingly enough, so did the predictions made in June 1991. Again, as in New Zealand, it appears that private-sector inflation forecasts are (at least partially) determined by lagged inflation; in other words, the regime change does not appear to have induced a revolution in expectations formation. However, both 12-month-ahead and 18-month-ahead inflation forecasts exhibit consistent downward trends over the remainder of the target period, with all forecasts made after target adoption lying within the target range (the six-month-ahead forecast dropped below the target range at one point, reflecting the one-time effect of the tax changes of 1994). Thus, as in New Zealand, the Canadian inflation targets appear to have gained credibility over time.

In the United Kingdom, inflation expectations at the longer horizon stayed stubbornly at the upper end of the 1% to 4% target range, even during periods when headline inflation was well within (or even near the bottom of) the official target range. For each of the four years following target adoption in Great Britain (1993 to 1996), inflation expectations were higher than the eventual outcome, and were revised downward continuously. Here again we observe a "learning" process in the private sector; or, as the private forecasters might have put it, a probationary period for the new policy. It is interesting that inflation expectations at the 18-month horizon did not increase during 1995, even though headline inflation had increased by almost 2%.

The Swedish disinflation during 1992 was partially anticipated, as shown by the 18-month forecast for inflation by the end of 1992; however, the adjustment of expectations again was not complete, as the successive downward revisions of inflation expectations reveal. Similarly, the impact of the devaluation of the krona in fall 1992 on inflation in 1993 was initially underestimated. From the end of 1993 until early 1996, inflation expectations in Sweden at all horizons remained around the upper end of the target range, and sometimes slightly above it, even though actual inflation was kept consistently inside the target range. Thereafter, while inflation expectations at the short horizon fell in line with actual inflation, which fell first to the bottom of the target range and finally below the range, inflation expectations at longer horizons remained around the center of the target.

The results for these four countries show that the adjustment of inflation expectations following the adoption of inflation targets was, for the most part, only gradual. To the extent that there was an initial impact of target adoption on private-sector expectations of inflation, it is most visible in the comparison with the non-targeting countries. For example, inflation expectations in Australia, a country which itself was moving toward adoption of inflation targeting, had until 1994 followed a course similar to that in New Zealand. Inflation expectations in Australia at all horizons exhibited a consistent downward trend, and in each year inflation expectations were successively revised downward. In contrast to New Zealand, however, during 1994 and 1995 inflation expectations in Australia at the 18-month horizon trended upward, although the actual inflation performance in Australia was not much different from that of New Zealand. In early 1996, expectations for inflation by the end of that year were 1% above Australia's target range of 2% to 3%, which had been adopted in late 1994. The divergence in medium-term expectations between the comparable nations of the Antipodes does suggest some difference between the anchoring effects of their medium-term targets, either due to the more informal nature of the target in Australia, or simply due to the fact that the adoption of the Australian target was so recent.

Italy, used for comparison with the other countries forced to devalue, Sweden and the United Kingdom, has been remarkably successful in containing the inflationary consequences of its massive devaluation following the exit from the ERM. That this came largely as a surprise to private-sector forecasters is shown by the 12-month forecast for inflation during 1993, which was revised upward (on average) from the 18-month forecast of 4.8% by 0.9%, only to be revised downward six months later by 1%. As the downward trend of inflation continued during 1993 and 1994, inflation expectations at the long horizon fell to 3.7%. This gain in lowering inflation expectations was largely lost, however, during the 1995 upsurge in inflation, with expectations at the 18-month horizon being almost 1.5% above the level a year earlier. From the beginning of 1996 on, inflation expectations in Italy fell rapidly, in line with actual inflation.

CPI inflation in the United States, which had been above 4% since 1988, fell rapidly during 1991 from more than 6% to 3% and remained around 3% for the following five years without discernible trend. Yet inflation expectations at the 18-month horizon, which had been above 4% in mid-1990, fell only gradually over the following three years, to reach 3.3% by mid-1993; this figure was slightly above actual inflation at that time.

The extent to which inflation in Germany rose during 1991 and 1992 appears, not surprisingly, to have been unexpected. The speed of the subsequent disinflation during 1993 and 1994 seems to have been underestimated; while at the time of German reunification inflation expectations (for the end of 1991) were barely above 3%, once inflation expectations had risen closer to 4% it took almost two years of disinflation (to mid-1994) before long-run inflation expectations returned to the vicinity of 2%. Thus inflation expectations in Germany give the impression of being heavily influenced by recent experience. A very similar picture emerges from the Swiss data: In mid-1990, while inflation was running above 5%, inflation in Switzerland during 1991 was still expected to be around 3.1%. Neither did long-term inflation expectations increase by much during 1991, when inflation peaked. Inflation expectations at the 18-month horizon then fell gradually from a peak of 3.7% to 2.4%, staying consistently above realized inflation rates during the past two years.

The experiences of Germany and Switzerland suggest that in a reliably proven targeting regime, inflation expectations exhibit a high degree of inertia, limiting both the upward motion in inflation after shocks and the speed of reaction to disinflation. The same appears to hold for the United States, despite the absence of explicitly announced targets. More telling, as seen in the experiences of the recent adopters of targets, and especially in the New Zealand-Australia and United Kingdom-Italy comparisons, inflation targets appear to be effective in anchoring medium-term inflation expectations. The resulting inertia of expectations may help the targeting country resist persistent increases in inflation after shocks to the price level, but at the same time may make additional disinflation more difficult.

Evidence from Interest-Rate Differentials

Another perspective on inflation expectations is given by interest rates. The panels in the left column of Figure 10.3 show the differentials between the yields on United States government debt (10-year government bonds and 3-month treasury bills) and the analogous yields for New Zealand, Canadian, and Australian public debt. The right column of Figure 10.3 presents the same differentials (but here relative to German government debt) for United Kingdom, Swedish, and Italian government securities.[16] Economic theory implies that cross-national interest-rate differentials are determined largely by expected relative changes in exchange rates, which in turn reflect expected differences in inflation rates. Thus, by observing the behavior of interest-rate differentials, we can obtain a market-based measure of inflation expectations in each country (or more precisely, the expectation of inflation in the home country relative to the comparison country, either the United States or Germany).

In New Zealand, the long-term interest-rate differential in particular mirrors very closely the course of the disinflation for the three years following target adoption. At its lowest point in early 1994, long-term investments in New Zealand dollars yielded a lower nominal return than comparable investments in U.S. dollars, while the 3-month New Zealand-U.S. differential had fallen below 2%. Interestingly, while New Zealand's headline inflation was well above target during 1995, both interest-rate differentials rose only modestly, apparently reflecting continued confidence in New Zealand's commitment to low inflation.

The enormous spike in short-term interest rates in Canada during late 1992 and in 1993 should be seen as a reflection of the general turmoil in world exchange markets that followed both the ERM shakeout and large price changes in the U.S. bond market, in conjunction with the subsequent constitutional crisis and election in Canada. Except for this spike, the Canada-U.S. rate differential on 3-month bills has trended consistently downward, and Canadian 3-month yields have actually been below the comparable U.S. rates since the beginning of 1996. More importantly, the long-term interest-rate differential has moved down markedly since the second half of 1995 and is now below the historical range

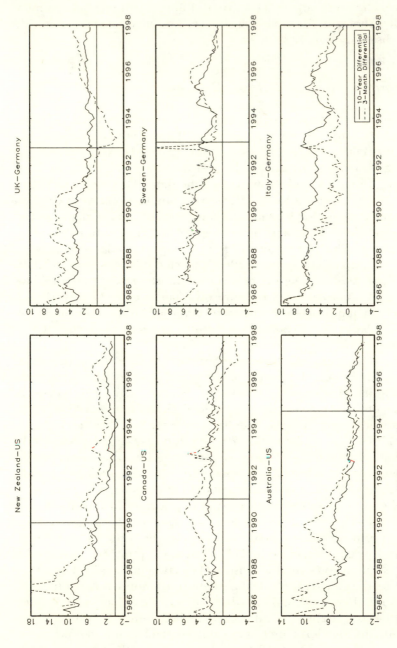

Figure 10.3. Interest rate differentials.

for the Canada-U.S. differential. The rather lengthy period that passed before the long-term differential began to narrow probably reflected fiscal and Quebecois-driven doubts about the quality of Canadian long-maturity government securities; only recently does this differential seem to have been dominated by monetary-policy commitments.

Following sterling's exit from the ERM, British official interest rates were repeatedly cut, while Germany decreased its official short-term rate (the repo rate) only cautiously. This behavior is reflected in a negative short-term interest-rate differential between the United Kingdom and Germany from late 1992 until mid-1994. Through this whole period the long-term interest-rate differential hovered around 1%, only briefly (in early 1994) dipping to 0.5%. Thereafter, the long-term differential rose above 1% and rose gradually from 1 to 2% between early 1995 and early 1997. It should be emphasized that these U.K.-Germany differentials are relatively low for the post-Bretton Woods period and suggest that for Britain, inflation targeting was largely successful in replacing ERM membership as the source of a nominal anchor for monetary policy.

Sweden's interest-rate differentials have behaved quite erratically. The Riksbank's efforts in September 1992 to defend the krona caused a sharp spike in the bill yield differential vis-à-vis Germany, and the differential between long-term bond yields also rose considerably. The subsequent cuts in the Marginal Rate following the krona's floating narrowed the short-term differential during the following months to 0.8% in September 1993. From then until the end of 1995 the short-term spread widened to almost 5% but then narrowed to below 1%. The long-term differential narrowed until February 1994, when it reached 0.8%. As in the case of the short-term spread, this narrowing was sharply reversed, and over the following six months the long-term differential rose to 4%, remaining in the 3% to 4% range for another year. Since the middle of 1995, however, the long-term differential has fallen steadily to below 2%.

The sharp rise in the differentials (particularly at the long horizon) during 1994 seems to indicate that by that point Sweden's inflation targets had not acquired much credibility. The narrowing of both interest-rate differentials since 1995, however, suggests important gains in credibility; although the prospect of European Monetary Union (to participation in which, however, the Swedish government is not committed) and the fiscal consolidation over recent years may have contributed to the narrowing as well.

Interest-rate differentials between Australian and United States government bonds and treasury bills respectively rose above their New Zealand counterparts from mid-1988 to mid-1990, when New Zealand headline inflation fell below that of Australia. Since 1991, however, the Australian short-term differential vis-à-vis the U.S. has been lower than that of New Zealand. Long-term bond differentials have behaved differently, and in a way that is quite interesting: Since 1991 the differential between yields on New Zealand and U.S. government bonds has been below the analogous Australia-U.S. spread, despite the almost identical inflation performance in Australia and New Zealand during those years. The New Zealand bond market is also arguably less liquid than the Australian, which, all else equal, would increase the New Zealand-U.S. spread. In particular, during the bond-market downturn of 1994, the differential between Australian and U.S. government bonds widened about 1.5% more than did its New Zealand counterpart. Only by 1997, following Australia's adoption of an inflation target in late 1994, have the two long-term differentials converged. Thus the relative performance of the long-term differentials in Australia and New Zealand tend to confirm the conclusion from the expectations surveys that inflation targets can be beneficial in anchoring inflation expectations.

Interest-rate differentials between Italian and German government securities have followed patterns very similar to those seen in Sweden. A sharp rise in both short-term and long-term differentials during the crisis of fall 1992 was eventually reversed, with both differentials falling to historic lows. As in Sweden, the narrowing of the short-term differential came to an end in August 1993, by which time it had reached 1%, while the long-term differential bottomed out in April 1994 at 2.2%. The short-term differential then rose steadily to reach 5.5% by October 1995 and has since fallen back to 1%. The long-term differential peaked in April 1995 at 6.3% and has since fallen below 1%. Anecdotal evidence suggests that the narrowing of both differentials in late 1997 was driven not only by Italy's excellent inflation performance but also (as a consequence) by expectations concerning European Monetary Union and the possibility (now a reality) of Italian membership in the Union from its inception.

Summary

The evidence from both the survey data and interest-rate differentials suggests that the adoption of inflation targeting does *not* establish immediate credibility for monetary policy. In particular, inflation expectations are slow to fall to the range established by the official inflation targets. This finding is consistent with the evidence presented in the first part of this chapter, which suggested that inflation targeting does not reduce the real costs of disinflation. Because credibility gains are slow to materialize, and because institutional arrangements (for example, for wage- and price-setting) do not change quickly following the adoption of inflation targets, inflation targeting does not provide a magic bullet for avoiding the real costs of disinflation. It appears that, for monetary policy-makers, announcements alone are not enough; the only way to gain credibility is to earn it.

On the other hand, both the survey data and the interest-rate differentials indicate that credibility, once earned, can provide better subsequent outcomes. After inflation targets have been met successfully for a period of time, inflation expectations remain low, even in the face of a business-cycle expansion. This evidence suggests that although the gains from inflation targeting are not high in the disinflation phase of inflation stabilization, inflation targeting does help to pin down inflation expectations as the new regime becomes established.

Does Inflation Targeting Change the Behavior of Inflation?

Even if the adoption of inflation targeting does not immediately improve the terms of the output-inflation tradeoff or moderate inflation expectations, it is possible that the adoption of inflation targeting might alter the dynamics of the inflationary process. For example, as the commitment to price stability by the central bank becomes established, the responses of actors in the economy to inflationary shocks may change, with the possible outcome that a given one-time shock to inflation may be less likely to induce a persistent rise in inflation. In other words, one potentially important benefit of inflation targeting is its ability to "contain" inflationary impulses, preventing them from affecting the trend or long-run rate of inflation.

We provide some tentative evidence on this question by means of a forecasting exercise, as follows: For each inflation targeter in our sample, we estimate a simple statistical model of the joint behavior of inflation and related variables. Specifically, for each country we estimate a three-variable, unrestricted vector autoregression (VAR) model of the behavior of core inflation, GDP growth, and the overnight interest rate controlled by the central bank (the policy instrument). Sample periods are from the second quarter of 1971 to the date of target adoption in each country. Using these estimated equations, we forecast the behavior of the three variables forward in time for five or more years from the time of target adoption. These forecasts are "dynamic" in that the model's forecast values (rather than actual data values) are used for the values of lagged variables in the forecast period.[17] Thus no data drawn from the period following target adoption are used in constructing the forecasts.

The purpose of this exercise is to evaluate whether the interaction among inflation, GDP growth, and short-term interest rates changes markedly following the adoption of inflation targeting.[18] The (unconditional) forecast of each variable generated by our statistical models can be thought of as representing how the system would have behaved (in the absence of new shocks) if the pre-adoption policy regime had been retained. This predicted behavior may be compared with the actual post-adoption behavior of the same variables. Since there do not appear to have been major aggregate supply or aggregate demand shocks since target adoption for the four inflation-targeting countries studied in this chapter, the comparison between what actually happened to these variables and their forecasted values, at least for the period of the early 1990s, is a worthwhile exercise.[19]

In the four countries that adopted inflation targets in the early 1990s (New Zealand, Canada, the United Kingdom, and Sweden), disinflation through tighter monetary policy had largely been completed by the time the target was adopted, allowing interest rates to come down. (The year or so of further disinflation that occurred in these countries appears to be attributable to the lagged effects of earlier policy actions.) This is consistent with our findings in the case studies that countries typically adopted targets in order to "lock in" inflation expectations at a low level after a disinflation. The key question here is whether, following the adoption of inflation targeting, positive shocks to the inflation rate lead to less permanent increases in inflation (with output and interest rates held constant) than would have been the case in the pre-adoption regimes.

Figures 10.4 through 10.6 plot the results of these simulations (dashed lines) versus the actual paths of inflation, GDP growth, and the instrument interest rate over the post-adoption period for each of our sample countries. Figure 10.4 compares New Zealand and Canada, two inflation targeters with small, open, resource-based economies, with Australia, a similar economy that adopted a less formal inflation-targeting regime, and that only in late 1994. Figure 10.5 compares the two European targeters that abandoned their exchange-rate pegs—the United Kingdom and Sweden—with Italy, a non-targeting European country that also was forced by speculative attacks to abandon its peg.

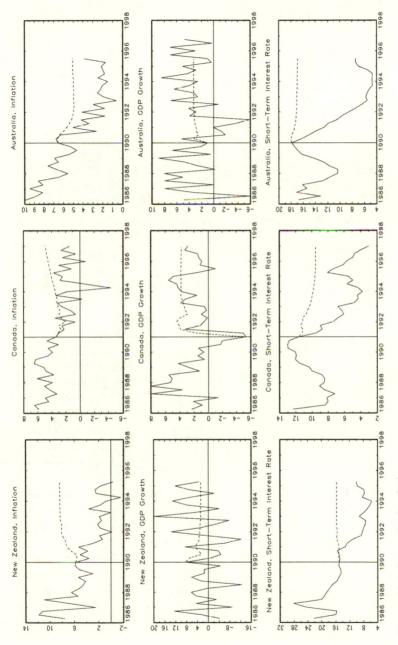

Figure 10.4. Dynamic simulations.

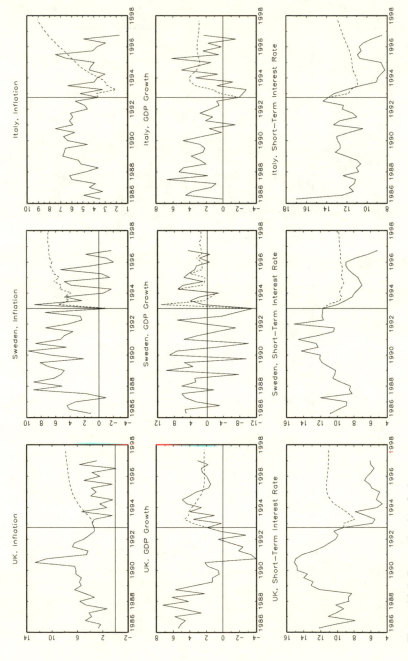

Figure 10.5. Dynamic simulations.

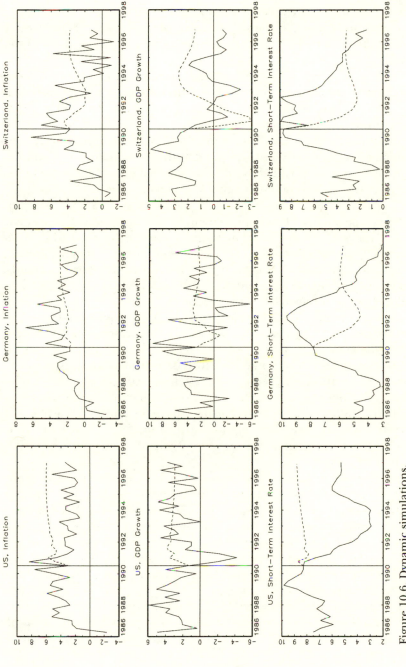

Figure 10.6. Dynamic simulations.

Figure 10.6 shows the results for Germany, Switzerland, and the United States. As should be expected, the simulated variables tend to "flatten out" over time, moving toward their sample means or toward a slight trend; this is the result of the absence of new shocks in the simulation.

Figures 10.4 and 10.5 show that, for all four inflation-targeters considered, actual inflation tends to be lower than forecast, especially during the period a year or more after adoption. Actual inflation in the targeting countries also exhibits a mild downward trend, as opposed to the slight upward trend typically seen in the simulations. Importantly, however, in all four countries except Sweden the lower-than-expected inflation rates are accompanied by substantial shortfalls in GDP growth over the two years following target adoption, as compared to the forecasted values. This pattern is another confirmation of our earlier result that there is no evidence of an improvement in the output-inflation tradeoff in the immediate aftermath of target adoption; instead, the initial disinflation is achieved only at the expense of short-run losses in output. Thereafter, however, GDP growth rates in all four targeters exceed the projections, while inflation and short-term interest rates remain at levels well below the forecasted values.

In the non-targeting countries included for comparison, the results are mixed. Like New Zealand and Canada (its comparison countries), Australia exhibits inflation below its out-of-sample forecast (Figure 10.4). Apparently, however, this disinflation came only at the cost of a substantial, entirely unpredicted shortfall in GDP growth over the first two years from the start of the simulation. Thereafter, the results exhibit the same pattern as in the comparison countries, with GDP growth on track, but with inflation and interest rates at new, lower levels. Thus, in Australia we see the effects of a disinflation without formal targets.

In contrast to all the other countries, Italy experienced inflation that was initially above the forecast, falling below the forecast only from 1994 onward (Figure 10.5). Meanwhile, Italian GDP growth fell substantially short of the projection until late 1994. Towards the end of the forecast horizon, while inflation and interest rates remain lower than predicted, GDP growth in Italy is below its forecast as well. The overall macroeconomic performance of Italy therefore seems less good than that of the other European countries.

In the United States (Figure 10.6), both the spike in inflation in late 1990 and the 1990-91 recession were largely unpredicted by our simple statistical model. By 1992, however, GDP growth had returned to its trend level, while inflation and short-term interest rates remained below their predicted levels for the rest of the forecast horizon. The results from our simulations for the United States therefore follow the basic pattern observed in the four inflation targeters and Australia.

The results for the other two baseline countries, Germany and Switzerland, are by contrast markedly different from those for the targeting countries, or for the United States, for that matter (Figure 10.6). The simulations for Germany clearly reflect the effects of monetary reunification, with both inflation and the monetary-policy instrument above their projections until early 1994. Likewise, following the upsurge in inflation in Switzerland during 1989-90, actual inflation was above its projection until the end of 1992; the Swiss interest rate also rose above its projection, and remained there for two years longer after inflation had returned to its expected level. GDP growth in both Germany and Switzerland exceeded the projections in the early part of the forecasting period, probably as a result of expanded aggregate demand; however, by 1992 and 1993 the effects of the increasingly restrictive monetary policy—as seen in interest rates well above those forecast into the second half of 1994—forced output growth below its projected trend. We interpret the return over time of inflation and the monetary-policy instrument to their projected levels after a surprise demand shock of great magnitude as characteristic of a successful targeting regime. Yet we also see that even a putatively credible monetary policy must tighten in response to shocks to such shocks, and that that policy tightness has real effects.

To assess the robustness of the results reported here, we also performed the simulations based on VARs estimated from 1980 on. One reason for doing so is that most of the countries in our sample conducted monetary policy during the 1970s much differently from the way they had after the second oil shock and the intellectual and political developments that followed it.[20] Another reason is that since the forecasts flatten out to their sample means, if we were to include the inflationary 1970s in the sample, we might bias the results and find inflation coming in below forecast. While there are only minor changes in the forecasts for GDP growth and short-term interest rates when we use the shorter data sample, in the alternative simulations the forecasts of inflation are lower in eight out of nine countries. Inflation still comes in consistently below forecast, however, for any of the inflation targeters and the United States. For Australia, the inflation forecast is higher, leading to a larger over-prediction of actual inflation.

Summary

For the inflation-targeting countries, the forecasting exercises described in this section indicate that inflation rates after the adoption of inflation targeting are lower than otherwise would have been expected. These disinflations are not costless, being accompanied by declines in output growth (relative to prediction), suggesting once again that adoption of inflation targeting does not eliminate the costs of reducing inflation. On the other hand, once disinflation has been achieved, inflation-targeting countries appear to have better inflation performance than might have been expected from their past experience, while output growth bounces back and for a short period may even exceed what would have been expected. Further, in the inflation-targeting countries, inflation rises less than would be expected during the subsequent period of renewed output growth, a finding consistent with our evidence that inflation expectations in these countries remain relatively tame in the face of strong business-cycle upturns.

The evidence from the remaining five countries suggests two important qualifications to these conclusions. First, as the results for Australia (prior to its target adoption) and for the United States show, better-than-expected inflation performance is not confined to countries operating under explicitly announced targets. Put differently, inflation targets are not a necessary condition for sustaining low inflation. Second, the results for Germany and Switzerland bring home the point that even for countries with a long record of credible targeting, reducing inflation comes at the price of significant output reductions in the short run.

The Effectiveness of Inflation Targeting: A Preliminary Assessment

All things considered, the adoption of inflation targeting as the framework for monetary policy in the countries examined here appears to have been a success. While we cannot know precisely what would have happened had they not adopted inflation targeting, these countries have seen inflation levels and inflation expectations fall below, and remain below, what would have been expected based on extrapolations of the past. On the other hand, the hopes of some adopting countries (Canada and New Zealand were particularly explicit on this point) that the costs of disinflation would decline as a result of inflation targeting were not fulfilled during the first post-adoption disinflations. It is difficult to say whether this should be seen as a failure of inflation targeting to create credibility, or simply as a confirmation of the finding of much previous research that changes in the structure of monetary policy have little effect on the inflation-output tradeoff in the short run.

The comparison of the adopting countries' inflation record with that of the respective "control" countries, Australia and Italy, underscores the favorable—albeit delayed—effect of inflation targeting on inflation expectations. Overall, though, we must admit that the economic performance of the non-targeters over the period considered is not appreciably different from that of the inflation targeters. While in all the inflation-targeting countries, inflation remains unexpectedly low as GDP growth returns to its predicted path, the same is true for Australia and the United States.

A comparison of the effect of inflation targeting in the sample countries to what longstanding targeters Germany and Switzerland have experienced brings home two crucial points. First, on the negative side, it may just be too much to expect monetary regimes, even highly credible ones, to alter the terms of the output-inflation tradeoff. So, perhaps, our findings for the inflation targeters should not come as a great surprise. Second, and more positively, there appears to be some evidence that a credible and transparent targeting regime is able to "lock in" low expectations of medium-term and long-term inflation in the face of temporary shocks to the price level. Thus we find a sort of asymmetry: The strength of a nominal targeting regime (*i.e.*, of either money growth or inflation) may be its ability to cope with and contain adverse inflationary developments, even though a policy of active disinflation remains costly. Thus, while inflation targeting may not reduce the costs of the transition to low inflation, it may help central banks sustain price stability in the longer run by increasing the transparency of policy and the accountability of the monetary policy-makers.

Part Three

CONCLUSIONS

11

What Have We Learned?

WE HAVE reviewed the experience with inflation targeting of a number of countries around the world, and we have reported the results of our attempts to measure the effects of this approach to monetary policy statistically. Now it is time to summarize what we have learned.

The evidence we have reported may help us to answer several important questions about the workings of an inflation-targeting regime. Three sets of questions stand out:

First are questions relating to design, implementation, and operation: Assuming that a country decides to adopt inflation targeting, how should it structure the policy regime? For example, who should be responsible for setting the inflation target, for meeting the target, and for explaining policy goals and actions to the public? How should the policy-makers respond to various shocks that threaten price stability or other economic objectives? Is there a best time (or set of economic and political circumstances) to introduce inflation targeting? Is there a consensus on what constitutes "best practice" in the day-to-day implementation of inflation targeting?

Second, how successful has inflation targeting been? What are the benefits of this approach? What are the costs? To what degree do the advantages and disadvantages of inflation targeting depend on the details of implementation, the political environment, and the state of the economy?

Third, are the advantages of inflation targeting unique to that approach, or might alternative approaches to monetary policy work as well or better?

This chapter addresses each set of questions. The reader will not be surprised to learn that we believe that a well-structured inflation-targeting regime—though neither a panacea nor a substitute for intelligent policy-making—will provide a useful framework for the making of monetary policy in modern economies.

The Design and Operation of an Inflation-Targeting Regime

To paraphrase Thomas Edison, good policy-making is one percent conceptualization and ninety-nine percent execution. Inflation target-

ing provides a useful conceptual framework for thinking about and implementing monetary policy. But the experience of countries that have taken
this approach suggests that a great deal depends on the details of implementation, including the choice of target, the means of communicating
with the public, the institutional arrangements that ensure central bank
accountability, and so on.

Our case studies suggest that a substantial degree of convergence has
taken place among the major inflation-targeting countries in the design
of their policy regimes. There seems indeed to be an emerging consensus on how to answer many of the operational questions posed in Chapter 3, and thus on what constitutes "best practice" in the implementation of inflation targeting. Many of the details of implementation have
differed from country to country, and such differences can provide us
with insight into what works and what doesn't within the inflation-targeting framework. We now consider a number of the key design and operational issues and some of the lessons that the international experience
with inflation targeting provides.

Introduction of the Inflation Target

When is the best time to introduce inflation targeting? Generally, major
changes in monetary policy regimes occur only under duress, and so it
might seem that the best time to start targeting inflation would be when
inflation is threatening to get out of control. Yet most inflation-targeting
countries have chosen to adopt the new regime only *after* having had
some initial success in lowering inflation from previously high levels.

This timing has usually reflected a tactical political decision that, in
order to gain credibility for the new regime, it is important to be able to
meet the initial inflation targets with high probability. It also reflects the
fact that one of the main benefits of inflation targets is that they may
help to "lock in" earlier disinflationary gains, particularly in the face of
one-time inflationary shocks. We saw this effect, for example, following
the exits of the United Kingdom and Sweden from the European Exchange Rate Mechanism and after Canada's 1991 imposition of the Goods
and Services Tax. In each case, the re-igniting of inflation seems to have
been avoided by the announcement of inflation targets that helped to
anchor the public's inflation expectations and to give an explicit plan
for and direction to monetary policy.

The specific impetus for the introduction of inflation targeting has
varied substantially. In some cases the introduction of the new approach

followed a discrete event, such as the collapse of an exchange-rate peg in the United Kingdom or Sweden, or the adoption of a much broader package of economic reforms, as in New Zealand. In other cases, the new approach to monetary policy has evolved gradually, in response to various dissatisfactions with the existing regime; we saw this pattern in Canada, Israel, and Australia. The central bank has usually played a key role in the move toward inflation targets, but the government has also taken the initiative in some countries, such as the United Kingdom and Spain. Formal legislative changes have played a role in only a few cases. Whatever the origins of the new policy, best results seem to be obtained when the inflation targets are introduced with some fanfare, in a way that makes clear to the public that a distinctly new approach is being adopted, rather than being quietly phased in. A clear signal that the new approach is supported by, and is the joint responsibility of, both the government and the central bank is also conducive to the framework's eventual success.

Choosing and Defining the Target

Despite the rhetoric about pursuing "price stability", all the countries studied here have chosen to target the inflation rate—that is, the rate at which prices are changing over time—rather than the level of prices *per se*. The reason is that policy-makers are concerned about the effect a price-level target might have on short-run macroeconomic stability. If they targeted a specific level of prices, and that target were overshot, there would have to be a period of falling prices—that is, deflation—as the price level was brought back to the target. As we saw in Chapter 3, there are good reasons to fear deflation, including the possibility that it might endanger the financial system and precipitate an economic contraction. Indeed, deflation has often been associated with deep recessions or even depressions, as in the 1930s. Thus policy-makers in the countries we have studied have concluded that a price-level target, which would likely require periods of deflation, might create unacceptable costs in terms of lost output and employment. Fortunately, the experience of inflation-targeting countries indicates that a full reversal of target misses, as would be required by a price-level target, does not appear to be necessary for the maintenance of low inflation or policy credibility.

For related reasons, no targeting country so far has chosen a zero midpoint for its inflation target range, as would be required by a literal application of the phrase "price stability." Even the Bundesbank, one of the world's most resolute opponents of inflation, chose as its normative inflation target 2% *per annum* for many years (now 1.5% to 2%), above most estimates of possible upward bias in official measures of inflation. A key rationale, again, is concern about possible deflation: Targeting values for inflation greater than zero makes periods of accidental deflation less likely. Also, many economists believe (though it remains controversial) that the benefits of low inflation may be fully realized when inflation reaches the 2% to 3% range, and that still lower rates could impede the functioning of the real economy. In any case, the evidence suggests that maintaining a target for inflation that is above (but not too far above) zero for an extended period, as even the Bundesbank has done, does not lead to instability in the public's inflation expectations or to a decline in the central bank's credibility.

Although targeting countries agree that inflation, not the price level, should be the target, and that the optimal target is not zero but a small positive rate of inflation, they exhibit important differences in the specific ways they choose to define their targets operationally. Perhaps most striking among these is that there is no clear consensus on what measure of inflation should be targeted. Some countries use the "headline", or all-items, CPI, presumably because it is the most familiar to the public. Others use a CPI inflation measure from which the prices of certain items (food and energy, for example) are excluded, in order to avoid reacting to the first-round effects (the direct effects on inflation) of transient supply shocks. Others use both types of measures.

We see here a manifestation of a central issue in the design of inflation targets: the short-run tradeoff between transparency (as promoted, for example, by the use of a simple, well-known measure of inflation) and policy flexibility (which, in this case, is enhanced by the use of inflation indexes that omit the first-round effects of supply shocks). The typical compromise has been to choose relatively simple and well-known indexes for defining the inflation target but to resort to complicated explanations of deviations from that target. There are exceptions: New Zealand, for example, uses an inflation target that explicitly excludes a variety of prices linked to supply shocks. That choice promotes policy flexibility but at some cost to transparency, since the public may find it difficult to understand the alternative index, particularly if its definition is not consistent over time (as has been the case in New Zealand). Overall, however, so long as the target inflation measure is not changed too often and does not deviate too widely from "headline" measures of inflation, it seems that the measure chosen is not critical to the success of the targeting program.

The tradeoff between transparency and flexibility is also an issue in deciding which agency will be responsible for measuring inflation. New Zealand has made the Reserve Bank accountable for meeting the targets and also for measuring (and adjusting) the official inflation numbers; presumably, giving the Reserve Bank some discretion in adjusting the inflation measure is intended to increase the flexibility of policy to deal with unforeseen events. In contrast, the other countries we have examined have chosen to separate responsibility for meeting the targets (vested in the central bank) from responsibility for measuring the target variable (vested in a separate statistical agency). Although allowing the central bank to measure and adjust the target variable may tend to heighten flexibility, it decreases transparency and erodes the public's confidence in the integrity of the regime. Assigning the measurement of inflation and the pursuit of the inflation target to separate agencies seems to be the wiser course.

Short-run Policy Flexibility and Multiple Objectives

Focusing monetary policy on inflation does not imply that traditional stabilization goals are ignored; the notion that monetary policy-makers under inflation targeting are indifferent to the performance of the real economy is simply incorrect. Central bankers responsible for inflation targeting continue to be concerned about fluctuations in output and employment, and in all the countries we have studied, the ability to accommodate short-run stabilization goals is, to some degree, built into the inflation-targeting regime. Evidence that output and employment remain concerns of policy-makers after the switch to inflation targeting can be seen in the fact that all the targeting countries have undertaken disinflation only gradually, to avoid putting undue pressure on the real economy. For example, a number of countries, including Canada and Sweden, set their initial inflation targets to take effect only with substantial delay, so as not to impose unnecessary short-run costs in terms of lost output or employment. A common practice has been to distinguish between the long-run inflation goal and short-run inflation targets, with the latter set to converge gradually with the former. By adjusting the speed of convergence with the long-run goal (or, nearly equivalently, the target horizon), the policy-makers can moderate the real costs of reducing inflation, and also reduce output fluctuations, while still maintaining a strong commitment to long-run price stability.[1]

The setting of a floor as well as a ceiling for the acceptable inflation rate, whether explicitly (through target ranges) or implicitly, also shows a concern for macroeconomic stabilization. This point has been emphasized most by the Bank of Canada, which has argued that inflation targeting that sets a floor as well as a ceiling can help protect the real economy from shocks to aggregate spending. In particular, declines in aggregate demand that cause the inflation rate to fall below the lower bound of the target range will automatically stimulate the central bank to loosen monetary policy without fearing that its action will trigger a rise in inflation expectations. Thus inflation targeting increases the flexibility of the central bank in responding to declines in aggregate spending. Insofar as aggregate demand shocks are the dominant source of cycles in a given country, this approach imparts a countercyclical tendency to monetary policy, in contrast to the destabilizing procyclical behavior of monetary policy seen in many countries in the past.

What about aggregate supply shocks? Unlike aggregate demand shocks, aggregate supply shocks are not automatically handled by the inflation-targeting framework. However, in all the countries we have examined, the monetary-policy authorities routinely allow deviations from inflation targets in response to supply shocks. Following (or in anticipation of) a supply shock, such as, for example, a change in value-added taxes, the normal procedure is for the central bank first to deviate from its planned policies as needed and then to explain the reasons for its action to the public. Among the countries we have considered, only in New Zealand has an explicit "escape clause" been invoked to justify such actions, although the Reserve Bank of New Zealand has also permitted target deviations that can be justified only on a more *ad hoc* basis. The ability to permit short-run deviations from the inflation target is beneficial if (1) they can be plausibly rationalized for the public, and (2) they do not threaten longer-run inflation goals. The capacity to deviate from the target if necessary allows the central bank a significant degree of flexibility in trying to stabilize the economy in the short run without sacrificing the benefits of low inflation and low inflation expectations in the long run.

A further source of policy flexibility lies in the power of the monetary authorities to adjust the inflation targets themselves (as opposed to deviating from established targets). All the targeting countries have adjusted the official inflation targets or target ranges gradually over time, both upward (as in the case of Germany after the 1979 oil shock and New Zealand after the 1996 election) and downward (as in all the countries we have examined, as their initial disinflations proceeded). So long as variations in the target path are announced far enough in advance that they do not appear to be merely an *ex post* rationalization of actual inflation outcomes, changes in the target path are generally perceived by the public to be a reasonable way of adapting to economic conditions. In particular, with adequate explanation from the central bank, the public seems able to distinguish a one-time, temporary shock to inflation—which may be accommodated by a transitory increase in the inflation target—from a change in trend inflation, which the inflation targets usually are (and should be) set to resist. This is a substantial benefit, since containment of inflationary expectations is the only means available, other than the painful solution of slowing the economy, for keeping inflation under control.

Information Variables and Intermediate Targets

Inflation-targeting central banks generally do not tie themselves to specific intermediate targets, such as the growth rate of the money stock or the exchange rate (although in some countries the exchange rate has provided a secondary objective for monetary policy). To the extent that intermediate targets are used, as in the hybrid regimes of Germany and Switzerland, conflicts between the intermediate target and the inflation goal are almost always resolved in favor of the inflation goal.

While the use of intermediate targets (other than the forecast of future inflation itself, as emphasized by Svensson [1997a]) does not fit comfortably with inflation targeting, many inflation-targeting central banks have emphasized particular macroeconomic indicators as information variables, *i.e.,* variables that contain information about the future course of the economy but which are not themselves targeted. Examples include the monetary conditions index in New Zealand and Canada and the broad money aggregate ALP in Spain. Considerable attention has been paid by some central banks to surveys that attempt to measure the public's expectations of inflation, as well as estimates of inflation expectations inferred from bond yields. Structural models of the economy play an important role in many countries. However, although the targeting countries differ in the degree to which they emphasize particular indicators of inflation in their decision-making, all rely on a variety of sources of information when deciding on policy. The result is a policy regime that exhibits what we have called "constrained discretion," a style of policy-making very different from the "automatic pilot" approach advocated, for example, by some monetarists. In particular, because it frees the central bank from mechanical rules and permits a distinction between short-run and long-run policy objectives, constrained discretion allows for objectives other than inflation to enter into decisions about monetary policy.

Point Target versus Target Range

A design decision that affects the short-run flexibility of policy is whether to set the inflation target as a single point (as, for example, in Switzerland's monetary targeting since 1975 and in the United Kingdom since 1995) or as a range of acceptable outcomes. The advantage of a range is that it provides more explicit flexibility to the targeting regime and also conveys to the public the important message that control of inflation is imperfect. However, the use of a range has certain drawbacks. As we saw in the case studies of countries that use a target range, and as we know from experience with exchange-rate targeting within a band, the range may "take on a life of its own." With target ranges in place, politicians, financial markets, and the public often focus on whether inflation is just outside or just inside the edge of the range, rather than on the magnitude of the deviation from the midpoint of the range. Furthermore, given the uncertainty of inflation forecasts, even with entirely appropriate monetary policy in place, the inflation rate may fall outside the target range. Missing an entire range may be perceived by the public as a more serious failure of policy than missing a point (which happens almost inevitably), leading to a possible loss of credibility for the inflation-targeting regime.

Another problem with the use of target ranges is that misses are particularly likely to occur if the target horizon is short, on the order of a year. In that case, "firm" target ranges for inflation may lead to the so-called instrument instability problem, in which the vigorous attempts of policy-makers to keep inflation within the target range cause the policy instruments—such as short-term interest rates or the exchange rate—to undergo undesirably large fluctuations. The problems of control errors in inflation and instrument instability have been particularly severe in New Zealand, but they have not been unknown in other inflation-targeting countries.

One solution to these problems is to widen the target range, as New Zealand did in November 1996. If the range is made wide enough to significantly reduce the instrument instability and control problems, however, the targeting regime may lose credibility. That is particularly likely if the public focuses on the edges of the range rather than on the midpoint, and if the range is made so wide that its upper limit seems unreasonably high. Indeed, the act of widening the range (as distinct from moving the midpoint of the range in response to events) might be seen as a sign that the monetary authorities have weakened their resolve, rather than as an indication that they are trying to improve the functioning of the system.

The alternative to using a target range is to set a point target for inflation. In order to avoid control problems and instrument instability, however, it is imperative that the public be made aware that, because of unavoidable uncertainties, even the best policies are unlikely to hold inflation consistently within a small tolerance around the point target. This need imposes a greater burden on the central bank to make its explanations persuasive. But, so long as the public believes the central bank's explanations, the bank has greater flexibility to cope with target misses without damaging its credibility. With a point target, success is no longer defined as hitting the target exactly (or as whether inflation has fallen just inside or outside the boundaries of the target range). Rather, it is defined as the bank's ability to keep inflation reasonably close to the target over long periods.

Transparency

A stress on "transparent" policy—policy that is clear, simple, and understandable—and on regular communication with the public characterizes (to a greater or lesser degree) all the inflation-targeting regimes we have considered. The central banks in inflation-targeting countries communicate in a variety of ways. They have frequent communications with the government, some mandated by law and some in response to informal inquiries, and their officials make public speeches on policy and the economy. Both channels are commonly used in countries that have not adopted inflation targeting, of course. Inflation-targeting central banks take public outreach a step further, however, through various types of informational campaigns and through the publication of regular "inflation reports." Inflation reports, first seen in the United Kingdom but now issued by virtually all inflation-targeting central banks, provide comprehensive information on inflation prospects and the central bank's plans and objectives, typically presented in a pedagogically clear and accessible style.

Through these channels of communication, central banks try to explain to both the general public and to narrower constituencies (such as participants in financial markets) (1) the goals and limitations of monetary policy, including the rationale for inflation targets; (2) the numerical values of the inflation targets and how they were determined; (3) how the inflation targets are to be achieved, given current economic conditions; and (4) reasons for any deviations from the targets. Even the independent Bundesbank, with its strong public support, makes great efforts along these lines.

Why spend so much effort on clarity and communication? The efforts by the inflation-targeting central banks to improve transparency and communication have been crucial to the success of the targeting regimes. They have improved private-sector planning by reducing uncertainty about monetary policy, interest rates, and inflation; they have promoted useful public debate of monetary policy, in part by educating the public about what a central bank can and cannot achieve; they have increased the central banks' freedom of action in the longer run, for example by making temporary deviations from target possible without adverse effects on inflation expectations; and they have helped clarify the responsibilities of the central bank and of politicians in the conduct of monetary policy. Transparency and communication together enhance accountability.

Accountability

A distinctive feature of all the targeting regimes discussed here is the tendency toward increased accountability of the central bank. The most extreme case is New Zealand, where the government and the central bank sign a formal agreement setting out the objectives of policy, and the government has the right to dismiss the Reserve Bank's governor if the inflation targets are breached. In other targeting countries, the central bank's accountability is usually less formalized. Still, transparency of policy associated with inflation targeting has tended to make the central bank highly accountable to both the public and the government. That high level of accountability has been evident in the majority of the inflation-targeting countries studied here.

Accountability has a number of advantages, both operational and political. We have seen throughout the case studies that sustained success in the conduct of monetary policy, as measured against a pre-announced and well-defined baseline (such as a path of inflation targets), can be instrumental in building public support for a central bank's independence and for its policies. This building of public support and accountability occurs even in the absence of a rigidly defined and legalistic standard of performance evaluation, as can be seen in the experience of the Bundesbank and Swiss National Bank, among others. A central bank that has the public's trust and support will be able to make policy with greater independence and a longer-run perspective, which generally leads to better economic outcomes. A trusted central bank may also provide a counterweight to the short-run influences affecting other dimensions of economic policy, such as fiscal policy. We have seen more than one example where the prestige and respect afforded the central bank by the public allowed it to exert a moderating influence on government budgetary decisions that threatened the achievement of the inflation objective.

Purely economic considerations aside, inflation targeting also has the virtue of being fully consistent with the role of a central bank in a democratic society. Though a central bank should be insulated from short-term political pressures on interest-rate decisions, over the longer term, it should be accountable to the political process for achieving its established goals. In other words, the central bank should be instrument-independent, but not goal-independent. When the goals of monetary policy, and the central bank's record in achieving them, are laid out clearly for the public, it becomes difficult for the central bank to pursue for any extended period policies that are inconsistent with the interests of society at large.

Macroeconomic Performance under Inflation Targeting: The International Record

How do economies respond to the adoption of inflation targeting? The clearest finding from the international experience is that inflation-targeting does indeed lead to lower inflation. In all the cases we have studied, countries using inflation targets significantly reduced both the rate of inflation and the public's inflation expectations relative to their previous experience and, probably, relative to what they would have been in the absence of inflation targets. Furthermore, once inflation is down, it stays down: Following disinflations, the inflation rate in targeting countries has not bounced back up during subsequent cyclical expansions of the economy. Inflation targeting does help policy-makers moderate and control inflation.

Economic theory and evidence both support the idea that low and stable inflation promotes economic growth and efficiency in the long run. Thus inflation targeting, perhaps together with other fiscal and structural reforms, can help create an environment in which the economy can prosper. Nor is the moderation of inflation the only benefit of targeting. The ability of a properly operated inflation-targeting regime to avoid deflation is equally important, since deflation appears to be extremely dangerous to the health of the financial system and of the economy in general. Finally, the forward-looking (as opposed to reactive) nature of inflation targeting has likely reduced the extent of procyclical, "stop-go" monetary policies. "Stop-go" policies (that is, monetary policies that react to inflation only after it has become a problem, then tighten sharply) have been an important source of cycles of boom and bust in a number of industrial countries, including the United States.

While the long-run economic benefits of lower and more stable inflation are clear, the balance of economic costs and benefits of inflation targeting in the short run is more ambiguous. Much economic theorizing suggests that commitment by a central bank to a plan for reducing inflation should improve its credibility and thereby reduce both inflation expectations and the output losses associated with disinflation. Experience (and the econometric evidence presented in Chapter 10) does not support this prediction, however. Inflation expectations, so far as we can measure them, do not immediately adjust downward following the adoption of inflation targeting. Instead, they respond only after a lag following declines in inflation. In other words, the public seems to take an "I'll believe it when I see it" attitude toward inflation reduction. So it appears that the only way for a central bank to achieve credibility is by earning it the hard way, by demonstrating that it can, in fact, achieve disinflation.

Consistent with the finding that inflation expectations respond slowly, there appears to be little if any reduction in the output loss associated with disinflation—the so-called "sacrifice ratio"—among countries adopting inflation targeting (see Chapter 10). Of course, there is always the hope that as inflation-targeting policies produce a continuing record of success in reducing inflation, both the pioneers and the later adopters of this approach will begin to enjoy a "credibility bonus" in the form of a lower real cost of achieving any given reduction in inflation.[2]

Although disinflation remains costly under inflation targeting, there does seem to be evidence that the effects of inflationary shocks are somewhat muted under this approach. For example, shortly after adopting inflation targets in February 1991, the Bank of Canada was faced with a large increase in indirect taxes, an adverse supply shock that in earlier periods might have led to a ratcheting up of inflation. Instead, the tax increase led to only a one-time increase in the price level; it did not generate second- and third-round rises in wages and prices, thereby creating a persistent increase in the inflation rate. Two other key examples are the experiences of Great Britain and Sweden following their departures from exchange-rate pegs in 1992. The normal expectation is that devaluation should have stimulated inflation in those countries, reflecting both the first-round direct effects of higher import prices and the subsequent effects on wage- and price-setting behavior. However, in the event, there was little inflationary impact of these two devaluations, a happy outcome that it seems reasonable to attribute to the adoption of inflation targets. The targets helped to focus public attention on the temporary nature of the devaluation shocks, while indicating the central banks' unwillingness to accommodate the shocks in the medium term. Both factors tended to short-circuit the second- and later-round effects of the initial inflationary shocks.

A common concern raised about inflation targeting is that the policy-makers' "excessive" attention to inflation will lead to low and unstable growth in output and employment. The evidence we have presented—both statistical and in the case studies—speaks quite clearly to this point. Inflation reduction *is* associated with below-normal output during the initial, disinflationary phase of an inflation-targeting regime. However, once low inflation levels have been achieved, output and employment return to levels at least as high as they were previously. A conservative conclusion is that, once low inflation is achieved, inflation targeting is not harmful to the real economy. Indeed, given the strong economic growth during the latter part of the 1990s in many countries that have adopted inflation targets, a case may be made that inflation targeting promotes real growth in addition to controlling inflation.

Once Again: A Framework, Not a Rule

A principal theme of this book is that inflation targeting does not fit within the "rules-versus-discretion" dichotomy of traditional monetary theory. According to that view, monetary policy must be either purely mechanical ("allow the money stock to grow by precisely 1% each quarter") or an exercise in unbridled discretion on the part of policy-makers. Some economists have characterized inflation targeting as just another type of policy rule. They have then cited the stock criticism of rules, which is that they place excessively tight limits on the ability of policy-makers to respond to unforeseen circumstances.

However, to reiterate, inflation targeting *as actually practiced* by modern central banks is in no sense a rigid policy rule. First, unlike classical monetary policy rules (such as the gold standard), inflation targeting does not give the central bank simple, mechanical instructions on how to conduct monetary policy. Rather, inflation targeting requires the central bank to use all available information in determining what actions to take in order to achieve the inflation target. Unlike policy rules, which typically direct the central bank's attention to a single key indicator (such as the monetary growth rate or the exchange rate), inflation targeting never encourages the central bank to ignore pertinent information in its policy-making.

Moreover, as we saw in the case studies, inflation targeting fosters a substantial degree of policy discretion, which permits the central bank to respond to economic developments quite flexibly so long as it remains within the constraints of long-run price stability. For example, as we mentioned above, there are a variety of mechanisms by which near-term inflation targets can be modified in response to changing economic circumstances, without abandoning the long-run inflation goal. Criticisms of inflation targeting based on the premise that it imposes too rigid a structure on monetary policy are therefore quite unfounded. Inflation targeting is not a rule. Rather, it is a framework that allows for the exercise of "constrained discretion."

Inflation targeting, conceived as a snug-fitting garment but not as a straightjacket for monetary policy, combines a number of the advantages traditionally ascribed either to rules or to discretion. Like rules, the inflation-targeting framework enhances policy transparency—the clarity with which policy objectives and planned actions are communicated to the public. Inflation targets are readily understood by the public and help keep the goal of price stability steadily in view. The inflation-targeting framework also creates a "nominal anchor" for the economy, convincing the public that low and stable inflation is the normal outcome and that deviations are likely to be transitory. Increased transparency, in turn, increases the accountability of monetary policy-makers to the public, thus making them less likely to engage in opportunistic behavior in the short run (for example, trying to create unsustainable employment gains, perhaps to support incumbent politicians).

Moreover, inflation targeting helps focus the political debate on what a central bank can do—control inflation—rather than on what it cannot do—raise economic growth permanently by pursuing expansionary policies. We mentioned a remarkable example of the salutary effects of inflation targeting on public debate in our chapter on Canada: In 1996, the president of the Canadian Economic Association criticized the Bank of Canada for pursuing monetary policy that he claimed was too contractionary. His criticism sparked widespread debate. Such debates often degenerate into calls for the immediate expansion or contraction of the economy with little reference to the long-run consequences of such policy changes. In this case, however, the very existence of the inflation target helped channel the debate into a substantive discussion over what should be the appropriate target level for inflation, with both the Bank and its critics obliged to make explicit their assumptions and estimates of the costs and benefits of various levels of inflation. In the end, the debate led to increased support for the Bank of Canada, and the conduct of monetary policy did not emerge as a major issue in the 1997 elections, as it had in the elections four years earlier.

Although inflation targeting is far more flexible than a simple policy rule, it does not permit the exercise of unbridled discretion by the central bank. The strategy of hitting an inflation target, by its very nature, forces policy-makers to be forward-looking rather than narrowly focused on current economic conditions. Further, through its transparency, an inflation-targeting regime increases the central bank's accountability, which in turn creates political pressures that prevent the central bank from ignoring, even briefly, the long-run consequences of its actions.

Alternatives to Inflation Targeting

We have argued that inflation targeting provides both a nominal anchor for monetary policy and a framework within which policy-makers can exercise "constrained discretion." However, there are other monetary regimes that in principle could provide similar advantages. We discuss briefly some advantages and disadvantages of the major alternatives to inflation targeting.[3]

Pegging the Exchange Rate

For any given country, particularly a small country, one strategy for monetary policy is to fix the exchange rate of its currency to that of a large, low-inflation country (usually a major trading partner). If the exchange rate is maintained at a fixed value, then eventually the domestic inflation rate should approach that of the other country, assuming that movements in the real exchange rate (that is, the relative prices of goods produced in the domestic and foreign economies) are not too large. Alternatively, the exchange rate might be allowed to depreciate at a fixed, predetermined rate (a "crawling peg"), which would permit the domestic inflation rate to be higher than that of the larger country.

An exchange-rate peg has some advantages, particularly if the authorities' commitment to it is reasonably credible. (A large stock of international reserves is a good indicator of a credible peg, but the central bank's demonstrated willingness to subordinate domestic policy goals to the maintenance of the peg is equally important.) An exchange-rate peg significantly constrains short-run opportunism on the part of the central bank, and hence, in principle, may reduce the inflationary bias of purely discretionary monetary policy. Another important advantage of an exchange-rate peg is its simplicity and clarity; the public easily understands, and typically supports, policies that promote a "strong" national currency. For example, the Banque de France has frequently cited the importance of the *franc fort* in justifying its tight monetary policies.

Exchange-rate pegs have helped even large countries to reduce their inflation rates. For example, whatever other concerns might be raised about the *franc fort,* it has succeeded in keeping French inflation low, and at about the same level as that of its German partner. Similarly, after pegging to the German mark in 1990, the United Kingdom was able to lower its inflation rate from 10% to 3% in just two years. (However, as we mentioned earlier, in 1992 the United Kingdom was forced to abandon the peg when the John Major government proved unwilling to raise interest rates high enough to stem a speculative attack on the pound.)

A particularly strong form of exchange-rate peg is the so-called currency board, designed in the nineteenth century as a means of controlling monetary policy in colonies. In a currency board system, the note-issuing authority announces both a fixed exchange rate with a particular foreign currency and its willingness to trade the foreign and domestic currencies at that rate in unlimited amounts. In order to make this promise credible, the authorities must maintain high levels of reserves of the foreign currency, sometimes exceeding 100% of the domestic currency issue. A currency board was successfully implemented by Argentina in 1990. Under the so-called "convertibility plan," Argentina's central bank was legally required to exchange Argentine pesos and U.S. dollars at a ratio of one to one. This strategy helped Argentina to bring inflation down from hyperinflationary levels in 1989 and 1990 to rates close to those of the United States by the mid-nineties. Currently, a number of countries (including several Eastern European transition economies) are experimenting with the currency board concept.

Exchange-rate pegs have serious disadvantages, however. Maintenance of the peg imposes severe constraints on the ability of the domestic monetary authorities to use monetary policy for other purposes, such as short-run domestic stabilization, especially if the domestic business cycle is "out of sync" with that of the nation's trading partners. The constraints on policy can be particularly onerous if the peg is imperfectly credible, since the lack of credibility will require domestic interest rates to be kept even higher than the interest rates of the country to which the currency is pegged. The strengthening of the domestic currency relative to that of trading partners, which often occurs following a successful peg, also tends to depress domestic economic activity, since it makes the country's exports less competitive in world markets. In addition, with a fixed exchange rate, shocks that strike the anchor country are quickly transmitted to the pegging country. For example, in response to economic problems engendered by the unification process in 1990, Germany tightened monetary policy and eased fiscal policy, actions that led to sharply higher interest rates. Those rates were transmitted, through the medium of exchange rates pegged to the mark, to members of the Exchange Rate Mechanism (ERM); the result was a significant slowing of growth in several of those countries.

Another disadvantage of exchange-rate pegs, as Obstfeld and Rogoff (1995) and others have emphasized, is that, in a world of highly mobile capital, a speculative attack on the pegged currency is always a possibility.[4] Indeed, the aftermath of German reunification was a crisis among members of the ERM in 1992. Since then, several other exchange-rate crises have occurred, including that of Mexico in 1994 and the widespread attacks on East Asian currencies in 1997.

Concerted speculative attacks on the currency of a country leave that country's central bank no attractive options: Either it can vigorously defend the peg, usually by raising interest rates sharply, or it can capitulate and devalue (or float) the currency. The former strategy can be highly damaging to the domestic economy, and may cost huge sums in international reserves. Abandoning the peg may also be destabilizing, by, for example, leading to a surge in inflation and increasing the domestic value of debts denominated in foreign currencies (a situation that arose both in Mexico and in East Asia).[5] Further, abandonment of the peg leaves monetary policy without the nominal anchor needed to maintain stable prices in the longer run.

A more general shortcoming of exchange-rate pegs is that they do not solve the problem of maintaining price stability. Rather, they shift the problem to another country (or to some international authority).

Even in a well-functioning system of fixed exchange rates, there must be a nominal anchor for the system as a whole. Under the gold standard, that anchor was provided by the world supply of monetary gold; unfortunately, shocks to the supply of or demand for gold could, and often did, lead to instability in the world price level. The Bretton Woods system of fixed exchange rates, which emerged after the Second World War and survived until 1971, was a "dollar standard" which tied the monetary policies of participants to that of the United States. That system collapsed when the monetary-policy objectives of the United States began to differ radically from those of Germany and other countries, just as the ERM came under extreme pressure in 1992 and 1993 when German monetary-policy goals diverged from those of other members. Finally, the proposed single European currency would require some type of system-wide nominal anchor (inflation targeting being at least one major possibility). Using the exchange rate as a nominal anchor is not an option for the system as a whole.

Targeting Money

A strategy for monetary policy that was popular from the mid-1970s (following the collapse of the Bretton Woods system) until the early 1980s was targeting a monetary aggregate. Both narrow measures of the money stock (the monetary base, M1) and broader measures (M2, M3) have been targeted in various countries. The intellectual roots of monetary targeting lie in Milton Friedman's monetarism, especially his (1959) recommendation that the central bank should maintain a constant rate of money growth. In practice, however, no central bank has ever adopted a rigid rule for determining money growth (Bernanke and Mishkin, 1992). As we have seen, even the most dedicated money-targeters (such as Germany and Switzerland) have demonstrated their willingness to deviate from their announced monetary targets in order to meet other short-term objectives, such as stabilization of output or the exchange rate. Further, the monetary targets themselves have been adjusted from year to year to reflect economic conditions and competing objectives of the central bank.

Compared with exchange-rate pegging, monetary targeting permits a central bank greater freedom to adjust monetary policy to domestic conditions, though at the same time it may impose less discipline on the central bank. Monetary targeting has other positive features as well: Monetary aggregates can be measured accurately and without too long a lag, and the ability of the central bank to control the rate of money growth is fairly good, at least for narrow monetary aggregates. The fact that deviations of actual money growth from targeted rates are fairly quickly detected should, in principle, have helped to build the credibility and accountability of central banks that engage in monetary targeting.

Ultimately, it appears that targeting money is a useful strategy *only* if there is a reliable relationship between money growth and goal variables such as inflation or the growth rate of nominal GDP. Despite early claims that velocity (the ratio of nominal GDP to the money stock) is constant, or at least predictable, in most countries, the relationship between money and the economy has proven to be highly unstable, as is evident from many of our case studies here. The reasons are not completely understood. Some observers have attributed velocity instability to financial innovation and other changes in banking systems. Others have suggested that the very attempt to target money caused historical relationships to break down. Whatever the reason, if the stock of money cannot be reliably linked to the behavior of goal variables such as inflation, then it is useless as a guide to monetary policy. In particular, given the frequency of velocity shifts, a money-targeting central bank must either constantly revise or miss its targets (thereby sacrificing any advantages of transparency, discipline, or accountability), or, alternatively, it must accept extremely poor outcomes for its goal variables.

This dilemma explains why the majority of monetary targeters abandoned this strategy in the 1980s;[6] and why even those few countries that continue to adhere to it do so in an extremely "flexible" and *ad hoc* manner. It also explains, not so incidentally, the upsurge of interest in inflation targeting. Under inflation targeting, the inflation rate is both the operating target and the ultimate goal variable, so the inflation-targeting central bank never faces the conflict between short-term target and longer-term objective routinely experienced by the money-targeting central bank.

Targeting Nominal GDP

As an alternative to inflation targeting, several economists have proposed that central banks should target the growth rate of nominal GDP (see, for example, Taylor [1985]; Hall and Mankiw [1994]). Relative to inflation, nominal GDP as a target has the advantage that it puts some weight on output as well as on prices in the policy-making process (although, as

Hall and Mankiw [1994] pointed out, there is no reason that the one-to-one weighting of output and inflation implicit in a nominal GDP target has to be the socially optimal one). With a nominal GDP target, a decline in projected real output growth would automatically imply an increase in the central bank's inflation target, which would tend to be stabilizing because it would automatically lead to an easier monetary policy. Cecchetti (1995) has produced simulations suggesting that attempting to stabilize nominal GDP growth should give better overall economic outcomes than targeting inflation would, in part because of the difficulty of forecasting inflation.

Nominal GDP targeting is close in spirit to inflation targeting and might provide a reasonable alternative. There are four reasons why inflation targeting is preferable to nominal GDP targeting, however.

First, having a nominal GDP target forces the government to make public its estimate of potential real GDP growth. Such an announcement raises difficult technical issues because estimates of potential GDP growth are far from precise, even in retrospect. From a political perspective, announcing a value for expected growth in potential real GDP is also problematic: A conservative estimate may lead to the accusation that the government or the central bank is excessively pessimistic and intends to prevent the economy from reaching its maximum potential; whereas a high estimate of potential growth, if it becomes viewed as an official target, can lead to excessively inflationary policies.

Second, information on prices is more timely and more frequently reported than data on nominal GDP (and could be made even more so)—a practical consideration that offsets some of the theoretical appeal of nominal GDP as a target. Although collection of data on nominal GDP also could be improved, measurement of nominal GDP requires data on current quantities as well as current prices and thus is perhaps intrinsically more difficult to accomplish in a timely manner.

Third, as we have argued in some detail, inflation targeting as it is actually practiced allows considerable flexibility for policy in the short run. Thus it is doubtful that, in practice, nominal GDP targeting would be more effective than inflation targeting in achieving short-run stabilization.

Finally, and perhaps most importantly, the concept of inflation in consumer prices is probably better understood by the public than is the concept of nominal GDP, which can easily be confused with real GDP. (Again, one can imagine a politician criticizing a low target for nominal GDP growth as being "anti-growth" when in fact the objective is to bring in a low rate of inflation.) Consequently, it seems likely that communication with the public and accountability would be better served by using an inflation target rather than a nominal GDP growth target. While a significant number of central banks have adopted inflation targeting, none to our knowledge has seriously considered adopting a nominal GDP target.

Just Do It: Preemptive Monetary Policy Without Explicit Targets

In recent years, the United States has achieved excellent macroeconomic performance (including low and stable inflation) without using an explicit nominal anchor (such as a target for the exchange rate, a monetary aggregate, or the price level). Although in the U.S. case, no explicit policy framework has been articulated, a coherent strategy for monetary policy does exist. That strategy consists of careful monitoring for signs of future inflation, coupled with periodic "preemptive strikes" by monetary policy against the threat of inflation.

Given the long lag between monetary-policy actions and their effects, as emphasized by Friedman, the preemptive strike strategy seems a sensible one. If the central bank waited until overt signs of inflation appeared, it would already be too late to maintain stable prices, at least not without a severe tightening of policy. Indeed, there is some evidence that inflation becomes much harder to control once it has been allowed to gather momentum, in the sense that higher inflation expectations become ingrained in various types of contracts and pricing agreements.

The main argument for the "just do it" strategy is, simply, its demonstrated success. In the United States, the inflation rate fell significantly over the decade of the 1980s, to around 3% by the end of 1991; since then, inflation has been stable at about that level or a bit below it. Although there was a mild recession in 1990-91, the subsequent lengthy expansion has brought unemployment rates down to levels not seen since the 1960s, and the overall growth rate has been good. Evidently, this strategy has helped the Federal Reserve to anchor expectations by convincing the public that it is concerned about future as well as current inflation, while at the same time retaining some discretion to deal with unforeseen events in the economy.

There are, however, some important problems with the "just do it" approach that would be ameliorated by the relatively modest change to inflation targeting. We leave the discussion of why inflation targeting improves on the "just do it" strategy, and of why we think that inflation targeting should be adopted in the United States, to the next chapter.

Conclusions

Our analysis suggests that targeting inflation, whether directly, as in New Zealand, Canada, the United Kingdom, Sweden, Australia, Spain, and Israel; or as the basis for a monetary targeting regime, as in Germany and Switzerland, is a useful strategy for the conduct of monetary policy. (Since the defining feature of both the German and the other monetary frameworks we have examined is a publicly announced numerical target for medium-term inflation, we do not draw as great a distinction between these targeting regimes as many do in more theoretically oriented discussions.) Transparency and flexibility, properly balanced in operational design, appear to be the foundations of a monetary-policy strategy that will achieve both output stability in the short run and price stability in the long run without imposing a straitjacket on policy. Inflation targeting demonstrably improves the accountability of central bankers to the public and to elected officials and fosters communication between the policy-makers and the public.

Inflation targeting is no panacea, however. In particular, it does not enable countries to wring inflation out of their economies without incurring costs in lost output and employment; nor is credibility for the central bank achieved immediately on adoption of an inflation target. Indeed, evidence suggests that the only way for central banks to earn credibility is the hard way: by demonstrating that they have the means and the will to reduce inflation and to keep it low for a period of time. Although this approach does not avoid the costs of achieving disinflation, we have seen that inflation targeting has been highly successful in helping Canada, New Zealand, the United Kingdom, Sweden, Spain, Australia, and others to achieve and maintain low inflation rates, something they were not always able to do in the past.

Finally, the adoption of inflation targets has not forced central banks to abandon their concerns about other important economic outcomes, such as the level of the exchange rate or the rate of economic growth, in order to achieve low inflation rates. Indeed, there is no evidence that inflation targeting has produced harmful effects on the real economy in the long run; more likely, low inflation rates have improved the prospects for sustained long-term growth. We conclude that inflation targeting is a highly promising strategy for monetary policy, and we predict that it will become the standard approach as more and more central banks and governments come to appreciate its usefulness.

12

Inflation Targeting for the United States and the European Monetary Union

WE HAVE described how inflation targeting has worked in practice and have indicated why we believe that it deserves consideration as a strategy for monetary policy. To date, however, the United States has chosen not to join the ranks of the inflation-targeting countries. Instead it has followed the "just do it" approach described in the preceding chapter. Granted, the United States has recently enjoyed excellent economic performance without benefit of explicit inflation targets. Will this strong performance necessarily continue? Or might the adoption of inflation targets promote even better monetary-policy outcomes for the United States in the future?

The Maastricht Treaty, which establishes the groundwork for the European Monetary Union (EMU) and the European System of Central Banks (ESCB), sets price stability as the primary goal of monetary policy. What has not been decided is precisely how the European Central Bank, supported by the national central banks that make up the ESCB, is to achieve that goal. Currently, both monetary targeting and inflation targeting are under consideration as policy strategies for the EMU. Should the European Central Bank follow the Bundesbank and choose monetary targeting as its monetary-policy strategy? Or would inflation targeting do a better job of promoting price stability in the new European context?

Our analysis of the international experience leads us to the conclusion that inflation targeting would be the better choice for monetary policy in both the United States and Europe. In policy-making, as in life, however, the "devil is in the details." So, in this final chapter, we use what we have learned about how inflation targeting has worked in practice to outline specific proposals for the implementation of inflation targeting in both the United States and the European Monetary Union.

Inflation Targeting in the United States

Friedman and Kuttner (1996) point out that U.S. monetary policy has performed quite well in the recent past without benefit of a formal rule or framework. The question arises, "If it ain't broke, why fix it?" Perhaps we should be satisfied with the flexibility of our current policy process, since we cannot know what challenges will confront monetary policy in the future.

Monetary policy in the United States as of the latter part of the 1990s is not "broke" to any serious degree, we agree. Still, it could surely be improved. Moreover, the experience of other countries suggests that now is the ideal time to make the requisite changes to ensure that the good performance of monetary policy in the United States will continue when the current Federal Reserve leadership passes from the scene.

If It Ain't Broke, Why Fix It?

Why tinker with a policy framework that is performing so well? We offer several answers to this question.

First, in our view, a major reason for the success of the Volcker-Greenspan Federal Reserve is that it has employed a policy-making philosophy, or framework, that is in many ways quite similar to inflation targeting. The Federal Reserve has expressed a strong preference for low, stable inflation; and policy discussions about short-run stabilization (both within the Federal Reserve and between the Federal Reserve and the legislative and executive branches) have featured consideration of the long-term inflation implications of current actions. So, along certain dimensions, adoption of inflation targeting would not be a major departure from what the Federal Reserve has actually been doing in recent years. Rather, it would serve to a large degree to formalize, and thus (it may be presumed) to perpetuate, some of the positive features of current practice.

Second, formal adoption of inflation targeting would increase the transparency of the Fed's policymaking. In this respect, it would build on a number of recent steps taken by the Fed, such as shortening the time before the minutes of Federal Open Market Committee (FOMC) meetings are released and the decision to announce immediately after the FOMC meeting the Committee's decision about whether to change the target for the federal funds rate. Greater transparency would promote better public understanding of the Fed's strategy and tactics. That better understanding would lead in turn to a more informed public debate and, ultimately, to better policy outcomes.

Our case studies have shown that inflation targeting encourages both public and politicians to focus on what monetary policy can do (maintain long-run price stability), rather than on what it cannot do (create permanent increases in output and employment through expansionary policies). Expansionary monetary policies have long been seen as a "quick fix" for the economy, because they create more output and more jobs in the short run. However, both experience and extensive research show that expansionary policies cannot sustain such increases for long. On the contrary, they may eventually lead to higher inflation, with harmful consequences for the economy in the long run. In the countries we have studied, the existence of an inflation-targeting framework has more than once nudged the political debate toward a longer-run perspective, in which the benefits of price stability are recognized. The result has been less pressure on the monetary authorities to pursue ill-advised policies that provide some temporary stimulus, but at the cost of higher inflation and impaired economic performance in the longer term.

The contrast between more and less transparent policy regimes is nicely illustrated by events during the spring of 1997 in the United States and the United Kingdom. At that time, following several previous reductions of the federal funds rate, the Federal Reserve reversed its policy and hiked the target for the funds rate by 25 basis points (one-quarter of a percentage point). Although that rise was quite modest, particularly given the rapid growth of the U.S. economy and the tight labor market at the time, it provoked a storm of criticism in Congress and elsewhere. Yet at about the same time, increases in interest rates engineered by the Bank of England, an established inflation-targeter, were received quite calmly by the British public. The difference, we suggest, lies in the use of inflation targeting in Britain. Because of this approach, the British public had a better understanding of the long-run objectives being pursued by their monetary authorities, and hence of the reason for their policy action, than did the U.S. public. The adoption of inflation targeting in the United States might reduce the attention paid to individual Federal Reserve policy moves and focus the public debate instead on whether the Federal Reserve has a sound long-run strategy for the conduct of monetary policy.

Increased transparency would also reduce the financial and economic uncertainty associated with the Fed's current procedures by giving the markets more information about what future monetary policies are likely to be. That would reduce substantially the costs incurred by financial analysts trying to guess what the Federal Reserve will do next and would make it easier for businesses and consumers to plan for the future, thus promoting economic efficiency.

Third, Federal Reserve adoption of inflation targeting would help to depersonalize U.S. monetary policy. True, monetary policy has been excellent in recent years under the leadership of chairmen Volcker and Greenspan. Moreover, the current members of the FOMC have demonstrated that they are convinced of the value of forward-looking monetary policy that focuses on price stability. This state of affairs has not always prevailed, however, and may not always exist in the future. Monetary policy-makers are quite capable of falling off the (anti-inflationary) wagon, as the experience of the 1970s illustrates. Adoption of inflation targeting would strengthen the central bank's commitment to the long-run goal of price stability and would make the achievement of low inflation less dependent on the competence or the convictions of a few individuals.

Fourth, an inflation-targeting framework seems more consistent than the current practice with democratic principles. Certainly there are good reasons, notably insulation from short-term pressures, for the central bank to have some degree of independence, as the Federal Reserve currently does. Indeed, the evidence is that economies with independent central banks enjoy lower rates of inflation than other countries, with no higher volatility in employment and output. Yet the practical economic arguments for central bank independence co-exist uneasily with the presumption that government policies should be made democratically, rather than by an elite group. Indeed, recent criticism of the Federal Reserve may have been prompted by the impression that the Fed, and particularly its chairman, has become too powerful. A political backlash against a "highhanded" Federal Reserve could have adverse consequences for the quality of U.S. monetary policy in the future.

To resolve the apparent conflict between the need for central bank independence on one hand and the regard for democratic principles on the other, it is useful to invoke once again the distinction made by Debelle and Fischer (1994) and Fischer (1994) between goal independence and instrument independence for the central bank. In brief, a goal-independent central bank is one that is free to set the objectives of monetary policy. An instrument-independent central bank is one that is free to set the instruments of monetary policy, such as the interest rate.

Because ultimately policy objectives in a democracy must reflect the popular will, they should be set by elected officials. Consequently, in a democracy, the central bank should not exercise goal independence. However, because the central bank has the best information and expertise on how to go about achieving policy objectives, it should be free to choose the settings of the instruments needed to do the job. That is, for efficient and accountable policy-making, the central bank should enjoy instrument independence.

Inflation targeting is consistent with, and indeed promotes, this way of organizing responsibility for monetary policy. In the standard inflation-targeting framework, the central bank is fully accountable to elected officials, who in turn typically have primary responsibility for setting the goals for monetary policy and then monitoring the economic outcomes. At the same time, the inflation-targeting framework ensures that the objectives set by the government are feasible and that they are considered within the appropriate long-run perspective. So, for example, this framework requires the government to choose objectives for the long-run inflation rate (which is potentially under the control of the central bank) rather than for, say, the long-run unemployment rate (which is not a feasible objective for the central bank). Finally, under inflation targeting as it has generally been practiced, short-term operational decisions belong solely to the central bank, as must be the case if it is to be accountable for achieving its assigned objectives. Thus, inflation targeting promotes instrument independence for the central bank.

An instructive example of how inflation targeting serves to reduce the tensions between central-bank independence and democratic policy-making is brought to light in our case study of the United Kingdom. Prior to 1997, monetary-policy decisions in the United Kingdom were made by the executive branch (the Chancellor of the Exchequer) rather than by the Bank of England. Then, on May 6, 1997, the Chancellor of the Exchequer, Gordon Brown, granted independence to the Bank of England, giving it the power to set the overnight interest rate. Brown made it clear that (in his view) his action had been made possible by the adoption of an inflation-targeting regime, which had increased the transparency of policy and the accountability of the Bank for achieving policy objectives. He pointed out that the inflation-targeting approach would enable the government to continue to set the goals of monetary policy, as is appropriate in a democratic society, and would also ensure the Bank the discretion it needs to achieve those goals.

Fifth, the adoption of inflation targeting would enhance the Fed's ability to deal with shocks to the economy, such as an unanticipated contraction in aggregate demand or instability in financial markets. As we saw in Chapter 6, for example, the Bank of Canada has claimed that the use of inflation targets has improved its ability to deal with shocks to aggregate demand. Because a decline in aggregate demand usually leads to lower-than-expected inflation also, the Bank is able to respond with a monetary easing, without causing the public to question its anti-inflationary resolve. Shocks to aggregate supply, as we have seen, can be handled through various devices, such as the exclusion of certain volatile prices from the targeted index. The use of inflation targets also appears to reduce the risk that supply shocks will create long-term increases in the rate of inflation.

Moreover, with inflation targets in place, the central bank can react more effectively to events that increase the risk of financial crisis. For example, following the failure of a large bank or corporation that rattles financial markets, the Federal Reserve would be able to inject needed liquidity into the financial system without being seen as jeopardizing its inflation goals. In response to problems in the banking sector and credit markets during the early 1990s, the Federal Reserve kept the federal funds rate fixed at the extremely low level of 3% (or about zero, in real terms, since inflation was also at about 3%) for more than a year. To rationalize this policy, Chairman Greenspan referred to the financial "headwinds" that were holding back the recovery of the U.S. economy. Still, some concern was expressed in financial markets that the Federal Reserve was losing its anti-inflationary resolve. That concern, which manifested itself in substantial increases in long bond rates when the Federal Reserve began raising the federal funds rate in February 1994, might have been less pronounced had an inflation-targeting regime been in place.

Given the likelihood that U.S. monetary policy, despite its generally good performance in recent years, could be improved by the adoption of inflation targets, we may still ask, why now? Why not wait until inflation starts to become a problem again before considering a shift in the Fed's framework for making monetary policy?

The answer, as suggested by the case studies, is largely political. We have seen that countries that have adopted inflation targeting have typically done so not when inflation is rising, but after they have already achieved some success in bringing the inflation rate down. That timing is advantageous because it increases the likelihood that the new regime will endure as it builds on already-established credibility of the central bank as an inflation fighter. Moreover, the public seems more willing to accept inflation targeting once it recognizes that low inflation can indeed be achieved, that it provides tangible economic benefits, and that additional short-run costs (in terms of lost output or employment) to bring down inflation may not be necessary.

The current conditions for adoption of inflation targeting in the United States thus seem highly propitious. Indeed, the political and economic situation is probably more favorable in the United States than it has been in other countries that have successfully adopted inflation targets. At the time of this writing, inflation has been low and stable for more than five years; the economy has been remarkably healthy, enjoying a balanced, long-lived expansion; the benefits of a low-inflation environment have become clear to the American public; and the success of inflation targeting in other industrialized countries is becoming increasingly apparent. Thus, the United States appears to have a window of opportunity in which a new monetary-policy approach could be adopted readily. With luck, the new framework could then be firmly established by the time the next difficult decisions about monetary policy have to be made.

A Proposal for Inflation Targeting in the United States

We turn now to a specific proposal. We first outline the elements of an inflation-targeting framework appropriate for the United States. We then explain how each element would work in practice and how it would improve the performance of monetary policy.

1. We recommend that the long-run inflation goal for the United States be defined as a rate of inflation slightly above (say one percentage point) the mean estimate of the upward measurement bias in inflation. This would be the effective definition of "price stability." Under current estimates of the measurement bias, that suggests a long-run inflation goal of about 2% per annum (1% above the estimated 1% measurement bias). The exact value for the long-run goal would not be specified in the original framework but would be established as part of an oversight process (see point 7 below).

2. A short-term inflation target would be set and announced once a year, at a regular time. This target might vary from year to year, depending on economic circumstances. The sequence of short-term targets would be required to converge with the long-run inflation goal, although convergence could be gradual.

3. The horizon for the inflation target would reflect the lag between the setting of policy and the effects of policy on the economy. Specifically, the target for inflation would be set not for the immediately following year, but for a year farther in the future. For example, at the end of 1998, the Federal Reserve might set the inflation target for inflation to be realized during the year 2000.

4. The inflation target would be a point target, rather than a target range. However, there would be appropriate discussion by the cen-

tral bank, for the benefit of the government and the public, of the inherent range of uncertainty around this target.

5. Inflation outcomes that fall below the target should be resisted just as strenuously as outcomes that exceed the target, except when particular developments such as favorable supply shocks justify acceptance of lower inflation.

6. The price index used for defining the inflation target would be the "core" CPI, from which the prices of food, energy, and other especially volatile items have been excluded.

7. The numerical value for the long-run inflation goal would be set with government involvement, possibly by a commission including participation by the Federal Reserve. Periodic revision of the long-run objective would be undertaken when conditions warranted. Determination of the long-run inflation goal should take into account biases in measuring inflation and provide safeguards against accidental deflation.

8. As mandated by the current Humphrey-Hawkins legislation, the Chairman of the Board of Governors of the Federal Reserve would be required to testify twice a year before Congress on the Federal Reserve's performance in achieving its inflation targets.

9. The Federal Reserve would produce a regular, comprehensive *Inflation Report*. It should use this report, and any other opportunities available to it, to outline developments relevant to inflation, the current status of monetary policy, and the Fed's proposed strategy for meeting the inflation targets.

We now look at each of these nine elements in greater detail.

1. Price stability and the long-run inflation objective

A key element in any inflation-targeting regime is the definition of what "price stability" means in practice. Our recommendation is that price stability be defined as an inflation rate slightly above the consensus estimate of the inflation measurement bias (which could change over time). If we take a figure on the order of 1% as the best estimate of the measurement bias, then add another 1% "margin of safety" (for reasons noted below), we obtain a recommended long-run inflation target of approximately 2% per year, a number that is consistent with worldwide practice.

Defining price stability in terms of a target for the long-run inflation rate, rather than in terms of a price-level target, is also consistent with worldwide practice, as we have seen throughout the case studies. The advantage of targeting an inflation rate rather than a price level is that targeting the latter might require periods of deflation, which could be harmful to the financial system and to the economy more generally. Some economists have pointed out that an inflation-rate target implies relatively greater volatility and unpredictability of the price level in the distant future, with possible adverse effects on long-term planning (retirement planning, for example). However, we believe that, in practice, such effects would be unlikely to be large (see, for example, McCallum [1996] for some illustrative calculations).

Federal Reserve Chairman Alan Greenspan reportedly has defined price stability as a situation in which inflation is not a consideration in household or business decisions. As we discussed in Chapter 2, measurement error for CPI inflation in the United States is estimated to be in the range of 0.5% to 2.0%, with a mean value in the vicinity of 1%. Thus an inflation goal of 2%—1% over the mean measurement error—is quite consistent with the Greenspan definition of price stability.

Yet, one might ask, why would a 2% goal for long-run inflation be better than a goal of zero inflation, which has the advantages of simplicity and the psychological appeal of the "magic number" of zero? Or why not a 1% long-run inflation goal, which is consistent with a "true" inflation rate of zero, once the estimated measurement error has been eliminated? The reason we need a margin of safety is that there are serious risks in setting an inflation target too low. Those risks, which we discussed in Chapter 2, include the possibility of reduced real-wage flexibility (if nominal wage cuts are not feasible) and possible financial instability if errors by the central bank cause the economy to slip into the range of negative inflation (deflation). A 1% target for true inflation provides some insurance against such risks.

2. Variation in the inflation target over time

A key issue in the design of an inflation-targeting regime is how flexible the inflation targets should be in the short and medium terms. As the case studies indicated, although central bankers are sometimes criticized for focusing too much on price stability, they are certainly concerned in practice with other aspects of economic performance, particularly fluctuations in output, employment, and exchange rates. Consequently, inflation targeters, even those most "hawkish" on inflation, have allowed their targets to vary over time in response to shocks to the economy, or as part of a disinflationary process. Indeed, much discussion of inflation targeting focuses on the setting of two parameters: the long-run inflation goal, and the length of time allowed for the convergence of actual inflation with that goal following a shock to the economy that drives inflation from its desired level. By setting paths for the short-term inflation target that gradually approach the long-run inflation goal, the central bank can help ensure that the economy does not suffer unnecessary losses in output and employment in the pursuit of price stability.

For example, suppose a jump in oil prices suddenly pushed inflation from low levels to a level well above the long-run goal. In this circumstance, the inflation-targeting approach would not require an immediate, draconian response. Instead, the short-term inflation target would be temporarily adjusted upward, with assurances that the target would follow a planned downward path over time. Such a response reflects both the reality that a short-term inflation bulge cannot be immediately eliminated (at least not without unacceptable costs), and also the presumption that inflation will be gradually returned to its long-run norm. During this process, the Federal Reserve would have to explain to the public that its actions were designed to keep output and employment losses to a minimum, while still maintaining the objective of long-run price stability. Experience suggests that this strategy would help to mitigate the second- and third-round effects of the oil price shock, as well as the effects on the public's expectations of inflation.

Another advantage of being able to adjust short-run inflation targets over time is that it would promote frankness among central bankers. Like their colleagues around the world, some Federal Reserve officials have been reluctant to admit that they are concerned about economic outcomes other than long-run price stability, or even that monetary policy can affect real variables like output and employment. They want to avoid giving the public the impression that they are being "soft" on inflation, an impression that might lead to higher inflation expectations. (That reticence appeared to be justified by the criticism evoked by Federal Reserve Vice-Chairman Alan Blinder in August 1994, when he dared to speak frankly about the inflation-output tradeoff in a speech at a conference in Jackson Hole, Wyoming.) The ability to adjust the inflation target over time (accompanied by public explanations) would encourage Federal Reserve officials to demonstrate their concerns about fluctuations in output and employment, without prompting the charge that they were ignoring their primary responsibility to control inflation in the long run. Politically, greater frankness in policy-making would tend to defuse the perception that the Federal Reserve is indifferent to the problems of the unemployed and other hard-pressed citizens. In short, a time-varying inflation target, rather than impeding the battle against inflation, would help the Federal Reserve to command public support for both its independence and its goal of stabilizing prices.

As an aside, we note that there is a trap into which some inflation targeters fall after a period of successful disinflation, when the inflation rate is close to its long-run objective. In this situation, inflation targets may remain unchanged for a prolonged period of time, giving the public the impression that the target has been fixed and will no longer vary. But tranquil periods do not last forever. Thus, in implementing an inflation-targeting framework in the United States, the Federal Reserve should remind the public that severe shocks to the economy always remain a possibility. To drive home this point, the Federal Reserve should make clear that it takes the annual review of the inflation target quite seriously, so that even a decision to leave the target unchanged must be carefully justified.

The flip side of the concern that inflation targets may not be changed often enough is that they may be changed too often and by too much. Some critics have suggested that, because targets might be changed frequently or on an *ad hoc* basis, the use of time-varying inflation targets may impair the credibility of the inflation-targeting framework itself. By accommodating any change in inflation by a change in its "target," they warn, a central bank or government might render the system meaningless. Experience suggests, however, that credibility is not damaged by varying targets over time, so long as the central bank explains its actions and reaffirms its commitment to long-run price stability. Indeed, because changes in inflation targets are so newsworthy and are so closely scrutinized (a result of the transparency of this approach), governments and central bankers probably change short-term inflation targets too infrequently, taking action only when the justification for change appears overwhelming. As our case studies demonstrate, policy-makers are often reluctant to change inflation targets even when a change in government occurs.

3. The horizon for which the inflation target is set

Monetary policy affects the economy only with long lags. Consequently, policy-making must be forward-looking, rather than purely reactive. The determination of the horizon for inflation targets should be based on research regarding how long it takes monetary policy to influence inflation: If, for example, research indicates that the lag is on the order of two years (a common estimate), then the inflation target should be set for the annual inflation rate two years hence. Such a practice would remind the public that price stability is a long-run, rather than a short-run, goal. In Canada, for example, the inflation targets were set to apply to a period beginning 22 months after the initial announcement. However, some inflation-targeting countries set the target for inflation only for the coming year, a short horizon which does not adequately reflect the lag between policy actions and their effects. In our case study of New Zealand, we saw that a short target horizon has resulted in problems of control and instrument instability. Even in the case of Canada, the fact that the inflation target is set annually and has remained essentially unchanged for a substantial period of time has made it more difficult to keep the public aware of the fact that the targets are supposed to be forward-looking in nature. Emphasizing that there is a relatively long horizon for targets seems essential.

4. A point target rather than a target range

Inflation targeters have made different choices on whether an inflation target should be expressed as a single point or as a range of acceptable outcomes. As we have seen, a target range allows for flexibility in responding to shocks to the economy and reflects the uncertainty in achieving any inflation target. A disadvantage of using a target range is that the upper and lower bands of the range may become the principal focus of public attention, leading the central bank to concentrate too much on keeping inflation just within the bands rather than trying to hit the midpoint of the range. For example, slight overshootings of the upper band of the target band have received tremendous attention in New Zealand, but inflation rates close to the upper end of the range but not breaching it have gone largely unremarked. In the United Kingdom in 1995, the inflation forecast exceeded the midpoint of the target range by more than one percentage point, but without breaching the upper band. In that case, probably too little attention was paid to the overshooting of the midpoint, and the fact that inflation had not actually crossed the upper end of the range was used as to justify the absence of any policy response. It is difficult to imagine policy objectives that would make sense of such asymmetric public reactions to inflation rates just inside and just outside the bands and the incentives that such reactions create for central bankers.

It is also not clear that the use of a target range is a good way for the central bank to convey how uncertain it is about its ability to hit the inflation target. Unfortunately, some estimates of the irreducible uncertainty around an inflation target are on the order of five to six percentage points (see for example, Haldane and Salmon [1995] and Stevens and Debelle [1995]).[1] The inflation-targeting central bank that employs a target range thus has the unattractive choice of making the target range very wide, which is likely to confuse the public about the central bank's intentions and reduce the credibility of policy; or of making the range so narrow that misses are inevitable, which has its own consequences for credibility.

To avoid such problems, we recommend a point target for inflation. We fully recognize that the control of inflation is inherently imperfect, and that the unavoidable range of uncertainty around the point target needs to be acknowledged in central bank analyses. However, we would like to see the Federal Reserve take the approach of the Bank of England: As we discussed in Chapter 7, in 1995 the Bank of England switched from a target range to a point target, and it has used the *Inflation Report* and other channels to communicate the inherent uncertainties in the control of inflation to the public, rather than leaving those uncertainties to be inferred from the target range. Finally, the use of a time-varying inflation target obviates the need for flexibility provided by the use of a target range.

5. Undershooting the target is just as undesirable as overshooting

Some central bankers have fallen into the "you can never be too rich or too thin" fallacy. It might be true that one can never be too rich—although some would disagree—but one surely can be too thin. Likewise, inflation can surely be too low. A decline in inflation below the inflation target, unless it arises from a beneficial supply shock, will exact a toll in terms of lost output and employment that is greater than necessary. Literal deflation, as we have seen, can be extremely harmful, particularly if it precipitates financial instability (see, for example, Mishkin [1997b]). An important advantage of inflation targeting is that it provides a floor for inflation as well as a ceiling.

6. Targeting "core" CPI inflation

Although the particular choice of the price index used in constructing the inflation target is perhaps not critical, we lean toward the use of a "core" CPI measure that excludes food, energy and other volatile items from the price index. The core CPI is likely to provide a better guide to monetary policy than other indices, since it measures the more persistent underlying inflation rather than transitory influences on the price level. Moreover, its use indicates to the public that the central bank will respond flexibly to inflationary shocks arising from supply shocks (such as sharp increases in the prices of oil or food). Use of a core CPI measure also helps the central bank to communicate to the public that not every shock that raises prices will lead to a permanent increase in inflation, and that short-term changes in inflation resulting from supply shocks will be treated differently from changes driven by aggregate demand.

The argument for using the CPI rather than some other price index (such as the GDP deflator) is that it is directly relevant to consumer living standards and is the price index best understood by the public and most widely reported in the media. It is also calculated more frequently and with less delay than other major price indices. Finally, measurement errors in this index are better understood by economists than those of alternative indices.

7. Responsibility for setting the inflation target

We have already mentioned in this chapter the useful distinction between goal independence and instrument independence for the central bank. We believe that inflation targeting is most effective and leads to the most democratically accountable policy-making when the central bank is instrument-independent but not fully goal-independent.

Inflation targeting, by its very nature, requires that the central bank have instrument independence. The central bank can hardly be held accountable for meeting the inflation targets if it is not given control of the policy instruments. Instrument independence takes advantage of the central bank's undeniably greater expertise in the implementation of monetary policy, and it enables the policy-makers to take into account the lag between policy and its effect without being handicapped by the myopic tendencies of politicians.

Inflation targeting does not, however, require that the central bank enjoy goal independence as well. Under our proposal, long-run inflation goals would be set by the government, possibly through a standing commission that includes the Federal Reserve as an active participant. Note that the commission might well decide to change the long-run inflation goal at some point, because of new research on measurement bias in the CPI or on the rate of "true" inflation that best promotes long-run economic growth and stability.

There are several reasons why the government should have substantial responsibility for setting long-run inflation goals. First, democratic accountability in the setting of goals not only legitimizes the policy-making process, but ultimately it protects the central bank from unwarranted criticism and attacks on its operational independence.[2] Second, government participation in setting long-run inflation goals obliges it to adopt a long-range view of the effects of monetary policy, rather than focusing solely on current cyclical conditions.

Another benefit of substantial government participation in setting inflation goals, one that has received relatively little attention, is that it may lead to sounder fiscal policy. A government that has committed itself to numerical inflation goals can better resist over-expansionary fiscal policies, large budget deficits, and excessive increases in public wages on the grounds that they are inconsistent with the government's own inflation goals. For example, in New Zealand, the setting of inflation targets by the Finance Minister seems to have helped that country keep government spending under control. Similarly, the role of the Canadian government in setting inflation targets may have helped it to resist salary increases in the public sector. Private-sector wage agreements may also be moderated if there is a strong government commitment to low inflation.

Because budget deficits in the United States are currently at very low levels (with even surpluses being possible), the salutary effect of inflation targets on fiscal discipline may not be so salient at the moment. However, serious fiscal imbalances may return in the future, particularly given the unfunded Social Security obligations that loom ahead.

Although the ultimate responsibility for setting long-run inflation goals should rest with the U.S. government, the Federal Reserve should not be left entirely out of the picture. Having the Federal Reserve participate in deciding the long-run inflation goal has much to recommend it. With a research staff of approximately five hundred economists, the Federal Reserve can provide valuable expertise on the economy and on monetary policy. Moreover, because the Federal Reserve is independent from the day-to-day political process, it would bring high prestige and the reputation of being an honest broker to the commission.

Once a long-run inflation goal has been established, the next step is to define a transition path of medium-term targets. In fact, because setting those targets will inevitably demand technical competence in determining the pace at which inflation can be moved toward the long-run goal without causing undue output fluctuations, it may be best to entrust this task solely to the Federal Reserve. In some inflation-targeting countries, medium-term inflation targets are set jointly by the central bank and the government, as represented (for example) by the finance minister. The most nearly analogous procedure for the United States would be to have the Secretary of the Treasury set the medium-term targets in consultation with the Federal Reserve. Empowering the finance ministry to establish medium-term inflation targets in consultation with the central bank may work well in a parliamentary system of democracy, in which the finance ministry represents both the executive and legislative branches of the government. That arrangement might not be suitable in the United States, however, where the Secretary of the Treasury functions as the representative of the executive branch but not the legislative branch. Thus, medium-term inflation targets set by the U.S. Treasury might reflect the political views of the President rather than the views of Congress.

8. Accountability

A key element of inflation targeting is the accountability to the public of the agency responsible for the conduct of monetary policy (the Federal Reserve, in the United States). The Humphrey-Hawkins legislation already provides some degree of accountability for the Federal Reserve by requiring the Chairman of the Board of Governors of the Federal Reserve System to testify before Congress twice a year on the performance of monetary policy. This testimony would remain an essential component of an inflation-targeting framework. However, under an inflation-targeting regime, the requirement to testify would impose greater accountability on the Federal Reserve than it does at present, because Congress would be able to measure the Fed's performance against a numerical benchmark. Inflation targeting should not be seen as a "free ride" for the central bank; on the contrary, the increased transparency of policy under inflation targeting would subject the Federal Reserve to more intense public scrutiny, as is appropriate in a democratic society.

Given the multi-year horizon of the medium-term inflation targets in our proposal, the Federal Reserve's testimony would be in two parts. In the first part, the Chairman would discuss current inflation performance, including the Federal Reserve's success or failure in achieving the inflation target set several years before. Key to this discussion would be an accounting of how the Federal Reserve had set its policy instruments in order to achieve that target, and an analysis of whether those settings were appropriate given the information then available. The Chairman would also indicate why any deviations from the inflation target had occurred and whether they could have reasonably been foreseen. An extremely important benefit to this discussion would be the opportunity it would provide to educate Congress about the lags in the effects of the policy instruments on inflation and the consequent need for forward-looking monetary policy.

In the second part of the testimony, the Chairman would discuss future inflation targets and their implications for current monetary policy and the Federal Reserve's general policy strategy. Again, this report would focus attention on the need to plan monetary policy over a long horizon. Engaging members of Congress in these discussions, with the media in attendance, would heighten the public's awareness and understanding of the goals and instruments of monetary policy. Further, it would provide the Federal Reserve with an opportunity to explain to the public its policy framework, the rationale for its current policies, and the need for attention to long-run as well as short-run objectives.

The Humphrey-Hawkins legislation now in effect appears to be sufficiently broad and non-specific to make new legislation unnecessary to implement the framework we have proposed here. (A parallel exists with the Canadian implementation of inflation targets, which were instituted without modifications to the Bank of Canada Act.) Nevertheless, some modification of Humphrey-Hawkins would probably be useful. The Act sets several goals for monetary policy, including high economic growth, low unemployment, and price stability; missing, however, is any specific reference to the time frame in which these goals are to be reached or to their order of priority. One might argue, for example, that a focus on long-run price stability is consistent with Humphrey-Hawkins, because price stability promotes high rates of economic growth and employment in the long run. It does not always promote "maximum employment" in the short run, however, which might lead some to interpret inflation targeting as inconsistent with the Act. It would be desirable to modify the Humphrey-Hawkins legislation in the direction of the Maastricht Treaty, which specifies that price stability is the overriding long-run objective of monetary policy, but also mandates attention to other important economic goals, so long as they are consistent with long-run price stability. Such modifications would clarify the role of price stability in the conduct of monetary policy and would provide a sounder foundation for the inflation-targeting framework.

Another problem with the Humphrey-Hawkins legislation is that it requires the Federal Reserve to set targets for the growth of the monetary aggregates and then to report to Congress on its success in meeting those targets. Because of the breakdown of the relationship between monetary aggregates and nominal spending and inflation in the 1980s, however, this focus on monetary targeting in the United States is now obsolete and is widely ignored both inside and outside the Federal Reserve System. Indeed, in the Humphrey-Hawkins testimony in July 1993, Chairman Greenspan indicated that the Federal Reserve would no longer use monetary targets as guides for monetary policy. The references to monetary targets should be struck from Humphrey-Hawkins as part of an overhaul of that legislation.

9. Communication

The monetary authorities must be accountable to the public directly, as well as to the government. Without public support, the central bank will ultimately fail to achieve its goals. As our case studies indicate, central banks in inflation-targeting countries strive mightily to convey to the public what monetary policy can and cannot do and to explain the rationale and strategy for the conduct of monetary policy. The Bank of England has been a leader in this effort with its *Inflation Report,* now copied by many other countries. Key features of the *Inflation Report* in Britain are clear and accessible writing, the use of color and graphics, and the employment of the best techniques of pedagogy, all in an effort to explain and clarify to the public how the policy framework works. We suggest that the Federal Reserve devote substantial resources to producing a similar, regular report, as well as using means such as speeches, brochures, exhibits, and videos to convey its message to the public.

The Federal Reserve is well prepared to take up this effort. The Board of Governors and the district Federal Reserve Banks all have substantial public information departments and similar resources already in place. Indeed, the Federal Reserve probably could do a better job of communicating with the public than other inflation-targeting central banks whose resources are far more limited.

Inflation Targeting in the European Monetary Union

For the European Monetary Union (EMU) to adopt inflation targeting would not be a radical step. Many of the fundamentals of inflation targeting have been codified in the Maastricht Treaty and have been stated in position papers published by the European Monetary Institute, the precursor to the European Central Bank. The Maastricht Treaty creates an institutional commitment to price stability by mandating that it be the primary long-run objective of monetary policy. Moreover, the European Monetary Institute (1997, p. 3) has issued the following guiding principles for monetary policy strategy:

- Effectiveness: The strategy should be effective in the pursuit of the final objective [price stability].

- Accountability: The strategy should involve the formulation and announcement of targets so that the central bank can be held accountable to the public for its actions.

- Transparency: The process of setting targets and of making decisions on the basis of the strategy should be made clear to the public.

- Medium-Term Orientation: The strategy should be able to deliver its final objective over the medium term, thereby providing an anchor to inflation expectations, but nevertheless provide the central bank with some discretion in response to short-term deviations from the target.

- Continuity: The strategy of the European System of Central Banks [ESCB] should build on the experience gained by participating national central banks before the start of Stage Three (when the European Monetary Union and the ESCB come into existence).

- Consistency with the Independence of the ESCB: The strategy must be consistent with the independent status granted to the ESCB by the treaty and should support it as far as possible.

Although these principles are fully consistent with inflation targeting, they are consistent with other approaches as well, notably monetary targeting as currently practiced in Germany, the anchor country for the European Exchange Rate Mechanism (ERM). Indeed, as the European Monetary Institute has emphasized, "differences between monetary and inflation targeting strategies are not overwhelming" (*Ibid.,* p. 6). The difference between the two strategies, as actually practiced, lies primarily in the degree of emphasis placed on monetary aggregates in formulating monetary policy and in communicating with the public. Although the EMI has taken a balanced position on the two strategies, we believe that the European Monetary Union should adopt inflation targeting rather than monetary targeting. We now outline a proposal for inflation targeting in the EMU.

A Proposal for Inflation Targeting in the European Monetary Union

Because the stage of development and the structure of money and capital markets of the countries that will make up the European Monetary

Union are similar to those of the United States, most of the recommendations in the U.S. proposal apply to the EMU as well.

1. We recommend a long-run CPI inflation goal for the EMU of slightly above (say one percentage point) the consensus estimate of the upward measurement bias in inflation.

2. The inflation target should be announced once a year and should be allowed to vary over time. In particular, gradual adjustment of the short-run targets toward the long-run goal should be permitted to moderate the output and employment effects of disinflationary policies.

3. The horizon for the inflation target should reflect the lags in the effects of monetary policy, which may differ from those observed in the United States. The lag of policy may also depend on which countries enter the European Monetary Union, since that will determine how large and open to trade the single-currency area will be. The European Monetary Institute is currently studying policy lags in the countries that are likely to join the EMU, as well as analyzing how monetary integration should be expected to affect those lags.

4. The inflation target should be a point target, rather than a range, with the uncertainty surrounding such a target being clearly communicated to the public. The uncertainty in predicting and controlling inflation in Europe may differ substantially from that in the United States.

5. Inflation outcomes below the inflation target should be considered as damaging as outcomes above the inflation target, except when economic developments (such as favorable supply shocks) justify lower inflation.

6. The price index used to specify the inflation target should be a "core"-type CPI from which the prices of food, energy, and other volatile items would be excluded. In particular, the index should exclude the direct effects of variations in mortgage interest rates.

7. The European Central Bank should issue an *Inflation Report* at regular intervals and should seize on every opportunity to inform the public of current inflation developments, the ease or tightness of current monetary policy, and the Bank's longer-run strategy for meeting its inflation targets.

8. Inflation and inflation targets should be the central consideration in discussions about monetary policy. The monetary aggregates should have no special role in formulating or explaining monetary policy.

9. As required by the Maastricht Treaty, the European Central Bank is to be goal-independent; that is, it is solely responsible for setting inflation targets. However, some mechanism should be devised for consultation with governmental bodies in setting those targets.

10. Under the Maastricht Treaty, the President of the European Central Bank is required to testify once a year to the European Parliament on the Bank's success or failure in achieving inflation targets. We propose that representatives of the European Central Bank also appear periodically before the national parliaments of the EMU countries.

The first seven elements of our proposal are essentially the same as those proposed for the United States. The last three elements, however, raise issues that require further comment.

8. The Role of Monetary Aggregates

Monetary targeting has been suggested as an alternative to inflation targeting for the European Monetary Union. Supporters of monetary targeting point out that Germany and Switzerland have used this approach successfully to control inflation over a substantial period of time. They argue that by adopting the same strategy, the European Central Bank will be able to inherit some of the Bundesbank's credibility. This view has been expressed by the European Monetary Institute [1997, p. 11]:

> the adoption of monetary targeting in Stage Three [of the unification process] would offer the advantage of ensuring continuity with the strategy of the EU central bank which has performed an anchor function in the ERM, in view of its long-term track record of fighting inflation. Following a monetary targeting strategy might therefore help the ESCB to inherit credibility from the start of its operations.

Although this argument is not without merit, it does not convince us that monetary targeting should be chosen as the basic monetary policy strategy for the European Central Bank. There are several reasons.

First, as we noted in the preceding chapter, monetary aggregates are not a particularly useful guide for monetary policy unless the relationship between monetary aggregates and inflation is strong and reliable. A stable relationship between money and inflation is, in fact, unlikely to exist in the fledgling EMU, since this relationship has never been particularly reliable in most of the constituent countries of the Union, including Germany (Estrella and Mishkin, 1997). As we saw in Chapter 4, the Bundesbank has not been unaware of the instability of the money-inflation relationship, which helps to explain why it has been willing to tolerate misses of its money-growth target range in more than half of the years for which targets have been set. Furthermore, the creation of the European Monetary Union and the ESCB at the start of Stage Three, together with ongoing financial deregulation and innovation, will cause major changes in the operation of the European financial system in coming years. Those changes will affect money and asset demands in unpredictable ways, making it likely that the relationship between monetary aggregates and inflation in the union as a whole will be even more unstable than it has been in the individual member countries.

The second objection to the adoption of monetary targeting by the European Monetary Union is that monetary targets are likely to prove a less effective vehicle of communication for the EMU than they have for pre-Union Germany and Switzerland. In our view, the Bundesbank and the Swiss National Bank have built their anti-inflationary reputations *despite* their use of monetary targeting. Indeed, the frequent target misses in those countries have typically been justified by reference to announced inflation goals and inflation trends, showing that Germany and Switzerland have followed what is, for most practical purposes, an inflation-targeting strategy. Masquerading their approach as a monetary targeting strategy has had some costs in terms of reduced coherence and transparency of policy, but these costs have been mitigated by the clarity of the explanations emanating from the Bundesbank and the Swiss National Bank, and by the fact that the policy framework includes a statement of the long-run inflation goal and regular evaluations of the progress being made toward that goal.

The (incorrect) claim that monetary targeting was the fundamental reason for success in these two countries, however, is proving destructive in current discussions about the choice of strategy for the nascent European Central Bank. Monetary targeting was serviceable in Germany and Switzerland because of public understanding, and strong support for, the anti-inflationary focus of the two central banks. The new European Central Bank has neither the anti-inflation credibility nor the unified political constituency of the Bundesbank and Swiss National Bank. Missing announced targets for money growth may thus be far more problematic for the European Central Bank, because the public will be less willing to accept at face value the ECB's explanations for these misses and its declarations of anti-inflationary determination. Furthermore, in many European countries, the public will have had no experience with a monetary policy focused on monetary aggregates, and thus may find the targets harder to understand and less relevant to their daily lives than targets for inflation. Because a key element of any successful targeting strategy is transparency and effective communication with the public, the better approach for the ECB would be to downgrade the attention to monetary aggregates and put inflation targets at the forefront instead. (Of course, to the extent that monetary aggregates do prove useful as information variables, there would be no objection to using them in that capacity.)

If the ECB chooses to adopt an inflation-targeting approach, it might well concentrate on educating the public to recognize that this approach is quite consistent with the monetary targeting approach followed by the pre-Union Bundesbank. The two approaches have several characteristics in common, including: a commitment to price stability; the specification of numerical inflation goals (both in the medium term and the long term); accountability of the central bank for meeting the goals; transparency of policy and effective communication with the public; a forward-looking approach that takes into account the lags inherent in monetary policy; and flexibility to respond to short-run economic developments. In short, in practice an inflation-targeting European Central Bank would function very much like the money-targeting Bundesbank, and the public should be helped to understand this basic continuity. The differences that exist—notably, the de-emphasis on money growth as an inflation forecaster under inflation targeting—favor the inflation-targeting approach.

9. Consultation in the Setting of Inflation Targets

Because the Maastricht Treaty gives the European Central Bank goal independence as well as instrument independence, consultation with the government is not an option for the European Monetary Union. Indeed, according goal independence to the European Central Bank may have been unavoidable, at least at the outset, since the relation of the European Parliament to the parliaments in the countries that will make up the EMU has not yet been clarified; thus it is not clear what governmental agency, other than the ECB itself, could be given the authority to set inflation targets for EMU. Still, some mechanism for consultation between the ECB and the constituent governments should be developed.

Enabling the national governments to participate in the setting of inflation targets would yield several benefits. First, it would keep the European Central Bank from being viewed as a non-democratic institution indifferent to the concerns of the public, helping to preserve its independence in the long run. Second, having the governments participate in setting inflation targets would help focus the political debate on monetary policy within the union on long-run issues, such as price stability, rather than on the "need" for short-run monetary stimulus, which politicians tend to believe always exists. Third, allowing the governments to take part in the inflation-targeting process would tend to sensitize them to the fact that large increases in public sector wages or unduly expansionary fiscal policies might interfere with the achievement of the union's inflation targets. Because fiscal deficits in Europe are already large, and because for demographic reasons public-pension obligations are likely to be relatively higher in Europe in coming years than even in the United States, the need for disciplined fiscal policy in the EMU is urgent.

10. Accountability

Within individual countries, numerical inflation targets increase the central bank's accountability by providing explicit objectives that make it easier to evaluate the bank's performance. However, accountability of the European Central Bank may be more difficult to achieve because the statutes of the European System of Central Banks cannot be changed by legislation, but only by alterations in the Maastricht Treaty. Moreover, it is not clear to whom the European Central Bank would be accountable. Although the President of the ECB is required to testify once a year to the European Parliament, this requirement may not guarantee sufficient oversight of ECB policies. Since the European Parliament is currently less powerful than the national parliaments of the countries that make up the union, scrutiny by that organization would not influence ECB behavior as strongly as would oversight by a more powerful body, such as a consortium of national parliaments, or the individual parliaments themselves.

In fact, the accountability of the European Central Bank under the Maastricht Treaty seems insufficient. The ECB should be required to justify its policy actions through periodic testimony, not only in the European Parliament, but in the national parliaments of the EMU countries as well. Besides increasing the Bank's accountability and visibility, such testimony would demonstrate to the public in each EMU country that the ECB is accountable to them, as well as to the EMU as a whole, which would increase popular support for the Bank's independence. This testimony would also provide the European Central Bank with an additional public forum in which to explain its policy and to emphasize the need for central bankers to adopt a long-run perspective when making policy decisions.

Our case studies have demonstrated that the accountability of central banks to the public is as important as its accountability to government. Despite its goal independence, the Bundesbank has devoted as much effort to public outreach as have central banks who are less independent. In taking up the mantle of the Bundesbank, the European Central Bank should make a concerted effort to communicate regularly and comprehensively with the public. This is why an *Inflation Report* or similar document should be produced by the European Central Bank, and why the ECB should take every opportunity to explain its policy actions and the reasons for its focus on inflation targets and price stability.

Conclusions

In this chapter we have tried to make the case for the adoption of inflation targeting by the United States and by the European Monetary Union. Inflation targeting would help both the public and its political leaders to focus on what monetary policy can do rather than on what it cannot do. By increasing the transparency of monetary policy, it would also reduce financial and economic uncertainty, thereby promoting economic efficiency. It would help to depersonalize monetary policy and make the role of the central bank more consistent with the principles of a democratic society. Finally, inflation targeting would also enhance the ability of monetary policy-makers to deal flexibly with adverse shocks to the economy, such as a contraction in aggregate demand or a period of financial instability, without sacrificing the long-range objective of low and stable inflation.

In this chapter, we have also outlined concrete proposals for the adoption of inflation targets in the United States and the European Monetary Union. We believe that now is the best time to implement these or similar proposals. Our case studies show that the public is most receptive to this approach once the central bank has demonstrated that it is capable of controlling inflation and the public has become aware of the benefits that accrue to a low-inflation economy. Both the United States and Europe are currently at that point. Furthermore, because the European Central Bank is an institution starting from scratch, now is the time that it will have the greatest flexibility in choosing what monetary policy strategy should be put in place. We are convinced that inflation targeting would be a highly successful approach for making monetary policy in both the EMU and the United States, as it has already proved to be in a number of countries around the world.

Notes

Chapter 1
Introduction

1. For earlier discussions of experiences with inflation targeting, see Goodhart and Viñals (1994), Leiderman and Svensson (1995), Haldane (1995), and McCallum (1996), among others. Bernanke and Mishkin (1997) discuss the idea of inflation targeting as a framework for policy, which we will emphasize here, and present some of the arguments discussed in more detail in this book.

2. H.R. 2360, 105th Congress, 1st session; see the language of Sec. 3(b)(2)(A) in particular. In an earlier session of Congress, Senator Connie Mack (R-Fla.) introduced a bill which, if it had passed, would have established price stability as the primary goal of the Fed, effectively forcing the U.S. central bank to adopt inflation targeting [S.R. 1266, 104th Congress, 1st sess.].

3. European Monetary Institute, 1997, p.2. See also Issing (1996).

4. Eichengreen (1992) presents a detailed account of the rise and fall of the gold standard, and of the contributions of monetary mismanagement to the Great Depression.

Chapter 2
The Rationale for Inflation Targeting

1. The Phillips curve's origin was the work of A.W. Phillips (1958), who discovered a negative relationship of wage inflation and unemployment in a century of British data. Numerous authors extended Phillips's results to the United States and other countries.

2. Of course, large transitory benefits can outweigh small permanent costs. Still, the thrust of Friedman's conclusion is to reduce the likelihood that activist expansionary policies will be desirable.

3. Indeed, the only rate of inflation that the public could expect at which there would be no incentive for the central bank to "cheat" by raising inflation still further would be the level of inflation at which the costs of further increases in inflation outweigh the benefits of the associated economic stimulus.

4. Under a gold standard, it is more precise to say that bread's price is measured in terms of the local currency, whose own value in terms of gold is fixed by the central bank.

5. It must be admitted that the rhetoric of some of the proponents of inflation targeting has encouraged thinking of this strategy as a rule.

6. McCallum (1995) argues that the central bank can simply choose not to behave myopically, in which case the public's expectations will come to reflect

its more farsighted behavior. This would appear to us to be more likely, however, under some institutional arrangements and policy strategies than others. McCallum also points out that to the extent that policy credibility is a problem, it will affect the government as well as the central bank; we agree, for reasons that we discuss below.

Chapter 3
Issues of Design and Implementation

1. Rotemberg and Woodford (1997) provide some simulation evidence in favor of this argument.

2. This debate is reminiscent of controversies over the use of "cones" or "tunnels" in establishing ranges for money growth. "Cones," which widen over time, were associated with a targeted rate of money growth with little offsetting of misses; "tunnels," which imply a constant forecast variance for the level of the money stock, are associated with level money stock targets and greater offset of target misses.

3. Technically, ensuring only that the inflation rate is stationary may leave a unit root in the price level, so that the forecast variance of the price level at more and more distant horizons grows without bound. This problem is analogous to the issue of "base drift" in monetary targeting; see Walsh (1986).

4. However, Svensson (1996) gives examples in which price-level targeting actually reduces the volatility of output. The practical relevance of these examples is an open question. One factor that bears strongly on the comparison of inflation and price-level targeting is the persistence of shocks to the economy; highly persistent shocks, which tend to induce a sequence of target misses in the same direction, would tend to make price-level targeting particularly costly. Persistence in price-level measurement errors would tend to have a similar effect, favoring an inflation target over a price-level target.

Chapter 4
German and Swiss Monetary Targeting: Precursors to
Inflation Targeting

1. For a brief, contemporary survey of the adoption of monetary targets, see Bank for International Settlements (1976), pp. 32–39. Later, in-depth accounts of the operation of monetary targeting in a number of countries may be found in Meek (1983) and Bernanke and Mishkin (1992).

2. There still existed some requirement for the Bundesbank to buy currencies participating in the bloc float, a multilevel arrangement of exchange rate bands similar to the European Monetary System, which arose some years later.

3. In a later account, Schiltknecht states, "Before the Governing Board of the Bank makes its final decision on the money-stock target, the Government is informed about the intentions of the Board. However, it must be emphasized

that the responsibility for establishing a money-stock target rests solely with the Governing Board." (Schiltknecht 1983, p. 73.)

4. There is no direct reference at the time or in the reminiscences of the participants to any exchange between Swiss and German policymakers on these issues. Whether the conditions surrounding adoption led to roughly one optimal conclusion, or whether there was an explicit meeting of the minds, is anyone's guess. The similarities of these countries' adoption of targeting regimes, however, are not seen in the respective regimes' operating procedures, as discussed below.

5. Neumann (1996) and Clarida and Gertler (1997) argue both points, that the Bundesbank has multiple goals and that it doesn't strictly target money. Von Hagen (1995) and Bernanke and Mihov (1997) focus on the latter point, while Friedman (1995) and Estrella and Mishkin (1997) discuss why the Bundesbank might not want to look at M3.

6. Von Hagen (1989) and Bernanke and Mishkin (1992) make some suggestions regarding this.

7. The resemblance between this approach and the approach called for in the EC Council of Ministers' statement of October 1972 quoted in the previous section is almost perfect.

8. See, for example, Deutsche Bundesbank (1981b, October, "Recalculation of the Production Potential of the Federal Republic of Germany").

9. The vast variety and depth of information provided by the Bundesbank in its *Monthly Report* and *Annual Report* would appear to be evidence that a wide range of information variables, far beyond M3, velocity, and potential GDP, play a role in Bundesbank decision-making (the work involved in producing the data and analysis makes it unlikely that it is merely a smokescreen or a public service). Nevertheless, monetary-policy moves are always justified with reference to M3 and/or inflation developments, rather than to these other types of data.

10. Although, on the other hand, neither is there a disclaimer of institutional responsibility, as one typically sees on articles written by Federal Reserve staff for official publications, for example.

11. Swiss National Bank (1994c, December, p. 272).

12. Posen (1995b) argues that German and Swiss support for central bank independence and pursuit of price stability is consistent with a general tendency for countries with politically effective financial sectors to have greater political support for low inflation.

13. The Bank's more recent response to large terms-of trade shocks will be discussed in the following section.

14. The issue of the susceptibility of M1 demand to changes in exchange rate expectations is analyzed in Rich (1985, pp. 60–69).

15. The Swiss National Bank also publishes a *Monthly Report,* which consists largely of data tables (mostly having to do with the financial system), as well as an *Annual Report* on the state of Switzerland's banks. Except for the short-term forecasts of SAMB growth published every three months in the

Monthly Report since 1991, neither of these has served the purpose of reporting on monetary policy since the publication of the first issue of *Geld, Währung, und Konjunktur* in 1983.

16. However, neither the Swiss National Bank nor the Bundesbank explicitly discusses private-sector inflation expectations, as many inflation-targeting central banks have done.

17. Actually, it was the third year of four in a row in which the 8.0% CBM monetary growth point target was exceeded by at least a percentage point (see Bernanke and Mishkin [1992, p. 201, Table 4]).

18. Two more technical developments also suggested the switch from CBM to M3 targets. The first was that minimum reserve requirements had changed substantially since 1974, so that CBM, computed on the basis of 1974 ratios, corresponded less and less to the monetary base and thus to "the extent to which the central bank has provided funds for the banks' money creation." The second was the increasing need to include, for control purposes, new components such as Euro-deposits held by domestic nonbanks, in some broadly defined money stock. Since these components had never been subject to minimum reserve requirements, the weight at which they should enter CBM was not clear, a problem that does not exist for an extended definition of M3.

19. "While officially the question of the correct exchange rate was still under discussion, the German Chancellor announced his decision on the exchange rate without informing Bundesbank President Karl-Otto Pöhl, although they had met only a few hours before" (Hefeker, 1994, p. 383). See Marsh (1992) for a longer historical account. For most East German citizens, personal assets were converted at the rate of 1 to 1. However, for larger holdings, a declining rate of exchange was employed.

20. We are grateful to Otmar Issing for emphasizing this shift to us. This change could be interpreted as a sign that the Bundesbank expresses greater confidence in its ability to achieve its desired inflation goal.

21. For two recent examples of this repeated argument, see Issing (1996) and Schmid (1995).

22. The reason behind lowering the medium-term target from 2% to 1% was the decline in the share in SAMB of banks' deposits at the Swiss National Bank from around 25% prior to 1988 to 9% to 11% from 1990 on, as a consequence of the institutional changes discussed earlier. Since the income elasticity of banks' deposits is higher than that of currency in circulation, the smaller fraction of the former translates into a smaller trend growth of SAMB.

Chapter 5
New Zealand: Inflation-Targeting Pioneer

1. "The role of monetary policy under [the new government's] approach is aimed in the medium term at achieving suitably moderate and steady rates of

growth in the major monetary aggregates. This is directed ultimately at the inflation rate, as control over the monetary aggregates is seen as a prerequisite for a lower, more stable rate of inflation" (Reserve Bank of New Zealand, 1985a, September, p. 513).

2. Before the passage of the Reserve Bank of New Zealand Act of 1989, the Reserve Bank was ranked comparatively low in its degree of independence. See, for example, Alesina and Summers (1993).

3. The problem of the treatment of housing costs was addressed in the beginning of 1994, when the share of the index based on existing dwellings in the CPI was largely replaced by an index of the cost of construction of new houses. Similar problems in the treatment of housing costs were a feature of the CPI in the United States before 1983.

4. Strictly speaking, the first PTA only allowed for, or required renegotiation of, the Agreement while the second and third PTAs explicitly required such a response to shocks.

5. We are grateful to Governor Brash for clarifying this point. The exclusion of the effects of taxes imposed by local authorities proved impractical given the difficulties of identifying policy changes at that level. The effect, however, remained potentially quite large, with the movement toward "user-pays pricing" of public services being part of the broader reforms.

6. This is not simply a matter of who guards the guardian, serious though that may be. "Because the Reserve Bank's estimate of underlying inflation relies on judgment in its construction, its validity cannot be directly verified [by outside observers]. In addition, there is room for disagreement concerning the proper model to be used in estimating the impact of one-time shocks" (Spiegel, 1995). The Reserve Bank itself has made note of this potential conflict of interest and its possible effect on its credibility in articles in the *Bulletin*.

7. Some bank documents, however, have made the contradictory claim that the move to targeting and central bank independence would be expected to have an effect on the costs of disinflation. For example, "in order to improve the prospects of monetary policy to remain—and be seen to remain—on the track of low inflation, and thereby help reduce the costs of disinflation, attention turned to possible institutional arrangements that would help improve monetary policy credibility" (Lloyd, 1992, p. 208). See Posen (1995a), Hutchison and Walsh (1996), and Chapter 10 for econometric assessments of this effect.

8. Again, this may be contrasted to the Bundesbank's approach, which does not address the short-run real effects of monetary policy in public statements but keeps all responsibility for the timing of disinflation within the Bundesbank.

9. The article cited here, while signed by Lloyd, not only appeared in the Reserve Bank's *Bulletin* under the authoritative title, "The New Zealand Approach to Central Bank Autonomy," but parts of it also appeared verbatim in other statements by Reserve Bank officials in 1992 and 1993. Thus it

seems reasonable to treat this statement as reflecting the official views of the Bank.

10. Following the introduction of the MCI, these assumptions would translate into an assumed path for the MCI over the forecast horizon.

11. Regarding financial stability, inflation targeting has an important advantage over an exchange rate peg in that the inflation targeting approach preserves the ability of the central bank to act as a lender of last resort. This option is not as available in a fixed-exchange-rate regime, as the Argentinean experience during the "tequila crisis" of 1995 demonstrates (*e.g.*, see Mishkin [1997a]).

12. A similar point about the gap between the perception and the operational realities of monetary targeting in Germany and Switzerland was made in Chapter 4.

13. See, for example, *New Zealand Herald* (1990a).

14. See *New Zealand Herald* (1990b). It is interesting that, after losing power, the Labour Party (which had instituted the inflation targets and the economic reforms more generally), announced its opposition to the 2% band for the inflation target. However, it continued to support keeping the center of the target at 1%.

15. The bill rate is indicative of the stance of the Reserve Bank's monetary policy, but unlike a true policy instrument, it is not directly controlled by the Bank. In March 1997, the Bank discussed moving to a more directly controlled instrument rate, but decided against such a change in June.

16. Until December 1993, the Bank's inflation forecasts assumed that the exchange rate would remain constant at the level present at the time of the forecast. The vindication of the statement above over the preceding two years led the Bank in June 1994 to assume from that point on an annual appreciation equal to the difference between the trade-weighted inflation forecasts for New Zealand's main trading partners and the midpoint of the 0% to 2% target range from June 1994.

17. See, for example, Louisson (1994).

18. We are grateful to Governor Brash for his discussion of these developments.

19. In that election multi-member proportional representation, which had been approved in a nationwide referendum, replaced majoritarian elections. Proportional representation was largely defended as a way for the public to put a brake on activist programs by the government, of either the left or right. (Under majoritarian parliaments, New Zealand had seen major shifts, such as Labour's "Rogernomics" reforms after 1984, and presumably such shifts would be less likely in a more fractured legislature.) The effect of multiple parties on inflation rates and fiscal policy (usually held by the economics literature to increase the former and loosen the latter) does not seem to have entered the discussions.

Chapter 6
Canada: Inflation Targets as Tools of Communication

1. To cite two examples of the belief in expectational sluggishness: "There is no doubt that Canadian markets are not at all supportive of inflationary actions nowadays. But it does take time for such reality to have an impact on market behavior, and on the costs and prices that flow from this behavior" (Crow, 1991, p. 13). And, "[t]he lags in the response of the Canadian rate of inflation to changes in monetary policy have traditionally been long, both as a result of institutional characteristics . . . and expectational sluggishness" (Freedman, 1994a, p. 21). Moreover, Longworth and Freedman (1995) explain how backward-looking expectations play a significant role in the current Bank of Canada forecasting model.

2. See similar statements in Jenkins (1990), Bank of Canada (1991b, March, pp. 3–21), and Freedman (1994a).

3. The example of New Zealand was probably not yet well established, and it was not acknowledged in public statements by senior bank officials until Freedman (1994a).

4. Thiessen (1994a, p. 86) makes an almost identical statement of these two points.

5. "Over longer periods of time, the measures of inflation based on the total CPI and the core CPI tend to follow similar paths. In the event of persistent differences between the trends of the two measures, the Bank would adjust its desired path for core CPI inflation so that total CPI inflation would come within the target range" (Bank of Canada, 1996c, November, p. 4).

6. "It is important to stress that the objective continues to be the control of inflation as defined by the total consumer price index" (Thiessen, 1996b, p. 4).

7. "Accommodating the initial effect on the price level of a tax change but not any ongoing inflation effects was the approach set out with the February 1991 inflation-reduction targets, and restated in the December 1993 agreement [extending the target framework]" (Thiessen, 1994a, p. 82). Of course, unlike the assessment of differences between core and headline CPI, the assessment of the size of a tax increase's impact effect on prices depends on an analyst's assumptions. The Bank does publish its own calculations of the price effects of tax changes.

8. "The targets continue to be expressed as a range or a band rather than a specific inflation rate because it is impossible to control inflation precisely" (Thiessen, 1994a, p. 86).

9. "Other sources of unexpected price increases, which are typically less significant than the three singled out for special attention, will be handled within the one percent band around the targets for reducing inflation" (Bank of Canada, 1991b, September, p. 4).

10. This may be due to the fact that, more than any other inflation-targeting country, Canada has had to cope with headline inflation falling below the target or reaching the target ahead of schedule; and, perhaps as a result, the Bank has faced greater public criticism of the targets as harmful to the real economy. These challenges are discussed in the next section.

11. See Thiessen (1994a, p. 89) and Freedman (1994a, p. 20) for examples.

12. This statement makes the assumption that the weakness in the Canadian economy reflects a gap between output and potential output, rather than a change in labor or product markets that has increased the "natural" rate of unemployment.

13. This statement is representative of the Bank's position. See also, for example, Bank of Canada (1995c, May, p. 3), which states: "The ultimate objective of Canadian monetary policy is to promote good overall economic performance. Monetary policy can contribute to this goal by preserving confidence in the value of money through price stability. In other words, price stability is a means to an end, not an end in itself."

14. This interpretation of short-run flexibility was raised in a different context in Bernanke and Mishkin (1992). In a more recent example, in the Bank of Canada's *Annual Report,* 1994, the Bank states that "in late 1994 and early 1995, the persistent weakness of the dollar began to undermine confidence in the currency, and the Bank of Canada took actions to calm and stabilize financial markets" (p. 7); the *Annual Report,* 1996 lists "promoting the safety and soundness of Canada's financial system" (p. 4) as the second part of its section "Our Commitment to Canadians." In short, the Bank found no inherent conflict between promoting (within limits) financial stability or more stable output on one hand and the pursuit of price stability over the long run on the other. In its attention to goals other than price stability, the Bank of Canada is similar to all the central banks we study in this volume, though perhaps more open about it.

15. "Real"—that is, inflation-indexed—bonds have been issued in Canada since 1991, following the example of the United Kingdom. One motive cited for the creation was precisely to obtain a measure of inflation expectations, which should be closely related in principle to the difference in yields between indexed and non-indexed bonds. As the Bank of Canada itself has pointed out, however, the market for real bonds to date has been relatively small and illiquid, and the experience with them has been relatively short. Thus, use of real bonds for measuring inflation expectations is viewed as difficult in practice.

16. This idea has been picked up since by a number of other countries and several private-sector forecasting groups as a compact means of expressing the relative tightness of monetary policy in open economies. For a more complete discussion of the MCI, see Freedman (1994b).

17. Freedman (1995, p. 30) offers the opinion that "it may well be that [the] most important contribution [of the *Monetary Policy Reports*] will be to signal prospective inflationary pressure and the need for timely policy action, at a time when actual rates of inflation (which are of course a lagging indicator) are still

relatively subdued." This scenario is premised on Canada's starting from a situation of "relatively subdued" inflation pressures, which was the case by 1995.

18. Citing New Zealand, the United Kingdom, and Sweden, Freedman (1995, pp. 29-30) notes, "These reports, which have both backward-looking and forward-looking perspectives, have received considerable attention and careful scrutiny by the press, the financial markets, and parliamentary committees." See also Thiessen (1995a, p. 56), who states: "This report will provide an account of our stewardship of monetary policy and will be useful for those who want to know more about monetary policy for their own decision-making."

19. This move may have seemed necessary after the October 1993 election was fought in part over the Bank's monetary policy, and Crow eventually decided not to be considered for a second term. The newly elected Liberal Government chose to extend rather than to replace the inflation targets.

20. According to Cukierman's (1992) index of central bank independence (based on the banks' formal legal standing), the Bank of Canada ranks, with the Danish central bank, just below the Federal Reserve in independence.

21. Laidler and Robson (1993, Chap.9) provide an extensive discussion of the Bank of Canada's practical independence and its limits through 1992.

22. See *Creating Opportunity: The Liberal Plan for Canada,* cited in Crane (1993).

23. The targets were intended to define the path implied by the various actual inflation targets at eighteen-month intervals of 3% by year-end 1992, 2.5% by mid-1994, and 2% by year-end 1995 (all range midpoints).

24. For example, "'the government is betting on its own inflation targets,' said Toronto-Dominion Bank chief economist Doug Peters, referring to Canada's target of 2 percent inflation in 1995" (Szep, 1991).

25. Sacrifice ratios attempt to measure the amount of real output lost for each point of disinflation.

26. See, for example, Ip (1991).

27. The academic literature has adopted the term "hysteresis" to describe situations in which increases in unemployment arising from transitory causes may tend to become permanent, for reasons such as loss of skills. Hysteresis has often been cited as a source of the persistently high unemployment rates observed for nearly two decades in Western Europe.

28. The committee's formal title was the Standing Committee on Finance, Subcommittee on the Bank of Canada, of the House of Commons, but it was called the Manley Committee after its chairman, John Manley. See its report, *The Mandate and Governance of the Bank of Canada,* February 1992.

29. It should be noted that, for all the attention central banks' written charters and legal mandates attract, only a few central banks have formal mandates for price stability. Not only have many inflation targeters—such as Canada, Sweden, Australia, and the United Kingdom—adopted largely successful inflation-targeting regimes without revision of their legal mission, but the Bundesbank is the only one of the three independent central banks with a long-standing suc-

cessful inflation record that has had such a clearly limited legal mandate (the Swiss National Bank and the U.S. Federal Reserve are the others).

30. The Liberal Party's campaign platform, *Creating Opportunity: The Liberal Plan for Canada,* included the statements: "Liberals believe that economic policies must not merely attack an individual problem in isolation from its costs in other areas. . . . The Conservatives' single-minded fight against inflation resulted in deep recession, three years without growth, declining incomes, skyrocketing unemployment, a crisis in international payments, and the highest combined set of government deficits in our history." See Crane (1993).

31. For a sample of private-sector reactions, see Marotte (1993).

32. For press coverage of Freedman's speech, see, among others, Ip (1993).

33. During the period of an announced downward path for inflation, the emphasis in the Bank of Canada's discussion was on the midpoint, whereas once the range of 1 to 3% range was reached, the emphasis shifted to the bands. We are grateful to Charles Freedman for discussion of this point.

34. Some press observers characterized the contemporaneous developments in transparency undertaken by the Bank as reflecting a desire to make the Bank seem more generally accountable rather than identified with a particular individual. See, for example, Vardy (1993) and McGillivray (1994).

35. The Bank had explained beforehand that it expected only a temporary blip in inflation in 1995 from the depreciation of the Canadian dollar. The fact that the depreciation did not lead to a persistent rise in inflation, even without a further tightening of monetary conditions, helped build the Bank's credibility.

36. The body of the *Monetary Policy Report* states, "Since the last *Report,* the Canadian economy has been weaker than expected and the degree of slack in labor and product markets has been correspondingly greater" (p. 3). And later, "Although a slowdown had been anticipated, the Bank was surprised (along with most others) by how abruptly the situation changed" (p. 6).

37. For example, "for the medium-term, a key issue is whether the trend of inflation might move below the 1 to 3 percent target range. . . . This in turn would imply an easing in the desired path of *medium-term* monetary conditions" (Bank of Canada, 1996c, May, p. 3). Governor Thiessen and other officers made similar statements to the press.

38. In addition to citing Akerlof, Dickens, and Perry (1996), Fortin also gives prominence to James Tobin's discussion of the macroeconomic significance of the nominal wage floor in his 1971 Presidential Address to the American Economic Association (p. 779).

39. See, for example, Crane (1996) and Fortin (1996b)

40. The speech, reprinted in Thiessen (1996a), was delivered before the Board of Trade of Metropolitan Toronto on November 6, 1996.

41. "However, inflation will work as a lubricant only if it fools people into believing that they are better off than they really are. There is, in fact, every reason to expect that people's behavior adapts to circumstances. In a low-inflation environment, employees are likely to come to understand the need for

occasional downward adjustments in wages or benefits" (Thiessen 1996a, pp. 68-9). Note that Thiessen does not assert that such wage flexibility has already occurred or is likely to arise quickly.

Chapter 7
United Kingdom: The Central Bank as Counterinflationary Conscience

1. This announcement was made official by the simultaneous delivery of a letter from the Chancellor to the Chairman of Parliament's Treasury and Civil Service Committee.

2. Speeches by officials of the Bank of Canada in the late 1980s leading up to that country's adoption of inflation targets made the same point, and with some of the same rhetorical spirit.

3. The Bank of England and the Chancellor were of course aware of the innovations in inflation targeting in New Zealand and Canada but they avoided mentioning them in public. Still, the U.K. adoption of inflation targeting may be thought of as part of a larger movement.

4. In a speech on June 14, 1995, Chancellor Kenneth Clarke (1995) announced that this objective would be extended indefinitely beyond the next general election. Without a change in the status of the Bank of England, however, the ruling party had no power to bind future governments, so the force of Clarke's statement was unclear. In late 1996, prior to the spring 1997 election campaign, Labour Party leaders indicated that they would continue the inflation-targeting framework (and the current targets) should they, as expected, win the election.

5. This is akin to the Swiss National Bank's rationale for its point target for monetary growth. As the Bank of England's own research suggests, however, if a target range were truly designed to capture some reasonable confidence interval of outcomes, given control problems, the range would be too wide for credibility with the general public. See Haldane and Salmon (1995).

6. See Clarke (1995). Note that the point target does not imply performance assessment on the basis of a backward-looking average. Instead, the inflation performance relative to the point target is explained as the result of past actions and intervening developments. We are grateful to Mervyn King for clarifying this point.

7. The Labour Party's commitment to the inflation target and to greater operational independence for the Bank of England was made explicit in the party's election platform. The rapid granting of independence—the day after Labour took office—nonetheless was a surprise to all observers.

8. The conveying of this information in an appropriate way to a nontechnical audience has challenged the staff of the *Inflation Report*. Initial efforts to depict the trend path of inflation with probability "cones" moving out from it were not widely understood. Recent renderings of a probability density for future inflation with shading from red (most likely) to pink (tail of distribution) appear to have been well received.

9. The statements quoted represent the Bank's official stance. In the same issue of the Quarterly Bulletin, the Bank's "General Assessment" echoes both statements—that "the achievement of price stability remained the ultimate objective of monetary policy" (p. 355), and that "had the United Kingdom remained in the ERM, it is quite possible that price stability would have been achieved during the next year. Although clearly desirable in itself, price stability attained too quickly might have intensified the problems of domestic debt deflation. Some easing of policy was, therefore, desirable" (p. 356).

10. At least, so long as an "optimal" contract for central bankers penalizing inflation performance alone is not in force.

11. There is now some requirement for the Bank and its senior staff to give testimony to the House of Commons Treasury Committee on a regular basis, as opposed to the by-request (though frequent) appearances in the past. Nonetheless, the record of these past testimonies—as well as the lack of incentives facing backbenchers on the committee to deviate from respective party leaderships' lines on monetary policy—suggests that these hearings are unlikely to influence Bank policy significantly.

12. The point should not be exaggerated, however, since Italy also managed to limit the pass-through effect of its ERM exit without adopting inflation targets (see Chapter 10).

13. See, for example, Economist (1994).

14. Svensson (1997a) makes clear the benefits of having the target of policy be the monetary policymaker's inflation forecast.

15. The Bank assumes in its projections that official interest rates will not change and that movements in the exchange rate will reflect the differential between U.K. short-term interest rates and trade-weighted overseas short-term interest rates.

16. Several British press commentators observed that the May meeting was postponed until after some local elections had taken place and took this as an indication that a rate hike was coming, since Clarke would not want to implement his policy the day before the elections. While the Bank-Chancellor meetings are monthly, the exact timing is not systematic, with occasional reschedulings occurring. In this instance, there was a widespread expectation before the meeting that the Chancellor would agree with the Bank's assessment; his later public overruling of the Bank, leaving rates unchanged, might be seen as an accommodation to broader Tory political reality, but one that emphasized the economic realities as well. As noted below, the U.K. press tends to look for politicization of monetary policy.

17. See Clarke (1995).

18. See, for example, Financial Times (1996). It should be noted that the British press tends to focus on the possibility that business and monetary cycles are governed by political and electoral developments. This is despite the fact that there is little econometric or other evidence to suggest that such cycles are

operative in the United Kingdom, an open economy with brief election campaigns on short notice.

Chapter 8
Sweden: Searching for a Nominal Anchor

1. The Riksbank's Governing Board consists of eight members, seven of whom are appointed by Parliament for the duration of the legislative period (3 years). These seven members appoint the Governor as the eighth member, but the Governor is appointed for five years and is not the Chairman. If a vote is tied, the Chairman, not the Governor, casts the decisive vote.

2. During the 1930s, monetary policy in Sweden followed a rule to stabilize the price level, a precursor to the monetary-policy strategy considered in this book. An account of this period may be found in Jonung (1979).

3. The Riksbank's decision to peg the krona to the ECU was part of a broader trend. On October 22, 1990, Norway adopted a peg to the ECU, and Finland followed suit on June 7, 1991.

4. In its own account of the speculative attacks and the ensuing floating of the krona, the Riksbank mentions all these factors behind the krona's susceptibility. See Sveriges Riksbank (1993a, 1, p.10).

5. The position papers referred to are those published in Sveriges Riksbank (1992c).

6. See, for example, the discussion in Svensson (1992), pp. 18–19. Certainly, for a small, open economy still undergoing the effects of financial liberalization, any form of monetary target was out of the question.

7. A detailed account of the political discussions concerning monetary policy during 1993 and 1994 may be found in Svensson (1995).

8. Berg and Grottheim (1997, pp. 171–175).

9. We are grateful to Claes Berg for discussion of this point. See Bäckström (1994).

10. Svensson (1997a) argues that inflation targeting should be interpreted as meaning that the central bank is using its inflation forecast as an intermediate target.

11. The issue of reform of the Riksbank is discussed in more detail in Svensson (1995).

12. Berg and Grottheim (1997, pp. 178–180).

13. This discussion is based on, and all relevant quotes are taken from, the summary of the Committee's report SOU 1993:20. We thank Lars Svensson for providing us with the English version of the summary.

14. See Berg and Lundkvist (1997) for a detailed examination of the structural adaptation of the Swedish economy to inflation targeting.

15. The Riksbank, unlike the Bank of Canada, does not have a monetary-conditions index that weights the effects of exchange and interest

rate movements in the economy. However, the influence of the krona's value on the economy is never overlooked in public discussion of the stance of policy.

16. Sveriges Riksbank (1997b, June, pp. 8-10). In Chapter 10 we report the results of a similar survey of a broad sample of targeting and non-targeting countries. Household expectations of headline CPI inflation averaged 6% to 7% annually in the 1980s in Sweden. Since 1992, those expectations have averaged 2%.

Chapter 9
Inflation Targeting in Three Small Open Economies

1. Ben-Bassat states, "About (1986), the Bank of Israel began setting an inflation target as a basis for monetary policy, without making this public" (Ben-Bassat, 1995, p. 38).

2. Chile also engaged in a form of inflation targeting when inflation was at double-digit levels, apparently quite successfully. See Morande and Schmidt-Hebbel (1997).

3. The economic stabilization program has received considerable academic attention. See, for example, the contributions in Bruno *et al.* (1991).

4. See, for example, the results reported in Table 1 of Ben-Bassat (1995).

5. Bufman and Leiderman (1997), p. 33.

6. This explicit commitment linking the choice of inflation target to future goals of disinflation represents a sharp change from the initial period of Israeli inflation targets, in which even government policy-makers interchanged the words "target" and "forecast" in their discussions. We are grateful to Ohad Bar-Efrat for discussion of this point.

7. This relationship assumes no change in the real exchange rate.

8. Quoted in Offenbacher (1996), p. 61.

9. Bufman and Leiderman (1997), p. 7.

10. *Ibid.*

11. See, for example, Edey (1997), p. 62.

12. "The motivation [from 1987 to 1989] was a growing discomfort (within and outside the Bank) with the degree of policy discretion, combined with the recognition that most other OECD countries had succeeded in getting inflation down: Australia, with inflation not far short of 10 per cent, looked out of step, and there were increasing calls for the Bank 'to do something about it'" (Grenville, 1997, p. 135).

13. For example, "In principle, systems with hard-edged bands and commitments to keep inflation continuously within a specified range, as in New Zealand, can be contrasted with systems such as those of Australia and Finland that focus on the average rather than the permitted range; however these differences can be easily exaggerated given the presence of caveats and exclusions in many systems" (Edey, 1997, p. 61).

14. Stated more generally, "In Australia, we did not adopt such a hard-edged band, because of concerns that the resulting discontinuity in the payoff func-

tion might induce instability in the instruments of monetary policy, and further may result in policy-induced business cycles" (Debelle, 1997, p. 119).

15. As stated in Laubach and Posen's (1997b) discussion of the lessons of Swiss and German monetary targeting (p. 43), "Severely limiting a central bank's discretion, the so-called 'binding of hands,' does not seem to be a necessary condition for sustained low inflation."

16. "The difference between 2 or 3 per cent inflation on average and something only slightly lower may be non-zero, but it is hard to believe that it is quite so crucial. Given that there are costs to reducing inflation further, and that the size of the additional gains is less certain, a practical course, for the time being, in Australia is to direct policy towards maintaining the current low but still positive rates of inflation" (Stevens and Debelle, 1995, p. 87).

17. Edey (1997), p. 62.

18. Chapter 10 discusses the Consensus Forecasts further and uses these data to study the credibility of several inflation-targeting regimes.

19. The announcement is reprinted in Banco de España, 1995b, January, pp. 5–13.

20. The English translation of the Law, from which this and all other quotes are taken, is provided on the Bank's website—http://www.bde.es

21. Almeida and Goodhart (1998), p. 12.

22. Almeida and Goodhart (1998), p. 20.

23. In addition to the *Inflation Report,* the Bank publishes every three months a "Quarterly Report on the Spanish Economy" in the *Economic Bulletin.* This report analyzes recent economic developments in great detail, but it does not discuss any policy decisions or provide any other forward-looking analyses.

Chapter 10
Inflation Targeting: How Successful Has It Been?

1. In our view, Huh's (1996) apparently similar comparisons are of apples to oranges. The focus of his analysis is a comparison of the experience of the United Kingdom to that of France—an ERM member which at the time had an overvalued exchange rate and rising policy credibility— and of the United States —a country without a declared nominal anchor, a different business cycle, and a smaller degree of openness.

2. See Svensson (1993), Ammer and Freeman (1995), Freeman and Willis (1995), and Huh (1996).

3. Ball (1994) explores some effects of labor-market structure on the sacrifice ratio. Because of data limitations, we omit this factor in our analysis.

4. Using alternatively the percent change of the middle month of the quarter or the average of the inflation rates of the three months within the quarter did not affect the results strongly.

5. Discrepancies between our results and those in Ball's Table 5.1 can be due either to differences in the timing of disinflations, or to differences in the measured output gap for a given episode. When performing the exercise of

using Ball's episodes and changes in inflation, our results are almost identical to his, which means that the measured output gaps are not the cause of the discrepancies. When instead using Ball's episodes, but our own measure of change in inflation, there are discrepancies between the ratios of the order of magnitude of 0.2 to 0.5. Finally, when we date the disinflationary episodes ourselves using Ball's criteria, we arrive at differences in the beginning and end dates of the order of 1 to 3 quarters. These differences in episodes have strong effects on the resulting sacrifice ratios. This suggests that Ball computed inflation in a different way, and therefore identified slightly different episodes.

6. Inflation for New Zealand and Australia was computed using the two Reserve Banks' underlying CPI series; for Canada using CPI excluding food and energy, for the U.K. using RPIX; and for Sweden using CPI excluding indirect taxes and subsidies. Except for New Zealand and Australia, CPI series for all countries are from the BIS. The measure of resource utilization was either the unemployment rate or residuals from Hodrick-Prescott filtered log GDP (meant to capture the output gap). Except for New Zealand, unemployment and real GDP are from the OECD *Main Economic Indicators*. Below we will report on the robustness of our results with respect to the choice of resource utilization measure. The nominal effective exchange rate and the U.S. dollars denominated commodity-price index, excluding energy prices, are from the Bank for International Settlements. (Replacing this with an index including energy prices made no difference in the results.)

7. Since we use these regressions exclusively for obtaining inflation forecasts, we do not include any contemporaneous variables on the right-hand side to avoid simultaneity issues. Neither do we impose a unit root on inflation by restricting the sum of the coefficients on lagged inflation to equal one. This prevents us from giving the estimated parameters a structural interpretation.

8. Box-Pierce tests did not indicate any autocorrelation in the residuals at one to 16 lags at the 5% level for any of the countries, either specification, and either choice of utilization measure.

9. The major changes to the results reported in the last paragraphs from choosing the alternative utilization measure are as follows: For New Zealand, the exchange rate is again significant, the significance of past inflation increases, and the output gap enters insignificantly. For Canada, the output gap enters significantly, and commodity prices are again included but insignificant. For Australia, neither the exchange rate nor commodity prices are included, and the lags of the output gap are jointly insignificant. For the United Kingdom, the exchange rate is now included in the regression, but the four lags are jointly insignificant. For Italy, the exchange rate is included and significant, while commodity prices are excluded. For the United States, the output gap enters significantly, and commodity prices are again included but insignificant. Finally, for Germany, lagged inflation enters now highly significantly, while both the output gap and commodity prices are insignificant, and the exchange rate is excluded. Since Swiss unemployment data start only in 1983, and the Swedish unemployment rate exhibits a break in the early 1990s, we do not report results for these two countries using unemployment.

10. Estimates are through 1995:3 for Italy, through 1995:2 for Australia, and through 1995:1 for New Zealand, due to data availability.

11. More precisely, the forecast error of a k-horizon out-of-sample forecast is a function of up to the k-th power of the estimated parameters.

12. The fact that the forecasts are overlapping introduces serial correlation between the forecast error at horizon j from forecast date k and the forecast error at horizon j-1 from forecast date k+1 [see Hansen and Hodrick (1980)]. The empirical standard deviation of the forecast errors at a specific horizon is nevertheless a consistent estimate of the true standard deviation at this horizon.

13. We discuss (and Figure 10.1 shows) only the results from the forecasts using the basic specification with four lags of all variables included, since the parsimonious specifications perform less well as forecasting equations.

14. For most countries, using the output gap instead of the unemployment rate as the utilization measure does not have a strong effect on the results. For Canada, the United Kingdom, Italy, the United States, and Germany, the respective average forecast errors become 0.38, -1.25, -1.35, -0.14, and -1.20. Except for Italy, inflation is even less often outside the one-RMSE band than before. For Italy, inflation is above the upper band in three out of eight quarters. For New Zealand and Australia, using the output gap instead of the unemployment rate leads to much higher over-prediction following target adoption. In New Zealand, inflation is below the lower band during the last three quarters, and the average forecast error rises to 4.06%. For Australia, inflation is below the lower band during all eight quarters, leading to an average forecast error of 5.80. These results should be treated with caution, however, as for all countries except the United Kingdom, Italy, the United States, and Switzerland the output gap enters the regression insignificantly, and thus there is effectively no Phillips curve found in the data.

15. The data on forecasts are from Consensus Forecasts, a monthly publication by London-based Consensus Economics, Inc. At the beginning of each month, Consensus Economics collects forecasts for a number of countries for up to 15 economic variables (output, employment, prices, and interest rates, to name a few) from a number of financial institutions and professional forecasters based in each country. The number of institutions polled varies with the size of the economy (for example, there are 30 respondents from the United States, 8 from Italy, and so on). The forecasts for inflation that we utilize in this section are forecasts for CPI inflation by the end of the current year and by the end of the following calendar year.

16. The 3-month interest rate for Germany is the 3-month FIBOR. The available treasury bill series for Germany is from the Bundesbank's operations in 3-month treasury bills (*Bundesschatzwechsel*), which were discontinued at the end of 1995. Besides this fact, the series exhibits the pattern of long periods of no change like the Bundesbank's discount and lombard rates, and therefore does not seem to be a good indicator of market conditions. The 3-month FIBOR, by contrast, behaves much like the overnight rate, except for a term premium.

17. Ammer and Freeman (1995) perform a similar exercise. They interpret their results as showing below-predicted GDP growth after targeting, as well as lower inflation and interest rates. Their simulations, however, were based on data series ending two years before the series presented here. As can be seen in the simulation results for New Zealand and Canada, GDP growth was initially below predicted values, probably due to disinflationary policies prior to target adoption. Over the whole post-target-adoption period, however, GDP growth rebounds and is at the predicted level on average.

For New Zealand, we use the discount rate rather than the overnight interest rate because it is the only continuously available series that can be seen as reflecting the stance of monetary policy. Since the late 1980s, the Reserve Bank has been keeping the discount rate 0.9% above the interbank overnight rate. For Sweden and Italy, we smooth out the spike in their short-term interest rates in September 1992 by interpolating neighboring values, since the forecasts would otherwise be dominated by these movements and would be meaningless for our purposes.

18. A formal test for structural breaks in monetary-policy reaction functions has three limitations that prevent its use in this assessment of inflation targeting's effectiveness: First, the tests would be of extremely low power given the limited time since adoption, even in New Zealand. Second, the tests would require us to impose a structural model of monetary policy-making for each country, which is beyond the scope of this analysis. Third, we are most interested in qualitative results, while the formal test would provide only a yes/no answer.

19. Country-specific shocks are not the only potential source of problems for this comparison. Another possible reason why inflation and interest rates could be lower than forecast would be the existence of a widespread disinflationary trend across many countries over this time period which drove these variables down in targeters and non-targeters alike. For this reason, we include Australia and Italy in our comparison. Again, treating Australia as a non-targeting country seems appropriate, given that our forecasts start almost five years prior to the adoption of an inflation target in Australia.

20. Clarida, Gali, and Gertler (1998), for example, show that after October 1979, the Federal Reserve became much more serious about fighting inflation, setting its monetary-policy instruments so that upward movements of inflation led to a rise in the real federal funds rate, rather than a fall as had occurred before 1979.

Chapter 11
What Have We Learned?

1. See Svensson (1997b) for a theoretical demonstration that gradual adjustment of the medium-term inflation target to the long-run goal is optimal for a policy-maker concerned about both output fluctuations and low, stable inflation.

2. It should be noted, however, that the relatively long records of low inflation compiled by Germany, Switzerland, and the United States have not produced detectable declines in the sacrifice ratios in those countries (Posen [1995a]).

3. This section draws heavily on Mishkin (1997a).

4. There is a debate about whether speculative attacks can be purely spontaneous, self-fulfilling prophecies, or whether there must be some "fundamental" problem with a country's policies before an attack occurs. The evidence is not clear as to whether countries experiencing attacks in the past decade had bad policy fundamentals; or, to the extent they did, whether these problems were the cause of the speculative attack.

5. Mishkin (1998) gives additional criticisms of the use of exchange-rate pegs in emerging-market countries.

6. Or, as an official of the Bank of Canada reputedly put it, "We didn't abandon the monetary aggregates; they abandoned us."

Chapter 12
Inflation Targeting for the United States and the European Monetary Union

1. It is possible that the adoption of inflation targeting, and the resulting stabilization of inflation expectations, may reduce this range of uncertainty. Clear evidence on this point is not yet available, however.

2. In practice, even central banks that do set inflation goals without formal government approval (Germany and Switzerland being the prime examples) are still not completely goal-independent. Even nominally goal-independent central banks know that choosing policy objectives that are inconsistent with the public's wishes will eventually have serious adverse consequences, because the independence of the central bank can be modified or taken away at any time through legislation (Posen, 1995b). Indeed, the Bundesbank, despite its reputation for being strongly committed to controlling inflation, has until recently used a numerical long-run inflation goal of 2% per year, which is the same as (for example) the midpoint of the Canadian inflation target, jointly set by the Finance Minister and the Bank of Canada. Thus, what appear to be very different processes for setting the long-run inflation target have led to the same quantitative result, a value for desired inflation which is low but recognizes the dangers to the real economy of making inflation too low.

References

Akerlof, George, Dickens, William, and Perry, George. 1996. "The Macroeconomics of Low Inflation." *Brookings Papers on Economic Activity* 1:1–59.

Alesina, Alberto, and Summers, Lawrence H. 1993. "Central Bank Independence and Macroeconomic Performance: Some Comparative Evidence." *Journal of Money, Credit, and Banking* 25(2):151–62.

Almeida, Alvaro, and Goodhart, Charles A. E. 1998. "Does the Adoption of Inflation Targets Affect Central Bank Behaviour?" Unpublished paper, London School of Economics, January.

Ammer, John, and Freeman, Richard. 1995. "Inflation Targeting in the 1990s: The Experiences of New Zealand, Canada, and the United Kingdom." *Journal of Economics and Business* 47:165–92.

Andersen, Palle, and Gruen, David. 1995. "Macroeconomic Policies and Growth." In Palle Andersen, Jacqueline Dwyer, and David Gruen, eds., *Productivity and Growth*. Sydney: Reserve Bank of Australia, 279–319.

Bäckström, Urban. 1994. "Monetary Policy and the Inflation Target." Speech given at the Stockholm Stock Exchange, December.

Ball, Laurence. 1994. "What Determines the Sacrifice Ratio?" In N. Gregory Mankiw, ed., *Monetary Policy*. Chicago: University of Chicago Press, 155–82.

Banco de España. 1994–95a. *Annual Report,* various issues.

———. 1995-97b. *Economic Bulletin,* various issues.

———. 1996–97c. *Inflation Report,* various issues.

Bank for International Settlements. 1976. *46th Annual Report 1975/76.*

Bank of Canada. 1991–96a. *Annual Report,* various issues.

———. 1991-94b. *Bank of Canada Review,* various issues.

———. 1995–97c. *Monetary Policy Report,* various issues.

Bank of England. 1994–97a. *Minutes of the Monthly Monetary Meeting,* various issues.

———. 1992–96b. *Inflation Report,* various issues.

Barro, Robert J., and Gordon, David. 1983. "A Positive Theory of Monetary Policy in a Natural Rate Model." *Journal of Political Economy* 91(4): 589–610.

Ben-Bassat, Avraham. 1995. "The Inflation Target in Israel: Policy and Development." In Andrew G. Haldane, ed., *Targeting Inflation,* London: Bank of England, 15–48.

Berg, Claes, and Grottheim, Richard. 1997. "Monetary Policy in Sweden Since 1992." Bank for International Settlements, Policy Papers no. 2.

Berg, Claes, and Lundkvist, Peter 1997. "Has the Inflation Process Changed?" Sveriges Riksbank *Quarterly Review* 2: 5–25.

Bernanke, Ben S., and James, Harold. 1991. "The Gold Standard, Deflation, and Financial Crisis in the Great Depression: An International Comparison." In Glenn R. Hubbard, ed., *Financial Markets and Financial Crises,* Chicago: University of Chicago Press, 33–68.

Bernanke, Ben S., and Mihov, Ilian. 1997. "What Does the Bundesbank Target?" *European Economic Review* 41(6): 1025–53.

Bernanke, Ben S., and Mishkin, Frederic S. 1992. "Central Bank Behavior and the Strategy of Monetary Policy: Observations from Six Industrialized Countries." In Olivier Blanchard and Stanley Fischer, eds., *NBER Macroeconomics Annual,* Cambridge, MA: MIT Press, 183–238.

_____. 1997. "Inflation Targeting: A New Framework for Monetary Policy?" *Journal of Economic Perspectives* 11(2): 97–116.

Bernanke, Ben S., and Woodford, Michael. 1997. "Inflation Forecasts and Monetary Policy." *Journal of Money, Credit, and Banking* 29(4): 653–84.

Birch, W.F. 1996. "NZ Monetary and Fiscal Policy Consistent and Has Reserve Bank Support." *Financial Times,* letter to the editor. January 9: 12.

Boskin, Michael J., Dulberger, Ellen R., Gordon, Robert J., Griliches, Zvi, and Jorgenson, Dale W. 1996. "Toward a More Accurate Measure of the Cost of Living." Final Report to the Senate Finance Committee. December 4.

Brash, Donald T. 1996a. "New Zealand's Remarkable Reforms." The Fifth IEA Annual Hayek Memorial Lecture. Institute of Economic Affairs Occasional Paper no. 100.

_____. 1996b. "Address to the Auckland Manufacturers' Association." February.

_____. 1997. "Address to the Canterbury Employers' Chamber of Commerce." January.

Bruno, Michael, and Easterly, William. 1998. "Inflation Crises and Long-Run Growth." *Journal of Monetary Economics* 41(1): 3–26.

Bruno, Michael, Fisher, Stanley, Helpman, Elhanan, and Liviatan Nissan, eds. 1991. *Lessons of Economic Stabilization and Its Aftermath.* Cambridge, MA: MIT Press.

Bryant, Ralph. 1996. "Central Bank Independence, Fiscal Responsibility, and the Goals of Macroeconomic Policy: An American Perspective on the New Zealand Experience." Unpublished paper, Victoria University of Wellington.

Bufman, Gil, and Leiderman, Leonardo. 1997. "Monetary Policy and Inflation in Israel." Unpublished paper, Bank of Israel, October.

Bufman, Gil, Leiderman, Leonardo, and Sokoler, Meir. 1995. "Israel's Experience with Explicit Inflation Targets: A First Assessment." In Leonardo Leiderman and Lars E. O. Svensson, eds., *Inflation Targets,* London: Centre for Economic Policy Research, 169–91.

Calvo, Guillermo. 1978. "On the Time Consistency of Optimal Policy in the Monetary Economy." *Econometrica* 46(6): 1411–28.

Cecchetti, Stephen G. 1994. "Comment." In N. Gregory Mankiw, ed., *Monetary Policy,* Chicago: University of Chicago Press, 188–93.

_____. 1995. "Inflation Indicators and Inflation Policy." In Ben S. Bernanke and Julio J. Rotemberg, eds., *NBER Macroeconomics Annual,* Cambridge, MA: MIT Press, 180–219.

Chote, Robert. 1997. "Treading the Line between Credibility and Humility." *Financial Times* June 13: 9.

Chote, Robert, Coggan, Phillip, and Peston, Robert. 1995. "Pound Hit as Clarke Fails to Lift Rates." *Financial Times* May 6–7: 1.

Clarida, Richard, Galí, Jordi, and Gertler, Mark. 1998. "Monetary Policy Rules in Practice: Some International Evidence." *European Economic Review* 42(6): 1033–67.

Clarida, Richard, and Gertler, Mark. 1997. "How the Bundesbank Conducts Monetary Policy." In Christina D. Romer and David H. Romer, eds., *Reducing Inflation: Motivation and Strategy,* Chicago: University of Chicago Press, 363–406.

Clarke, Kenneth. 1995. Mansion House Speech to the City, June 14. Excerpted in *Financial Times,* June 15, p. 10.

Coote, Michael. 1996. "Price Stability Requires a Tight, Not Loose, Inflation Target." *New Zealand Business Review* p. 70.

Cozier, Barry, and Wilkinson, Gordon. 1991. "Some Evidence on Hysteresis and the Costs of Disinflation in Canada." *Bank of Canada Technical Report no. 55.*

Crane, David. 1993. "John Crow Deserves to Be Fired, Not Rehired." *Toronto Star,* November 14, p. D4.

_____. 1996. "Bank of Canada Should Rethink Zero Inflation." *Toronto Star,* September 5.

Crow, John W. 1988 "The Work of Canadian Monetary Policy." The Hanson Lecture. *Bank of Canada Review* February: 3–17.

_____. 1989. "Targeting Monetary Policy." *Bank of Canada Review* December: 21–8.

_____. 1990. "Current Monetary Policy." *Bank of Canada Review* September: 33–41.

_____. 1991. "Method and Myth in Monetary Policy." *Bank of Canada Review* July: 9–14.

Cukierman, Alex. 1992 *Central Bank Strategy, Credibility, and Independence: Theory and Evidence.* Cambridge, MA: MIT Press.

Debelle, Guy. 1997. "Discussion." In Philip Lowe, ed., *Monetary Policy and Inflation Targeting,* pp. 118-23. Sydney: Reserve Bank of Australia.

Debelle, Guy, and Fischer, Stanley. 1994. "How Independent Should a Central Bank Be?" In Jeffrey C. Fuhrer, ed., *Goals, Guidelines, and Constraints Facing Monetary Policymakers.* Federal Reserve Bank of Boston Conference Series 38, 195–221.

Deutsche Bundesbank. 1974-96a. *Annual Report,* various issues.

_____. 1974-96b. *Monthly Report,* various issues.

_____. 1995c. *The Monetary Policy of the Bundesbank.* October.

Easton, Brian. 1994. "Economic and Other Ideas Behind the New Zealand Reforms." *Oxford Review of Economic Policy* 10(3): 78–94,.

Economist. 1994. "Willkommen Herr Clarke." September 17.

Edey, Malcolm. 1997. "The Debate on Alternatives for Monetary Policy in Australia." In Philip Lowe, ed., *Monetary Policy and Inflation Targeting,* Sydney: Reserve Bank of Australia, 42–67.

Eichengreen, Barry. 1992. *Golden Fetters: The Gold Standard and the Great Depression, 1919-1939.* New York and Oxford: Oxford University Press.

Estrella, Arturo, and Mishkin, Frederic S. 1997. "Is There a Role for Monetary Aggregates in the Conduct of Monetary Policy?" *Journal of Monetary Economics* 40(2): 279- 304.

European Monetary Institute. 1997. *The Single Monetary Policy in Stage Three: Specification of the Operational Framework.*

Fallow, Brian. 1996. "Wider Inflation Target Is Risky Policy—Brash." New Zealand Herald, June 28.

Feldstein, Martin. 1997. "The Costs and Benefits of Going from Low Inflation to Price Stability." In Christina D. Romer and David H. Romer, eds., *Reducing Inflation: Motivation and Strategy,* Chicago: University of Chicago Press, 123–56.

Financial Times. "Shares Hit as Rates Rise to 6%." October 31, 1996.

Fischer, Andreas M., and Orr, Adrian B. 1994. "Monetary Policy Credibility and Price Uncertainty: The New Zealand Experience of Inflation Targeting." *OECD Economic Studies* 22 (spring): 155–79.

Fischer, Stanley. 1993 "The Role of Macroeconomic Factors in Growth." *Journal of Monetary Economics* 32(3): 485–512.

____. 1994. "Modern Central Banking." In Forrest Capie, Charles A. E. Goodhart, Stanley Fischer, and Norbert Schnadt, eds., *The Future of Central Banking: The Tercentenary Symposium of the Bank of England,* Cambridge: Cambridge University Press, 262–308.

Fortin, Pierre.1996a "The Great Canadian Slump. " *Canadian Journal of Economics* 29(4): 761–87.

____. 1996b. "Raise the Inflation Target and Let Canada Recover." *Globe and Mail* September 26.

Fraser, B. W.1993. "Some Aspects of Monetary Policy." *Reserve Bank of Australia Bulletin* April: 1-7.

____. 1994a. "Managing the Recovery." *Reserve Bank of Australia Bulletin* April: 20-28.

____. 1994b. "Sustainable Growth in Australia." *Reserve Bank of Australia Bulletin* July: 17–23.

____. 1994c. "The Art of Monetary Policy." *Reserve Bank of Australia Bulletin* October: 17-25.

____. 1995. "Economic Trends and Policies." *Reserve Bank of Australia Bulletin* April: 20- 27.

Freedman, Charles. 1994a. "Formal Targets for Inflation Reduction: The Canadian Experience." In J. A. H. de Beaufort Wijnholds, S. C. W. Eijffinger, and L. H. Hoogduin, eds., *A Framework for Monetary Stability,* Dordrecht and Boston: Kluwer Academic, 17–29.

_____. 1994b. "The Use of Indicators and of the Monetary Conditions Index in Canada." In T. Balino and C. Cottarelli, eds., *Frameworks for Monetary Stability: Policy Issues and Country Experiences,* Washington, D.C.: International Monetary Fund, 458–76.

_____. 1995. "The Canadian Experience with Targets for Reducing and Controlling Inflation." In Leonardo Leiderman and Lars E.O. Svensson, eds., *Inflation Targets,* London: Centre for Economic Policy Research, 19–31.

Freeman, Richard, and Willis, John. 1995. "Targeting Inflation in the 1990s: Recent Challenges." Board of Governors of the Federal Reserve System International Finance Discussion Papers, no. 525.

Frenkel, Jacob A. 1996. "Interview: Jacob Frenkel." *Central Banking* VII(3): 50–57.

Friedman, Benjamin M. 1994. "Comment." In N. Gregory Mankiw, ed., *Monetary Policy,* Chicago: University of Chicago Press, 182–88.

_____. 1995 "The Rise and Fall of the Money Growth Targets as Guidelines for U.S. Monetary Policy." Paper prepared for the Bank of Japan Seventh International Conference. Preliminary draft.

Friedman, Benjamin M., and Kuttner, Kenneth. 1996. "A Price Target for U.S. Monetary Policy? Lessons from the Experience with Money Growth Targets." *Brookings Papers on Economic Activity* 1: 77–125.

Friedman, Milton. 1959. A Program for Monetary Stability. The Millar Lectures. New York: Fordham University Press.

_____. 1968. "The Role of Monetary Policy." *American Economic Review* 58: 1–17.

_____. 1977. "Nobel Lecture: Inflation and Unemployment." *Journal of Political Economy* 85(3): 451–72.

Friedman, Milton, and Schwartz, Anna J. 1963. *A Monetary History of the United States, 1867- 1960.* Princeton: Princeton University Press.

Fuhrer, Jeffrey C. 1995. "The Phillips Curve Is Alive and Well." Federal Reserve Bank of Boston, *New England Economic Review* March-April: 41–56.

George, Eddie. 1995a. "Monetary Policy Realities." *Bank of England Quarterly Bulletin* 35(4): 388–94.

_____. 1995b. "The Prospects for Monetary Stability." Speech to the City, June 14. Reprint, *Bank of England Quarterly Bulletin* 35(3): 295–6.

Goodfriend, Marvin. 1993. "Interest Rate Policy and the Inflation Scare Problem: 1979-1992." Federal Reserve Bank of Richmond, *Economic Quarterly* 79(1): 1–24.

Goodhart, Charles A. E., and Viñals, José. 1994. "Strategy and Tactics of Monetary Policy: Examples from Europe and the Antipodes." In Jeffrey C. Fuhrer, ed., *Goals, Guidelines, and Constraints Facing Monetary Policymakers.* Federal Reserve Bank of Boston Conference Series 38: 139–87.

Gordon, Robert R. 1985. "Understanding Inflation in the 1980's." *Brookings Papers on Economic Activity* 1: 263–302.

Grenville, Stephen. 1997. "The Evolution of Monetary Policy: From Money Targets to Inflation Targets." In Philip Lowe, ed., *Monetary Policy and Inflation Targeting*, Sydney: Reserve Bank of Australia, 125–58.

Groshen, Erica L., and Schweitzer, Mark E. 1996. "The Effects of Inflation on Wage Adjustments in Firm-Level Data: Grease or Sand?" *Federal Reserve Bank of New York Staff Reports*, no. 9.

Haldane, Andrew G., ed. 1995. *Targeting Inflation*. London: Bank of England.

Haldane, Andrew G., and Salmon, Christopher K. 1995. "Three Issues on Inflation Targets." In Andrew G. Haldane, ed., *Targeting Inflation*, London: Bank of England, 170–201.

Hall, Robert E., and Mankiw, N. Gregory. 1994 "Nominal Income Targeting." In N. Gregory Mankiw, ed., *Monetary Policy* Chicago: University of Chicago Press, 71–94.

Hall, Terry. 1995. "NZ Bank Chief Admits Price Rise Slippage." *Financial Times*, June 30, p.6.

____. 1996a. "NZ Central Bank Hints at Monetary Easing." *Financial Times*, October 25, p.6

____. 1996b. "NZ Bank Cautious on Wider Inflation Target." *Financial Times*, December 18, p.8.

Hansen, Lars Peter, and Hodrick, Robert J. 1980. "Forward Exchange Rates as Optimal Predictors of Future Spot Rates: An Econometric Analysis." *Journal of Political Economy* 88(5): 829–53.

Hefeker, Carsten. 1994. "German Monetary Union, the Bundesbank, and the EMS Collapse." *Banca Nazionale del Lavoro Quarterly Review* 47: 379–98

Heikensten, Lars. 1997. Address before Conference of the Stockholm Chamber of Commerce and Veckans Affärer, January 29. Mimeo.

Hess, Gregory D., and Morris, Charles S. 1996. "The Long-Run Costs of Moderate Inflation." Federal Reserve Bank of Kansas City, *Economic Review*, second quarter: 71–88.

Hörngren, Lars. 1992. "Swedish Economic Policy under New Conditions." In Sveriges Riksbank, *Monetary Policy with a Flexible Exchange Rate*, pp. 67-76.

Huh, Chan. 1996. "Some Evidence on the Efficacy of the UK Inflation Targeting Regime: An Out-of-Sample Forecast Approach." *Board of Governors of the Federal Reserve System International Finance Discussion Papers*, no. 565.

Hutchison, Michael M., and Walsh, Carl E. 1996. "Central Bank Institutional Design and the Output Cost of Disinflation: Did the 1989 New Zealand Reserve Bank Act Affect the Inflation-Output Tradeoff?" *Reserve Bank of New Zealand Research Paper* G96/6.

Ip, Greg. 1991. "Inflation War is Won, Bank of Canada Says." *Financial Post*, October 15, p.40.

____. 1993. "Drop in Inflation Rate Beats Expectations." *Financial Post*, December 8, p.5.

Issing, Otmar. 1996. "Is Monetary Targeting in Germany Still Adequate?" In Horst Siebert, ed., *Monetary Policy in an Integrated World Economy: Symposium, 1995*, pp. 117–30. Tübingen: Mohr.

_____. 1997. "Monetary Targeting in Germany: The Stability of Monetary Policy and of the Monetary System." *Journal of Monetary Economics* 39(1): 67–79.

Jenkins, W. 1990. "The Goal of Price Stability." *Bank of Canada Review* July: 3–7.

Jonung, Lars. 1979. "Knut Wicksell's Norm of Price Stabilization and Swedish Monetary Policy in the 1930's." *Journal of Monetary Economics* 5(4):459–96.

Judson, Ruth, and Orphanides, Athanasios 1996. "Inflation, Volatility, and Growth." *Board of Governors of the Federal Reserve System Finance and Economics Discussion Series*, no. 96/16.

King, Robert G., and Watson, Mark W. 1994. "The Post-War U.S. Phillips Curve: A Revisionist Econometric History." *Carnegie-Rochester Conference Series on Public Policy* 41: 157–219.

König, Reiner, and Willeke Caroline. 1995. "German Monetary Reunification." *Central Banking* 6(1): 29–39.

Kydland, Finn, and Prescott, Edward. 1977 "Rules Rather than Discretion: The Inconsistency of Optimal Plans." *Journal of Political Economy* 85(3): 473–92.

Laidler, David, and Robson, William. 1993. *The Great Canadian Disinflation.* Montreal: C. D. Howe Research Institute.

Lamont, Norman. 1992. Mansion House Speech to the City, October 29. Reprint, *Financial Times,* October 30, p.14.

Laubach, Thomas. 1997. "Signalling with Monetary and Inflation Targets." Unpublished paper, Federal Reserve Bank of Kansas City, October.

Laubach, Thomas, and Posen, Adam S. 1997a. "Some Comparative Evidence on the Effectiveness of Inflation Targeting." *Federal Reserve Bank of New York Research Paper* no. 9714.

_____. 1997b. "Disciplined Discretion: Monetary Targeting in Germany and Switzerland." *Essays in International Finance* no. 206, December. International Finance Section, Princeton University.

Leiderman, Leonardo, and Svensson, Lars E. O., eds. 1995. *Inflation Targeting.* London: Centre for Economic Policy Research.

Leigh-Pemberton, Robin. 1984. "Some Aspects of UK Monetary Policy." *Bank of England Quarterly Bulletin* 24(4): 474–81.

_____. 1990. "Some Remarks on Exchange Rate Regimes." *Bank of England Quarterly Bulletin* 30(4): 482–4.

_____. 1991. "Stability and Economic Policy." *Bank of England Quarterly Bulletin* 31(4): 496–7.

_____. 1992. "The Case for Price Stability." *Bank of England Quarterly Bulletin* 32(4): 441–8,.

Lloyd, Michele. 1992. "The New Zealand Approach to Central Bank Autonomy." *Reserve Bank of New Zealand Bulletin* 55(3): 203–20.

Longworth, David, and Freedman, Charles. 1995. "The Role of the Staff Economic Projection in Conducting Canadian Monetary Policy." In A. Haldane, ed., *Targeting Inflation,* London: Bank of England, 101–12.

Louisson, Simon. 1994. "New Zealand Inflation May Burst Target." *Reuters World Service,* December 6.

Lucas, Robert E., Jr. 1976. "Econometric Policy Evaluation: A Critique." *Carnegie-Rochester Conference Series on Public Policy* 1: 19–46.

Lusser, Markus. 1991. Referat (Address) to the General Assembly of the Swiss National Bank. *Geld, Währung, und Konjunktur,* June: 167-72.

Macfarlane, I. J. 1992. "Making Monetary Policy in an Uncertain World." *Reserve Bank of Australia Bulletin,* September: 9–16.

____. 1995. "Inflation and Changing Public Attitudes." *Reserve Bank of Australia Bulletin,* December: 9-15.

Marotte, Bertrand. 1993. "Markets Endorse New Governor: Central Bank to Continue Inflation Battle." *Ottawa Citizen* December 23, p.D6.

Marsh, David. 1992. *The Bundesbank.* London: William Heinemann.

McCallum, Bennett T. 1995. "Two Fallacies Concerning Central-Bank Independence." *American Economic Review,* 85(2): 207-11.

____. 1996. "Inflation Targeting in Canada, New Zealand, Sweden, the United Kingdom, and in General." *NBER Working Paper No. 5579,* May.

McGillivray, Don. 1994. "Bank Still Headed in Wrong Direction." *Calgary Herald,* January 4, p.A4.

McIver, Greg. 1996. "Swedish Consumer Prices Fall." *Financial Times,* November 15, p.3.

Meek, Paul, ed., 1983. *Central Bank Views on Monetary Targeting.* New York: Federal Reserve Bank of New York.

Mishkin, Frederic S. 1991. "Asymmetric Information and Financial Crises: A Historical Perspective." In Glenn R. Hubbard, ed., *Financial Markets and Financial Crises,* Chicago: University of Chicago Press, 69–108.

____. 1996. "The Channels of Monetary Transmission: Lessons for Monetary Policy." *Banque de France Bulletin Digest* 27 (March): 33-44.

____. 1997a. "Strategies for Controlling Inflation." In Philip Lowe, ed., *Monetary Policy and Inflation Targeting,* Sydney: Reserve Bank of Australia, 7–38.

____. 1997b. "The Causes and Propagation of Financial Instability: Lessons for Policymakers." In *Maintaining Financial Stability in a Global Economy,* Kansas City: Federal Reserve Bank of Kansas City, 55–96.

____. 1998. "Exchange Rate Pegging in Emerging Market Economies?" *International Finance* 1(1): September.

Montagnon, Peter. 1995 "Bank Governor Passes First Inflation Test." *Financial Times,* October 22, p.4.

Morande, Felipe, and Schmidt-Hebbel, Klaus. 1997. "Inflation Targets and Indexation in Chile." Unpublished paper, Central Bank of Chile, August.

Moulton, Brent R. 1996. "Bias in the Consumer Price Index: What is the Evidence?" *Journal of Economic Perspectives* 10(4): 159-77.

Neumann, Manfred. 1996. "Monetary Targeting in Germany." Paper prepared for the Bank of Japan Seventh International Conference.

New Zealand Herald. 1990a. "Pressure on Government to Relax Inflation Target." August 4.

____. 1990b. "Most Voters Back Target of Lower Inflation." October 25.

Nicholl, Peter W. E., and Archer, David J. 1992. "An Announced Downward Path for Inflation." *Reserve Bank of New Zealand Bulletin* 55(4): 315–23.

Obstfeld, Maurice, and Rogoff, Kenneth. 1995. "The Mirage of Fixed Exchange Rates." *Journal of Economic Perspectives* 9(4): 73–96.

Offenbacher, Akiva. 1996. "How Inflation Has Come Down." *Central Banking* VII(3): 61–66.

Organisation for Economic Co-Operation and Development (OECD). 1975. *Economic Survey: Switzerland.* Paris: OECD.

Ortega, Eloisa, and José-Maria Bonilla. 1995. "Reasons for Adopting an Inflation Target." In Andrew G. Haldane, ed., *Targeting Inflation,* London: Bank of England, 49–58.

Phelps, Edmund S. 1968. "Money-Wage Dynamics and Labor-Market Equilibrium." *Journal of Political Economy* 76(4): 678–711.

Phillips, A.W. 1958. "The Relation Between Unemployment and the Rate of Change of Money Wage Rates in the United Kingdom, 1861-1957." *Economica* 25 (November): 283–99.

Posen, Adam S. 1995a. "Central Bank Independence and Disinflationary Credibility: A Missing Link?" *Federal Reserve Bank of New York Staff Reports,* no. 1, May.

———. 1995b. "Declarations Are Not Enough: Financial Sector Sources of Central Bank Independence." In Ben S. Bernanke and Julio J. Rotemberg, eds., *NBER Macroeconomics Annual,* Cambridge: MIT Press, 258–74.

Reddell, Michael 1988. "Inflation and the Monetary Policy Strategy." *Reserve Bank of New Zealand Bulletin* 51(2): 81–4.

Reserve Bank of Australia. 1994–95. *Bulletin,* various issues.

Reserve Bank of New Zealand. 1985–90a. *Bulletin,* various issues.

———. 1990b. *Annual Report.*

———. 1991–95c. *Monetary Policy Statement,* various issues, .

Reuters Financial Service. 1991. "Lower NZ Dollar Not a Threat to Inflation—Bolger." October 24.

Rich, Georg. 1985. "Die Inflationsbekämpfung als Aufgabe der schweizerischen Geldpolitik." *Geld, Währung, und Konjunktur* March: 60–69.

———. 1989. "Geldmengenziele und schweizerische Geldpolitik: Eine Standortbestimmung." *Geld, Währung, und Konjunktur,* December: 345–60.

———. 1992. "Die schweizerische Teuerung: Lehren für die Nationalbank." *Geld, Währung, und Konjunktur* March: 73–88.

———. 1997. "Monetary Targets as a Policy Rule: Lessons from the Swiss Experience." *Journal of Monetary Economics* 39(1): 113–41.

Rogoff, Kenneth. 1985. "The Optimal Degree of Commitment to an Intermediate Target." *Quarterly Journal of Economics* 100(4): 1169–89.

Rotemberg, Julio J., and Woodford, Michael. 1997. "An Optimization-Based Econometric Framework for the Evaluation of Monetary Policy." In Ben S. Bernanke and Julio J. Rotemberg, eds., *NBER Macroeconomics Annual,* Cambridge, MA: MIT Press, 297–361.

Samuelson, Paul, and Solow, Robert. 1960. "Analytical Aspects of Anti-Inflation Policy." *American Economic Review* 50(May): 177–94.

Sarel, Michael. 1996. "Nonlinear Effects of Inflation on Economic Growth." *IMF Staff Papers* 43 (March): 199–215

Schiltknecht, Kurt.1983. "Switzerland—The Pursuit of Monetary Objectives." In Paul Meek, ed., *Central Bank Views on Monetary Targeting*, New York: Federal Reserve Bank of New York, 72–79.

Schlesinger, Helmut.1983. "The Setting of Monetary Objectives in Germany." In Paul Meek, ed., *Central Bank Views on Monetary Targeting*, New York: Federal Reserve Bank of New York, 6–17.

Schmid, Peter. 1995. "Monetary Policy: Targets and Instruments." *Central Banking* 6(1): 40–51.

Shapiro, Matthew D., and Wilcox, David W. 1996. "Mismeasurement in the Consumer Price Index: An Evaluation." In Ben S. Bernanke and Julio J. Rotemberg, eds., *NBER Macroeconomics Annual*, Cambridge, MA: MIT Press, 93–154.

Shiller, Robert. 1996. "Why do People Dislike Inflation?" *Cowles Foundation Discussion Paper no. 1115.* March.

Spiegel, Mark. 1995. "Rules vs. Discretion in New Zealand Monetary Policy." *Federal Reserve Bank of San Francisco Economic Letter,* no. 95–09, March 3.

Stevens, Glenn, and Debelle, Guy. 1995. "Monetary Policy Goals for Inflation in Australia." In Andrew G. Haldane, ed., *Targeting Inflation*, London: Bank of England, 81–100.

Summers, Lawrence. 1991 "How Should Long-Term Monetary Policy Be Determined?" *Journal of Money, Credit, and Banking* 23(3): 625–31.

Svensson, Lars E. O. 1992 "Targets and Indicators with a Flexible Exchange Rate." In Sveriges Riksbank, *Monetary Policy with a Flexible Exchange Rate*, 15–24.

_____. 1993. "The Simplest Test of Target Credibility." *NBER Working Paper* no. 4604.

_____. 1995. "The Swedish Experience of an Inflation Target." In Leonardo Leiderman and Lars E. O. Svensson, eds., *Inflation Targets*. London: Centre for Economic Policy Research.

_____. 1996. "Price Level Targeting vs. Inflation Targeting: A Free Lunch?" *NBER Working Paper* no. 5719, August.

_____. 1997a "Inflation Forecast Targeting: Implementing and Monitoring Inflation Targets." *European Economic Review,* 41(6): 1111–46.

_____. 1997b. "Inflation Targeting: Some Extensions." *NBER Working Paper* no. 5962, March.

Sveriges Riksbank. 1992-94a. *Quarterly Review,* various issues.

_____. 1994-97b. *Inflation and Inflation Expectations in Sweden* (until November 1995) and *Inflation Report* (since March 1996), various issues.

_____. 1992c. *Monetary Policy with a Flexible Exchange Rate,* December.

Swiss National Bank. 1975a. *Rapport.*

_____.1975b. *Monatsbericht.*

_____. 1986-94c. *Geld, Währung, und Konjunktur,* various issues.

Szep, Jason. 1991. "Canada Plans to Introduce Inflation-Indexed Bonds." *Reuters Financial Service*, May 28.

Tait, Nikki. 1995. "NZ Bank Chief Sticks to Policy." *Financial Times*, May 3.

____. 1996. "NZ Deal Gives Rise to Faith and Doubt." *Financial Times*, December 20.

Taylor, John B. 1985. "What Would Nominal GNP Targeting Do to the Business Cycle?" *Carnegie-Rochester Conference Series on Public Policy* 22: 61–84.

Thiessen, Gordon. 1991. "Notes for Remarks by Gordon G. Thiessen, Senior Deputy Governor of the Bank of Canada." *Bank of Canada Review* July: 15–21.

____. 1994a. "Further Direction for the Bank of Canada and Monetary Policy." *Bank of Canada Review* Spring: 85–90.

____. 1994b. "Opening Statement before the Standing Senate Committee on Banking, Trade, and Commerce." *Bank of Canada Review* Spring: 81–90.

____. 1995a. "Uncertainty and the Transmission of Monetary Policy in Canada." The Hermes-Gordon Lecture. *Bank of Canada Review* Summer: 41–58.

____. 1995b. "Notes for Remarks by Gordon G. Thiessen, Governor of the Bank of Canada." *Bank of Canada Review* Summer: 65–70.

____. 1996a. "Does Canada Need More Inflation to Grease the Wheels of the Economy?" *Bank of Canada Review* Winter: 47–62.

____. 1996b. "Towards a More Transparent and More Credible Monetary Policy." Remarks delivered at the Ecole des Hautes Etudes Commerciales.

Vardy, Jill. 1993. "Crow Out, Thiessen In: New Bank of Canada Governor Will Continue Inflation-Fighting Policies." *Financial Post*, December 23, p.1.

von Hagen, Jürgen. 1989. "Monetary Targeting with Exchange Rate Constraints: the Bundesbank in the 1980s." *Federal Reserve Bank of St. Louis Review*, 71(5): 53–69.

____. 1995. "Inflation and Monetary Targeting in Germany." In Leonardo Leiderman and Lars E. O. Svensson, eds., *Inflation Targets*, London: Centre for Economic Policy Research, 107–21.

Walsh, Carl E. 1986. "In Defense of Base Drift." *American Economic Review* 76(4): 692–700.

Woodford, Michael. 1994. "Nonstandard Indicators for Monetary Policy: Can Their Usefulness Be Judged from Forecasting Regressions?" In N. Gregory Mankiw, ed., *Monetary Policy*, Chicago: University of Chicago Press, 95–115.

Index

accountability of central bank, 296-97; Bank of Canada, 116, 122, 130,132, 144, 344; Bank of Israel, 214, 251; Bundesbank, 61; of central bank in fixed-term targeting, 77; and inflation targeting, 283; inflationary pressures of German monetary union, 74-75; New Zealand, 87, 91, 100-102; proposed for EMU, 332-33; proposed for inflation targeting in United States, 324-26; Reserve Bank of Australia, 219, 251; Spain, 237, 251; Sweden, 186; United Kingdom/Bank of England, 153, 159, 162-63, 169; vs. credibility in New Zealand, 114

accounting to the public, in inflation targeting, 24

adjusted monetary base (AMB), 62

adoption of inflation targeting: in Australia, 218-23; in Canada, 116-20; in Israel, 205-09; in New Zealand, 87-92; in Spain, 235-40; in Sweden, 174-82; in United Kingdom, 147-53

adoption of monetary targeting, factors in Germany and Switzerland, 43

adjusted monetary base (AMB) and SAMB growth and annual targets 1980-90 in Switzerland (graph), 54

advantages of monetary targeting, 304-05

aggregate demand shocks, and inflation targeting, 292

aggregate shocks, responding to, 35

aggregate supply shocks , 24; vs. aggregate demand shocks, 292

ALP, in Spain, 236-37, 242

alternatives to inflation targeting, 301-07

AMB, *see* adjusted monetary base

analysis of inflation targeting, control group strategy, 252-253; measures used for, 252-54; OECD countries, 252; Phillips-curve equations in, 253; sacrifice ratios in, 253

analysis of operational framework in Germany and Switzerland, 56-57

Annual Report: in Australia, 227-228; of Bundesbank, 61, 337; in Canada, 117, 120, 127, 128, 130, 133, 135, 136, 137; in Israel, 212-13; in New Zealand, 101; in Spain, 243; of Swiss National Bank, 338

anti-inflation policy in United Kingdom, 151

approach to study, 7-8

Australia
—analysis: lessons from, 250-51; Phillips curve, 226
—central bank: accountability, 251; cash and long-term interest rates in, 230 (graph); credibility, 222; flexibility, 221; nominal effective exchange rate (graph), 230; transparency of policy in, 205, 251
—communication to public, 225; *Annual Report,* 227-28; *Bulletin,* 226-27; Quarterly Report, 227, 232
—GDP growth rates in, 229, 230 (graph), 235
—inflation targeting: adoption of, 218-23; experience under, 228-35; key features of, 203-05; operational framework for inflation targeting, 223-38; and price stability, 221, 222, 224-25; real-side goals in, 226; setting inflation target, 204; "thick point" target in, 204, 223, 224; underlying inflation targeted, 221-22, 230 (graph)
—monetary policy: compared with New Zealand, 220-21; critical episode in, 228, 229-32; fiscal consolidation, 205; monetary targeting abandoned, 219
—unemployment in, 226, 229
—wage-bargaining mechanisms in, 204
—wage increases in, 234-35

balancing transparency and flexibility, 26

Ball's sacrifice ratio method, 349

Banco de España: and adoption of inflation targeting in Spain, 235-36; credibility of, 239; flexibility of, 240; independence of, 242; and operational framework, 239; and price stability, 204

Bank of Canada Act, 141

Bank of Canada Review, 120

Bank of Canada: accountability, 130, 344; *Annual Report, 1993,* 136; *Annual Report, 1994,* 127, 137; credibility, 344; and disinflationary policy of 1980s and early 1990s, 116-17; emphasis on floor and ceiling for inflation, 136; flexibility in, 144; and Governing Council of, 128; government, 129; independence of 134, 343; internal organization of, 128-29; and price stability, 116, 342; rationale for inflation targeting approach, 119; responsibility for meeting targets, 115; short-run goal of, 118; transparency, 344

Bank of England, 158-59; conflict with Chancellor of the Exchequer, 162, 164-67, 168, 169; exchange rate index, 161; given operational independence, 169; independence of, 146; inflation forecasts of, 157; lack of goal independence, 170; responsibilities of, 145; subordinate status of, 165

Bank of Israel Law of 1954, 213

Bank of Israel: accountability, 214; credibility of, 206, 209, 217; independence of, 213-14; and inflation targeting, 348; instrument interest rate of, 210; measures of inflation expectations, 212

base drift in monetary targeting, 336

behavior of core inflation, VAR model of, 275-82

benefits of inflation targeting, 298

benefits of low inflation, 16-19

Beveridge curve, in Sweden, 198

bill rate, vs. true policy instruments, in New Zealand, 340

Black Wednesday, effects of: in Sweden, 177; in United Kingdom, 147, 152

bloc float, 336

Boletín Económico, 243

Box-Pierce tests, 350

Bretton Woods system, 304, 305

Bretton-Woods fixed-exchange-rate regime, 43, 51, 174, 304, 305

British Labour Party, and inflation target, 155

British monetary policy under inflation targeting, 159-71

Bulletin; in Australia, 226-227; in New Zealand, 89, 90, 100

Bundesbank Act of 1957: Article 3, 45; Section 13, 60; Section 18, 60-62

Bundesbank, 44-51; and 1979 oil supply shock, 70, 72-73; accountability of, 61; central bank money stock (CBM), 45; credibility of, 50, 73; free liquid reserves in, 45; growth of production potential, 58; M3 vs. CBM, 57, 59-60; monetary policy of in 1970s and 1980s, 68-69; normative judgments made by, 58-59; responsibility for monetary expansion, 60; transparency in, 61, 72-73

—and German reunification, 68, 70-72; stance on monetary union in Germany, 71

—communication with public: *Federal Gazette,* 60; *Monthly Report,* 61, 337; *Annual Report,* 61, 337

—price stability in, 45; unavoidable price increases, 58

—targets in: adoption of target range, 59; asymmetrical responses to target misses, 69-70; effect of monetary targeting on wage-setting behavior, 50; horizons for inflation target, 31; information variables used in, 337; problems with M3 target, 75-76; reformulation of target range by, 59; target growth rate derivation, 57-59

Canada

—analysis: lessons from, 144; Phillips curve, 124; bias in inflation measurement, 121; sacrifice-ratio calculations, 134

—central bank: accountability, 116, 122; credibility, 124; effect of Quebec referendum on sovereignty on interest rates, 138-139; effects of tax increase on CPI, 341; flexibility, 116, 123, 342; inflation expectations in, 126; policy transparency, 124-25, 127

—communication to public, 122, 127; *Annual Report*, 130, 133, 135; *Monetary Policy Report*, 126, 130, 138
—inflation targeting, 115-44; compared to New Zealand, 123; core CPI in, 133, 137; critical junctures of inflation targeting framework, 132; development of, 115; first horizon for, 115; Governor Crow's views on, 118-20; headline CPI in, 137; lack of escape clauses, 123; target range, 116, 123; timetable for reducing inflation in, 120; total vs. core CPI in, 341
—monetary policy, 130-43; expectational sluggishness in, 341; fiscal policy and monetary contraction in, 140; goods and services tax in, 118; inflation-indexed bonds in, 133; lags in effect of monetary policy in, 119; M1 and M2 in, 125-26; monetary conditions index (MCI), 126, 342; real economy and prices, 124; real-return bonds, 133; reducing vs. maintaining inflation, 142; risk premiums in long-term interest rates, 118; under Conservative Government, 134
—unemployment in, 130-32
Canadian Conservative Party, and formal targets, 117
Canadian dollar, 135, 136
Canadian Economic Association, 132, 133
Canadian economic indicators, 131 (graphs)
Canadian exports, and economy, 133
Canadian GDP, stagnation of, 139
Canadian monetary policy under inflation targeting, 130-43
Canadian target distinctions, compared with Bundesbank, 118
Canadian-U.S. interest rate differential, 141
cash and long-term interest rates in Australia, 230 (graph)
Cash Rate instrument, of Reserve Bank of Australia, 229, 231, 232
CBM *see* central bank money
central bank as counterinflationary conscience, in United Kingdom, 145-71
central bank independence: Cukierman's index of, 343; in Germany and Switzerland, 337; in New Zealand, 339

central bank: accountability of, 37-38; discussion of limited discretion, 349; effect on inflation rate, 14, 23; and inflation, 3-4; and inflation reports, 37; and goal vs. instrument independence, 38; independent vs. subordinate, 38; opportunistic behavior of, 15, 16; responsibility to communicate with public, 37
central bank money (CBM), in Germany, 45-46; 57-58; 68-69; vs. monetary base, 57
centralized wage-setting mechanisms, in Sweden, 194
Chancellor of the Exchequer, conflict with the Bank of England, 162, 164-67, 168, 169
Chicago School, 4
Chile, inflation targeting in, 348
commodity price inflation, relationship to inflation, 262
communication with public, 31, 34, 42, 295-96; in Australia, 225; in Bank of England, 146, 153, 157, 158-59; in Canada, 122, 127, 132, 133; in New Zealand, 89, 102; proposed for EMU, 329; proposed for United States, 326; role of in inflation targeting, 23; in Sweden, 177, 197
communications issues, 36-38
comparison of Bundesbank response to 1979 oil shock and reunification, 72-73
conclusions regarding inflation targeting, 308
cones, for establishing ranges for money growth, 336
conflict of interest, in Reserve Bank of New Zealand, 339
conflict, Bank of England and Chancellor of the Exchequer, 162, 164-67, 168, 169
consensus forecasts of inflation, 276 (graphs)
Consensus Forecasts, 349, 351; in Australia, 227; as measure of inflation expectations in Canada, 126, 139
Conservative Government, in Canada, 134, 135
Conservative Party
—and formal targets in Canada, 117
—in United Kingdom, 147; effect on interest rates, 162; role in adoption of inflation targeting, 147, 148

constrained discretion policy regime, 293-
94, 301; and inflation targeting, 22-23
consumer price index , *see* CPI
control group strategy, for analyzing inflation targeting, 252-53
control problems, in New Zealand, 87, 92,
112
coordination of expectations of economic
agents, in Bundesbank, 50
core CPI, *see* CPI
core inflation, 27; in Canada, 115; as price
index for inflation target in New
Zealand, 93; in Spain, 247, 248; vector
autoregression (VAR) model of behavior,
275-82; vs. headline inflation in United
Kingdom, 146
cost of disinflation under inflation targeting, 254-66; at high levels, 16-17; at low
to moderate levels, 18; in Canada, 142
countercyclical tendency to monetary
policy, in Canada, 123
counterinflationary conscience, Bank of
England as, 159
country-specific shocks, effects of, 352
CPI, 290
—actual inflation rates, 266-71
—core, in Canada, 121-22, 130, 131 (graph),
133, 137; in Israel, 209; proposed as price
index for EMU, 328; proposed as price
index for inflation targeting in the
United States, 316, 321-22; vs. headline
CPI, in Sweden, 183-184, 185, 202; vs.
total CPI in Canada, 341
—and housing costs in New Zealand, 339
—as inflation target, 27; in Australia; in
Canada, 115, 117, 121-22; 131 (graph);
in Israel, 215 (graph); in Spain, 283
(graph); in Sweden, 175 (graph), 183;
in Switzerland, 53 (graph); in New
Zealand, 87
—and unavoidable / normative inflation in
Germany, 47 (graph)
credibility, in Australia, 222; Banco de
España, 239; Bank of Canada, 124, 344;
Bank of England, 170-71; Bank of Israel,
209, 217; and exchange rate peg, 303;
and inflation targeting, 266-75; linked to
transparency and flexibility, 73; of monetary policy and adoption of inflation

targeting, 274-75; in New Zealand, 95,
112, 114; and quantitative goals, in
Canada, 124; and sacrifice ratio, 255; in
Sweden, 179-81, 184-85, 195 in United
Kingdom, 145, 152, 153, 155
Cukierman's index of central bank independence, 343
currency board, as exchange rate system,
302
cyclical factors in inflation forecasts, 259

de-emphasis on monetary targets in United
Kingdom, 151
deflation, 29-30
demand shock vs. supply shock, 35, 72
depersonalization of U.S. monetary policy,
311-12
derivation of monetary targets in Germany
and Switzerland, 63-66
deviations from target, 35-36
direct inflation targeting, 4
disadvantages of monetary targeting, 305
discount and long-term interest rates in
New Zealand, 103 (graph)
Discount and T-bill rates in Israel, 215
(graph)
discretion vs. rules, 4
discretion-based monetary policy, 5-6
disinflation
—Ball's definition of, 255
—costs of, under inflation targeting, 253,
257, 298-99; in Canada, 134; in Israel,
210, 218; in New Zealand, 90
—and inflation targeting, 254-66
disinflationary trend, effects of, 352
domestic vs. exchange-rate objectives, in
Spain, 245
"dual economy," in United Kingdom,
165
dynamic simulations of inflation, vs. actual
paths of inflation (graphs), 277-79

EC, *see* European Community
Ecole des Hautes Etudes Commerciales,
141
econometric studies of inflation, 18
Economic Bulletin, in Spain, 243, 349
economic crisis in New Zealand, effect on
monetary policy, 95

economic growth prospects in 1988, effect on Swiss National Bank, 80-81

economic performance, impermanence of, 3-4

economic stabilization program, in Israel, 206

effectiveness of inflation targeting, 282-83

effects of tax increase on CPI in Canada, 341

employment growth in Canada, 136

employment, and inflation targeting, 254, 299

EMU, *see* European Monetary Union

ERM, 259, 271, 273, 346; and Spain, 241, 245, 248, 249

escape clause, 292; in Canada (lack of), 123; to deal with supply shocks, 24; in Israel, Australia, and Spain (lack of), 204; in New Zealand, 94; in Sweden, 182, 185; in Switzerland, 62, 81-82; in United Kingdom, 168

European Central Bank, 4, 241–42, 326; goal independence of, 329; and *Inflation Report,* 328

European Community (EC), 43-44, 49; and Sweden, 176-77

European Exchange Rate Mechanism (ERM), *see* Exchange Rate Mechanism

European Monetary System, 6; and Sweden, 177; tensions in, 75

European Monetary Institute, 4, 326; principles of monetary policy strategy, 326-27

European Monetary Union (EMU), 274, 309, and Bundesbank, 76, 77; inflation targeting in, 326-33, 353; proposal for inflation targeting in, 327-33

European System of Central Banks (ESCB), 309

exchange rate, in Canada, 126, 131 (graph); effect on future inflation in New Zealand, 98; and inflation targeting in Israel, Australia, and Spain, 203-04; as intermediate variable in Israel, 210; as policy objective in Spain, 237

exchange rate index, of Bank of England, 161

Exchange Rate Mechanism (ERM) parities, 76, 147, 327; in Spain, 236; and United Kingdom, 151

exchange rate peg, advantages of, 302; as alternative to inflation targeting, 301-04; and credibility, 303; criticism of, 353; currency board as, 302; disadvantages of, 303; and ERM, 303; nominal anchor for, 304; and price stability, 303-04; in Sweden, 201

exchange-rate crises of 1992 and 1993, 6

exchange-rate targeting, in Sweden, 172

Exchequer, responsibilities of in United Kingdom, 145, 146

expansionary policies: benefits of, 14; costs of, 14

expectational sluggishness, in Canada, 341

extended money stock M3, 76

extension of inflation target, in Canada, 121

features of inflation targeting: Australia, 203-05; Canada, 115-16; Israel, 203-05; Spain, 203-05; Sweden, 172-73; United Kingdom, 145

Federal Gazette, required announcements in, 60

Federal Reserve Bank, ability to deal with shocks to the economy, 313-14

financial stability, as objective of monetary policy in New Zealand, 99

Finland, and ECU, 347

fiscal consolidation, in Israel, Australia, and Spain, 205

fiscal policy , 3; and monetary contraction in Canada, 140; under Governor Thiessen in Canada, 136

fixed exchange rate as nominal anchor in Sweden, 174

fixed-term inflation targeting, effect of tying to specific event, 76-77

flexibility, 26; Australia, 221, 223; Banco de España, 240; Bank of Canada, 116, 123, 129, 144, 342; Bank of Israel, 250; importance of in targeting regime, 85; in inflation targeting, 292; and monetary policy in Germany during reunification, 75; New Zealand, 92; in Riksbank inflation targeting, 184; short-run, and multiple objectives, 291-93; Spain, 250; Sweden, 172, 179-80, 182, 184, 185, 197; Swiss National Bank, 84; and transparency, balancing, 26-27, 290-91; United Kingdom, 146, 153; United States, 317-19

forecast of inflation at the target horizon, as intermediate target, 33

forecasting inflation from Phillips curves, 260-261 (table)

foreign-exchange crisis of September 1992, in United Kingdom, 145

formal statistical analysis, limitations of, 7

forums for communication with public, 37

framework for inflation targeting in the United States, 315-26

framework for monetary policy, 6

franc fort, 302

free liquid reserves, in Bundesbank, 45

GDP deflator, in Canada, 121

GDP growth
—in Australia, 229, 235; in Canada, 133, 352; in New Zealand, 352; in Sweden, 174-76
—and unemployment rate: in Australia, 230 (graph); in Canada, 131 (graph); in Germany, 47 (graph); in Israel, 215 (graph); in New Zealand, 103 (graph); in Spain, 238 (graph); in Sweden, 175 (graph); in Switzerland, 53 (graph); in United Kingdom, 151, 160 (graph), 163, 168

GDP growth targeting, vs. inflation targeting, 306

GDR marks, conversion to deutschemarks, 71

Geld, Währung, und Konjunktur, 67, 338

German and Swiss monetary targeting, 336-38

German Democratic Republic (GDR), 70

German monetary reunification, disputes over, 338; effects on inflation, 281

German monetary targeting, key features of, 42

German reunification, effects on economy in Spain, 237

Germany, lessons from 84-85; monetary targets in, 211; pursuit of price stability in, 337

goal independence, 38; vs. instrument independence, 312-13

goal of price stability, initial definition in New Zealand, 92

gold standard, 5, 19, 335; and relative marginal values, 19; and Sweden, 174

goods and services tax (GST): in Canada, 118, 132, 133; in New Zealand, 94

Governing Board of Riksbank, 347

Governing Council of Bank of Canada, 128

government policy, and economic growth, 3

government responsibility, and monetary policy, 3

gradual adjustment of medium-term inflation target, 352

Great Depression, contributions of monetary mismanagement to, 335

growth of production potential, use of by Bundesbank, 58

growth rate, and rate of inflation, 18

GST, *see* goods and services tax

Hanson Lecture, in Canada, 119-20

headline CPI, 290; in Canada, 115, 121-22, 137; in Israel, 204, 209; as measure of inflation in Spain, 240, 247; as price index in New Zealand, 93; in Spain, 204; in Sweden, 173, 200; in Switzerland, 55

headline inflation: and core CPI, in Sweden, 183-184, 185, 202; and core inflation, in United Kingdom, 146, 151; in New Zealand, 108, 110; in Sweden, 193

high inflation, costs of, 16-17

horizons for inflation targets, 31; compared in Bundesbank and Swiss National Bank, 63; proposed for EMU, 328; proposed for United States, 315, 319-20

housing costs, and CPI in New Zealand, 339

Humphrey-Hawkins legislation, 316, 324-26

hyperinflation, 16

hysteresis, in academic literature, 343

implementation of inflation targets, 36

incomes policies, in United Kingdom, 148

independence: Banco de España, 242; Bank of Canada, 129, 134, 343; Bank of Israel, 213; Federal Reserve in United States, 312; Reserve Bank of Australia, 223-24, 228; Reserve Bank of New Zealand, 89-90; Swiss National Bank, 67

indexation, complete, 18
indicator variables, 34-35
inflation, actual vs. dynamic simulations, 277-79 (graph); benefits of low, 16-19; and commodity price inflation, 262; definition of, 17; econometric studies of, 18; effects of central bank's intentions on, 23; effects of high inflation on economy, 16-17; in Germany after reunification, 70; and growth rate, 18; interactions with monetary policy and real GDP in inflation targeting, 253; and nominal exchange rate, 262; promoting economic efficiency and growth, 16-17; public confusion about, 17; rate of, 289-90; role in market-driven growth, 3; as stimulant to economy, 13; and unemployment, 11, 12, 13, 130-32
Inflation and Inflation Expectations in Sweden, 186
inflation bias, 15
inflation control target, in Canada, 118, 129-30, 138
inflation expectations, and adoption of inflation targeting, 266-275; in Canada, 119, 126; and interest-rate differentials, 271-274; market-based measure of, 271-74; response to inflation targeting, 298
inflation forecasts: from estimated Phillips curves, 259-66; from Phillips curves, 265 (graphs)
inflation goal, balanced with other goals in New Zealand, 96
inflation-indexed bonds, in Canada, 133, 342; in the United Kingdom, 342
inflation rate, as macroeconomic variable, 10; and unemployment, 29; vs. price level, 30
inflation-reduction targets, in Canada, 118, 120
Inflation Report, in Spain, 243, 246; in Sweden, 173, 186-87, 191-92, 194, 195, 198, 200, 201; in United Kingdom, 146, 147, 155, 157-59, 161-63, 166-69, 170, 171; proposed for United States, 316
inflation reports to public, by central bank, 37
inflation scares, 20

inflation target, in Australia, 204, 218-223; in Canada, 121, 127-28, 131 (graph); and consumer price index, 27; deviations from, 35-36; in EMU, 331-32; horizons for, 31; implied vs. measured, 28; in Israel, 204, 205-09, 215 (graph), 348; in New Zealand, 87, 99; numerical value of, 28-30; optimal, 30; as point or range, 32; in Spain, 240, 241; in Sweden, 174-82; timing of introduction, 288; too high or too low, 28-30; in United Kingdom, 146, 149; in United States, 317-19; varying over time, 31; when to implement, 36
inflation targeting, 4-8, 287, 308
—alternatives to, 301-07
—in Australia, and exchange rate, 203-04; key features of, 203-05; operational framework for, 223-28
—benefits of, 6, 26, 298
—in Canada, 115-44, 341-44; adoption of, 116-20; critical junctures of framework, 132; features of, 115-16; monetary policy under, 130-43
—in Chile, 348
—as a conceptual framework for monetary policy, 4, 21-25, 287-88, 299-301, 335; consensus on operational questions, 288; rationale for, 10-25
—design, implementation, and operation of, 26-38, 287-97
—effects on economy: behavior of inflation, 275-82; disinflation vs. economic cost in, 253; effect of tying fixed term to specific event, 76-77; employment, 254, 299; inflation expectations, 266-275; international macroeconomic performance of, 297-99; macroeconomic stability, 292; other macroeconomic variables, 35, 253; output, 299; price stability, 254; private-sector inflation expectations in, 253, 254; real costs, 22, 266; real output, 254; supply shocks, 24; wage- and price-setting, 275;
—features of: reduction of inflation, 254, 275; accountability, 24, 295-96; advantages of, 26; combining elements of rules and discretion, 6; credibility, 266-75, 282-83; information variables, 293-94; forestalling rise in inflationary ex-

pectations, 91; interaction among inflation, GDP growth, and short-term interest rates, 276; intermediate targets, 293-
94 ; nominal anchor, 6, 20; policy-maker
accountability in, 6; short-run policy
flexibility, 291-93; transparency, 23, 283,
295-96
— in Israel, 214-18; and exchange rate, 203-
04; key features of, 203-05
— in New Zealand, 114, 339-340; adoption
of, 87-92; key features of, 86; and Policy
Targets Agreements (PTAs), 92-95
— public involvement in, 6, 24; communication with public, 4, 34, 295-96
— in Spain, 244-50; adoption of, 235-40; and
exchange rate, 203-04; key features of,
203-05
— in Sweden, objectives of, 180; monetary
policy under, 189-200
— in the European Monetary Union (EMU),
326-33, 353
— in the United Kingdom, 145-71, 345-46;
adoption, 147-53; monetary policy under,
159-71; reasons for, 145
— in the United States, 309-26, 353; and
democratic principles, 312; proposal for,
315-26
— risks of: circularity, 34; disinflation, 254-
66; problems with exclusive focus on, 21;
self-fulfilling prophecies, 34; tradeoffs in,
26
— vs. exchange-rate targeting, 250
inflationary expectations, and inflation targeting, 91
information: to be used for policy-making, 32-35; to communicate to public,
36-37
information variables 34-35; of Bundesbank,
337; in Canada, 125; and intermediate targets, 293-94; of Riksbank, 185
instrument independence, 38; vs. goal independence, 312-13, 322-23
instrument instability, in New Zealand, 87;
with target ranges, 294
interest-rate differentials, 272 (graphs); and
inflation expectations, 271-74
interest rates, in Canada, 131 (graph); cash
and long-term in Australia, 230 (graph);
effect on future inflation in New Zealand,

98; marginal and long-term, in Sweden,
175 (graph); and MCI in Canada, 126
intermediate target, 33; conflict with price
stability in the United Kingdom, 149;
forecast of inflation as, 33; money growth
as, 33; in New Zealand, 99; in Spain, 236
intermediate target variable, CBM as, 45
intervention and long-term interest rates,
in Spain (graph), 238
introduction of inflation target, timing of,
288
inverted yield curve, 69, 74
IPSEBENE series, in Spain, 247, 248
Israel
— analysis: lessons from, 250-51
— central bank: accountability in, 251;
disinflation and recession in, 218; economic stabilization program in, 206; flexibility in, 250; transparency in, 205, 251
— communication to public: "Recent Economic Developments" report, 212
— inflation targeting: adoption of, 205-09;
CPI inflation target, 205-06; experience
under, 214-18; inflation target and
disinflation, 348; inflation targets and CPI
inflation, 215 (graph); key features of,
203-05; operational framework under,
209-14; price stability, 217; relationship
with exchange-rate target, 207-08, 212,
216; responsibility for setting, 204; target
range in, 210; use of headline CPI, 204;
wage-bargaining mechanisms in, 204
— monetary policy: discount and T-bill rates
in, 215 (graph); exchange-rate target,
206; fiscal consolidation in, 205
— GDP growth and unemployment rate
(graph), 215
Israeli monetary policy, compared to German policy, 211-12

key features of inflation targeting: in New
Zealand, 86; in Sweden, 172-73; in
United Kingdom, 145
key lessons: from Australia, 250-51; from Israel, 250-51, from Spain, 250-51; from
Sweden, 201-02; from United Kingdom,
171
Kohl, Chancellor Helmut, accountability
for inflationary pressures, 74-75

krona: depreciation of, 181; influence on economy in Sweden, 347

Labour Party: in New Zealand, 86, 88, 91, 110, 111, 340; and inflation targeting in United Kingdom, 345
lags, in effect of monetary policy, 119
Law on the Banco de España, 235, 242, 243-44
lessons: from Australia, 250-51; from Canada, 144; from Germany and Switzerland, 84-85; from Israel; from New Zealand, 113-114; from Spain, 250-51; from Sweden, 201-02; from United Kingdom, 171
Liberal Government, in Canada, 121-22, 132, 135, 136, 343, 344
limitations of test for structural breaks in monetary-policy reaction functions, 352
Lombard credit, in Bundesbank, 46; after German reunification, 71-72, 73, 74, 75
long-run inflation, effect on monetary policy, 23; goal proposed for United States, 315, 316-17
long-run price stability, as a nominal anchor, 20
long-run vs. short-run inflation targets, 291
long-term interest rates: in Canada, 131 (graph); in Spain, 238 (graph); in Sweden, 175 (graph); in United Kingdom, 160 (graph)
low inflation, benefits of, 16-19; and economic growth in Canada, 143; and nominal interest rates, 29; permanent and transitional costs of, 141; vs. targeting framework in Canada, 134

M0, in United Kingdom, 149, 155, 158
M1 money stock, 23; in Canada, 125; in Israel, 210; in Switzerland, 52, 62, 79; susceptibility to changes in exchange rate expectations, 337
M2, in Canada, 125-26
M3, definition of, 57; effect of monetary unification on in Germany, 71-72; as monetary target in Germany, 57; problems with in Bundesbank, 75-76; in United Kingdom, 148, 149
M4, in United Kingdom, 155, 158

Maastricht Treaty, 4, 204, 236, 239-40, 241, 247, 248, 309, 326, 329, 331, 332
macroeconomic developments in New Zealand, 102, 103 (graph)
macroeconomic performance under inflation targeting, international, 297-99
macroeconomic policy, goals of, 10
macroeconomic significance of nominal wage floor in Canada, 344
macroeconomic variable, inflation rate as, 10; and inflation targeting, 253
majoritarian elections vs. multi-member proportional representation in New Zealand, 340
Manley Committee, in Canadian House of Commons, 134, 343
marginal and long-term interest rates in Sweden, 175 (graph)
Marginal Rate, in Sweden, 176, 178, 190; replaced by repo rate in Sweden, 191
market-based measure of inflation expectations, 271-274
market-driven growth, 3
MCI, see monetary conditions index
measure of inflation in inflation targeting, 290
measurement of distribution of forecast errors in analysis of inflation targeting, 263-64
measures of capacity utilization, in Sweden, 191
Medium Term Financial Strategy, in United Kingdom, 149
medium-term forecast, in United Kingdom, 164
medium-term growth path for SAMB, in Switzerland, 63, 83-84
medium-term monetary conditions and target range in Canada, 121-22, 344
medium-term nominal framework, in United Kingdom, 152
medium-term projections for inflation in New Zealand, 98-99
Mexican crisis, in Spain, 245
midpoint of inflation target range, 289-90; in Canada, 116
minimum reserve requirements, in Switzerland, 52

moderate inflation rate, and economic efficiency, 10
monetarism, 12
monetarism, effect on Bundesbank, 49-50
monetary aggregates, in New Zealand, 339; proposed role of in EMU, 329-31
monetary base, use of in Switzerland, 66
monetary conditions index (MCI), 226; in Canada, 116, 126,138, 139, 342; in New Zealand, 98, 100, 340
monetary contraction, and fiscal policy in Canada, 140
Monetary Policy Committee, of Bank of England, 159, 170
monetary policy
—in New Zealand: during 1970s and 1980s, 88; and monetary conditions index, 98; need for clarification of, 89; and real economy, 97
—in Sweden: from adoption to May 1994, 189-91; from January 1996 to December 1997, 189, 193-200; from May 1994 to December 1995, 189, 191-93
—monetary policy in United Kingdom under inflation targeting, 146
Monetary Policy Report, in Canada, 126, 127, 128, 129, 130, 138, 342, 344
Monetary Policy Statement, in New Zealand, 93-94, 100, 102, 104, 105, 106, 107
monetary policy, activist, 11; in Canada, 124-25, 130-43; case study approach to, 7-8; critical episode in Australia, 228, 229-32; effects on output and employment, 15; and flexibility in Germany during reunification, 75; as government responsibility, 3; and inflation, 3; limitations of in Sweden, 197-98; linked to medium- and long-term horizons, 24; and medium-term stabilization, 3; and nominal anchor, 11, 20; over-manipulation of, 13; as political issue in New Zealand, 109; price stability in, 10; principles of European Monetary Institute, 326-27; and public expectations, 12; and short-run fluctuations in the economy, 10; in Sweden, 189-200; in United Kingdom, 159-71; without explicit targets, 307; and unemployment, 11

monetary reunification in Germany, 338; effects on inflation, 281
monetary targeting, 4
monetary targets: and outcomes in Germany, 48 (graph); abandoned in United Kingdom, 151; de-emphasis on in United Kingdom, 151
money growth, "cones" or tunnels for, 336
money growth, as intermediate target in Spain, 236
money growth, as intermediate target, 33
monetary rule, 5
monetary targeting, 41-85; as alternative to inflation targeting, 304-05; definition of, 41; flexibility in, 304-305; lessons from, 84-85; underlying conflict of, 74
—in Germany, 336-38; adoption, 43; and monetary policy, 68-77
—in Switzerland, 336-38; adoption, 43, 51; and monetary policy in Switzerland, 77-84
—in EMU: vs. inflation targeting, 327, 329-31
monetary targets, as frameworks for monetary policy, 68; predictive ability of in Switzerland, 82; use of in United Kingdom, 150
Monthly Report: of Bundesbank, 61, 76, 337; of Swiss National Bank, 338
multi-member proportional representation vs. majoritarian elections in New Zealand, 340
multi-year horizon, used in Switzerland, 63

narrow monetary aggregate, use of in Switzerland, 62
National Debt Office, in Sweden, 178
National Party, in New Zealand, 104, 106-07
New Zealand First Party, 110, 111
New Zealand Herald, 340
New Zealand
—analysis: lessons from, 113-14
—central bank: accountability, 114; control problems in, 87, 112; credibility, 95, 112 (lack of); flexibility, 92; independence of, 339; transparency in, 95
—communication to public: 102

—GDP growth and unemployment rate in (graph), 103

—inflation targeting, 86-114, 339-40; adoption of 87-92; inflation as sole intermediate target, 99; initial goal of price stability defined, 92; instrument instability in, 87; Labour Party and, 110, 111; monetary conditions index in, 98; National Party and, 104, 106-07; open-ended targets in, 96; price index for inflation target, 93; reasons for narrow price stability focus, 96; target range established in, 92; underlying and headline inflation and targets in, 103 (graph); use of narrow target range in, 87; zero inflation vs. low, positive inflation in, 113

—monetary policy: balancing inflation goal with other goals, 96; discounted and long-term interest rates in, 103 (graph); economic reform in, 86; effect of economic crisis on, 95; effect of goods-and-services tax on, 94; effect of tax levies on, 95; effect of terms of trade on, 94; government control over speed of disinflation, 97; importance of exchange rates to economy, 98; inflation forecasting in, 99-100; macroeconomic developments in, 102, 103 (graph); nominal effective exchange rate in, 103 (graph); relationship of monetary policy and real economy, 97; as small, open economy, 92; under inflation targeting, 102-13; underlying inflation in, 104

nominal anchor: in Australia, 204; in Canada, 119; forms of, 19-20; and inflation targeting, 19; in Israel, 204; and long-run price stability, 20; for monetary policy, 11; and monetary targeting, 42, 43; need for, 19-21; in Spain, 204, 236; in Sweden, 172, 174; in United Kingdom, 145

nominal effective and DM/SFR exchange rate in Switzerland, 54 (graph)

nominal effective exchange rate: Australia, 230 (graph); Canada, 131 (graph); Germany, 48 (graph); New Zealand, 103 (graph); relationship to inflation, 262; Spain, 238 (graph); Sweden, 175 (graph); United Kingdom, 160 (graph)

nominal interest rates, effect of low inflation on, 29

nominal targeting regime, strength of, 283

normative rate of price increase, 31

Norway, and ECU, 347

numerical goals for inflation, in Germany and Switzerland, 42

numerical value of inflation target, 28-30

objectives of inflation targeting in Sweden, 180

OECD countries: analysis of inflation targeting in, 252; inflation in, 348; and Israel, 210

OECD Economic Report, 102, 130

Office for National Statistics, in United Kingdom, 154

oil crisis of October 1973: and Bundesbank, 49; and Swiss National Bank, 55

oil price shock of 1991, 104

oil-price increases, concerns in Canada, 118

operational framework for inflation targeting: Australia, 223-228; Canada, 120-30; Israel, 209-14; New Zealand, 92-102; Spain, 240-44; Sweden, 182-89; United Kingdom, 153-59

operational framework for monetary targeting, in Germany, 56-62

operational framework for monetary targeting, in Switzerland, 62-68

operational issues in inflation targeting, 27-36

operational questions of inflation targeting, consensus on, 288

optimal control method of policy-making, 12

ostmarks, conversion to deutschemarks, 71

output, and inflation targeting, 299

over-manipulation of monetary policy, 13, 23

overnight and long-term interest rates (graphs): Canada, 131; Germany, 47; Switzerland (graph), 53; United Kingdom (graph), 160

paper-money standard, unbacked, 19-20

parallel structure, of case studies, 7-8

parameter instability tests, 262-64

Phillips curve, 11; in analyzing inflation targeting, 253; in Australia, 226; in Canada, 124; inflation forecasts from (graphs), 265; methodology of Gordon and Fuhrer, 259; origin of, 335; and Riksbank, 200

point target, 32; and credibility, 295; and flexibility, 295; proposed for EMU, 328; proposed for United States, 315-16, 320-21; in United Kingdom, 146, 154; in Switzerland, 42, 64; vs. target range, 32, 294-95, 345

policy activism, arguments against, 11-16

policy credibility problem, 14-15

policy discretion, in inflation targeting, 300

policy lags: effect on policy-making methods, 12-14; and monetary policy, 12

Policy Targets Agreement (PTA) in New Zealand, 86, 88, 91, 92-95, 97; irregular timing of, 95-96

policy transparency, in Canada, 127; goals of, 26; in Israel, Australia, and Spain, 203

policy-making framework: information used for, 32-35; and price stability, 10

political pressure, effect on monetary policy, 23

politicization of monetary policy in United Kingdom, 346

precursors to inflation targeting, 41-85

preemptive monetary policy, 307

price index for inflation targets in New Zealand, 87, 93

price index: consistent use of, 28; to be targeted, 27-28

price level: establishing a nominal anchor for, 19-21; vs. inflation rate, 30

price stability, 283; in Australia, 221, 222, 224-25; in Canada, 119, 121, 122, 124, 134, 135, 342; definitions of, 28; in Germany, 45, 337; in Israel, 217; mandates for, 343; in New Zealand, 88, 89; as primary goal in monetary policy, 10; proposed as primary goal of Federal Reserve Bank, 335; in Spain, 237, 239; in Sweden, 178-79, 186, 188-89, 192, 347; in Switzerland, 65, 337; in United Kingdom, 146, 149152, 153, 156-57, 345-46; in United States, 316-17; and responses to inflationary shocks, 275; as target for measured inflation, 42; vs. inflation targeting, 254, 289

price-level targeting, 336; use of in Sweden, 180

prices, and real economy in Canada, 124

private enterprise, and prosperity, 3

private-sector inflation expectations in inflation targeting, 253

probability cones, and communication in the United Kingdom, 345

production potential, and Bundesbank, 58

Progressive Conservative Party, in Canada, 135

proposal for inflation targeting in the European Monetary Union, 327-33

prosperity, and private enterprise, 3

PTA, see Policy Targets Agreement

public expectations: in inflation scares, 20; and monetary policy, 12

public involvement monetary policy, in inflation targeting, 24

public sector borrowing requirement (PSBR) in United Kingdom, 148

public support for monetary policy: in New Zealand, 92; in Swiss National Bank, 67

public, maintaining credibility with, 36-37

publicity, maximized in Canadian inflation targeting, 117

quantitative goals and credibility, in Canada, 124

quantity theory of monetary targeting, 43-44

Quarterly Bulletin, in United Kingdom, 157, 345-46

Quarterly Report, in Australia, 227, 232

Quebec referendum on sovereignty, and interest rates in Canada, 138-39

range, of inflation target, 32

range vs. point target, practical implications of, 32

rate of inflation, 289-90; and growth rate, 18

"rational expectations" models of inflation, in United Kingdom, 152

rationale for Canadian inflation-reduction targets, 120

reader's guide to text layout, 8-9

real bonds in Canada and the United Kingdom, 342

real economic costs under inflation targeting, 266

real economy: and monetary policy in New Zealand, 97; and prices in Canada, 124

real output, and inflation targeting, 254

real-return bonds, in Canada, 133, 139

real-side costs of trading off disinflation, in United Kingdom, 156-57

real-side goals, in Australia, 226

reasons for changing U.S. policy, 310-15

"Recent Economic Developments," published in Israel, 212

recession, as result of restrictive monetary policy, 11

relative marginal values, under gold standard, 19

repo rate: after German reunification, 71-72, 73, 75; use of in Sweden as policy instrument, 191, 193

Reserve Bank Act of 1959, Section 10, in Australia, 219

Reserve Bank of Australia: accountability, 219; Cash Rate instrument, 229, 231, 232; flexibility, 223; independence of, 223-24, 228; "Semi-Annual Statement on Monetary Policy," 228

Reserve Bank of New Zealand Act of 1989, 87-88, 96; and independence, 339

Reserve Bank of New Zealand Bulletin, 101

Reserve Bank of New Zealand: and exchange rates, 98; flexibility in, 87; potential conflict of interest in, 339; as relatively "rule-oriented," 97

responsibility for setting inflation target, in United States, 322-324

retail price index (RPI), in United Kingdom, 148

retail price index excluding mortgage interest payments (RPIX), in United Kingdom, 146

reunification of Germany, effect on monetary policy, 68, 70-72

revision of commercial bank liquidity requirements in Switzerland, 78-79

Riksbank Committee, report of, 188

Riksbank, 173; accountability, 186; adoption of inflation target as nominal anchor, 174, 179; commitment to price stability, 179; control of, 173; credibility, 195; defense of krona's exchange rate peg, 177; and ECU, 347; flexibility, 184; Governing Board of, 347; inflation forecast of, 187; information variables for inflation targeting, 185; and Phillips-curve estimation, 200; relationship to Parliament, 186

risk of circularity, in inflation targeting, 34

risk of self-fulfilling prophecies in inflation targeting, 34

risk premiums in long-term Canadian interest rates, 118

risks of targeting too high or too low, 28-30

RPIX, 165, 350; and RPI inflation and targets in United Kingdom, 55, 146, 153-54, 160 (graph), 161, 162, 163, 164, 167-168

RPIY, use of in United Kingdom, 146, 154, 162, 164

rules-versus-discretion and inflation targeting, 4, 21, 299-301

rules-based monetary policy, 5-6

sacrifice ratios, 254-59, 298, 343, 349-350; in analyzing inflation targeting, 253, 254-59; in Canada, 134; and credibility, 255; definition of, 254; and their determinants, 258 (table); and inflation rate, 255; and low inflation, 353; Ball's methodology for, 255-56, 257-59

SAMB, 62 in Switzerland: after changes in financial markets, 79, 82; after stock-market crash of October 1997, 78; and medium-term growth paths, 54 (graph); use of by Swiss National Bank, 62 (graphs)

scope of information provided to public, 36-37

seasonally adjusted monetary base, see SAMB

"Semi-Annual Statement on Monetary Policy," in Australia, 228

shekel, speculative attacks against, 207

short-run policy flexibility: in Canada, 342; and multiple objectives, 291-93

short-run stimuli, effect on monetary policy, 23

short-term inflation target, proposed for EMU, 328; proposed for United States, 315, 317-19 short-term interest rates in 1988, effect on Swiss National Bank, 80-81

Social Democrats, role in Swedish target inflation, 191-92

sources of data for analyses, 350

Spain
—analysis: lessons from, 250-51
—central bank: accountability, 251; flexibility in, 250; transparency in, 205, 239, 251
—communication to public: *Annual Report*, 243; *Economic Bulletin*, 243; *Inflation Report*, 243
—GDP growth and unemployment rates in (graph), 238
—inflation targeting, 244-50; adoption of, 235-40; core inflation in, 247; CPI inflation and targets in, 238 (graph); domestic vs. exchange-rate objectives in, 237, 245 ;Exchange Rate Mechanism in, 236; intermediate target in, 236; key features of, 203-05; price stability in, 237; responsibility for setting inflation target, 204; underlying inflation measures in, 247; use of headline CPI, 204; wage-bargaining mechanisms in, 204
—monetary policy: fiscal consolidation in, 205; inflation target vs. exchange-rate target, 241; intervention and long-term interest rates in, 238 (graph)

Spanish Parliamentary Committee on Economic Affairs, 242

speculative attacks, 353

Statistics New Zealand, 95

stock-market crash of October 1997, and Swiss National Bank, 78

success of inflation targeting, 349-52

success of inflation targeting, analysis of, 252-83

supply shock vs. demand shock, 72; and inflation targeting, 24; responding to, 35

Survey of Forecasters, in Canada, 139

surveys, of inflation expectations, 266-71; used to canvas public expectations in New Zealand, 100

Sweden
—analysis: lessons from, 201-02; Phillips-curve estimation, 200

—central bank: accountability, 186; and Black Wednesday, 177; credibility, 179-80, 185, 195; flexibility, 172, 179-80, 184; influence of krona on economy, 347; transparency, 197
—communication to public, 197; *Inflation Report,* 186-187, 191-192, 194, 195, 198, 200, 201
—GDP growth and unemployment rate in (graph), 175
—inflation targeting, 172-202, 347-48; adoption of, 174-82; CPI inflation in, 175 (graph); features of, 172-73; headline CPI in, 173, 200, 348; headline vs. core CPI in, 183-84, 185, 202; increasing importance of trend inflation in, 173; Marginal Rate in, 190; motives for adopting, 179; nominal anchor in, 172; objectives of, 180; operational framework in, 182-89; price stability in, 347; target range in, 173
—monetary policy: abandonment of exchange-rate peg, 178; centralized wage-setting mechanisms in, 194; exchange-rate targeting in, 172; marginal and long-term interest rates in, 175 (graph); use of exchange-rate peg, 201; value-added tax, 195
—unemployment in, 198-99

Swedish monetary policy under inflation targeting, 189-200

Swiss and German monetary targeting, 336-38

Swiss Economic Indicators, 52, 53

Swiss economy, effects of exchange rate on, 77-78

Swiss inflation performance through 1992, 77

Swiss Interbank Clearing (SIC), 78, 79

Swiss monetary targeting, key features of, 42

Swiss National Bank: *Annual Report,* 338; accountability of, 67; and adoption of monetary targeting, 51; change to medium-term growth path, 83-84; changes affecting demand for SAMB, 78-79; flexibility in, 84; focus on headline CPI, 65; independence of, 67; introduction of ceiling on growth of bank credit, 52; *Monthly Report,* 338; and narrow monetary aggregate, 62; public support for,

67; and revision of commercial bank liquidity requirements, 78-79; and SAMB, 338; and stock-market crash of October 1997, 78; transparency in, 79-80; use of M1, 62; use of monetary base, 66; use of point targets, 64; use of SAMB, 62

Switzerland: 1975 recession, 55-56; lessons from, 84-85; pursuit of price stability in, 337; as small, open economy, 83-84

symmetrical responses, proposed for EMU target misses, 328; proposed for U.S. target misses, 321

T-bill rates in Israel (graph), 215

target adoption: in Canada, 117-18; in Spain, developments leading to, 236; and parameter instability, 262-63

target bands, in Australia, 348

target breach, result of in New Zealand, 87, 108, 109

target growth rate, derivation of in Bundesbank, 57-59

target horizon, in Sweden, 184

target range, 4; in Canada, 120-21, 123, 135-36, 144, 341; and credibility, 294-95; in Germany, 42; and instrument instability, 294; in Israel, 210; in New Zealand, 87, 92; reformulation of by Bundesbank, 59; spread of, 32; in Sweden, 172, 180, 184-85; in United Kingdom, 146, 154; vs. point target, 294-95, 345

target thresholds, in United Kingdom, 146

target, choosing and defining, 289-91

targeting a point or range, 32

targeting core CPI, proposed in United States, 321-22

targeting framework, vs. low inflation in Canada, 134

targeting inflation rate vs. price level, 30

targeting money growth, 304-05

targeting nominal GDP, 305-07

tax code, change in Sweden, 176

tax levies, effect on monetary policy in New Zealand, 95

tax-related distortions, social costs of, 18

taxes, and monetary policy, 132-33

terms of trade, effects on monetary policy in New Zealand, 94, 95

"The Great Canadian Slump," 139, 143

The Monetary Policy of the Bundesbank, 61

"thick-point" inflation target, in Australia, 204, 223, 224

time horizon for inflation target, 31; in Australia, 222, 224; proposed for EMU, 328; proposed for United States, 315, 319-20

time inconsistency problem, 14-15

timetable for reducing inflation, in Canada, 120

total vs. core CPI in Canada, 341

tradeoff, between costs and benefits of activist policies, 14, 15

transparency in monetary policy, 295-96; in Australia, 205, 251; in Bank of England, 170; in Bundesbank, 61; in Canada, 124-25, 127, 132, 144, 344; defined, 26; and flexibility, balancing, 26-27, 290-91; importance of in targeting regime, 84; and inflation targeting, 23, 283; in Israel, 205, 251; in New Zealand, 95; in Spain, 205, 239, 251; in Sweden, 197; in United States, 310-11

trend inflation, and one-time shocks in Canada, 144

tunnels, for establishing ranges for money growth, 336

unavoidable price increases, in Bundesbank, 58

underlying and headline inflation and targets in New Zealand (graph), 103

underlying CPI: defined in Australia, 225; used in New Zealand and Australia, 350

underlying inflation: in New Zealand, 93-94, 95, 104; measures in Spain, 247; use in Australia, 204

unemployment rate: in Australia, 226, 229, 230 (graph); in Canada, 131 (graph); and hysteresis in Canada, 343; and inflation, 11, 12, 13; in Israel, 215 (graph); and monetary policy, 11; in Spain, 238 (graph); in Sweden, 174-76, 175 (graph), 198-99; in United Kingdom, 160 (graph), 163, 165, 168

United Kingdom

—analysis: lessons from, 171

—central bank: accountability, 153, 159, 162-63; and Black Wednesday, 152; credibility, 145, 148-49, 152, 153; flexibility, 153; inflationary pressures in, 164; September 1992 foreign exchange crisis in, 152

—communication to public, 153; *Inflation Report*, 155, 157-59; Quarterly Bulletin, 157, 345-46

—GDP growth and unemployment rate in, 151, 160 (graph)

—inflation targeting, 145-71, 345-46; adoption of, 147-53; and Conservative Party, 147, 148; headline inflation in, 151; key features of, 145-46; nominal anchor in, 145; operational framework in, 153-59; point target in, 154; price stability in, 152; retail price index in, 148; RPIX, 153-54; RPIX and RPI inflation and targets in, 160 (graph); RPIY, 154; target range in, 154; target range vs. point target in, 146; target thresholds in, 146; use of headline and core inflation in, 146; use of M3 as target aggregate, 148

—monetary policy: and anti-inflation policy, 151; "national interest" control over, 170; and Exchange Rate Mechanism, 151; and probability cones, 345; and probability density, 345; incomes policies in, 148; Medium Term Financial Strategy in, 149; nominal effective exchange rate in, 160 (graph); overnight and long-term interest rates in, 160 (graph); use of monetary targets in, 150; value-added tax in, 162; wage-price controls in, 148

—unemployment rate in, 163

United States: depersonalization of monetary policy in, 311-12; flexibility in, 317-19; independence of central bank, 312; inflation targeting and democratic principles, 312; inflation targeting in, 353; point target proposed for, 315-16, 320-21; proposed framework for inflation targeting, 315-26; transparency of policy in, 310-11

upward bias of inflation expectations in Canada, 119

USD/new shekel exchange rate (graph), 215

utilization measure, effect on analyses, 351

value-added tax (VAT) in Spain, 237-239, 240–41; in Sweden, 195; in United Kingdom, 162

variation in inflation target over time, in United States, 317-19

VAT, *see* value-added tax

vector autoregression (VAR) model of behavior of core inflation, 275-82

velocity shocks, 44

volatility of relative prices, and uncertainty, 23

Volker-Greenspan Federal Reserve, 310

wage- and price-setting, and inflation targeting, 275

wage-bargaining mechanisms, in Israel, Australia, and Spain, 204; in Sweden, 187

wage flexibility, in Canada, 344

wage increases, in Australia, 234-35

wage-price controls, in United Kingdom, 148

yield curve, in New Zealand, 100, 107

zero rate of inflation, problems with, 28; risk of deflation with, 29-30; vs. low, positive inflation in New Zealand, 113